Out of Africa

African influences in Atlantic Creoles

Mikael Parkvall

Denna tror jag knappast du kommer att läsa, men skulle du göra det tillhör du en liten exklusiv krets...

2000
Battlebridge Publications

This volume is dedicated to the memory of

Chris Corne
and
Gunnel Källgren

two of my main sources of inspiration and support
during the preparation of this thesis
who sadly died before its completion.

Published by: Battlebridge Publications,
37 Store Street, London WC1E 7QF, United Kingdom

<parkvall@ling.su.se>

ISBN 1-903292-05-0

Cover design: Mikael Parkvall

Printed by Hobbs the Printers Ltd, Brunel Road, Totton, Hampshire, SO40 3WX, UK.

Contents

3. Phonology, continued

4. Grammar

6. Demographic data, continued

7. Summary and discussion of the results, continued

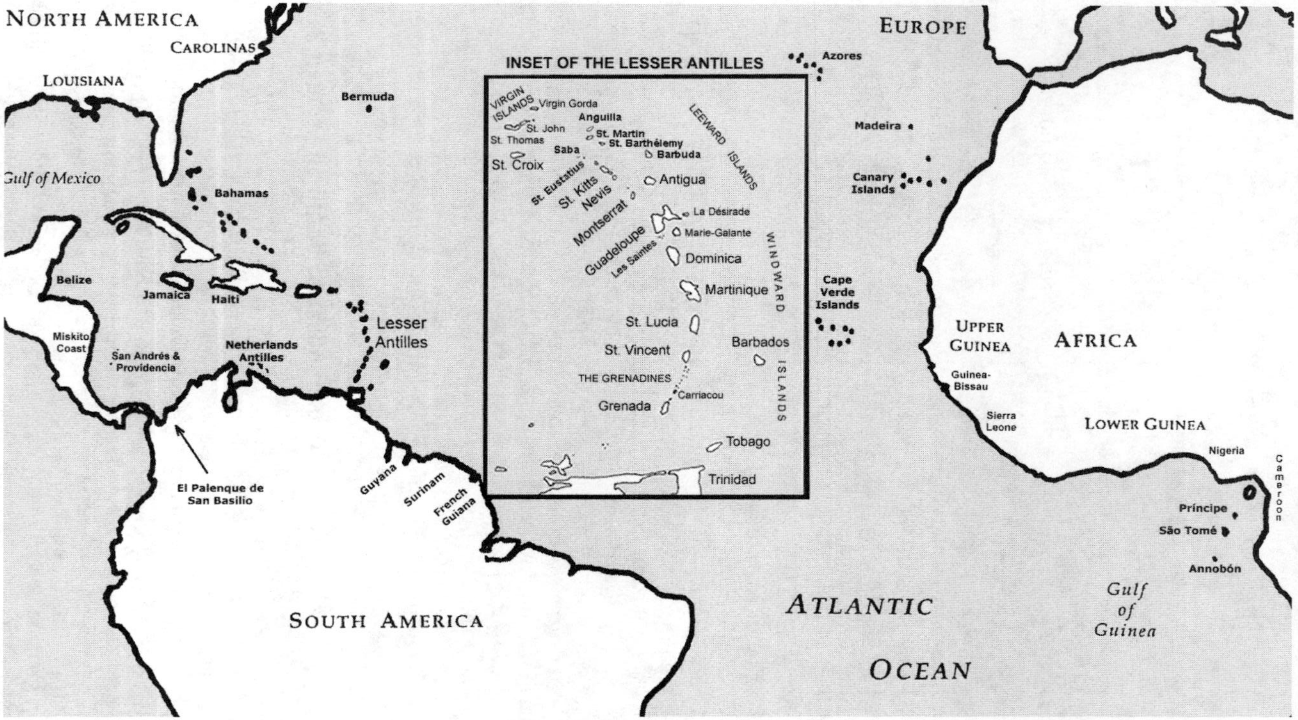
North America
Carolinas
Louisiana
Gulf of Mexico
Bermuda
Bahamas
Belize
Jamaica
Haiti
Miskito Coast
San Andrés & Providencia
Netherlands Antilles
Lesser Antilles
El Palenque de San Basilio
Guyana
Surinam
French Guiana
South America
INSET OF THE LESSER ANTILLES
VIRGIN ISLANDS
Virgin Gorda
St. John
St. Thomas
St. Croix
Anguilla
St. Martin
St. Barthélemy
Saba
Barbuda
St. Eustatius
St. Kitts
Nevis
Antigua
LEEWARD ISLANDS
Montserrat
La Désirade
Marie-Galante
Guadeloupe
Les Saintes
Dominica
WINDWARD ISLANDS
Martinique
St. Lucia
Barbados
St. Vincent
THE GRENADINES
Carriacou
Grenada
Tobago
Trinidad
Europe
Azores
Madeira
Canary Islands
Cape Verde Islands
Upper Guinea
Africa
Guinea-Bissau
Sierra Leone
Lower Guinea
Nigeria
Cameroon
Príncipe
São Tomé
Annobón
Atlantic Ocean
Gulf of Guinea

Chapter 1

Introduction

1.1 Aim and scope of the study

The present study concerns the presence of substrate features in Atlantic Creoles. The aim is first and foremost to identify features that can be reliably ascribed to substrate influence, and secondly to examine whatever correlations there may be between those findings and what is known about the historical and demographic development of the communities where Atlantic Creoles are spoken.

The Creoles studied here are those which are spoken on both sides of the Atlantic Ocean, which derive most of their vocabulary from one of five European languages (English, French, Portuguese, Dutch and Spanish), whose substrate languages are spoken along the West African coast, and which arose as a result of European colonisation ventures and slave trade between the late 15th and early 18th century. Thus excluded are contact languages of non-European lexicon (which in the Atlantic area are in any case Pidgins or semi-Pidgins rather than Creoles). Similarly, varieties that do not seem to have originated in the relevant period, such as *français tirailleur* (West African Pidgin French) are not taken into account, and nor are moderately restructured varieties such as Brazilian Vernacular Portuguese, Caribbean Vernacular Spanish or African American Vernacular English, New Jersey Black Dutch,[1] *Français Populaire d'Abidjan* and the French dialects of St Thomas, St Barts, and Missouri, and the Englishes of e.g. Bermuda, the Cayman Islands, the Bay Islands of Honduras, Saba, St Helena, and Tristan da Cunha. Furthermore, varieties which seem to represent unstable xenolects rather than stable Pidgins, such as the *Habla Bozal* of Cuba are also excluded, as are languages with a substrate not belonging to the Niger-Congo phylum, such as Pidgins and (possible) Creoles of Dutch and Afrikaans lexicon in South Africa. Although these varieties are not within the actual scope of this dissertation, sporadic reference will be made to them whenever appropriate.

Note, finally, that while I have earlier included the so-called Isle de France Creoles of the Indian Ocean among the Atlantic Creoles (Parkvall 1995c, 1998, 1999a, 1999c), given the documented West African input in the formation of Mauritian (Baker & Corne 1982), this is not done in the present work.

The full list of Creoles considered in this study (ignoring minor offshoots) is given in the table overleaf, while the map which follows the table will help the reader to identify where these languages are spoken.

Most previous comparative work on Atlantic Creoles has included only languages of a single lexifier.[2] With the exception of Van Name (1869-70) – one of the first ever publications on Creole languages – it was not until the second half of the 20th century that comparisons across the lexifier boundaries were made, notably in Loftman (1953), Valkhoff (1966), Taylor (1971, 1977), Baudet (1981), Bickerton (1981), Boretzky (1983), Green (1988) and Holm (1988). Although several of these dealt with substrate influences, most were not concerned exclusively with this, and the scope of this dissertation is considerably wider in its study of substrate influences than any of these.

1 Although this variety has sometimes confusingly been referred to as "Negerhollands" (e.g. Ginneken 1913:287-88), it is not likely to be identical with the Dutch-lexicon Creole of the same name spoken on the Virgin Islands.

2 E.g. Herskovits & Herskovits (1936:117-75), Cassidy (1962), Alleyne (1980), Hancock (1987), McWhorter (1995), Baker (1999a) (on English-lexicon Creoles), Adam (1883), Göbl (1934), Goodman (1964), Hull (1979), Parkvall (1995c) (on French-lexicon Creoles), Ferraz (1987) and Bruyn & Veenstra (1993) (on Portuguese- and Dutch-lexicon Creoles, respectively).

Principal Creole language varieties considered in this study

GROUP	LOCATION	VARIETIES
English-lexicon varieties	North America	**Gullah** (Carolinas, Georgia), **Bahamian**
	Western Caribbean	**Jamaican, Belizean, Miskito Coast Creole** (Nicaragua), **San Andrés & Providencia Creole** (Colombia)
	Lesser Antilles	Spoken on the Leeward Islands such as **Antigua, St Kitts, Nevis, and the Virgin Islands**, as well as on the Windward Islands of **St Vincent, Barbados,** and **Trinidad.**
	The Guianas	**Guyanese**, **Sranan** (Surinam), **Ndyuka** (Surinam), **Saramaccan** (Surinam)
	West Africa	**Krio** (Sierra Leone), **Nigerian**, **Cameroonian**
French-lexicon varieties	North America	**Louisianais**
	Western Caribbean	**Haitian**
	Lesser Antilles	Numerous varieties, spoken on islands such as **Guadeloupe, Martinique, Dominica, St Lucia, Grenada** and **Trinidad**.
	The Guianas	**Guyanais** (French Guiana), **Karipuna** (north-eastern Brazil)
Portuguese-lexicon varieties	Upper Guinea	**Cape Verdean, Guinea-Bissau Creole** (Guinea-Bissau and Senegal)
	Gulf of Guinea	**Sãotomense** (São Tomé), **Angolar** (São Tomé), **Principense** (Príncipe), **Fa d'Ambu** (Annobón)
Dutch-lexicon varieties		**Negerhollands** (US Virgin Islands), **Skepi** (Guyana), **Berbice** (Guyana)
Spanish-lexicon varieties		**Papiamentu** (Netherlands Antilles), **Palenquero** (village of El Palenque de San Basilio, Colombia)

Apart from this introduction (chapter 1), this thesis comprises six chapters. Chapter 2 is a Creolistic manifesto of sorts, in which certain methodological considerations are discussed, along with an attempt at defining the very concept of 'substrate-induced feature'. The following three chapters (2-4) deal, respectively, with substrate influences in phonology, syntax, and lexicon, while chapter 5 attempts to trace the geolinguistic origins of those who created the Atlantic Creoles. The final chapter treats the relationship between the linguistic and the demographic data presented. The focus of attention is on whether or not linguistic substrate influences can be predicted on the basis of the origins of the founder population.

1.2 Methodology

The features included here are those I regard as being probably of neither European origin, nor the result of language universals. One of the things I discovered while identifying these features was that there were fewer of them than I had expected there to be, and while I started out with what might be called a substratist approach, it is now more obvious to me that both substratists and superstratists have grossly exaggerated the contributions to Atlantic Creole grammar of non-European and European languages, respectively. On the other hand, I have examined the Atlantic Creoles from a European standpoint, pondering upon features in these languages that do not seem to be European. If the question asked had been "How much is there in the Atlantic Creoles that is of European origin?", the result might perhaps have been different. Clearly, many basic traits cannot with certainty be ascribed to either source; to just take one example, the basic SVO word order of Atlantic Creoles could be seen as a generalisation of either a European or a West African pattern. These problems, together with an outline of my methodological approach, are discussed in chapter 2.

Since carrying out the research presented here, the focus of my interest in Creole languages has shifted from substrate influences to the reduction associated with pidginisation. As there are several non-Creole languages which are more "mixed" (in the sense of presenting features from more than one language), this mixedness cannot and should not, as I now see things, be considered the essence or Creolehood. Rather, the traces of broken transmission (pidginisation), which can still be seen in the languages known as Creoles, are what sets Creoles apart from non-Creoles (McWhorter 1998, *forthcoming*; McWhorter & Parkvall 1999; Goyette 2000).

The collection of substrate features discussed is probably not exhaustive. I am sure that there are more traits that can be ascribed to substrate influence, but which have escaped me. In particular, I was troubled by the fact that so much of what could be found is ascribed to Lower Guinean languages, and in particular those of the Kwa group. In Creoles among whose creators there were few Kwa speakers, such as Palenquero SC or the Upper Guinea PCs, few syntactic "Kwaisms" have been found. Hitherto, I had suspected that the Kwa bias in creolistics in general was due to the expectations of the observers - since Creolists have expected to find Kwa features, Kwa features is generally what they have found. If only I could be less prejudiced, I would certainly be able to change that picture, given the vast numbers of other Africans which were taken to the Caribbean. And yet, even in this thesis, there is a notable Kwa bias. I cannot claim to be able to explain this. Is it a *founder effect* (Mufwene 1996)? Is it a coincidence? Is it due to the availability of grammars and dictionaries being more satisfactory for certain languages than for others? Or does it perhaps have something to do with the structure of Kwa languages somehow being more unmarked, and thereby more fit for survival in a restructuring context?[3] These issues are discussed in chapter 6.

After each section dealing with a particular feature suggested to be substrate-induced, the discussion is summarised in a table, where the feature is assigned to a specific substrate or group of substrates. The combination of these tables then form the basis of the concluding discussion in chapter 6.

1.2.1 Defining substrate influence

Chapter 1 is devoted to a detailed discussion of what I consider to be a convincing case of substrate influence. As will be apparent, I am trying to use the term more restrictively than many of my predecessors. Nevertheless, I have chosen to include a couple of features that fail to meet my own criteria (e.g. in not being cross-linguistically uncommon). This is done for a variety of reasons; in some cases, I did so since I felt I had something to add to the discussion on the origins of these features. In some other cases, the feature was considered interesting in highlighting the differences between various otherwise rather similar Atlantic Creoles. For yet others (e.g. §3.2.7 and §4.1), specific reasons for my decision to include the feature in question are given in the text.

1.2.2 Choice of substrate languages

It is necessary to consider a large number of potential substrates, since even closely related languages may exhibit far-reaching differences. Limiting ourselves to Europe, we find that e.g. West Germanic have some word orders quite unlike their relatives to the north, whose basic word orders in turn are far from identical. Whereas the definite article is a free preposed morpheme in English, Dutch and German, it is suffixed in Scandinavian. Many Scandinavian dialects also have phonological systems which, apart from having some quite exotic phonemes, make use of a

[3] An implicit assumption in some creolistic work, and explicitly claimed by Mufwene (1991c). And yet, serial verbs (§4.6), is only one example of a Kwa (or, at least, Lower Guinean) feature which has been transferred into many Creoles, but which is marked at least in the sense of being cross-linguistically uncommon and diachronically unstable.

complex interplay between stress and tone. Unlike many other Germanic languages, English preserves its SV order even in sentences introduced by an element other than the subject, and normally also in subordinated clauses. Among the Romance languages, we find striking differences even between the closely related Spanish and French, with vowel inventories of five and fifteen phonemes respectively. On the other hand, Spanish has systems of demonstratives and verb conjugations which are more complicated than their French counterparts. Needless to say, similar differences between otherwise closely related languages occur in Africa as well.

Unfortunately, the entire set of potential substrates of Atlantic Creoles includes several hundred languages and, even if all of these were satisfactorily documented, it would be far beyond the scope of a thesis such as this to examine every one of them. Therefore, much of the following discussion will be concerned with rather general areal features and tendencies that can be discerned from the study of a limited number of hopefully representative Niger-Congo languages. Nevertheless, I believe that I have made reference to a larger number of West African languages than any other author who has ever studied Atlantic Creoles comparatively. This is necessary in order to be as unbiased as possible for, in my view, substratist studies of Atlantic (and other) Creoles suffer from two main problems, both involving some wishful thinking.

Some scholars have had recourse to the so-called "cafeteria principle", in that they have examined a number of African languages of varying relevance until the desired feature has been detected and, once detected, this is claimed to be the origin of the Creole feature.

On the other hand, others appear to have decided in advance which African language they want their Creole to resemble, and the entire Creole is described in terms of the structure of the chosen substrate. Thus, most of the structure of Haitian, for instance (including what could with equal ease be derived from French!), is presented as essentially the result of the relexification of Fon and related languages in the works of the UQAM[4] "relexificationist" group (e.g. Lefebvre 1993, 1998; Lumsden 1999). In the works of practically all currently active Creolists specialising in the Surinamese Creoles, usually only Fon and Kikongo (and, to a lesser extent, Akan)[5] are considered at all. Similarly, much substratist research on Jamaican has concentrated on Akan to the virtual exclusion of other languages. Even otherwise impressive works such as Boretzky (1983) and Holm (1988, 1989) suffer from these problems. Boretzky completely ignores Upper Guinean languages, and Holm (except when referring to Boretzky) basically examines only Bambara and Yoruba, despite speakers of Yoruba being rather late arrivals in the New World, and probably too late to have had a significant impact on Atlantic Creole formation (see §6.1.2 and §6.7.4 below). When the choice of substrates is conditioned by inadequate sociohistorical and demographic data, the results must be called into question. On the other hand, a reliance on areal features is equally dangerous. Holm (1987, 1992:53) uses languages such as Tsonga and Zulu, spoken in South Africa and Mozambique (and thus far away from the areas from which most slaves were taken to the Americas) to account for structures in New World Afro-American speech varieties, with the implicit assumption that the features discussed are of a pan-Niger-Congo character. This is by no means an exception, but it is somewhat comparable to using Bulgarian or Persian as approximations of the lexifier languages of Jamaican and Haitian – they are, after all, Indo-European!

In addition to this, the absence of a wider typological overview is often painfully obvious, as discussed in chapter 2 below.

In order to be as unbiased as possible, I have chosen to regard any African language spoken close to the coast between Senegal and Angola as a potential substrate of virtually any Atlantic Creole, and have consulted as many descriptions of languages from this area as feasible. As far as demographic data are available, it seems that there were a few slaves from every major area in each colony, and given that a group can have a disproportionate influence on Creole formation under favourable circumstances, no group should be aprioristically excluded. In other words, one of the basic methodological features underlying this thesis is that the Creoles should first be examined without reference to demographical data. Demographics and history should *only later* be taken into account, and then used to exclude implausible substrate languages. After all, there are cases such as the Dutch Creole of Berbice where the demographic data would not lead us to

---

4 The *Université du Québec à Montréal*.

5 Akan is the collective name for Twi, Fante, and a number of other closely related languages.

expect the universally accepted overwhelming dominance of Ijo in the substrate-derived parts of the language (see §7.1.1).

I confess to having two (deliberate) presuppositions, however. One is that the Portuguese Creoles off the African coast constitute a special case. For obvious geographical reasons, only Upper Guinean languages can be expected to have influenced the Upper Guinean Portuguese Creoles, and similarly, only Lower Guinean and Bantu languages are relevant for the Gulf of Guinea Creoles. The other deliberate preconception is that Creoles did not necessarily arise where they are currently spoken, and that many of them may owe quite a lot of their structure to proto-Creoles that arose elsewhere. This conclusion is based on linguistic similarities, rather than on the basis of history or demographics (see e.g. Parkvall 1999c; Baker 1999a; McWhorter 1999b). Clearly, the investigation of the social and demographic circumstances of Creole genesis presupposes that one is investigating the setting where the Creole was actually born, rather than one to which is was imported from elsewhere.[6]

Apart from these two exceptions, it is only after the linguistic comparison of the Creoles and their putative substrate languages that history and demographics are taken into account (chapter 6). In the concluding discussion, then, I have tried to follow what Smith (1999:252) calls "Bickerton's edict", i. e. that speakers of the substrate language suggested to have influenced the Creole be present "at the right place and at the right time".

Data from 168 African languages have been considered.[7] These are listed in the table which occupies the following three pages (pp 6-8).

1.2.3 Sources used

Because of the large number of languages involved (five European lexifiers, dozens of Creoles, and hundreds of African languages), I have almost exclusively relied on written sources of data, and only to a very limited extent on informants. Also, I myself do not speak any of the African languages, and have only reading competence in the Creoles involved. This is bound to upset those who advocate that only native speakers of Creole languages should be entrusted to study them, but such a requirement would obviously rule out any large-scale comparative work, since no one speaks dozens, let alone hundreds of languages well.

Given the wide scope, there are unfortunately bound to be quite a few errors in what follows. Faulty data is a subject that has been discussed extensively in Creolist circles recently (e.g. DeGraff 1999b; Déjean 1999; discussions on CreoLIST during the summer of 1999).[8] I can only regret any errors that there may be in what follows, and express the hope that fellow Creolists will draw these to my attention in a friendly manner and in a spirit of collegiality.

Apart from a large number of African reference grammars and previous creolistic work (both of which are of course listed in the bibliography), United Nations (1999)[9] proved to be a valuable corpus for the section on phonotactics (§3.4).

---

6 Although I have earlier (Parkvall 1995a, c) to some extent lent support to Afrogenetic theories, the working hypothesis here is that New World Creoles all emerged in the Americas rather than in Africa. As discussed in §7.2.2, this need not be a correct assumption.

7 Because of the large number of languages, I have not examined an entire reference grammar for each of these, but some data from each of the languages listed have been taken into account. As for some comments on my terminological choices, the reader may consult §1.3.2 below. It may be worth noticing at this early a stage, however, that "Delto-Benuic" is *not* suggested to be taken as a language family in the genetic sense, but only used for convenience.

8 An e-mail discussion list with 400+ subscribers. For details, see <www.ling.su.se/Creole/CreoLIST>.

9 This material contains translations into 29 West African languages of the United Nations declaration of Human Rights, which equals about 2 150 words for each languages.

African languages considered in this study

	Name	Area	Family
1	Adamawa Fulfulde	Cameroon	Atlantic
2	Balanta	Guinea, Guinea-Bissau	Atlantic
3	Banyun	Guinea-Bissau	Atlantic
4	Biafada	Guinea-Bissau	Atlantic
5	Bijago	Guinea-Bissau	Atlantic
6	Bullom	Sierra Leone	Atlantic
7	Diola	Senegal	Atlantic
8	Ejamat	Guinea-Bissau	Atlantic
9	Fulfulde	Guinea	Atlantic
10	Gambian Wolof	Gambia	Atlantic
11	Kasanga	Guinea-Bissau	Atlantic
12	Kisi	Guinea, Liberia, Sierra Leone	Atlantic
13	Kobiana	Guinea-Bissau	Atlantic
14	Konyagi	Senegal	Atlantic
15	Lebu	Senegal	Atlantic
16	Limba	Sierra Leone	Atlantic
17	Manjaku	Guinea Bissau, Senegal	Atlantic
18	Mankanya	Guinea-Bissau, Senegal	Atlantic
19	Papel	Guinea-Bissau	Atlantic
20	Serer	Senegal	Atlantic
21	Sherbro	Sierra Leone	Atlantic
22	Temne	Sierra Leone	Atlantic
23	Wolof	Senegal	Atlantic
24	Bambara	Mali	Mande
25	Bisa	Burkina Faso, Ghana	Mande
26	Bobo Madaré	Burkina Faso	Mande
27	Dan	Ivory Coast	Mande
28	Dyula	Ivory Coast	Mande
29	Gambian Mandinka	Gambia	Mande
30	Guro	Ivory Coast	Mande
31	Kong Dyula	Ivory Coast	Mande
32	Kpelle	Liberia, Guinea	Mande
33	Kuranko	Sierra Leone, Guinea	Mande
34	Loko	Sierra Leone	Mande
35	Malinke	Mali	Mande
36	Mandinka	Senegal, Gambia	Mande
37	Maninka	Guinea	Mande
38	Maukakan	Ivory Coast	Mande
39	Mende	Sierra Leone, Liberia	Mande
40	Susu	Guinea, Sierra Leone	Mande
41	Vai	Sierra Leone, Liberia	Mande
42	Wojenekakan	Ivory Coast	Mande
43	Worodugukakan	Ivory Coast	Mande
44	Abri	Ivory Coast	Kru
45	Bete	Ivory Coast	Kru
46	Godie	Ivory Coast	Kru
47	Grebo	Liberia	Kru
48	Kru	Liberia	Kru
49	Tepo	Liberia, Ivory Coast	Kru
50	Dogon	Mali, Burkina Faso	Dogon
51	Bariba	Togo	Gur
52	Dagaari	Burkina Faso, Ghana	Gur
53	Dagbani	Ghana	Gur
54	Gurenne	Ghana	Gur
55	Kabiye	Togo	Gur
56	Moore	Burkina Faso	Gur

	Name	Area	Family
57	Senufo	Ivory Coast	Gur
58	Supyire	Mali	Gur
59	Tampulma	Ghana	Gur
60	Vagla	Ghana	Gur
61	Adangme	Ghana	Kwa
62	Akpose	Togo, Ghana	Kwa
63	Anum	Ghana	Kwa
64	Anyin	Ivory Coast, Ghana	Kwa
65	Awutu	Ghana	Kwa
66	Basila	Benin	Kwa
67	Baule	Ivory Coast	Kwa
68	Ebrie	Ivory Coast	Kwa
69	Efutu	Ghana	Kwa
70	Gã	Ghana, Togo	Kwa
71	Gonja	Ghana	Kwa
72	Guang	Ghana	Kwa
73	Late	Ghana	Kwa
74	Lelemi	Ghana	Kwa
75	Nkonya	Ghana	Kwa
76	Nzema	Ghana, Ivory Coast	Kwa
77	Okere	Ghana	Kwa
78	Asante	Ghana	Kwa (Akan)
79	Fante	Ghana	Kwa (Akan)
80	Twi	Ghana	Kwa (Akan)
81	Aja	Togo, Benin	Kwa (Gbe)
82	Ewe	Ghana, Togo	Kwa (Gbe)
83	Fon	Benin, Togo	Kwa (Gbe)
84	Gẽ	Togo, Benin	Kwa (Gbe)
85	Gun	Benin, Nigeria	Kwa (Gbe)
86	Bekwarra	Nigeria	Delto-Benuic (Cross)
87	Efik	Nigeria	Delto-Benuic (Cross)
88	Gokana	Nigeria	Delto-Benuic (Cross)
89	Ibibio	Nigeria	Delto-Benuic (Cross)
90	Mbembe	Nigeria	Delto-Benuic (Cross)
91	Obolo	Nigeria	Delto-Benuic (Cross)
92	Oron	Nigeria	Delto-Benuic (Cross)
93	Edo	Nigeria	Delto-Benuic (Edoid)
94	Engenni	Nigeria	Delto-Benuic (Edoid)
95	Epie	Nigeria	Delto-Benuic (Edoid)
96	Etsako	Nigeria	Delto-Benuic (Edoid)
97	Ibilo	Nigeria	Delto-Benuic (Edoid)
98	Isoko	Nigeria	Delto-Benuic (Edoid)
99	Urhobo	Nigeria	Delto-Benuic (Edoid)
100	Wano	Nigeria	Delto-Benuic (Edoid)
101	Ekpari	Nigeria	Delto-Benuic (Idomoid)
102	Idoma	Nigeria	Delto-Benuic (Idomoid)
103	Ekpeye	Nigeria	Delto-Benuic (Igboid)
104	Igbo	Nigeria	Delto-Benuic (Igboid)
105	Izi	Nigeria	Delto-Benuic (Igboid)
106	Ijo	Nigeria	Delto-Benuic (Ijoid)
107	Kalabari	Nigeria	Delto-Benuic (Ijoid)
108	Kolokuma	Nigeria	Delto-Benuic (Ijoid)
109	Amo	Nigeria	Delto-Benuic (Kainji)
110	Bassa-Nge	Nigeria	Delto-Benuic (Nupoid)
111	Ebira	Nigeria	Delto-Benuic (Nupoid)
112	Gbari	Nigeria	Delto-Benuic (Nupoid)
113	Nupe	Nigeria	Delto-Benuic (Nupoid)
114	Birom	Nigeria	Delto-Benuic (Platoid)

	Name	Area	Family
115	Jukun	Nigeria	Delto-Benuic (Platoid)
116	Kpan	Nigeria	Delto-Benuic (Platoid)
117	Tarok	Nigeria	Delto-Benuic (Platoid)
118	Isekiri	Nigeria	Delto-Benuic (Yoruboid)
119	Yoruba	Nigeria	Delto-Benuic (Yoruboid)
120	Ngbaka	Congo-Kinshasa	Adamawan
121	Hausa	Nigeria	Afro-Asiatic
122	Margi	Nigeria	Afro-Asiatic
123	Akwa	Congo-Brazzaville	Bantu
124	Babole	Congo-Brazzaville	Bantu
125	Bafut	Cameroon	Bantu
126	Balundu	Cameroon	Bantu
127	Bamileke	Cameroon	Bantu
128	Bangi	Congo-Kinshasa	Bantu
129	Basaa	Nigeria	Bantu
130	Bembe	Congo-Brazzaville	Bantu
131	Benga	Gabon	Bantu
132	Beti	Cameroon	Bantu
133	Bobangi	Congo-Kinshasa	Bantu
134	Chokwe	Angola, Congo-Kinshasa	Bantu
135	Duala	Cameroon	Bantu
136	Ejagham	Nigeria, Cameroon	Bantu
137	Ewondo	Cameroon	Bantu
138	Fang	Cameroon, Equatorial Guinea	Bantu
139	Herero	Namibia	Bantu
140	Kikongo	Congo-Brazzaville, Congo-Kinshasa, Angola	Bantu
141	Kimbundu	Angola	Bantu
142	Kituba	Congo-Kinshasa	Bantu
143	Kwambi	Namibia	Bantu
144	Lam-nso	Cameroon	Bantu
145	Lingala	Congo-Kinshasa	Bantu
146	Luvale	Angola	Bantu
147	Mbangala	Angola	Bantu
148	Mbere	Gabon, Congo-Brazzaville	Bantu
149	Mbunda	Angola	Bantu
150	Mpongwe	Gabon	Bantu
151	Ndingi	Angola	Bantu
152	Ndonga	Angola, Namibia	Bantu
153	Ngemba	Cameroon	Bantu
154	Ngom	Gabon, Congo	Bantu
155	Ngwe	Cameroon	Bantu
156	Njebi	Gabon, Congo	Bantu
157	Ntandu	Congo-Kinshasa	Bantu
158	Shira	Gabon	Bantu
159	Suga	Cameroon	Bantu
160	Teke	Gabon, Congo-Brazzaville	Bantu
161	Tiene	Congo-Kinshasa	Bantu
162	Tiv	Nigeria	Bantu
163	Tsogo	Gabon	Bantu
164	Umbundu	Angola	Bantu
165	Yaka	Angola	Bantu
166	Yambasa	Cameroon	Bantu
167	Yans	Congo-Kinshasa	Bantu
168	Yemba	Cameroon	Bantu

1.2.4 Other issues

It may be useful for readers to know that I – in contrast to e.g. Mufwene (1997b) and DeGraff (1999a, 2000) – subscribe to the view that Creoles derive from Pidgins. (For arguments in favour of this hypothesis, see e.g. McWhorter & Parkvall 1999, McWhorter 1998, *forthcoming*, and Baker 1999b). However, provided one believes that substrate languages had any constructive effect at all, this should – with one possible exception – not matter much in this particular context. The exception is that although a Pidgin may be expanded (the process I would label *creolisation*) by adults regardless of its adoption as an L_1 by children (*nativisation*), nativisation without *expansion* seems not to have been attested. Therefore, I take it that creolisation can have taken place no later than when there was a group of people for whom the Pidgin/Creole was the first and main vehicle of communication (cf §6). It is thus only the period between the start of language contact and the emergence of a group of native speakers (preferably with limited competence in their ancestral languages) that can properly be considered the formative period of a Creole. Thereafter, I see no reason to doubt that a Creole would change in any other way than would a non-Creole under similar circumstances.

1.3 Terminological issues and transcription conventions

1.3.1 Names of contact languages

As just mentioned, the precise meaning of the term *Creole* has been increasingly questioned in recent times, and the issue of whether the concept is only historically motivated (for references, see e.g. McWhorter & Parkvall 1999) or whether the languages called Creoles can be synchronically defined on language-internal grounds alone (McWhorter 1998, *forthcoming*; Goyette 2000) has been vigorously debated. Although I have publicly taken a stand in that debate (in favour of the latter opinion), it is of little importance in the present context, since there is more or less universal agreement in designating the languages discussed here as Creoles.

Some varieties (e.g. the English-lexicon variety spoken in Barbados today) are such that I would normally hesitate to apply the label 'Creole' even to the basilectal poles of their continua. Here, however, I have, for the sake of convenience and in order not to distract the readers attention through terminological discussions that are irrelevant in this particular context, opted for the traditional labels, so that even e.g. mesolectal Barbadian and Cape Verdean are considered Creoles.

There has also been a good deal of discussion regarding the distinction between Pidgins and Creoles, and it is increasingly recognised that nativisation is not a *sine qua non* for creolisation. It is nowadays usually acknowledged that Pidgins may expand into fully-fledged languages through frequent usage alone, and it is on this basis that the "Pidgins" of e.g. Nigeria, Cameroon and Guinea-Bissau are treated as Creoles rather than as Pidgins.[10]

Again for the sake of simplicity, most Creoles under discussion are designated through a combination of the name of the location where they are spoken (in its nominal rather than adjectival form) and a letter combination denoting the lexifier language. Therefore, albeit at the risk of offending native speakers, the names in the right column in the upper part of the following table are consistently employed instead of the autoglossonyms (or lexifier forms) such as those in the left column. The main reason for adopting this system is that I believe it facilitates rapid identification on the part of the reader – all the more so since many of the languages in question are simply known as Creole (*Kreol, Kriol, Kreyol, Kweyol,* etc.) or Patois (*Patwa*, etc.) to their speakers. The only cases where I have made exceptions to this practice is for languages which have a name so well-known that the system above would do little but cause confusion. These are set out in the lower part of the table which follows.

10 All three have a number of L_1 speakers, but are for the majority of their users second languages.

List of names of Creoles adopted in this thesis

NOT USED HERE	USED HERE
Dominiken	Dominica FC
Bajan (< Bar*badian*)	Barbados EC
Creolese	Guyana EC
Kamtok (< Cameroon Talk)	Cameroon EC
Enpi (< NP < Nigerian Pidgin)	Nigeria EC
Kabuverdianu	Cape Verde PC
Louisianais	Louisiana FC
Principense	Príncipe PC
Sãotomense	São Tomé PC
Aisyen	Haiti FC
Patwa	Jamaica EC
Kriyol	Guinea-Bissau PC
Virgin Islands DC	Negerhollands DC
Sierra Leone EC	Krio EC
São Tomé Maroon PC (?)	Angolar PC
Netherlands Antilles SC	Papiamentu SC
Colombia SC	Palenquero SC
Coastal Surinam EC	Sranan EC

EC = English-lexicon Creole
FC = French-lexicon Creole
PC = Portuguese-lexicon Creole[11]
DC = Dutch-lexicon Creole
SC = Spanish-lexicon Creole.

1.3.2 Names of African languages

For African languages, I have tried to follow the naming conventions of Moseley & Asher (eds.) (1994) and of SIL's *Ethnologue* database.[12] The internal family relationships of the Niger-Congo phylum are subject to debate every now and then. In contrast to most other Creolists, I have followed the classification now used by most Africanists, in which languages such as Yoruba, Igbo and Efik are no longer regarded as Kwa. The new classification (with the remaining Kwa languages labelled, as is sometimes done, "New Kwa", in order to avoid confusion with the former, larger family) is illustrated in the table below (based on the *Ethnologue*), where "New Kwa" refers to the languages remaining in this family, as opposed to the no-longer-Kwa languages, which are now treated as subbranches of Benue-Congo alongside the huge Bantoid family. In the following, "Kwa" is used for "New Kwa".

However, I have chosen to use other, partly different labels to refer to some of the African languages involved in Atlantic Creole formation. Since several interesting features are areally rather than genetically distributed, and since I felt the need for a convenient cover term for the no-longer-Kwa group, I decided to introduce the term "Delto-Benuic" for these languages. "Delto-Benuic" could in genetic terms thus be interpreted as either "no-longer-Kwa plus Ijo", or "Benue-Congo-minus-Bantu-but-including-Ijoid". This is illustrated in the figure which follows.

11 Not to be confused with P/C '(any) Pidgin and/or Creole' or P/Cs 'Pidgins and Creoles (in general)'.

12 <www.sil.org/ethnologue> (SIL=*Summer Institute of Linguistics*). When the Ethnologue and Mosely & Asher (eds) (1994) differed in their naming practices, I have used whatever seems to me to be the best known.

The Niger-Congo languages

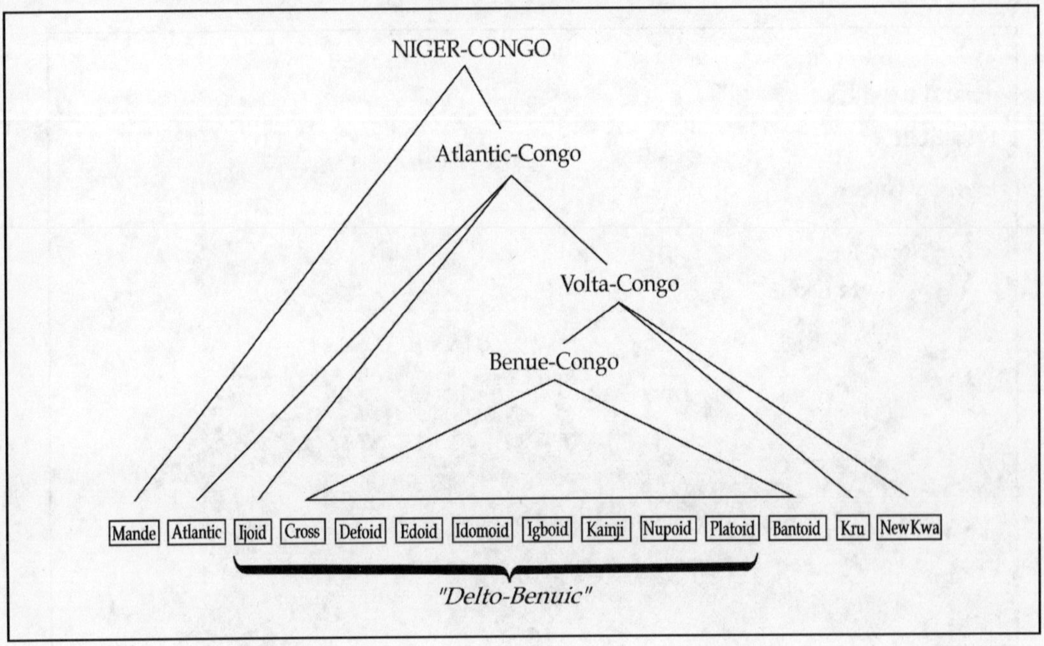

The only other groupings that the reader needs to be aware of are Akan and Gbe, two subdivisions of (New) Kwa. These are introduced not mainly because of being warranted by typological discrepancies, but rather because the great role that Kwa has played in creolistics (and apparently also in Creole genesis) makes a more fine-grained distinction convenient. A map showing the locations of many of the languages and groups of languages to which frequent reference is made will be found on page 13.

1.3.3 Names of geographical regions

The terms *Upper Guinea* and *Lower Guinea* will appear from time to time, and will be used approximately as they were in the days of the slave trade. Upper Guinea refers to the West African coast between the River Senegal and Cape Palmas (on the frontier between Liberia and Côte d'Ivoire), whereas Lower Guinea stretches from that Cape as far as the Biafra region in Nigeria. Slaves exported from Upper Guinea would thus have spoken Atlantic, Mande or (occasionally) Kru languages, while slaves from Lower Guinea were mainly speakers of Kwa and Delto-Benuic languages.

Within Upper and Lower Guinea, the following subdivisions are mentioned in the text:

Area	**Roughly corresponding to**
Windward Coast	Liberia
Ivory Coast	Côte d'Ivoire (Ivory Coast)
Gold Coast	Ghana
Slave Coast	Togo, Benin, south-western Nigeria
Biafra	South-eastern Nigeria

The locations of these areas are indicated on the map overleaf.

Location of geographical regions to which reference is made in the text

The third major region, stretching from Cameroon to Angola, is thoroughly Bantu-speaking. I had some trouble finding an appropriate term for it, since "the Bantu-speaking areas of West Africa" would be too cumbersome. After discussions with Philip Baker and the Bantuist Michael Mann, I decided that my original 'Bantuland' might carry with it unfortunate colonial connotations, and I therefore opted for Mann's suggestion 'Buntu', consisting of the same root *ntu* as in *Bantu*, but equipped with the prefix of noun class 11, used to denote (among other things) territories.[13] *Buntu* is thus used here for the area in which Bantu languages are spoken.

1.3.4 Linguistic terminology

Needless to say, my linguistic terminology is a product of what I happen to have read in linguistics. So, while I agree whole-heartedly with e.g. Winford (1996) that Creolists ought to adapt their terminology to that of general linguistics unless there are good reasons not to do so, I am sure that there are instances where I have failed to observe his advice. Whenever in doubt, however, I have tried to comply with the suggestions of Trask (1993).

13 Naturally, the phonetic realisation of this prefix varies from one Bantu language to another.

Location of the more important languages, language families and linguistic groupings to which reference is made in the text

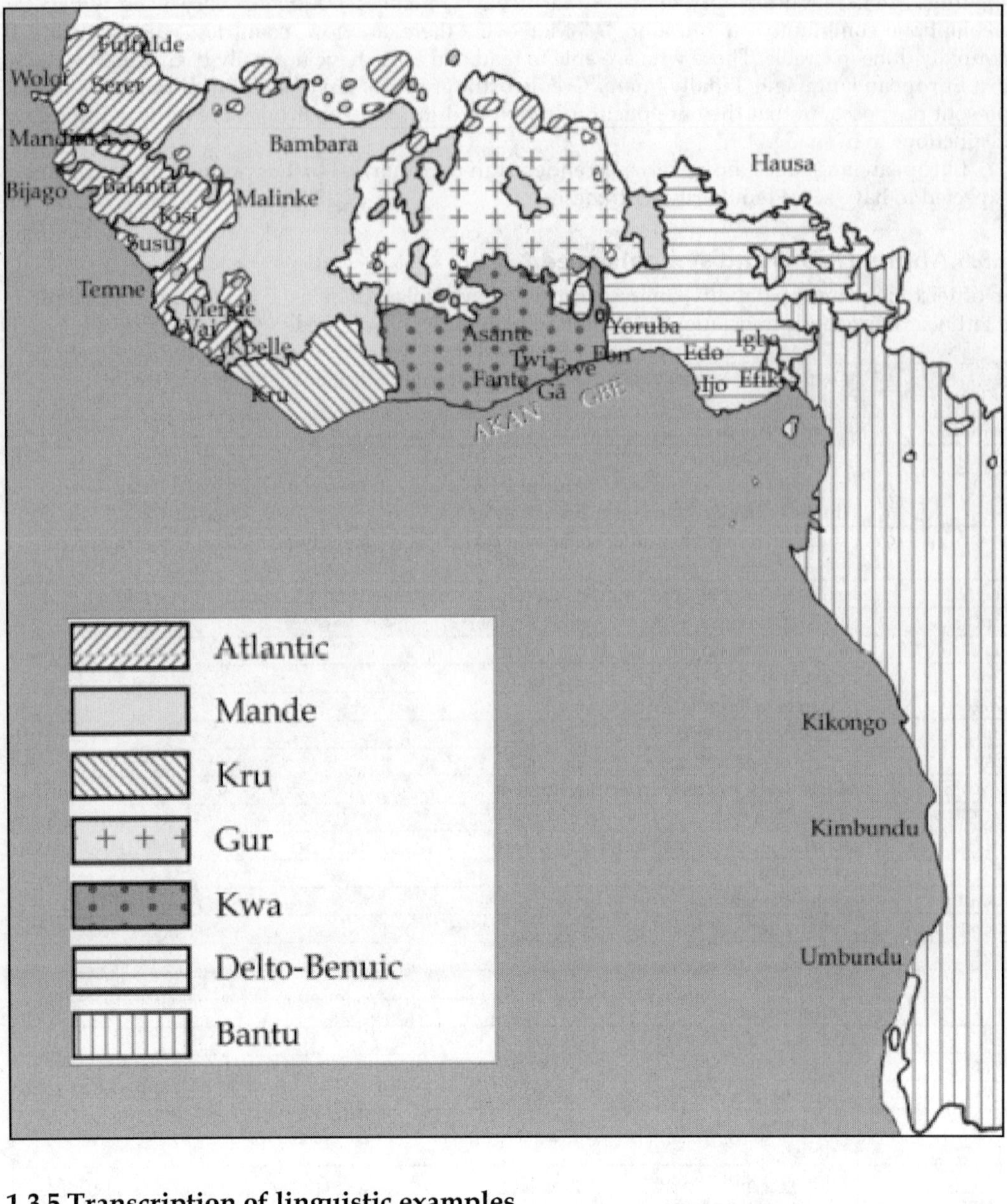

1.3.5 Transcription of linguistic examples

I have decided to transcribe contemporary Creole and African examples in IPA rather than in the orthographies normally employed.[14] The reasons for this are manifold. First, they might constitute an obstacle in a comparative study, since they differ from one another, often depending

14 The transcription is intended to be basically phonemic, but in order to facilitate comparison, I have sometimes consciously indicated purely phonetic features. This goes for e.g. final /n/ in Papiamentu (which is automatically velarised, but which is here nevertheless indicated as /ŋ/) and for other automatic subphonemic processes, such as palatalisation.

on what the official language of the country is (e.g. /u/ might be rendered <u> in a country having English, Spanish or Portuguese as its official language, but <ou> in a Francophone country, and <oe> in officially Dutch-speaking territories). In many cases, the choice of spelling conventions are the result of intricate political and ideological considerations. Secondly, these spellings are in fact often only semi-standardised. Practices frequently vary even within the creolophone community in question.[15] Moreover, there are few countries where writing is normally done in Creole. Those who are able to read and write have normally been taught to do so in a European language. Finally, many Creole orthographies are less practical than IPA for the present purposes, in that they are peculiarly rich in digraphs, sometimes preventing important distinctions to be made.

European languages, however, are rendered in their normal orthographies, as the reader is expected to have some familiarity with these.

1.3.6 Abbreviations and symbols used

In order to improve readability, abbreviations and symbols will be used sparingly, and mainly in interlinear morphemic translations. The following will be encountered:

–	suggests absence of substratal influence from [a particular source] (in the tables concluding each section)
#	word boundary
$	syllable boundary
(...)	suggests possible but weakly supported substratal influence from [a particular source] (in the tables concluding each section)
+	suggests substratal influence from [a particular source] (in the tables concluding each section)
†	extinct or archaic, or example taken from non-contemporary source
1pl	1st person plural
1sg	1st person singular
2pl	2nd person plural
2sg	2nd person singular
3pl	3rd person plural
3sg	3rd person singular
AAVE	African-American Vernacular English
ADJ	adjective
AUX	auxiliary
C	consonant
COMP	complementiser
CONJ	conjunction
COP	copula
CPLTV	completive
D	Dutch
DC	Dutch-lexifier Creole
DEF	definite
DEM	demonstrative
DET	determiner
E	English
EC	English-lexifier Creole
EMPH	marker of emphasis
F	French
FC	French-lexifier Creole
FUT	future
IMPERF	imperfective
IMPERS	impersonal pronoun

15 E.g. Aruban versus Curaçaoan Papiamentu.

INANIM	inanimate
INDEF	indefinite
INF	infinitive
IRR	irrealis
L	liquid
Lg(s)	language(s)
LOC	locative adposition
M	masculine
N	nasal consonant
NEG	negation
NP	noun phrase
OBJ	object
P	Portuguese
PASS	passive
P/C(s)	Pidgin and/or Creole language(s)
PC	Portuguese-lexifier Creole
PERF	perfective
PL	pluraliser
POSS	possessor
PRES	present
PROG	progressive
Q	question marker
S	semi-vowel *or* Spanish (when indicating etymologies)
SC	Spanish-lexifier Creole
SUBJ	subject
TMA	tense/mood/aspect
UPSID	UCLA Phonological Segment Inventory Database
V	vowel
Ṽ	nasal vowel
VP	verb phrase

1.4 Acknowledgements

I would like to extend a heartfelt thanks to the following people who have helped me during the writing of this thesis:

Enoch Aboh, Jeff Allen, Marlyse Baptista, Adrienne Bruyn, Jean-Robert Joseph Cadely, Vincent Cooper, Greville Corbett, Eva Eckkrammer, Emmanuel Faure, Rick Goulden, Tjerk Hagemeijer, Charles Harvey, George Huttar, Tore Jansson, Silvia Kouwenberg, Carla Luijks, Jouni Maho, Kevin Moore, Salikoko Mufwene, Peter Patrick, Mathias Perl, Nicolas Quint, Robin Sabino and **Jack Sidnell** for generously sharing with me some of their knowledge on their respective areas of expertise, **Clancy Clements, George Lang** and **David Sutcliffe** for helping me out of a Sticky Situation in Guyana, **Gabriele Sommer** for being kind enough to comment on the part about negations, **Karl-Erland Gadelii** for introducing me to creolistics in the first place, **Tom Klingler** for information on Louisiana FC and for lodging in New Orleans, **Östen Dahl** for making a linguist out of me, **Robert Chaudenson, Fred Field, Kate Green, Ron Kephart, Gerardo Lorenzino, Bill Samarin, Peter Stein, Thomas Stolz** and **Henri Wittmann** for sending me multitudes of articles and books, **Dany Adone, Peter Bakker, Angela Bartens, Louis-Jean Calvet, Tucker Childs, Robert Fournier, Stéphane Goyette, Anthony Grant, Magnus Huber, John Ladhams, Heliana Mello, Bethanie Morrissey, Sarah Roberts, Cefas van Rossem, Armin Schwegler, Jeff Siegel** and **Norval Smith** for generally enlightening discussions on issues concerning contact linguistics (and every once in a while also on personal matters), and both **Lotta Hedberg** and Bethanie Morrissey for last-minute proofreading of parts of the manuscript. Among Creolists, however, I am most indebted to **Philip Baker** and **John McWhorter**, who provided invaluable moral support and good advice, and with whom I have had numerous rewarding discussions, without which this thesis would be considerably poorer.

Although their impact is less evident here than in the papers I am currently preparing, they have more than anybody else forged my view of contact languages. Philip Baker also sacrificed a great deal of time in preparing the publication of the whole thing.

I would also like to thank all the people who made my stays in Mauritius, Martinique and other Creole-speaking countries pleasant, **Céu Fonseca** for housing and company in Lisbon, **my parents** for funding some of my conference trips when no none else would, **Johanna Bäckström, Kjell Carlsson, Gunnar Eriksson, Päivi Juvonen, Ásta Magnúsdóttir, Anna Palm, Tina Renkl, Gurutze Uría** and **Annica Westerberg**, among others, for brightening up my life through simply being friendly for the past couple of years.

Angela Bartens, Philip Baker, Stéphane Goyette, Anthony Grant and Magnus Huber were kind enough to read and comment upon earlier versions of the manuscript, something that resulted in some improvements. Unfortunately, time constraints prevented me from taking all their comments into consideration.

Alas, two of my main sources of inspiration and support, **Gunnel Källgren** and **Chris Corne**, sadly passed away during the time I spent working on this dissertation. I would like to dedicate it to their memory.

Chapter 2

Epistemology, methodology and terminology in Creolistics

It seems impossible to improve our understanding of how language contact and language restructuring functions – the ultimate goal of Pidgin and Creole studies, in my view – without determining from where the various features that make up the subsystems of these languages stem. When discussing the linguistic features that make up a Creole, it would presumably not be very controversial to claim that these can, at least potentially, derive from one or several of the following four sources:[1]

(1) The lexifier[2]
(2) The substrates
(3) Universals of restructuring[3]
(4) Independent development, including post-crystallisation changes either internally motivated or brought about by adstratal influence.

To determine the origin of a particular feature in a given Pidgin or Creole (henceforth P/C), we should therefore compare it to the linguistic systems likely to reflect these four possible sources, namely:

(a) The lexifier language, including obsolete forms and non-standard varieties likely to have been present in the restructuring situation
(b) A number of potential substrates chosen on the basis of reliable historical documentation – difficult though it is to find such data
(c) P/Cs in other parts of the world unrelated to the one investigated
(d) A large number of typologically divergent languages unrelated to any of those involved in the restructuring situation.

Note that each of (a) - (d) corresponds to one of (1) - (4) in the sense that the presence or absence of a given feature in any of (a) to (d) strengthens or weakens the possibility that the same feature in the P/C under investigation derives from any of the sources (1) to (4).

Considering the totality of features present in a given Creole, the following table illustrates the *a priori* possible combinations:

---

1 It seems to have become increasingly popular in recent years to acknowledge the possibility of multiple origins of Pidgin and Creole features (e.g. Kihm 1988; Stolz 1987a; Thomason & Kaufman 1988). Insofar as substrate languages can function as filters to sort out the lexifier material best suited for survival in the new linguistic ecology, this is certainly correct. In this paper, however, I use *origin* and similar words in a stricter sense.

2 It is crucial, in order to improve our understanding of P/C formation, to distinguish between lexifier features that are actual retentions, as opposed to those that have been (re)introduced later as a consequence of most Creoles' continued coexistence with their respective lexifiers. This is not the place to go into details on this subject, but see Goyette (2000) for an excellent demonstration of how this can in some cases be done.

3 I might be justified in dividing (3) into *universals of pidginisation* and *universals of creolisation* (the expansion of a Pidgin possibly but not necessarily causally related to nativisation), where the former would include e.g. morphological reduction, and the latter e.g. the development of a set of highly grammaticalised preverbal TMA markers (and in particular combinations of such markers). This division would of course require (c) below to be split into Pidgins and Creoles. One reason why I have chosen not to do so here, is that there is a dearth of data on stable but non-expanded Pidgins. Also, since pidginisation is associated with reduction, and Creolisation with expansion, assigning a given feature to either of these groups, even without taking the comparative perspective into account ought not be controversial – the feature would simply speak for itself.

Possible combinations of the presence or absence of particular Creole features in the lexifier (a), substrates (b), other P/Cs (c), and whether or not they are cross-linguistically common (d)

	LEXIFIER (a)	SUBSTRATES (b)	OTHER P/CS (c)	CROSS-LINGUISTICALLY COMMON (d)
1	+	+	-	-
2	+	-	+	-
3	+	+	+	-
4	+	-	-	-
5	-	+	-	-
6	-	-	+	-
7	-	+	+	-
8	-	-	-	-
9	+	+	-	+
10	+	-	+	+
11	+	+	+	+
12	+	-	-	+
13	-	+	-	+
14	-	-	+	+
15	-	+	+	+
16	-	-	-	+

Features which are cross-linguistically common should be put aside in creolistic discussions, assuming that they represent universals in the sense that they are manifestations of human cognition and processing capacity (in the case of semantics and syntax), articulatory capacity (in the case of phonology and phonetics) and/or economy principles versus expressive needs and perceptual salience. Examples would include arguably trivial features such as the presence of pronouns and consonants in a language, but also what to the untrained eye may seem less trivial, such as palatalisation (but cf §3.2.7) and the grammaticalisation of names of body parts into adpositions (and ultimately perhaps locative case affixes). With a "this could have happened to any language anywhere", we can thus eliminate cases 9 to 16 from our table above. This leaves cases 1 to 8, which are examined more closely in the table opposite.[4]

Obviously, there is also the question of quantity and quality. Finding evidence of a certain structure being used in a limited number of contexts by a limited number of people speaking a language variety which may or may not have been present in the restructuring situation cannot be considered enough, especially not if there are other more plausible sources of the same feature in the P/C. Still, this has been done repeatedly in the history of Creole studies (as we shall see below).

The term *Cafeteria Principle* was coined by Dillard (1970) for scholars picking a feature more or less at random from an Atlantic P/C and assigning it to almost any African language which happened to share it. Although coined with reference to substratists, the very same principle has been abused by writers emphasising the lexifier contribution to Creole genesis. Of course, what Smith (1999:252) has called *Bickerton's Edict* should be carefully observed, and any language variety which is invoked as the source of a given feature must have had speakers present *at the right place in the right time* (Bickerton 1984).

4 In the table, only features that are *present* in a given P/C are discussed. As pointed out in Parkvall (1999a), a lot can also be learned from studying features that are *absent*, and from asking why that should be so. Although this is not done here, the present methodology can, of course, easily be applied for such purposes.

CROSS-LINGUISTICALLY COMMON	PRESENT IN LEXIFIER	PRESENT IN SUBSTRATES	COMMON IN OTHER P/CS	SUGGESTED INTERPRETATION
-	+	+	-	Possibly present in the P/C because of lexifier/substrate convergence. *Examples*: Cliticised PAST marker /-ba/ in Upper Guinea Portuguese Creoles; basic SVO word order in Atlantic Creoles.
-	+	-	+	A lexifier feature possibly retained in the P/C because of unmarkedness, for instance semantic transparency. A lexifier origin is likely (though not certain) on the basis of its cross-linguistic rarity; after all, the same few European languages have been involved, or at least present, in the majority of all documented restructuring situations.
-	+	+	+	Cross-linguistically uncommon feature which by chance occurs in both the lexifier and the substrates of this particular P/C. Just like in the case above, the cross-linguistic rarity seemingly conflicts with its presence in Creoles in general, so that it may again be suspected that an Atlantic (and thus Indo-European/ Niger-Congo) bias in Creole studies in general is responsible.
-	+	-	-	An obvious lexifier retention. *Examples*: Position of adjectives vis-à-vis the nouns they determine in most Romance Creoles; most of the lexicon of any P/C.
-	-	+	-	An obviously substrate-induced feature (Africanism, in the case of Atlantic Creoles). *Examples*: dative serialisation and co-articulated stops in Atlantic Creoles; pronominal systems including dual forms and inclusive/exclusive distinctions in Pacific P/Cs (such as Tok Pisin, Philippine Spanish Creoles and Pidgin Yimas); 3pl used as nominal pluraliser in both groups.
-	-	-	+	A feature associated with restructuring. *Example*: Zero prepositions; limited allophony and allomorphy; almost complete lack of morphology; transformational shallowness. Possibly also features of the Creole TMA system. Again, there is a risk in basing generalisation on Atlantic and Pacific P/Cs alone, not only because the both share western European lexifiers, but also since some features *happen* to be shared by certain Melanesian and West African languages, such as prenasalised stops, verb serialisation, and the use of 3pl as a nominal pluraliser mentioned above.
-	-	+	+	A possible convergence between substratal and universal features. *Examples*: Bimorphemic interrogatives in many P/Cs.
-	-	-	-	This is a logical possibility, but it is difficult to come up with a good example. The closest I can get is OSV word order in Mobilian Jargon which, however, can be said to have a parallel in Muskogean (Drechsel 1996:250, 1997:128, 301-02). One might also include the opposition between short and long verb forms in Mauritian.

In addition to this, my claim is that the other two factors mentioned above, viz. universals of restructuring and independent development (as manifested through cross-linguistic frequency), should by definition be considered as omnipresent in *any place* at *any time*.

This may seem trivial to many readers, but the history of Creolistics – including fairly recent contributions – nevertheless abounds with examples of violations of these principles. Below follow a few examples intended to illustrate this.

2.1 First example: Universals, not substrate

Ferraz (1983:124) believed that the lack of passives in the Gulf of Guinea PCs was due to substrate influence. While some potential substrates, such as Ewe, Edo, Igbo, Kalabari, Kolokuma and Yoruba lack passive constructions (Lafage 1985:280; Thomas 1910:139; Westermann & Bryan 1952:93; Faraclas 1990:111; Ward 1952:172-73), others, including Ijo, Kikongo, Umbundu, and Kimbundu do have them (Williamson 1969b; Bentley 1887:621; Valente 1964:204; Maia 1964:91). More to the point, voice distinctions are liable to disappear in *any* restructuring process. In the Atlantic area, no basilectal Creole has retained the passives of its lexifier, a feature shared by most P/Cs elsewhere, including - to mention but a few - Tayo, Tok Pisin, Chinese Pidgin English, Tay Boi, and Pidgin Hawaiian (Ehrhart 1993:169; Shi 1991:19; Holm et al. 1997; Reinecke 1971:53; Roberts 1995:113). Indeed, Sebba (1997:39) and others include lack of passives as one of the most typical features of Pidgins. When passives do appear in P/Cs, they have usually been grammaticalised anew from other material, as in Papia Kristang PC, Kenyan Kinubi, Louisiana FC, and Seychelles FC (Baxter 1988; Owens 1996:165-66; Corne 1999:114; Bollée 1993:95). It is thus more than feasible that voice distinctions would disappear even in a situation where all languages involved have such a distinction. Although I do not know of any restructuring situation involving only languages having passives, a parallel may be seen in Koriki Trade Motu (Dutton 1983), which lacks overt transitive marking despite this being a feature of both of its input languages. Reasonably grammaticalised passives are by definition indicated by means of grammatical morphemes, and grammatical morphemes are precisely those which tend to disappear in a restructuring situation.

This is particularly true for more idiosyncratic areas of grammar; contrary to what was suggested by naïve observers in the early stages of Creolistics, such as Adam (1883), lack of such a feature as gender in a P/C does not require a substratal explanation. Both the European lexifiers (with the exception of English) and most of the Niger-Congo substrates of the Atlantic Creoles do have gender,[5] but since the systems are not anywhere near being compatible (i.e. a gender assigned to a certain noun in language X cannot be identified with that of language Y),[6] and - perhaps even more importantly - since grammatical gender distinctions, devoid of lexical content as they are, are not essential to makeshift communication, gender disappears from any reasonably radical Pidgin, and is hence also absent from their Creole descendants.

The Pidgins based on North American Indian languages, in particular those used more by Indians than by whites, such as Mobilian Jargon and Chinook Jargon, provide an excellent testing ground. Most languages native to this part of the world are excessively inflected to by European standards, and still, the resulting Pidgins are virtually devoid of morphology. And when nativising Chinook Jargon (Grant 1996), the Creole creators - mostly from synthetic-language backgrounds - did not develop inflexions, but rather kept the analytical system so typical of Creoles. Even in Bantu-speaking parts of Africa, where languages such as Lingala and Kituba have developed among varieties so closely related that quite a few idiosyncrasies have been able to survive - enough for McWhorter (1999a) to question their Pidgin status - the complex Bantu morphology has been severely reduced. Similarly, although pro-drop is a feature of both Romance languages and Arabic, Lingua Franca - the Pidgin which resulted mainly from contact between these two - preferred overt subject pronouns.

Some authors, in particular Mufwene (e.g. 1991a, 1991b, 1993, 1996), claim that Creoles are made up of features selected from a pool to which first and foremost the lexifier, but also to some extent the substrates, contributed. What the examples of morphological reduction just discussed suggest, however, is that substrate languages do not simply act as a filter through which lexifier material passes, but that the development of Pidgins operates in part independently from what the input components have to offer.

---

5 Though usually referred to as 'noun classes' in Niger-Congo languages.

6 Interestingly, even in contact situations where the input languages do have to some extent compatible systems (because they are genetically related), gender or class systems are severely reduced or abandoned altogether. Prime examples hereof include the Bantu Pidgins of Africa (Heine 1973; Stolz 1986:121).

The lack of inherited passives in P/Cs, for which Ferraz invoked substrate influence, should therefore not surprise us. Rather, given the low semantic content of the stylistic device of passivisation, its absence is an expected outcome of pidginisation.

In a similar vein to Ferraz, Lipski (1999:223-24) suggests that the lack of articles and copulas in "Chinese-Cuban Pidgin Spanish"[7] might be due to influence from Macao PC. In fact, a global perspective of Pidgins and Creoles would lead to a rather different conclusion, as articles and copulas are more often lost than retained. Obviously, both copulas and articles, just like many other grammatical items, are vulnerable in any Pidgin (or L_2 variety), even if all or most of the input components obligatorily express them.

Other features for which substrate influence has been invoked, but where, following the logic outlined in the table above, universal tendencies would seem to provide as plausible an explanation, include analytic counting systems (e.g. *ten-and-two* for 'twelve'; cf §5.1.1.4) and bimorphemic interrogatives (e.g. *what person* for 'who' or *what place* for 'where').[8]

The lack of inherited features such as passives, copulas, gender marking, articles and several other highly grammaticalised categories in most P/Cs should thus not call for a substratist explanation, but is rather a perfectly natural consequence of pidginisation.

Some attempts at explaining Creole features in terms of substrate transfer are not necessarily attributable to universals of pidginisation, but might equally well be the result of independent post-crystallisation developments. While Winford (1999) claims that important features of the Sranan TMA system are derived directly from the language's West African substrates, its organisation contains little that might not have emerged even if Sranan had developed in isolation from these languages.

2.2 Second example: again universals, not substrate

Holm (1992:62; see also Holm 1987) claims that there is "abundant evidence" that non-standard Brazilian Portuguese derives in part from São Tomé PC, citing as support a number of not spectacularly remarkable features of Brazilian Portuguese. Some of these, such as the lack of inversion in interrogative sentences, palatalisation[9] of alveolar stops (both Holm 1987:414), lack of certain kinds of agreement (p 407) and reduction of verbal morphology (p 420) are such that it is equally difficult to find languages which lack the "Brazilian" traits, as languages which have them. In other words, contact with almost any language, and not only Sãotomense, would have produced the same results. Moreover, it is far from certain that profound language contact must be responsible for these developments. Several languages could be cited which have undergone similar developments under conditions involving only moderate contact. Swedish, for instance, has during the past eight hundred years or so had its gender system reduced from three genders to two, has lost the accusative and dative case inflexions, the subjunctive and conditional verb paradigms, and completely abandoned verbal person and number agreement, thereby reducing the forms in the remaining paradigms from six to one, and as a result thereof introduced obligatory subject pronouns. Definite and indefinite articles have also emerged, quite predictably derived from demonstratives and the numeral 'one' respectively. Despite the somewhat longer time span - an additional three centuries - this is not unlike what has happened to non-standard Brazilian Portuguese and, presumably, few people would admit that it constitutes "abundant evidence" that Swedish is descended from Sãotomense.

Admittedly, Holm also mentions more substantial features, but these can alternatively be derived from the lexifier (circumverbal negation, mutual exchanges of /l/ and /r/, existential copula *tem*), or are ontologically dubious (serial verbs, preverbal TMA markers), or may have been

7 The glossonym appears between quotation marks because it is not obvious from the data that Lipski presents that the variety under discussion is a Pidgin rather than L_2 Spanish.

8 Muysken & Smith (1990:893) make the excellent point that, while some languages in West Africa do have bimorphemic interrogatives, the only forms in the Saramaccan interrogative paradigm that can unequivocally be shown to be of African origin are precisely those that are opaque (see §5.1.1.2 below).

9 Again, cf §3.2.7 below.

caused by contact with languages other than Sãotomense (syllable structure simplification, object marking *para*).

My claim here is that, in order to demonstrate the influence of one language on another, be it a Creole or not, the features adduced as proof need to display some degree of idiosyncraticity. This is generally accepted in historical linguistics but, although acknowledged in language contact studies such as Givón (1979:25) and Thomason & Kaufman (1988), it is often overlooked in Creolistics, and even explicitly denied in Lefebvre (1998). Most of the features discussed by Holm, on the other hand, tend to be cross-linguistically common to the point of being trivial.

2.3 Third example: lexifier, not substrate or universals

P/C phonology provides us with another typical illustration of epistemological slips in Creolistics. Macedo (1979:72), in his study of Cape Verde PC, claims that the presence of /t͡ʃ/ and /d͡ʒ/ in that language (in many other accounts of Cape Verdean phonology represented as /c/ and /ɟ/ respectively) is due to substratal influence, since the two phonemes are not present in (modern standard European) Portuguese. They do exist in the phoneme inventories of many Mande and Atlantic languages which are putative substrates of Upper Guinea Portuguese Creole (e.g. Bella 1946:731; Campbell 1991; Colley 1995:3; Ladefoged 1968; Maddieson 1984; Rowlands 1959:9; Ruhlen 1975), and this, of course, makes Macedo's account plausible. However, a closer look at the data suggests that he was in fact mistaken.

The first clue is that only the instances of /ʃ/ which correspond in modern Portuguese to orthographical <ch> – and not those spelt <x> or <s> – are realised as /c/ in Upper Guinea PC (the others have resulted in /s/). Since the P/C creators must have acquired their Portuguese lexicon through oral contact rather than through writing, this suggests that various kinds of /ʃ/ must once have been distinguished even in spoken Portuguese. This is indeed the case, as can be seen in the table below.

PORTUGUESE ORTHOGRAPHY	CURRENT STANDARD EUROPEAN PORTUGUESE	16TH CENTURY PRONUNCIATION	REFLEX IN UPPER GUINEA PORTUGUESE CREOLE
s$	ʃ	s	s
x	ʃ	ʃ	s
ch	ʃ	t͡ʃ	c

In the standard, <ch> changed from an affricate to a fricative in the 16th century, but even today, some dialects, especially in north-western Portugal, retain this distinction (Ferronha [ed.] n. d.:32; Carvalho 1984c:155).

Furthermore, a look at modern English and French loan-words in Wolof and Mandinka (Peace Corps 1995a, 1995b), important substrates of Upper Guinea Portuguese Creole, reveals that instances of English /t͡ʃ/ consistently result in /c/, whereas both English and French /ʃ/ instead yield /s/. This suggests that speakers of Wolof and Mandinka at least would have depalatalised all instances of Portuguese <ch> if only it had been pronounced /ʃ/ in the formative period of Upper Guinea Portuguese Creole – given, of course, that the substrates did not undergo any drastic changes in the time span between their first contacts with the Portuguese and their first contact with English and French.

Quite clearly, Upper Guinea Portuguese Creole /c/ is not the direct reflex of modern Portuguese /ʃ/, but rather of an older Portuguese /t͡ʃ/. Obviously, then, the presence of /c/ in Upper Guinea Portuguese Creole (and its voiced counterpart /ɟ/, the story of which is parallel to that of /c/, i. e. it is derived from an older Portuguese /d͡ʒ/, today rendered as /ʒ/) is due not to substratal influence, but simply represents a direct carryover from the lexifier.

Now that we know that older Portuguese did have /t͡ʃ/ and /d͡ʒ/, and that the only underwent a moderate mutation into /c/ and /ɟ/ respectively in Upper Guinea Portuguese Creole (according to some accounts; as noted above, many represent the same phonemes as affricates rather than as plosives, something that leaves no room at all for substrate influence), it may seem tempting to assume that all instances of /ɟ/ reflect 16th century Portuguese. However, Modern Portuguese /ʒ/ is not the only sound which corresponds to /ɟ/ in Upper Guinea Portuguese Creole. Portuguese also has a palatal lateral /ʎ/. When Portuguese comes into contact with languages lacking this, the recipient language (in cases of borrowing) or the P/C creators (in cases of restructuring) had the choice of retaining either the feature [+PALATAL], or the feature [+LATERAL] (or, of course, using both sequentially, resulting in /lj/).[10] We do find both strategies in languages outside Europe which have been in contact with Portuguese, with the former being the most common. The palatal option, in turn, makes both a glide /j/ and a plosive /ɟ/ possible. In most cases, /j/ has been the favoured option, and it is for instance the normal reflex of /ʎ/ in the Lower Guinea PCs (and also the descendant of /ʎ/ in French). In Upper Guinea, however, Portuguese /ʎ/ constantly corresponds to /ɟ/, with the exception of recent loans and upper mesolects. This is not attested for any variety of Portuguese, which makes a superstratal model less plausible. Portuguese dialects which have lost the phoneme have usually replaced it by /j/, as for instance that of São Miguel in the Azores (Révah 1963:447). The fact that /ɟ/ is not a reflex of /ʎ/ in PCs outside this area suggests a substratal explanation, and indeed French loans in Wolof and Bambara (Peace Corps 1995a, 1995b) such as *médaille* 'medal', *ail* 'garlic' and *paillasse* 'straw mattress' prove that French <il ~ ille>, cognate with Portuguese <lh>, and once similarly pronounced, has yielded precisely /ɟ/.

Thus, taking into account more language varieties than just modern standard Portuguese and the local African languages, the origin of /c/ and the multiple origins of /ɟ/ can be determined. The presence of the former has little to do with substrate influence, whereas those instances of the latter that correspond to Portuguese <lh> (but only those!) do.

2.4 Fourth example: substrate, not lexifier

Working in a vein similar to that of Robert Chaudenson (e.g. 1979, 1992, 1995), Mufwene (1996) and Wittmann & Fournier (1983:194) suggest that serial verb constructions (SVCs), often considered typical of Atlantic Creoles, are not of African origin, as many before them would have it, but rather overgeneralisations of European prototypes. European languages are not normally considered to be serialising, but constructions such as *go get a doctor* or *allez chercher un médecin* are reminiscent of SVCs, and sufficiently so, according to Mufwene (1996:115-16) for them to gain a foothold in the nascent Creoles, in which they expanded and constituted a pattern after which other serial constructions were formed. There are, however, a few additional facts, which Mufwene and Wittmann & Fournier apparently did not consider, and which alter the picture significantly. First (and this, Mufwene and Wittmann & Fournier do themselves admit), the SVC-like constructions in European languages are limited to lative heads, in English to *come* and *go*. Most Atlantic Creoles have at least three other important types of SVCs (instrumental, benefactive and comparative; see §4.6), which have no apparent prototypes in European languages.[11] This speaks against a European origin. Secondly, SVCs are rare cross-linguistically, and apart from East Asia and New Guinea, few languages other than those of West Africa and Creoles with such substrates display extensive serialisation. This indicates that SVCs are unlikely to have emerged independently of one another in a large number of Atlantic Creoles and their substrates.[12] Thirdly, many P/Cs - interestingly enough precisely those with non-serialising substrates, as pointed out by Muysken & Veenstra (1995:291) - do not have SVCs. This suggests that there is no causal connexion between SVCs and the restructuring process. Finally, most SVCs of the Atlantic Creoles, often together with others, can be found in African languages, spoken, as it happens, in

---

[10] Something similar to this, viz. /lɟ/, has been attested in the Portuguese Creole of Sri Lanka (Dalgado 1900:15).

[11] In addition to these constructions, most ECs, some PCs and DCs in the Atlantic area use a serial verb meaning 'to say' (or an item which originates from such a serialisation) in a complementiser function (see §3.4).

[12] The so-called *Isle de France* Creoles of the Indian Ocean (Mauritius, its dependencies, and the Seychelles) might seem to constitute an exception; however, there were indeed West Africans among their creators (Baker & Corne 1982), and it also seems that Eastern Bantu is more serialising than has been assumed (Corne et al. 1996). For the ontological status of SVCs in Isle de France Creoles, see also Bickerton (1989, 1990), Seuren (1990a, 1990b) and Corne (1999:181-88).

the very areas from which most slaves were exported to the plantation colonies.[13] This too speaks in favour of an African origin.

In other words, the comparison between the Creoles and the lexifiers only might well lead to the conclusion arrived at by Mufwene and Wittmann & Fournier. However, when account is taken of the relevant substrates, as well as other restructured languages, and when a global typological perspective is adopted, a very different picture results.[14]

2.5 Conclusion

This list could be extended. For instance, several features of Bickerton's (1981) bioprogram are conspicuously similar to West African languages, and, interestingly, Creoles outside the Atlantic and Hawaii look strikingly less like Bickerton's Creole prototype. Since this has been commented extensively on elsewhere (e.g. Singler 1986, McWhorter 1997b), I will refrain from repeating what others have already pointed out.

The moral of the story, then, is that the Creolist must take into account not only lexifier and substrate but also general properties of P/Cs and the findings of linguistic typology and historical linguistics. I hereby suggest:

- that a linguistic feature of a P/C be regarded as a **certain lexifier retention** iff (=if and only if) it is *present in the lexifier, absent from the substrates, cross-linguistically uncommon* and *not generally present in other, unrelated P/Cs.*

- We are dealing with a **certain substrate transfer** iff the feature is *present in the substrates, absent from the lexifier, cross-linguistically uncommon* and *not generally present in other, unrelated P/Cs.*

- Similarly, a feature is a **certain restructuring universal** iff it is *absent from both the lexifier and the substrates* and *cross-linguistically uncommon,* but *generally present in other, unrelated P/Cs.*

- A **certain case of independent development**, finally, is characterised by being *absent from all the input components* as well as from *other, unrelated P/Cs.*

I believe that paying due attention to this division is essential in order to arrive at an understanding of language restructuring and other outcomes of far-reaching language contact. And – to end on a positive note – let me emphasise that some publications, notably Hancock (1980), Bickerton (1986:228) and Rooij (1997:316), quite explicitly do make the distinctions called for in this chapter.

---

13 For examples of non-lative SVCs in West African languages, see e.g. Agheyisi (1971:107-09), Armstrong (1984:331), Baudet (1981:112), Bellon (1983:23), Boretzky (1983:177-78), Creissels (1991:323), Fagerli (1995), Huttar (1981), Lafage (1985:279), Lord (1993), Manfredi (1984:353), Muysken & Veenstra (1995), Redden et al. (1963:67), Sebba (1987, 1997:195), Taylor (1971:294-95), Ward (1952:3), Welmers (1946:41), Westermann & Bryan (1952:92).

14 For more examples of the same kind criticising particularly the substratist school of thought, see McWhorter & Parkvall (1999).

Chapter 3

Phonology

In this chapter, the phonemic inventories of Atlantic Creoles will be compared with those of their lexifiers and putative substrates, the admittedly somewhat simplistic working hypothesis being that whenever a lexifier phoneme is lacking in the Creole, this is due to it being absent also from the dominant substrate(s).

Whenever claims regarding the presence or absence of phonemes in West African languages are made in the following section, and no other reference is given, the claim is based on a private database including the complete segment inventories of about 80 such languages. It is based on data given in Anon. (1961), Armstrong (1984), Arnott (1969b), Bamgbo̥se (1966, 1969), Bella (1946), Bentley (1887), Campbell (1991), Childs (1995), Clements (1985), Colley (1995), Cook (1969), Delafosse (1929), Derive (1990), Elugbe (1984), Eynde (1960), Faraclas (1984), Houis (1963), Innes (1966, 1967), Kelly (1969), Ladefoged (1968), Laman (1912), Laver (1969), Maddieson (1984), Maddieson (1984), Mafeni (1969), Manessy & Sauvageot [eds] (1963), Marchese (1984), Meier, Meier & Bendor-Samuel (1975), Ndiaye (1996), Opubor (1969), Rowlands (1959), Ruhlen (1975), Schadeberg (1982), Smith (1967, 1969), Swift & Zola (1963), Söderberg & Wikman (1966), UPSID, Ward (1952, 1963), Welmers (1952, 1973, 1976), Westermann (1924), and Williamson (1969b).

3.1 Vowels

3.1.1 Vowel aperture

While English is difficult to classify, the lexifier languages concerned here, with the exception of Spanish, have vowel inventories which distinguish four degrees of aperture, with contrasting open-mid (i.e. /ɛ/, /ɔ/) and close-mid (i.e. /e/, /o/) vowels. Some Atlantic Creoles, however, have three degrees of aperture rather than four. Since five-vowel systems are exceedingly common, this need not necessarily be due to substrate influence, but the fact that most Caribbean ECs and FCs have more phonemic vowels than ECs and FCs of the Indian and Pacific Oceans, coupled with the fact that the same is broadly true of their respective substrates, suggests that this may indeed be the case.

The following Atlantic Creoles, excluding those lexified by Spanish,[1] are said to distinguish only three degrees of aperture in their vowel systems:

- Sranan EC (Adamson & Smith 1995:221).
- Ndyuka EC (Alleyne 1980:35).
- Basilectal Louisiana FC (Neumann 1985:84).[2]
- Guinea-Bissau PC (Scantamburlo 1981:21; Kihm 1994:14; Rougé 1988:12, 1994:139)
- Annobón PC (Post 1995:193).
- Negerhollands DC (Stolz 1986:42).

Lalla (1986) and Alleyne (1980:42) also hypothesise that Jamaica EC and Krio EC, respectively, originally belonged to this class. Both now have a seven-vowel system, but the five vowels of Sranan EC (from an earlier form of which both are partly descended) and its close relative Ndyuka EC would seem to support the hypothesis. A problem, however, is that Saramaccan EC, a more direct descendant of proto-Sranan than Krio which has had less contact with its lexifier

1 Palenquero has a five-vowel-system, just like Spanish. Basilectal Papiamentu SC has seven vowels (the mesolect having nine), but there, of course, a large part of the lexicon is from Portuguese and Dutch.

2 Valdman & Klingler (1997:113), however, describe a four-level system.

than any other EC after its birth, has an opposition between open-mid and close-mid vowels which is manifested in etymologically motivated positions in lexemes of English origin (Holm 1988:114). It should be noted, though, that the Sranan vowel system has been analysed as containing both five and seven oral vowels, and that there are some few minimal pairs opposing /e ~ ɛ/ and /o ~ ɔ/, such as /seri/ 'to sail' versus /sɛri/ 'to sell' (Holm 1988:114). Berbice DC, finally, is another borderline case, since the number of minimal pairs is small indeed and, moreover, the distinction only concerns front vowels (Kouwenberg 1994c:277-79)

Of a total of more than 80 West African languages whose phonemic inventories I have examined, about two thirds make a distinction between open-mid and close-mid vowels, with the distribution being as follows (percentages are relative to the total number of languages within each grouping):

LANGUAGE GROUP	THREE DEGREES OF APERTURE	FOUR DEGREES OF APERTURE
Atlantic	33%	67%
Mande	25%	75%
Kru	0%	100%
Kwa	3%	97%
Delto-Benuic	37%	64%
Bantu	41%	59%
All	**32%**	**68%**

Two remarks are in order here, as some groupings are highly heterogeneous in this respect. Firstly, the southern Delto-Benuic languages (spoken in areas from which most slaves from this region were drawn) tend to have four degrees or aperture, whereas the northern languages do not. For Bantu languages, on the other hand, it is the ones spoken furthest away from the slaving areas which have the most complex vowel systems. Taking this into account, we could revise the above table as follows:

LANGUAGE GROUP	THREE DEGREES OF APERTURE	FOUR DEGREES OF APERTURE
Atlantic	33%	67%
Mande	25%	75%
Kru	0%	100%
Kwa	3%	97%
most relevant Delto-Benuic	5%	95%
most relevant Bantu	100%	0%
All	**32%**	**68%**

What we see, thus, is that the substrate speakers most likely to reduce the European vowel inventories would be Bantu speakers and of some few speakers of Atlantic and Mande languages[3]. Lower Guineans, on the other hand, would not be expected to carry out this reduction.

AREA	FEATURE	LANGUAGE	GROUP	SUGGESTED SUBSTRATE INFLUENCE
Phonology	Vowel aperture	Sranan EC	EC	+Bantu, -Kwa, -Delto-Benuic
Phonology	Vowel aperture	Ndyuka EC	EC	+Bantu, -Kwa, -Delto-Benuic
Phonology	Vowel aperture	Louisiana FC (basilect)	FC	+Bantu, -Kwa, -Delto-Benuic
Phonology	Vowel aperture	Guinea-Bissau PC	PC	+ various Atlantic and Mande languages
Phonology	Vowel aperture	Annobón PC	PC	+Bantu, -Kwa, -Delto-Benuic
Phonology	Vowel aperture	Negerhollands DC	DC	+Bantu, -Kwa, -Delto-Benuic

3 The only Atlantic languages with only three degrees of aperture in my sample are Konyagi and Fulfulde. Annoyingly, all the Mande languages distinguishing only three degrees of aperture are claimed to distinguish four by at least one other source!

Although Mande and Atlantic languages normally have four degrees of aperture, we obviously have to recognise other possibilities than Bantu for Guinea-Bissau PC. There are a few languages in the relevant area with only three degrees of aperture, though there seems to be no systematic distribution.

For the FCs, there is (as in French) a tendency to use close-mid vowels (/e, o/) in open syllables, and open-mid (/ɛ, ɔ/) vowels in closed syllables. With few exceptions, therefore, the minimal pairs in FCs occur where the loss of an etymological /r/ has made a previously closed syllable open, as is illustrated below:

LANGUAGE	WORD	ETYMOLOGY	GLOSS	WORD	ETYMOLOGY	GLOSS
Haiti FC	/ve/	(< F *vœux*)	'wish'	/vɛ:/	(< F *vert, verre*))	'glass', 'green'
	/ke/	(< F *queue*)	'tail'	/kɛ:/	(< F *cœur*)	'heart'
	/ne/	(< F *nœud*)	'knot'	/nɛ:/	(< F *nerf*)	'nerve'
	/lo/	(< F *lot*)	'lot'	/lɔ:/	(< F *l'or*)	'gold'
	/fo/	(< F *faux*)	'false'	/fɔ:/	(< F *fort*)	'strong'
	/se/	(< F *c'est*)	'it is'	/sɛ:/	(< F *sœur*)	'sister'
Dominica FC	/le/	(< F *vouloir*)	'to want'	/lɛ:/	(< F *l'heure*)	'hour, time'
	/pe/	(< F *peux*)	'to be able'	/pɛ:/	(< F *peur*)	'to be afraid'
	/mo/	(< F *mot*)	'word'	/mɔ:/	(< F *mort*)	'dead; to die'

Sources: Amastae (1979:85), Green (1988:429), Valdman (1970).

The same thing in part applies to São Tomé PC (Green 1988:429). It is not obvious how these items should be treated. It is possible, of course, that the languages concerned originally retained post-vocalic /r/,[4] and that the subsequent loss of this turned a system with five oral vowels into a seven-vowel one by making a previously allophonic variation phonemic. Under this analysis, all Atlantic French Creoles, as well as São Tomé PC (and thus possibly also earlier forms of its relatives) would also count as languages with (originally) vowel systems distinguishing only three degrees of aperture, with the more open forms found before etymological /r/ being purely allophonic.

3.1.2 Denasalisation

In principle, the Atlantic Creoles whose lexifiers had nasal vowels (i.e. French and Portuguese) have preserved these. This is by no means self-evident, since other French-based Pidgins and Creoles, such as Tayo (Ehrhart 1993),[5] Burundi Pidgin French (Niedzielski 1989:86) and Congolese Tirailleur Pidgin French (Queffelec & Niangouna 1990:17-8) either replace nasal vowels with their oral counterparts (Tayo) or with a V+N sequence (the two varieties of African Pidgin French). Denasalisation is also attested in the speech of 16th century Portuguese Blacks (Raimundo 1933:21).

However, almost no Atlantic Creoles systematically lack the nasal vowels of their lexifier. One exception is Saramaccan EC, in which Portuguese /ẽ/ and /ɛ̃/ are denasalised (Stolz 1986:87). Since Saramaccan does have nasal vowels (Bakker, Smith & Veenstra 1995:170), this denasalisation may have operated in the hypothesised Djutongo PC, whose merger with proto-Sranan EC led to the formation of Saramaccan (Ladhams 1999a).

Louisiana FC too has nasal vowels, but is nevertheless remarkable in that cases of denasalisation are more frequent than in other FC varieties (Neumann 1985:88).

4 This is still found in some New World FCs (Orjala 1970:32; Maher 1993:410; Corne 1999:131), as well as in Príncipe PC (Ferraz & Valkhoff 1975:23). Green (1988:429, 431) also suggests that an underlying /r/ may still be present in the varieties presently under discussion.

5 Corne (1999:41; p c), however, vehemently disputes this, claiming that Tayo does indeed have phonemic nasal vowels.

Denasalisation of mid nasal vowels is relatively frequent in Dominica FC, but may be a 20th century development (Amastae 1979:107), something that is supported by the rarity of denasalisation in its closest relatives.

Similarly, Angolar PC has phonemic nasal vowels, but appears to frequently use oral vowels where São Tomé PC has retained nasals (for examples, see e.g. Lorenzino 1998:85). The comparison with the closely related São Tomé PC confirms that we are dealing with an - if not recent - at least post-formative,[6] development.

In Guinea-Bissau PC, Portuguese nasal vowels are often realised as a sequence of oral vowel and nasal consonant, but simple denasalisation is also documented (Scantamburlo 1981:27).

A majority of all West African languages have phonemic nasal vowels,[7] and a number of those which do not, nevertheless allow them on the phonetic level. The Mande, Kru and Kwa families are homogeneous in having nasal vowels, to the extent that it is rather difficult to find exceptions (Campbell 1991; Delafosse 1929:56; Duthie 1996:12; Houis 1963:22; Innes 1967:4; Maddieson 1984; Marchese 1984:128; Ruhlen 1975; Welmers 1976; UPSID).

Likewise, Atlantic languages typically lack nasal vowels (Ruhlen 1975; Manessy & Sauvageot [eds] 1963:2; UPSID).

Gur is mixed in this respect (Welmers 1952:83; Maddieson 1984:289), as is Bantu (Arnott 1969b:147; Guthrie 1953; Maddieson 1984; Ruhlen 1975; Schadeberg 1982:110; UPSID).

Many less relevant Delto-Benuic languages in the north lack nasal vowels (Ruhlen 1975; Maddieson 1984). However, more or less all Delto-Benuic languages closer to the coast have them (Bamgboṣe 1966:7; Blench 1984:313; Faraclas 1984:388; Kelly 1969:156-57; Mafeni 1969:107; Opubor 1969:127-28; Ruhlen 1975).

Of the main potential contributors to Atlantic Creole formation, it is thus mainly Atlantic and some Bantu languages that might have contributed to denasalisation.

Not unexpectedly, it is from African languages lacking nasal vowels that we have evidence of denasalisation in L_2 varieties of European languages or in European loan words. Speakers of Wolof, for instance, often replace French nasal vowels with corresponding oral vowels, and somewhat less often with VN (David 1975:57; Dialo 1990:64; Gamble 1963:135; Kwofie 1978:71; Ndiaye 1996:110; Peace Corps 1995a; Rambaud 1963:15). In Kikongo and closely related languages, French and Portuguese nasal vowels are often denasalised, but sometimes also replaced by VN (Bal 1979; Swift & Zola 1963; David 1975:168; Swartenbroeckx 1973). Similar developments are attested in other Western Bantu languages, such as Kimbundu, Myene and Teke (Mendonça 1933:65; Calloc'h 1911:65; Anon. 2000).

Since no Atlantic Creole whose lexifier has nasal vowels lack them altogether, substrate influence in this area must be regarded as slight, as indicated by the brackets in the following summary.

AREA	FEATURE	LANGUAGE	GROUP	SUGGESTED SUBSTRATE INFLUENCE
Phonology	Denasalisation	Saramaccan EC	EC	(+Atlantic), (+Kikongo), (+Kimbundu)
Phonology	Denasalisation	Louisiana FC	FC	(+Atlantic), (+Kikongo), (+Kimbundu)
Phonology	Denasalisation	Guinea-Bissau PC	PC	(+Atlantic), (+Kikongo), (+Kimbundu)
Phonology	Denasalisation	Angolar PC	PC	(+Atlantic), (+Kikongo), (+Kimbundu)

3.1.3 Front rounded vowels

World-wide, front rounded vowels occur in 12% of all languages, but most of these are found in Europe and Asia, and only 3% of the languages of Africa have front rounded vowels (Ruhlen 1976:148). This, together with the fact that oppositions between them are acquired by children later than those between their unrounded counterparts (Ingram 1989:194), makes this phoneme series a highly marked one. Indeed, it can also be shown on a cross-linguistic basis to be diachronically unstable (Hock 1991:143).

6 Post-formative with regard to creolisation, that is. As noted in §5.4.2, Angolar PC is just a partial relexification of São Tomé PC.

7 53% of all Niger-Kordofanian languages (Ruhlen 1976:159), as opposed to 22% world-wide.

Three of the five lexifier languages, French, Dutch and some dialects of Portuguese,[8] have a set of rounded front vowels. In West Africa, on the other hand, front rounded vowels are exceedingly rare. They have been attested – often merely as allophones of other vowels – in Wolof, Kru, some Mande languages (Malinke, Vai, Dyula, and some Ivorian Mande languages) and some Bantu languages (Ngwe, Yans) (Sauvageot 1965:24; Derive 1990:115, 135; Ruhlen 1975:234, 248; Westermann & Ward 1933:41; Welmers 1976:15; Delafosse 1929:55; Holm 1988:119). In the UPSID database, phonemic front rounded vowels are represented only in Wolof (Atlantic) and Ejagham (Bantu) out of 39 relevant West African languages.

It is thus not surprising that front rounded vowels are all but absent from Afro-European language varieties. They are certainly absent from the Portuguese Creoles in Africa, but there is nothing to suggest that front rounded vowels were ever present in the superstratal input, i.e. that the Portuguese dialects that have them were well represented in the original restructuring situation.

They are also missing from Skepi DC and Berbice DC, and apparently only present in the acrolectal variety of Negerhollands DC spoken by whites (Stolz 1986:119), and even the moderately restructured New Jersey Black Dutch (Prince 1910) displayed unrounding tendencies.[9]

Dutch has imposed front rounded vowels on the now obsolete *Church Creole* register of Sranan EC and on Papiamentu SC (Voorhoeve 1971:312; Kouwenberg & Murray 1994:7). This seems to be a recent phenomenon, though, in the former case because only Dutch loan-words are affected, and in the latter because monolingual speakers born before about 1910 lack such vowels (Baum 1976:86).

In the French Creoles, bilingual speakers of urban dialects occasionally use front rounded vowels (e.g. St-Jacques-Fauquenoy 1974:30; Valdman 1971:61), as do speakers of the strongly French-influenced Creoles of Louisiana and St Barts/St Thomas (Neumann 1985; Highfield 1979; Maher 1997:247), but, interestingly, they have also been attested in the speech of monolingual informants in rural areas of northern and south-western Haiti (Pompilus 1979:120; Valdman 1971:61, 1973:517; Ariza 1991). A few observers claim to also have found front rounded vowels in Grenada FC (Hazaël-Massieux 1990:99), but this finding seems more controversial, and has not been corroborated by others. Some also question the existence of front rounded vowels in northern Haitian. Be that as it may, the fact remains that almost all known Atlantic Creoles do *not* have a front rounded series.

Front rounded vowels are usually replaced by their unrounded counterparts in FCs and DCs[10] and in basilectal Papiamentu SC, thus keeping the feature [+FRONT] rather than [+ROUNDED]. In some varieties, however, the opposite strategy is employed. This is especially true of Guiana FC and, to a lesser extent, Haiti FC (Hall 1966:28; Lefebvre 1998:401; Fauquenoy-St-Jacques 1979; Green 1988:439; Tinelli 1981:124), and Berbice DC (Stolz 1986:85). Some examples may also be found in 19th century Louisiana FC (Corne 1999:151). Saramaccan EC also has a tendency to back front rounded vowels in words of Dutch origin (Stolz 1986:87), but since the age of these loans remains unknown, African influence cannot be invoked with certainty.

For FCs, it may be significant that the reflex of the French 3pl *eux* (or dialectal forms of this) is /je/ in Guiana, Louisiana and Grenada, but /jɔ/ in Haiti and all Lesser Antillean varieties except Grenadian.

French loan-words in African languages, as well as documentation of West African L_2 French suggests that the unrounding strategy is used in Wolof, Senegalese languages in general, Fulfulde, Mandinka, Guinean languages in general, Susu, Ivory Coast languages,[11] Akan, Gã,

8 The dialects spoken around Castelo Branco and Portalegre, as well as that of the Lagos area in the south-west have /y/ and /ø/ (Ferronha [ed.] n. d.:33), as does the Portuguese spoken on São Miguel (Azores) (Cunha & Cintra 1985:13).

9 Holm (1989:337) makes the reservation that this applies to certain dialects of European Dutch as well. However, Prince mentions items which do have front rounded vowels in the white, but not in the black ethnolect, such as /zu:y̥ə/ 'seven' (D *zeven*; white ethnolect /zø:y̥ə/) and /nu:t/ 'nut' (D *noot*; white ethnolect /nø:jt/.

10 Definitely so in Negerhollands DC (Stolz 1986:43, 84), and probably also in Skepi DC, where, however, the number of attested words (Robertson 1983) containing an etymologically front rounded vowel only amounts to four.

11 That is, where front rounded vowels are not kept; Lafage's data show a surprisingly high rate of retention even among people only moderately proficient in French.

Bete, Myene, Kituba, Kikongo (Dialo 1990:64; Ndiaye 1996:109; David 1975:56; Rambaud 1963:15; Peace Corps 1995a; Kwofie 1978:64; Anon. 1961; Swift & Zola 1963:xvii; Swartenbroeckx 1973; Diallo 1998:118; Houis 1963; Anon. 2000; Lafage 1979:212, 1990; Zang Zang 1998:95; Arensdorff 1913:266).

Some languages also make use of mixed systems. The few French loan-words in Bambara mentioned by Blondé (1979:381) present a mixed pattern; on the one hand, /alimeti/ 'match' (< F *alumette*) displays unrounding, but on the other, in /dute/ 'tea' (< F *thé*), the vowel is backed. The same applies to Mandinka, another Mande language, where Peace Corps (1995b) has on the one hand /ni:moro:/ 'number' (< F *numéro*), /dipite:/ 'member of parliament' (< F *député*), and /piki:ro:/ (< F *piqûre*) 'injection', and on the other /lune:to:/ 'glasses' (< F *lunettes*) and /penturo:/ 'paint' (< F *peinture*). In Wolof, too, we find /pi:r/ 'pure' (< F *pure*), /isin/ 'factory' (< F *usine*), /kɔsti:m/ 'suit' (< F *costume*), and /iniwɛrsite/ 'university' (< F *université*) alongside /su:jɛ:/ 'July' (< F *juillet*), /lundi/ 'Monday' (< F *lundi*), /wuloɔr/ 'value' (< F *valeur*), and /ləjum/ 'vegetables' (< F *légumes*) (Peace Corps 1995a). Bal's (1979) examples from French loans in Ntandu also suggest a varied treatment of French front rounded vowels, and there are even varying realisations for one and the same word, as in /muzíki ~ mizíki/ 'music' (< F *musique*) (Bal 1979:52).

David (1975:171) suggests that the backing strategy is used by Bantu speakers in Congo-Kinshasa, and this is the only case for which I have seen data or explicit claim that backing is the preferred strategy. Note, however, that this does not seem to apply to neighbouring Kikongo and Kituba.

It is not clear what determines the choice of replacement strategy, although it does appear likely that substrate influences would have played a role.[12] As no clear geographical pattern can be discerned, the evidence presented above does not seem sufficient, however, to make any statements with respect to the treatment of etymological front rounded vowels in FCs and DCs.

3.1.4 High nasal vowels

As shown in §3.1.2, some of the nasal vowels provided by the European lexifier languages have been lost in the Atlantic Creoles. On the other hand, two new ones, /ĩ/ and /ũ/, have developed in some varieties.

Cross-linguistically, Ruhlen (1973) has shown that close vowels are the least likely to have phonemic nasalised counterparts. And indeed, of the two European lexifier languages having phonemic nasal vowels, one, namely French lacks only a closed set of nasal vowels (the other, Portuguese, does have such a set). The relative rarity of high nasal vowels thus makes a substrate derivation more likely.

At least phonetically, /ũ/ and /ĩ/ exist in a number of Atlantic Creoles. As for their phonemic status in Haiti FC, there is some disagreement.[13] Nasal closed vowels occur underlyingly in slightly more than a dozen Haitian words of clearly African origin, and if one chooses to consider them phonemic, they are clearly marginal to the phonemic system of Haiti FC. Yet, it is noteworthy that while many African words in the Haiti FC lexicon have been Europeanised, in the sense that they have lost conspicuously African features such as prenasalised and coarticulated stops, /ĩ/ and /ũ/ remain, albeit in mostly in words of African origin. Tinelli (1981:7), who considers close nasal vowels phonemic in Haiti FC, also points out that they are present in some lexical items of French origin such as /fĩm/ (< F *film*) 'film', but so far as I can understand, it would not be difficult to account for these by the regressive nasalisation rules of Haitian.

Jamaica EC has [ĩ] and [ũ] on the phonetic level, as does Krio EC, and all the Surinamese ECs (Bailey 1966:15; Berry 1961:4 cited in Tinelli 1981:10; Fyle & Jones 1980:xix; Adamson & Smith 1995:221; Alleyne 1980:35; Bakker, Smith & Veenstra 1995:170). The same goes for Dominica FC and Grenada FC, where their phonemic status is explicitly denied by Amastae (1979:85) and

---

12 In L_2 Swedish, for instance, unrounding is universally preferred for /y/, while both strategies are used with regard to /ø/ (Bannert 1990), the choice usually being predictable from the speaker's background.

13 For various points of view on this issue, see Hall (1953:250-264), Goodman (1964:50), Brousseau (1994), Corne (1999:143), Valdman (1978:62), Tinelli (1981:7) and Green (1988:430).

Phillip (1988:34, 44) respectively. Both close nasal vowels are furthermore attested in Papiamentu SC (Tinelli 1981:9), whereas only [ĩ] exists in Negerhollands DC (Stolz 1986:48). They are not phonemic in either of these languages.

The sources I have consulted usually give details only on the phonemic inventories of African languages, and not the precise phonetic realisations. In others, the two levels are not consistently kept apart. This means that there may well be other languages with closed nasal vowels on the phonetic level only which could have contributed them to the Atlantic Creoles. Available evidence, however, suggests that closed nasal vowels are rare in Atlantic and Bantu languages (though Schadeberg 1982:110 shows that they occur phonetically in Umbundu).[14]

On the other hand, they are present, and for the most part even phonemic in almost all Kwa and Mande languages in my sample. The Delto-Benuic languages present a more complex picture. Closed nasal vowels are phonemic in Urhobo, Igbo, Yoruba, Kpan, Jukun, Nupe and some dialects of Ijo – all spoken in a geographically continuous area bordering on Kwa – but not in Efik, Gbari, Amo, Tiv, Isoko, Kohumono, Tarok, Birom, Mbembe, Hausa and most Idomoid languages.

It is difficult to ascribe the presence of /ĩ/ and /ũ/ in Creoles to any specific source, partly because these may be phonetically present in African languages without this being indicated in my sources. The evidence provided in this section must therefore be taken as weak.

AREA	FEATURE	LANGUAGE	GROUP	SUGGESTED SUBSTRATE INFLUENCE
Phonology	High nasal vowels	Jamaica EC	EC	(+Mande), (+Kwa), (+SW Delto-Benuic)
Phonology	High nasal vowels	Krio EC	EC	(+Mande), (+Kwa), (+SW Delto-Benuic)
Phonology	High nasal vowels	Surinam ECs	EC	(+Mande), (+Kwa), (+SW Delto-Benuic)
Phonology	High nasal vowels	Haiti FC	FC	(+Mande), (+Kwa), (+SW Delto-Benuic)
Phonology	High nasal vowels	Lesser Antilles FC	FC	(+Mande), (+Kwa), (+SW Delto-Benuic)
Phonology	High nasal vowels	Papiamentu SC	SC	(+Mande), (+Kwa), (+SW Delto-Benuic)
Phonology	High nasal vowels	Negerhollands DC	DC	(+Mande), (+Kwa), (+SW Delto-Benuic)

3.2 Consonants

3.2.1 Lack of /z/

/z/ has phonemic status in English, French, Portuguese and Dutch.[15] Apart from the Surinamese ECs (see §3.2.6), the related West African EC basilects consistently devoice occurrences of lexifier /z/, as does basilectal Guinea-Bissau PC (Holm 1988:135; Hancock 1969; Rougé 1988:12; Scantamburlo 1981:19-20; Kihm 1994:15). The same goes for Berbice DC (Kouwenberg 1994c:283), which is a little surprising, since Ijo, claimed to be its dominant substrate, has both /s/ and /z/ (Williamson 1969b:98). According to Kouwenberg (p c), however, /z/ is confined to loan-words in Ijo.

About half of the West African languages have an opposition between /s/ and /z/, but one of those which do not is Balanta (Ruhlen 1975:165), the most widely spoken indigenous language of Guinea-Bissau. Neighbouring Wolof also lacks this opposition, and French /z/ is frequently devoiced, both in Wolof loans from French, and in Wolof-speakers' L_2 versions of French (Sauvageot 1965:34; Peace Corps 1995a; Dumont 1990:110). The Sotavento varieties of Cape Verde PC, closely related to Guinea-Bissau PC, display a variable devoicing of /z/ (Carvalho 1984b:28-29). Apart from the Atlantic languages mentioned above, /z/-less potential substrates of Upper Guinea PC include the Mande languages Dyula, Loko, Mandinka, Mende, and Susu (Ladefoged 1968:46, 48, 49; Colley 1995:3; Rowlands 1959:9; Houis 1963:27).

---

14 I have not come across close nasal vowels in any Atlantic language. The only Bantu languages in the UPSID database with closed nasal vowels is Bembe.

15 Though only marginally or not at all in some Dutch lects, particularly on the Atlantic seaboard. /z/ is also phonemic in some conservative varieties of Spanish (Munteanu 1996:233), but not in any known overseas varieties.

A variable devoicing (20% of all tokens in Josselin de Jong 1926) is also apparent in Negerhollands DC (Stolz 1986:90).

The absence of any Atlantic FC in this category is striking.

The general geographical pattern in Africa is that while all relevant substrates have /s/, /z/-lessness predominates heavily among the Atlantic languages. The other high concentration of /z/-less languages that there is, is found in the Kwa-speaking area, where the general trend is that Akan lacks /z/, while Gbe has it. Lack of /z/ is thus most plausibly ascribed to influence from Atlantic or Akan languages, with possible reinforcement from some members of the Mande and Delto-Benuic groups.

For the Surinamese ECs, we may attempt at tracing the origins of /z/-lessness more precisely. The most commonly invoked substrates (and these are indeed the languages which provided the vast majority of African words in the Surinamese ECs) are Kikongo and the Kwa clusters Gbe and Akan. Both Kikongo and Gbe languages do distinguish between /s/ and /z/, whereas Akan does not. Akan also has in common with the Surinamese ECs a lack of postalveolar fricatives (see §3.2.6) and the affricates /t͡ʃ/ and /d͡ʒ/. Other West African languages with a similar fricative / affricate configuration – i.e. which have /s/, but lack /z, ʃ, ʒ, t͡ʃ, d͡ʒ/ – include Balanta, Serer and some varieties of Wolof (Atlantic), Dyula, Loko, Mandinka and Susu (Mande), and Efik (Delto-Benuic). However, most of these have palatal plosives, which, if available, would be more faithful representations of the affricates. This leaves us with Susu and Efik, neither of which have left any lexical impact on the Surinamese Creoles. It is in other words likely that the merger of six lexifier phonemes into /s/ mentioned above is a development due to Akan influence.

AREA	FEATURE	LANGUAGE	GROUP	SUGGESTED SUBSTRATE INFLUENCE
Phonology	Lack of /z/	Surinam ECs	EC	+Akan
Phonology	Lack of /z/	West African ECs	EC	+Atlantic, +Akan, -Gbe, +Ijo
Phonology	Lack of /z/	Guinea-Bissau PC	PC	+Atlantic, +Akan, -Gbe, +Ijo
Phonology	Lack of /z/	Cape Verde PC	PC	(+Atlantic, +Akan, -Gbe, , +Ijo)
Phonology	Lack of /z/	Negerhollands DC	DC	(+Atlantic, +Akan, -Gbe, , +Ijo)
Phonology	Lack of /z/	Berbice DC	DC	+Atlantic, +Akan, -Gbe, , +Ijo

3.2.2 Interdental fricatives in Angolar

Angolar PC has /θ, ð/ as reflexes of São Tomé PC /s, z/ (Lorenzino 1998:71). In West Africa, as in the world as a whole, these phonemes are rare. In my sample, only Balanta and Papel (Atlantic) and the Bantu languages Herero, Mbunda, Ndonga, Kwambi and the Ndingi dialect of Kikongo have them (Quintino 1961:745; Cardoso 1902:122; Ferraz 1979:10; Lorenzino 1998:76). The first two are for geographical reasons out of the question as substrates of Angolar. So are the Bantu languages mentioned, with the exception of Ndingi, for they are all spoken in southern Angola, or even beyond its borders, in Namibia or Zambia, and from these regions, virtually no slave trade took place. It is therefore difficult to avoid the conclusion that the interdental fricatives in Angolar must stem from Ndingi, unless they formerly were present in other Bantu languages. Needless to say, independent development cannot be completely excluded – the very existence of marked phoneme series in human languages of course shows that they indeed can emerge without any outside input, and yet their cross-linguistic rarity proves that they usually do not. Unfortunately, I do not know whether Ndingi or any of the other Bantu languages with interdental fricatives lacks /s, z/, but if so, that would, of course, strengthen the case.

AREA	FEATURE	LANGUAGE	GROUP	SUGGESTED SUBSTRATE INFLUENCE
Phonology	/θ, ð/	Angolar PC	PC	Ndingi Kikongo

3.2.3 Apicals

Many of the Atlantic Creoles fail to make the distinction between the laterals and rhotics of European languages, or show traces of a possible earlier non-distinction.

The Ibero-Romance distinction between a flap and a trill (or rather a flap and a fricative in modern standard Portuguese) is not maintained in any basilectal Creole.[16] In Latin America, it is even lost in non-Creole varieties such as Dominican and Puerto Rican Spanish (Green 1997:5.2.4; Megenney 1993:155; Munteanu 1996:243-44). This is hardly surprising, since the distinction is rare cross-linguistically and, in West African languages I have examined, something similar exists only in Urhobo, Adamawa Fulfulde and Hausa (Kelly 1969:154; Ruhlen 1975:195, 203), none of which can be considered an important substrate of any Atlantic Creole.

Once having been merged with the flap, some variation between this and the alveolar /d/ is only to be expected for reasons of articulatory proximity; indeed this is precisely what has happened in many varieties of Spanish and Portuguese spoken by descendants of Africans in the Atlantic area. Since it is relatively unsurprising, I will not make any more comment on this.

More interesting are the cases of interchanges between /ɾ ~ r ~ d/ on the one hand and /l/ on the other. To be sure, many languages around the world lack a distinction between laterals and rhotics, but the distinction is generally maintained in Pidgins and Creoles *if and only if* it is found in the substrates, and is hence of interest to the present discussion.

3.2.3.1 Rhotic sounds

Many of the potential substrates, and hence also some Creoles, lack a rhotic phoneme, i.e. what in Western European orthographies is rendered <r> or <rr>, corresponding phonetically to [ɹ, r, ɾ, ʁ, ʀ]. Other West African languages do have rhotic sounds, but often have no phonemic distinction between this and a lateral. Presumably for this reason, several Creoles either regularly or sporadically interchange European liquids, diachronically speaking.

No EC presents a synchronic allophony of liquid phonemes (though cf the discussion about Surinamese ECs below) but, in a diachronic perspective, there seems to have been quite a lot of fluctuation between /l/ and /r/ in many of the more radical varieties, witness the table below. Note that substitutions in both directions are attested for all these varieties. This is potentially of some importance, since /l/ is in general more diachronically stable than /r/ in the world's languages (Hock 1991:129).

LANGUAGE	/l/ > /r/	/r/ > /l/
Jamaican EC	/brufil/ 'Bluefields'	/flitaz/ 'fritters'
Jamaican Maroon Spirit EC	/brib/ 'believe'	/blada/ 'brother'
St Kitts	/beri/ † 'belly'	
Sranan EC	/bɔri/ 'boil'	/alen/ 'rain'
Ndyuka EC	/pori/ 'spoil'	/fele/ 'afraid'
Saramaccan EC	/kɛtrɛ/ 'kettle'	/lepi/ 'ripe'
Krio EC	/brit͡ʃ/ 'bleach'	/lapa/ 'wrapper'
Ghanaian Pidgin English	/bɔtru/ 'bottle'	/blit͡ʃ/ 'bridge'
Cameroon EC	/krabas/ 'calabash'	/tumalo/ 'tomorrow'

While the process is rather sporadic elsewhere, the Surinamese ECs provide a more systematic picture. In Sranan EC, /l/ and /r/ are distributed in an interesting way (cf §3.9). In the core (English-derived) vocabulary, /l/ with few exceptions occur only word-initially, and /r/ only intervocalically or as the second consonant of a complex onset. As is illustrated by the following

[16] It is kept, though, in the conspicuously mesolectal Barlovento dialects of Cape Verde PC (Cardoso 1989:89; Macedo 1979:102).

examples (from Hancock 1969, 1987), this is implemented regardless of the etymological distribution of liquids:

ITEM	ETYMON (AND GLOSS)	ITEM	ETYMON (AND GLOSS)
/lepi/	'ripe'	/priti/	'split'
/leti/	'right'	/puru/	'pull'
/liba/	'river'	/ɔri/	'hold'
/lutu/	'root'	/bere/	'belly'

A similar tendency may possibly be observed in Jamaica EC,[17] as well as in Jamaica Maroon Spirit EC,[18] but in neither language is this consistly implemented, and counter-examples are easily found.

Although I suspected this situation to be substrate-induced, it is not found in any of the 29 languages in United Nations (1999). One possible reason for the observed pattern is a universal tendency for liquids to be realised as rhotics when in contact with vowels, and otherwise as laterals (Bhat 1974:82). This pattern fits Sranan even better if, as has been suggested, initial clusters are diachronically contractions of earlier CVCV structures (Holm 1988:112; Devonish 1989:27).

Another explanation is that the distribution of liquids in Sranan is indeed identical to that in one or several of its substrates, although this is not indicated in writing, the two sounds being regarded as allophones of one and the same phoneme. This could be the case of the Kwa languages, were [l] and [r] are in allophonic variation in some dialects of Akan (Christaller 1875:4). Even more promising is Ansre's (1971:158-59) claim that this is traditionally also the case also for Ewe[19] where, moreover, [l] occurs in syllable-initial position, and [r] elsewhere. Problematic, however, is the fact that many syllable-initial liquids would occur intervocalically, if preceded by a vowel-final syllable. In addition, Ansre points out that in clusters, there is a tendency to use [r] with dentals, apicals and palatals (presumably, then, [l] elsewhere). In Sranan, however, /r/ is found in all clusters, even if the other part of it is velar or labial.

In any case, the picture sketched above largely applies to the other Surinamese ECs (though subsequent development has deleted most or all intervocalic liquids), and is altered in Sranan EC mainly through the influence of Dutch. It can therefore be assumed that /l/ and /r/ stood in an allophonic relationship in proto-Sranan, from which Ndyuka EC and Saramaccan EC are descended.

Among the Portuguese Creoles in Africa, the basilects of São Tomé and Annobón lack /r ~ ɾ/ completely, and replace etymological /r/ and /ɾ/ with /l/ (or Ø) (Valkhoff 1966:88-89, 92; Barrena 1957:20), whereas several Cape Verdean PC dialects display sporadic interchange of /l/ and /r ~ ɾ/ (both have phonemic status, though; Silva 1957:100, 103). A few examples are also attested in Brazilian Vernacular Portuguese (Elia 1994:565; Holm 1987:417; Mello 1996:106).

The fact that Príncipe PC, as opposed to its sister languages of São Tomé and Annobón, maintains /r/ in etymologically correct positions is interesting, and agrees well with Ferraz' (1979:9) and Maurer's (1997:431) claim that Delto-Benuic languages (Edo in particular) had a greater impact on Príncipe PC, while Kikongo was more important on São Tomé. Unless extensive decreolisation has taken place on Príncipe (in which case we would expect some hypercorrections), and presuming that the Gulf of Guinea PCs are related, this could be taken to imply that /r/ was definitively lost in São Tomé PC after the settlement of Príncipe, but before the colonisation of Annobón, as suggested in Parkvall (1999d).

/l/~/r/ alternation has been attested in both Papiamentu SC (though to such a limited extent that it must be considered marginal) and Palenquero SC (Granda 1994:403), as well as in a large number of dialects of Latin American Spanish, including those of Panama, Puerto Rico, Cuba,

17 E.g. /talabred/ 'thoroughbred', /prajmali/ 'primary', /brufil/ 'Bluefields' (Cassidy & Le Page 1980:lxi).

18 E.g. /ara/ 'all', /fraga/ 'flog', /weri/ 'while' (Bilby 1992:2-3).

19 Today, both are phonemic, however, due to the influx of English loan-words.

Coastal Ecuador, Eastern Venezuela, Chincha (Peru), and the Dominican Republic (Lipski 1994). Outside the areas of African influence, the same phenomenon also occurs in Chile, and it is attested even in some varieties of European Spanish (Perl 1992:544; Lipski 1994:126; Munteanu 1996:164, 173). It is only in the Caribbean and in Eastern Venezuela, however, that /r/ can replace /l/; everywhere else, the substitutions are done at the expense of the former. Mathias Perl (p c) informs me that the use of /l/ for etymological /ɾ/ in word-final position found in the speech of Cuban Blacks, is paralleled in Andalusian Spanish. Given that this, as mentioned above, is the cross-linguistically unmarked development, it can be explained without recourse to a substrate hypothesis. The substitution of /r/ for /l/, however, is more unexpected, and largely confined to areas with a large Afro-Hispanic population.

Liquid alternation was not the rule in any DC, but examples are attested in all known varieties: Berbice DC /bluru/ 'brother' (< D *broeder*), Skepi DC /blur/ *idem*, Negerhollands DC /wɔltər/ 'root' (< D *worter*), /hulkan/ 'hurricane' (< D *orkaan* + E *hurricane*), and New Jersey Black Dutch /sxəutərgɑfəl/ 'fork' (< D *schotel* + archaic D *gaffel*) (Robertson 1989; Josselin de Jong 1926:13; Stolz 1986:65; Prince 1910).

Meanwhile, there are very few examples of liquid interchange in FCs, and most of those known to me have attested parallels in non-standard French. It is tempting to explain this as a lexifier inheritance, since the French <r> is a uvular fricative, and hence phonetically less similar to a lateral. Yet, wherever French is used in the formerly slave-exporting areas of West Africa today, even by illiterate speakers (where influence from the orthography would be negligible), French [ʁ] is replaced not by a fricative, but – almost invariably – by a trill [r] or a flap [ɾ] (e.g. Faïk 1979:453; Dialo 1990:64; Lafage 1985, 1990:775, 777), and in several areas, merger of French /l/ and /r/ is indeed attested in L_2 varieties of French, or in French loan words (Faïk 1979:453; Swift & Zola 1963:xvii; Laman 1912; Frey 1993:252; Dialo 1990:64).

The transition from [r] to [ʁ] via [ʀ] was underway in western France when the overseas settlements were established, witness the variation between these two forms in some areas, such as Canada and Louisiana. The variety of French which provided the superstratal input of the Atlantic FCs must have had a uvular <r>, since in almost all Atlantic FCs,[20] French <r> corresponds to a velar fricative /ɣ/ with various labialised allophones ([ɣ, ɣ^w, w]) rather than to a liquid. Of the potential substrates I have examined, only Malinke has /ʁ/, i. e the current standard French realisation, and no substrate language is claimed to have its progenitor /ʀ/.

French loan-words suggest that /l/ is the preferred substitute for French <r> for speakers of the Bantu languages Kikongo, Kituba, Lingala and Ntandu (Bal 1979; Dzokange 1979; Swartenbroeckx 1973; Swift & Zola 1963). The Senegambian languages Wolof and Mandinka mostly represent French <r> by <r> (Peace Corps 1995a, b), which in Mandinka seems to imply [r], and in Wolof either [r] or [ɹ].[21]

Since most West African speakers of French from non-Bantu areas seem to realise <r> as a trilled /r/, while many Bantus prefer /l/, the FC fricative /ɣ/ – if at all the result of substrate influence – would be expected to be due to a language having /ɣ/, but not /r/. This is true for a number of small languages, but particularly worthy of mention are Ewe, Gẽ, Isekiri, Kpelle, Bete and Godie, some dialects of Ijo, and perhaps also Efik, Wolof and Bambara, though /ɣ/ is but an allophone of other sounds in this latter group of languages. Of these, Wolof is a less likely source of the FC realisation, given that Dumont (1990:130) indicates that speakers of this languages tend to prefer an apical realisation of French /r/. Further support for Ewe as the origin of FC /ɣ/ is lent by the fact that /ɣ/ has a labial allophone [w] before back vowels (Duthie 1996:17),

---

20 Except in most varieties of Louisiana FC, where the predominant variant /r/ is probably due to contact with Cajun French, which retains the trilled realisation once normal in European French. The Cajun origin is suggested by the fact that 1) Louisiana FC is deeply influenced by Cajun on all other levels, 2) that this is not only the sole FC to have a trilled rhotic, but also the only one to have been in contact with a variety of French having the trill, and 3) that some few speakers of Louisiana FC use a fricative in its place, while the opposite fails to obtain for other FCs.

21 Dialo (1990:64) reports, however, that Senegalese speakers commonly use /l/ for French <r>. While not indicating any specific L_1 for these speakers, Wolof is the most widespread language of the country.

mirroring perfectly the pattern of most FCs.[22] The fact that /ɣ/ is also the reflex (though without a labial allophone) of French <r> in Indian Ocean FCs, however, where there was less West African input, could be taken to support a lexifier origin.

Among the potential substrates of West Africa, most languages of Upper Guinea have a phonemic distinction between /l/ and a sound which may be considered an acceptable approximation of the European /r/ realisations. This is also the case of most of the Delto-Benuic languages. However, most languages of Ghana as well as most Western Bantu languages do not make such a distinction, as is illustrated in the table below:[23]

	GROUP 1 Having both a rhotic and /l/	GROUP 2 Having /l/, but no rhotic	GROUP 3 Having a rhotic, but not /l/	GROUP 4 Lacking both a rhotic and /l/
Creoles	*Most*	Saramaccan EC, Ndyuka EC, São Tomé PC, Annobón PC	*None*	*None*
Atlantic	Wolof, Balanta, Adamawa Fulfulde, Temne, Serer	Kisi		
Mande	Wojenekakan, Susu, Maukakan, Mandinka, Malinke, Loko, Kpelle, Kong Dyula, Bisa, Bambara	Worodugukakan, Vai, Mende, Loko, Dan		
Kru	Bete, Godie	Kru, Grebo		
Gur	Tampulma, Bariba	Dagbani		
Kwa	Gẽ, Gã, Baule, Basila, Late	Lelemi, Okere, Fon, Efutu, Ebrie, Ewe[24]	Asante, Fante, Twi	
Delto-Benuic	Yoruba, Tarok, Nupe, Mbembe, Kalabari, Isekiri, Isoko, Ijo, Gbari, Edo, Izi, Igbo, Etsako, Ibilo		Urhobo, (Efik)	(Efik[25]), Birom, Amo
Bantu	Yaka, Ngemba, Kimbundu, (Ngwe)	Teke, Kituba, Kikongo, Ewondo, Bembe, Chokwe, Umbundu, Luvale	Tiv, (Ngwe)	

There is evidence that the presence or absence of liquids to some extent does predict the realisation of European words by speakers of African languages. As we would expect, loans displaying /l/ for European /r/ abound in languages from all over West Africa. And indeed, the L_2 English of Twi-speakers, as we would expect from the table above, but contrary to any single-liquid Atlantic Creole, replaces /l/ by /ɹ/ (Gyasi 1991:27).

It is difficult to judge the importance of the sporadic interchanges between /l/ and /r/ noted above for a large number of Atlantic Creoles. For one thing, it is not regular, and usually not even particularly common. It could also potentially be ascribed to a large number of substrates. It is furthermore possible that distributional restrictions of the type described for Sranan above played a role, and that even substrates with two phonemic liquids can give rise to fluctuation. One of the most interesting observations here is the fact that FCs differ strikingly from Creoles of other lexifiers in not displaying the phenomenon in question.

The complete merger of /l/ and /r/, however, as evidenced in most Creoles of Surinam and the Gulf of Guinea, is likely to have been caused by substrate influence.[26] Putative sources for this are most Bantu and Gbe languages. Atlantic and Delto-Benuic languages, however, most of which have a contrast between laterals and rhotics, would not be expected to have generated such a merger. Nor would most Akan varieties, since they generally have /r/, but not /l/. The fact that no Atlantic Creole has a rhotic phoneme, but no /l/ is interesting in view of the importance often attached to Akan dialects in substratist argumentation.

---

22 In many FC varieties, this labial allophone has during the 20th century spread to the virtual exclusion of [ɣ]. However, conservative varieties of Guiana FC, at least, lack labialised allophones altogether (Corne 1999:151).

23 Languages appearing twice and between brackets indicate conflicting data or differing analyses.

24 /r/ is now phonemic due to modern loans from English (Ansre 1971:158-9).

25 Efik has both /ɣ/ and /ɾ/, but apparently, neither is phonemic.

26 All the more so since there is no lexifier prototype for it, other than in isolated lexical items.

AREA	FEATURE	LANGUAGE	GROUP	SUGGESTED SUBSTRATE INFLUENCE
Phonology	Merger of /r/ and /l/	Surinamese ECs	EC	+Bantu, +Gbe, -Akan, -Atlantic, -Delto-Benuic
Phonology	Merger of /r/ and /l/	Gulf of Guinea PCs (except Príncipense)	PC	+Bantu, +Gbe, -Akan, -Atlantic, -Delto-Benuic

Syllable-final /r/ is lost in most Atlantic Creoles, which is not particularly surprising. For one thing, it is cross-linguistically unstable (Hock 1991:129), and some or all instances of it had furthermore already been lost in some lexifier varieties (many dialects of English and Andalusian Spanish) before Creoles started forming. Of possible interest, however, is the fact that while some FCs allow post-vocalic /r/s, others do not. The former group includes Louisiana FC, Northern Haiti FC and Guiana FC, while standard Haiti FC and Lesser Antilles FC varieties belong to the latter (Parkvall 1995c:11).

Among the West African languages that have /r/ in the first place, most do not seem to tolerate it word-final position. The main exceptions to this are the Atlantic languages, and in United Nations (1999), Wolof, Guinean Fulfulde and Serer, all seem to permit word-final /r/. If the difference within the group of FCs is substrate-induced, it might point to a stronger representation of speakers of Atlantic languages in Louisiana, northern Haiti and French Guiana than elsewhere.

AREA	FEATURE	LANGUAGE	GROUP	SUGGESTED SUBSTRATE INFLUENCE[27]
Phonology	Post-vocalic /r/	Louisiana FC	FC	+Atlantic
Phonology	Post-vocalic /r/	Northern Haiti FC	FC	+Atlantic
Phonology	Post-vocalic /r/	Guiana FC	FC	+Atlantic

If the variability of liquids is relatively predictable because of the phonetic similarities, and because it is cross-linguistically common, the occasional non-maintenance of the distinction between nasal and non-nasal alveolars is less so. The nasality of vowels is normally conditioned by consonants, but in a number of West African languages, the opposite is true. In the Kwa language Guro, for instance, nasal consonants such as [n] are allophones of non-nasal phonemes, such as /l/, which appear before nasal vowels (Creissels 1989:105). Precisely the same thing applies to Yoruba (Bamgbo̩se 1969:163), and in Ewe too, vowels determine the nasality of consonants, rather than vice versa (Duthie 1996:17).[28]

Other West African languages in which [n] varies with /l ~ ɾ ~ r ~ d/ include the Upper Guinean languages Wolof, Bambara, north-western Mande, Mandinka and Susu, the Kru languages Grebo and Klao, and the Lower Guinean languages Twi, Ewe, Gã, Edo, Igbo, Yoruba, Urhobo and Isoko and the Bantu language Chokwe (Ansre 1971:158; Bamgbo̩se 1966:7; Boretzky 1983:65; Campbell 1991:1454; Christaller 1875:11; Delafosse 1929:74-75; Derive 1990:69; Eynde 1960:10, 34; Holm 1988:135; Innes 1966:20; Kelly 1969:156; Mafeni 1969:121; Omoruyi 1986:72; Rowlands 1959:9; Schmied 1991:143). Note that most Bantu languages are conspicuously absent from the list.

In the Atlantic Creoles, this kind of variability is relatively uncommon. I have not come across any examples at all from ECs or DCs, and those I have encountered from FCs seem to be patterned on European French dialectal forms.

Papiamentu SC has a form /lãda/ 'to swim' (< S/P *nadar*), which also appears in São Tomé PC (Taylor 1977:191), but Anthony Grant (p c) informs me that the same form is also found in European dialects of Spanish. Ferraz (1979:37) and Granda (1994:430) attest a few more

27 Since the substrate influence here is not positive, "+Atlantic" must in this table and the one in §3.4.1 be interpreted as mere shorthand for "-all others", i.e. the suggested impact of Atlantic is only relative to that of other African language groupings.

28 Duthie's examples do not include apical sounds, however.

examples from São Tomé PC and its daughter dialect Annobón PC, but do not suggest that it is widespread.

In some varieties of Louisiana FC, in Haiti FC, and Lesser Antilles FC (Klingler 1992:103; Carrington 1984:43, 55-56; Valdman 1978:82-83; Green 1988:422; Alleyne 1996:145), the initial phoneme of the definite article /la/ appears either as [n] or as [l] (or as zero) depending on the phonological environment. In Haiti FC (but apparently not other varieties), this allophony extends also to object forms of the 3sg pronoun, so that /li pɣã l/ 'he takes it' appears as [li pɣã n] (Tinelli 1981:67). Note that this is limited to these particular items, and does not affect the rest of the lexicon.

Granda (1994:418) claims that Portuguese loan-words in Kikongo tend to display /d/ before /i/, and /l/ before other vowels, regardless of the Portuguese etymon – thus /pudisi/ 'police' (< P *polícia*, F *police*), but /sáabala/ 'Saturday' (< P *sábado*) – and draws parallels between this and the treatment of Spanish apicals in Palenquero SC. Indeed, in a sample of almost 15 000 Kikongo syllables in Swartenbroeckx (1973), I found /d/ used to the near exclusion of /l/ before /i/, whereas /l/ is four times as common as /d/ before other vowels. The tendency was the same, though *far* less pronounced, among the 6 669 Palenquero syllables examined.[29] In order to verify whether this tendency in Palenquero actually differs from other Creoles with an allegedly less pronounced Kikongo influence, I also examined corpora of Jamaica EC, Guinea-Bissau PC (for the latter of which a Bantu substrate is out of the question) and Dominica FC.[30] Interestingly, these too display a dominance of /d/ before /i/, and in fact an even stronger such dominance than does Palenquero. All three except Dominica FC (presumably because of the frequency of the determiner /la/) prefer /l/ before other vowels. This reduces the value of Granda's observation, and it is not immediately obvious that this constitutes proof of Kikongo influence in Palenquero.

The sporadic fluctuation and allophony involving nasal and non-nasal apicals in Atlantic Creoles may well be substrate-induced, but this is by no means certain, and it is in any case impossible to establish links to any specific region in Africa with regard to this feature.

As an aside, it could be mentioned that replacement of etymological /r/ by the glide /j/ is reported mainly from Spanish- and Portuguese-speaking areas (Bartens 1996:100), though Lalla & d'Costa (1990:41, 60) mention some cases in older Jamaican texts.

3.2.4 Coarticulated stops

Coarticulated stops, entirely absent from all five lexifier languages involved, are certainly exotic not only from a European point of view, but are highly marked cross-linguistically. Nevertheless, they do occur in some Atlantic Creoles, where their presence can hardly be explained without resorting to substratist arguments. For although rare among the world's languages, and only occasionally found outside Africa (Maddieson 1984:37; Ruhlen 1976:154),[31] West Africa abounds with languages having these phonemes. Cutting across genetic frontiers, they occur chiefly between the equator and 10°N (Creissels 1989:55), i.e. roughly the region here referred to as Lower Guinea, although Welmers (1973:48) points out that they are lacking in many languages along the coast.

Among ECs and related varieties, coarticulated stops occur in a few varieties, viz. Gullah EC, Ndyuka EC, Saramaccan EC, Krio EC, Liberian English, Nigeria EC, and Cameroon EC (Alleyne 1980:50-51; Holm 1988:127, 1993:319; Dwyer 1966; Mafeni 1971:107, 110; Bakker, Smith & Veenstra 1995:170; Turner 1949:241). One coarticulated stop, /g͡ɓ/, also turns up in

29 Before /i/: 43,6% /l/, 56,4% /d/; before other vowels: 64,2% /l/, 35,8% /d/. The corresponding Kikongo numbers are: 6,4%, 93,6%, 79,3%, 20,7%. The Palenquero corpus was kindly provided by Armin Schwegler. The copy of Swartenbroeckx (1973) from which I worked has been scanned from the printed original, a technique which unfortunately is bound to generate some errors. I hope, though, that the large number of tokens examined will minimise the effects thereof.

30 Jamaica EC: 2 261 syllables from Le Page & De Camp (1960), Guinea-Bissau PC: 1 159 syllables from Scantamburlo (1981), Dominica FC: 823 syllables from Durand (ed.) (1989).

31 In Ruhlen's (1976:154) sample, 71% of all Niger-Kordofanian languages had coarticulated stops, as opposed to 6% in the world as a whole.

Príncipe PC (Ferraz 1975:155), and it is possible that Sranan EC once too had /k͡p/ and /g͡b/ (cf Boretzky 1983:61-62; Alleyne 1980:55).

In most Creoles, these stops occur only in some lects, and usually only in a limited number of lexemes, mostly of African origin (but see e.g. Holm 1988:127 for some examples of European-derived words with coarticulated stops). It is also true that several of the varieties having coarticulated stops (viz. the West African ECs) are still in contact with West African languages, but apparently, this phoneme series did find its way to at least three plantation colonies (Surinam, Príncipe and the Carolinas).

The imposing of coarticulated stops on European lexical items seems to be conditioned either by the lack of simple stops, as in older Yoruba (Ansre 1971:158-9),[32] or by West African phonotactic rules, since some languages only allow a coarticulated allophone of stops or labialised stops in certain positions (e.g. Welmers 1973:48; Guthrie 1953: 78). And indeed, one finds coarticulated realisations of European stops in present-day L2 varieties of English and French in several areas in West Africa (Bamgboṣe 1969:169; Cook 1969:44; Lafage 1985:183; Alleyne 1980:177).

In Upper Guinean languages, coarticulated stops are rare in the Atlantic family, though occurring in Balanta, Kisi and Temne (Childs 1995:22; Ruhlen 1975:165; Maddieson 1984:37). They are common, however, in Mande languages, although lacking in major northern representatives of the family, such as northern Bambara, Dyula, Mandinka, and in most Kru languages (Rowlands 1959:9; Maddieson 1984:287; Ladefoged 1968:46; Welmers 1973:48; Marchese 1984:127; Ruhlen 1975:200, 226; Innes 1966:14).

In Lower Guinea, most Kwa languages have /k͡p/ and /g͡b/ (the main exception being the Akan dialects [Clements 1985:56-57; Welmers 1946; Ladefoged 1968:51-52]), as do virtually all major Delto-Benuic languages and the members of the Gur family (Welmers 1952:83; Maddieson 1984:290; Ruhlen 1975:186; Maddieson 1984:289).

Bantu languages relevant to this study generally lack coarticulated stops, the exceptions in this family being those spoken in the north-western areas, bordering on the Delto-Benuic group.

In short, then, and despite exceptions, the coarticulated stop series is found in a *relatively* well-defined area of West Africa, whence it must have been introduced to the Creoles which have such a series.

AREA	FEATURE	LANGUAGE	GROUP	SUGGESTED SUBSTRATE INFLUENCE
Phonology	Coarticulated stops	Gullah EC	EC	+Lower Guinea, -Akan
Phonology	Coarticulated stops	Surinam ECs	EC	+Lower Guinea, -Akan
Phonology	Coarticulated stops	West African ECs	EC	+Lower Guinea, -Akan
Phonology	Coarticulated stops	Príncipe PC	PC	+Lower Guinea, -Akan

3.2.5 Prenasalised stops and fricatives

Much of what was said about coarticulated stops above applies to prenasalised stops as well. This phoneme series is cross-linguistically quite uncommon. Most well-represented in Africa (where one in four of the Niger-Kordofanian languages has it, as opposed to one in ten globally; Ruhlen 1976:154), it also occurs in Hakka, and in certain South American and Melanesian languages (Maddieson 1984:67-68). Of the languages in the UPSID database, almost 12% feature prenasalised stops, while less than 2% (mostly African languages) also have prenasalised fricatives.

On a *phonetic* level, prenasalised stops are far more common, as in e.g. French [ʃɑ̃ːᵐb], 'chambre', but since that is irrelevant to the present study, it seems reasonable to focus attention on word-initial occurrences. Even there, however, prenasalised stops may surface without being phonemic. This is the case of for instance Haiti FC sequence-initial nasal + stop strings, as in [m̥paːle] 'I spoke' and [n̥dɔ̃ːmĩː] 'We slept' (Green 1988:437), but since these are merely sandhi-

[32] Whence loan-words such as /k͡pánũ/ 'pan' and /k͡pɛ̀tɛ́ɛ̀sì/ 'storeyed building' (< E *upstairs*) (Banjọ 1986:537). Note that <p> in Yoruba orthography normally corresponds to /k͡p/.

reduced phonetic realisations /mwẽ pale/ and /nu dɔmi/ respectively, no claim that Haitian FC would have phonemic prenasalised stops has to my knowledge been forwarded. The same is true for Upper Guinea PC, where similar strings can be heard initially, but are considered non-phonemic by Green (1988:437) and Kihm (1994:16), since the nasal element has become syllabic after near-complete erosion of a preceding vowel.[33] Similar examples from various dialects of Cape Verde PC are given by Bartens (1996:111), Cardoso (1989:85) and Lang (1999:1), but prenasalised stops are not phonemic in in-depth analyses of Cape Verdean phonology, such as Nunes (1963).

Among the other Atlantic Creoles, the distribution of prenasalised stops is similar to that of coarticulated stops. We find them in Gullah EC, Jamaican Maroon Spirit EC, Sranan EC, Ndyuka EC, Saramaccan EC, Krio EC, Cameroon EC, São Tomé PC, Angolar PC, Annobón PC, and Palenquero SC (Holm 1988:128-130; Stolz 1986:77-8; Turner 1949:241; Bakker, Smith & Veenstra 1995:170; Hancock 1969; Schwegler 1998a:264; Bilby 1983:79, 81, 1992:2, 9; Dwyer 1966:519, 529; Post 1995:194; Lorenzino 1998:71; Granda 1994:402, 427), and perhaps in a few others as well. Stolz (1986:76) and Sabino (p c) suggest that Negerhollands DC once had prenasalised stops as well, and the same may be true of Papiamentu SC and Black ethnolects of Caribbean Spanish (Munteanu 1996:249). Lipski (1994:98) adds that prenasalised stops are frequent in 16th century attestations of Spanish as spoken by Africans. Also, a modern restructured variety with a homogenous (Bantu) substrate, Congolese Tirailleur Pidgin French, contained items such as /ŋ͡ganze/ 'to hire' (< F *engager*) (Queffelec & Niangouna 1990:17-18).

Like the coarticulated phonemes, the prenasalised stops prototypically occur in words of African origin, but African phonological rules have evidently in some cases been extended to European-derived lexical items as well, as in the following examples:

LANGUAGE	ITEM	GLOSS	ETYMOLOGY
Sranan EC	/cin͡di/	'knee'	(< D *knie*)
Saramaccan EC	/n͡dofu/ /m͡beti/ /n͡deti/ /piŋ͡gu/ /m͡bói/ /ŋ͡gɔ́tɔ/	'abundant' 'meat' 'night' 'pig' 'to cook' 'ditch'	(< E *enough*) (< E *meat*) (< E *night*) (< E *pig*) (< E *boil*) (< E *gutter*)
Jamaican Maroon Spirit Language EC	/m͡blada/ /drown͡di/ /in͡di/	'blood' 'to drown' 'in'	(< E *blood*) (< E *drown*) (< E *in*)
São Tomé PC	/ŋ͡gaba/ /ŋ͡gaɲa/ /m͡põ/ /ŋ͡glãdʒi/	'to praise' 'hen, chicken' 'bread' 'big'	(< P *gabar*) (< P *galinha*) (< P *pão*) (< P *grande*)
Annobón PC	/n͡tela/ /pen͡dé/ /fen͡de/ /n͡da/ /ŋ͡gia/ /ŋ͡gaɲia/	'star' 'to lose' 'to smell' 'to go' 'chain' 'hen, chicken'	(< P *estrela*) (< P *perder*) (< P *feder*) (< P *andar*) (< P *grilhão*) (< P *galinha*)
Palenquero SC	/n͡dolo/ /n͡gande/ /n͡dulo/	'pain' 'big' 'hard'	(< S *dolor*) (< S *grande*) (< S *duro*)

Sources: Hancock (1969), Kramer (1998), Bilby (1983, 1992), Morais-Barbosa (1975:137), Ferraz (1979:95), Stolz (1986:77), Granda (1994:402, 427).

33 Tinelli (1981:9), however, sees initial nasal+stop sequences as phonemic in words of the Senegalese dialect of Guinea-Bissau PC such as /ⁿtẽde/ 'understand' (< P *entender*) and /ⁿjẽta/ 'together' (< P *junta*), while Carvalho (1984b:29) recognises both possibilities for Cape Verde PC.

Note that, as opposed to most Upper Guinea PC examples such as /ᵐbarka/ 'to emigrate' (< P *embarcar*), most of the items above did not etymologically contain a nasal + stop sequence, and the possible prenasalised stop can therefore not simply be the result of syllable boundary reanalysis. Therefore, substrate influence appears to be a plausible explanation, and more called for than in the case of the Upper Guinean Creoles. In the Upper Guinean examples which did not historically contain a nasal + stop string, spread of nasality present elsewhere in the word is usually able to account for the prenasalised surface realisation.

However, in several of the Creoles which do have prenasalised stops, their phonemic status is marginal. They often occur in a limited number of lexemes, and are frequently in free distribution with non-nasal stops.

Nevertheless, the absence of FCs in the above list is once again striking. This can hardly have anything to do with French itself, since French loan-words in Bantu languages frequently contain prenasalised stops (Parkvall 1999c:37). Not only have stops in French-derived words not become prenasalised, but African words originally containing prenasalised stops have lost them in FCs, witness Africanisms such as Haiti FC /ogũ/ 'god of war and iron' (< Yoruba /n͡gũ/) and Lesser Antilles FC /gẽbo/ 'bat' (< Kikongo /n͡gembo/) (etymologies from Cérol 1991:72 and Baker 1993:142, 148).

African languages having prenasalised stops include quite a few of the Atlantic and Mande families, but virtually none of the Kru, Gur, Kwa or Delto-Benuic ones. In the Bantu area, the north-western Bantoid varieties again align themselves with the Delto-Benuic languages in not having prenaslised stops, whereas the southern Bantu languages in general seem to have them. Without too much oversimplification, then, Lower Guinea, as opposed to Buntu is clearly an area whose languages does *not* make use of prenasalised stops, whereas the picture in Upper Guinea is complex, with both the Atlantic and the Mande families being split in two, seemingly without any areal or genetic tendencies. Of the major potential substrates of this area, Fulfulde, Limba and Sherbro (all Atlantic) and Loko, Mandinka, Mende, and Vai (all Mande) have prenasalised stops, whereas Balanta and Temne (Atlantic), and Bambara, Kpelle and Mandinka (Mande) do not (Arnott 1969a:58; Bella 1946:731; Childs 1995:22; Delafosse 1929:60; Houis 1963:8-19; Innes 1967:4; Manessy & Sauvageot [eds] 1963:167; Ladefoged 1968:46-49; Maddieson 1984:286; Rowlands 1959:9; Spears 1967:168; Welmers 1976; Westermann 1924:1). Wolof, the Atlantic language in Senegambia with the largest number of speakers, belongs to the former group according to Tinelli (1981:9), Ndiaye (1996:108) and Campbell (1991:1454), but to the latter according to Ladefoged (1968:46), Ward (1963:63) and Maddieson (1984:288). In any case, English *biscuit* when borrowed into Wolof has indeed resulted in the form /mbiskit/ (Peace Corps 1995a). Similarly, its close relative Serer also has prenasalised stops according to Ladefoged (1968:46), but not in the analysis of Manessy & Sauvageot (eds) (1963:165). The same problem obtains for Kisi (Atlantic) and Susu (Mande), neither of which has prenasalised stops according to Ladefoged (1968:48), but both do have them in the accounts of Childs (1995:22) and Houis (1963), respectively.

According to Rougé (1988:14), the languages of Guinea-Bissau – the relevant substrates of Guinea-Bissau PC – *all* have prenasalised stops.

A major problem in determining the status of initial nasal + stop is that nasals are allowed as syllable nuclei in a great many languages. A sequence [#NC-] could thus either be analysed as /#N$C-/ or /#NC-/ depending on the phonotactics of the language concerned. Nasals are explicitly said to be syllabic in at least a score of the languages concerned here, including most Lower Guinean languages, but few Upper Guinean or Bantu languages.[34] Thus, even if occurring word-initially, /NC-/ need not represent a prenasalised phoneme (see e.g. the discussion in Welmers 1973:70-73).

---

34 Dan, Kpelle, Mandinka, Susu (all Mande), Bariba (Gur), Akan, Baule, Ewe, Gã (all Kwa), Efik, Igbo, Izi, Nupe, Yoruba (all Delto-Benuic), Hausa (Afro-Asiatic), Benga, Balundu, Basaa, Ngwe, Tiv (all peripheral north-western Bantu) (Anon. 1961:5; Arnott 1969b:147-48; Bamgboṣe 1966:8; Dunstan 1969:39; Duthie 1996:10; Green & Igwe 1963:3; Guthrie 1953:16, 24, 28; Hoffmann & Schachter 1969:78-79; Houis 1963:16; Meier, Meier & Bendor-Samuel 1975:35; Rowlands 1959:16; Ruhlen 1975:167, 187, 248; Smith 1969:137-38; Welmers 1952:84, 1973:66-67). For the syllabicity of nasals in African languages in general, see also Creissels (1989:112-17).

Furthermore, standard orthographies of several Bantu languages indicate a non-existent vowel, so that a sequence /NC-/ is written as <NVC-> (Jouni Maho, p c), and this obviously further complicates the use of a written corpus such as United Nations (1999). In United Nations (1999), word-initial NC-clusters are found in a number of Lower Guinean languages, including Aja, Asante, Baule, Adangme, Ewe, Fante, Fon, Gã, Gẽ, Gonja, Nzema and Twi, and the failure of my sources to consider prenasalised stops phonemic is probably due to nasals being syllabic.

While there seems to be little reason to assume that a speaker of a language with word-initial /#N$C-/ (typically a Lower Guinean language) would *introduce* prenasalised stops even on the phonetic level in Creole formation, it does seem reasonable that s/he would tolerate them if they were introduced by others (typically Upper Guineans or Bantus) – in other words, speakers of both types of languages might use the same phonetic realisation for a particular word, while having different underlying segmentations of it.

To sum up, word-initial nasal + stop sequences occur in most parts of Africa that concern us here. We would not, however, expect Lower Guineans to introduce this feature into words of European derivation, whereas speakers of some Upper Guinean languages and of most of the major Bantu tongues might do so.[35] Not unexpectedly, then, European consonant-initial loan-words in Lower Guinean languages do not seem to be equipped with prothetic nasals, as have been attested among Bantu and Upper Guinean languages.

AREA	FEATURE	LANGUAGE	GROUP	SUGGESTED SUBSTRATE INFLUENCE
Phonology	Prenasalised stops	Gullah EC	EC	+Upper Guinea, +Bantu
Phonology	Prenasalised stops	Jamaican Maroon Spirit EC	EC	+Upper Guinea, +Bantu
Phonology	Prenasalised stops	Surinam EC	EC	+Upper Guinea, +Bantu
Phonology	Prenasalised stops	West African EC	EC	+Upper Guinea, +Bantu
Phonology	Prenasalised stops	Gulf of Guinea PC	PC	+Upper Guinea, +Bantu
Phonology	Prenasalised stops	(Negerhollands DC†)	DC	+Upper Guinea, +Bantu
Phonology	Prenasalised stops	(Papiamentu SC†)	SC	+Upper Guinea, +Bantu
Phonology	Prenasalised stops	Palenquero SC	SC	+Upper Guinea, +Bantu

3.2.5.1 Prenasalised fricatives

In common with many other authors, Welmers (1973:70-73) doubts whether Kikongo word-initial combinations of nasal + fricative should be considered phonemic (he suspects not). In any case, both Kikongo and the closely-related Ntandu have Portuguese loan-words in which an etymologically word-initial fricative is preceded by a prothetic nasal, as in the following examples:

LANGUAGE	ITEM	GLOSS	PORTUGUESE ETYMON	SOURCE
Ntandu	/nsáalu/	'salt'	*sal*	Bal (1979:54)
Ntandu	/nsáaku/	'bag'	*saco*	Bal (1979:54)
Kikongo	/nzêta/	'salad oil'	*azeita*	Swartenbroeckx (1973)
Kikongo	/nsàmpátu/	'shoe'	*sapato*	Swartenbroeckx (1973)

I have not come across this in non-Bantu languages, although in United Nations (1999) word-initial strings consisting of nasal + fricative are found not only in the Bantu languages Kituba, Beti, Ndonga, Chokwe, but also in a number of Kwa languages[36] and Igbo.[37] Note, however, that

35 This, of course, would apply in particular to languages which have prenasalised stops, but which lack the corresponding oral plosives. This has been claimed to apply for voiced stops in Fulfulde, Serer (Atlantic), Mende (Mande), Chokwe and Luvale (Bantu).

36 Asante, Nzema (few tokens), Twi, Baule, Fante, Gonja, Gẽ (few tokens).

as noted above, most Lower Guinean languages allow syllabic nasals, and the same observations as above regarding the role of Lower Guinean languages therefore apply here as well.

As opposed to what is the case in Buntu, I have no indications that European loan-words with initial fricatives receive prothetic nasals in Lower Guinean languages.

If prenasalised fricatives can indeed be seen as typical of Bantu, it is perhaps significant that the only Atlantic Creole in which they have been attested is Palenquero SC, where Schwegler (1999) suggests that they once were more common than today, restricted as they now are to *"archaizing ... funeral chants"* (Schwegler 1999:5.2.4.1). If prenasalised fricatives are of Bantu origin, their absence in all other Creoles may be taken to suggest that Bantu impact was nowhere as decisive as in the case of Palenquero SC, and possibly also that Bantu alone would at least not have been enough to introduce the prenasalised *stops* just discussed – if it were, we would expect the corresponding fricatives to appear at least somewhere else than in Palenquero SC, as is the case with prenasalised stops. Somewhat speculatively, this can therefore be seen as indirect evidence that the presence of prenasalised stops in certain other Creoles owes more to Lower Guinean languages than to Bantu.

AREA	FEATURE	LANGUAGE	GROUP	SUGGESTED SUBSTRATE INFLUENCE
Phonology	Prenasalised fricatives	Palenquero SC	SC	+Bantu?

3.2.6 Depalatalisation

Depalatalisation in this context refers to the process whereby the postalveolar fricatives /ʃ, ʒ/ are replaced by their alveolar counterparts /s, z/. The postalveolar fricatives now exist in all five lexifier languages except Spanish, which, however, had /ʃ/ (corresponding to modern velar /x/) until the 17th century. On the other hand, modern Portuguese /ʃ, ʒ/ were /t͡ʃ, d͡ʒ/ in the standard until the 16th century, as they still are in some dialects. The French postalveolar fricatives derive from the same source, but had changed from affricates to fricatives before overseas expansion began.

Ingram (1989:183, 194) considers /s/ less marked than /ʃ/, and the opposition between postalveolar and alveolar fricatives is acquired relatively late by children. This is also reflected in both European and African languages (but holds globally as well) in that any language having the palatoalveolar fricatives (i.e. /ʃ, ʒ/) almost invariably has at least one of the alveolar ones (i.e. /s, z/) as well, with unvoiced variant being more common than voiced ones. The distribution of the relevant phonemes among the 451 languages of the UPSID database illustrates this:

ANY OF /s, z, ʃ, ʒ/	/ʃ/	/ʒ/	/s/	/z/	/ʃ/ or /ʒ/	/s/ or /z/	/s/ or /ʃ/	/z/ or /ʒ/
397	189	63	378	135	192	380	396	146
88%	42%	14%	84%	30%	43%	84%	88%	32%

Given the somewhat marked status of postalveolar fricatives, and in particular the voiced ones, we would expect the distinction between these and their alveolar counterparts to be neutralised in some Creoles, and this is indeed what we do find.[38]

The etymological postalveolar fricatives are consistently replaced in the Gulf of Guinea PCs by the alveolars /s, z/ (with the exception of modern Portuguese loans). The radical Surinamese ECs have gone one step further in that /s/ corresponds not only to etymological /s/ and /ʃ/, but also to /z, ʒ, t͡ʃ, d͡ʒ/, i.e. six lexifier phonemes are merged into one. Basilectal Guinea-Bissau PC

37 Only a few tokens in Igbo. In the same corpus, word-initial nasal + stop sequences were absent from the following languages: Wolof, Guinean Fulfulde, Serer (Atlantic), Kpelle, Susu, Maninka (Mande), Kabiye, Moore, Dagaari, Bariba, Dagbani (Gur), Adangme, Aja, Ewe, Fon, Gã (Kwa), Yoruba (Delto-Benuic).

38 One factor which might facilitate this (but which I have not been able to take into account) is the fact that the precise realisation of /s/ in many languages is further back than it is in English, approaching the pronunciation found in e.g. Dutch or Finnish. This is the case, for instance, of many Mande languages (Westermann & Ward 1933:82).

too has lost the lexifier distinction between /s/ and /z/. In Krio and other West African ECs, the lexifier distinctions are largely retained, but there are indeed examples such as /was(i)/ 'wash' and /kisi ~ kas/ 'catch', and Jones (1971:71) suggests that this was once more common, although he does not suggest that early Krio lacked postalveolar fricatives and affricates altogether.[39]

More or less frequent substitution of /ʃ, ʒ/ by /s, z/ is reported from older Jamaica EC, St Kitts EC, Krio EC, Cameroon EC, older Louisiana FC, Negerhollands DC, and Vernacular Brazilian Portuguese (Jones 1971:71; Stolz 1986:72; Neumann-Holzschuh 1987; Cable 1886; Hancock 1969; Vincent Cooper, p c; Lalla & d'Costa 1990:58; Mendonça 1933:62-63).

It was also a feature of the Portuguese of blacks, as manifested in 16th century Portuguese theatre (Naro 1978:327). Isolated examples of depalatalisation of etymological /ʃ, ʒ/ can also be found in just about all insular Caribbean FCs, but only *very* rarely, and without any regularity.[40] Given the sporadic occurrence of this in FCs, it is possible that it is related to the attested depalatalisation that can be found in a small number isolated lexemes (some quite possibly *hapax legomena*) in most varieties of North American French, as well as in the French of Pondicherry (India).

Apart from the occasional example in overseas varieties of French, Lalla & d'Costa (1990:58) suggests that some English (especially nautical) varieties, once also displayed a certain instability in this respect. In essence, though, depalatalisation of alveolar fricatives, in particular when occurring regularly, must be attributed to substrate influence.

As for the substrates, depalatalisation in L_2 European or in European loan-words is attested from Wolof, Fulfulde, Bambara, Senegalese languages in general, Mandinka, Guinean languages (L_1 not given), Akan, Gã, Yoruba, Bantu languages of Congo-Kinshasa, Kituba, Umbundu, Ntandu, Kikongo, and Malagasy (Ndiaye 1996:109; Rambaud 1963:15; Peace Corps 1995a, 1995b; Dumont 1990:110; Schmied 1991:143; Anon. 1961; Diallo 1993:238; Redden et al. 1963; Kwofie 1978:67; Christaller 1875; David 1975:168; Faïk 1979:453; Arensdorff 1913:266; Blondé 1979:380; Dialo 1990:64; Delafosse 1929; Swift & Zola 1963; Valente 1964:66; Bal 1979; Swartenbroeckx 1973; Bavoux 1993:181).

On the basis of the phonological inventories of the about 85 African languages examined, the pattern that emerges is the following:

LANGUAGE FAMILY:	LANGUAGES LACKING POSTALVEOLAR FRICATIVES:	LANGUAGES HAVING AT LEAST ONE POSTALVEOLAR FRICATIVE:	CONFLICTING DATA OR DIALECT DIFFERENCES:
Atlantic:	Adamawa Fulfulde, Balanta, Wolof, Kisi, Serer	Temne	
Mande:	Bisa, Dan, Dyula, Kong Kpelle, Loko, Mandinka, Maukakan, Mende, Susu, Vai, Wojenekakan	Malinke, Worodugukakan	Bambara
Kru:	Bete, Godie, Grebo, Kru		
Gur:	Bariba, Tampulma		Dagbani
Kwa:	Akan in general, Basila, Baule, Ebrie, Ewe, Fante, Fon, Gẽ, Late, Lelemi, Twi	Okere	Asante,[41] Gã
Delto-Benuic:	Efik, Efutu, Etsako, Igbo, Isoko, Izi, Kalabari, Mbembe, Nupe, Edo	Amo, Birom, Ijo, Yoruba, Gbari, Tarok, Urhobo, Ibilo	Isekiri
Bantu:	Bembe, Ewondo, Kituba, Ngwe, Teke, Yaka	Tiv, Luvale, Ngemba, Chokwe, Kimbundu, Umbundu	Kikongo

39 Given that Krio seems to have formed through koinéisation of Gullah EC and some kind of Jamaican Maroon speech with Gullah as the dominant component (e.g. Baker 1999a; Huber 1998c), it could be that the instances of /s/ corresponding to English /ʃ/ are survivals from Sranan introduced by way of the Jamaican Maroon Spirit EC.

40 Southern Lesser Antilles FC, Haiti FC, and Western Guiana FC all replace word-final /ʒ/ and /z/ with /j/ with some regularity, but this may possibly reflect a French pronunciation /j̊/, which can still be heard in some varieties of Louisiana French (e.g. /vwazinaj/ 'neighbourhood' [< F *voisinage*]).

41 As is evidenced by the very name of the language, variously spelt *Asante* and *Ashante*.

For several of the languages above indicated as lacking postalveolar fricatives, there is also additional evidence in the form of SLA data or European loan-words, which show that /s, z/ are indeed substituted for European /ʃ, ʒ/.

In short, substrate speakers from Upper Guinea and most Bantus can be expected to have contributed to the depalatalisation of the palatoalveolar fricatives of the lexifier languages, whereas Lower Guinea is quite mixed. On a regional level, it is difficult to draw any conclusions out of these data. Presuming that most slave deliveries from Lower Guinea were relatively mixed, slaves from pretty much any region could have contributed to the merger of /s/ and /ʃ/.

3.2.7 Palatalisation

As pointed out in chapter 1, palatalisation is so common a process (e.g. Bhat 1978; Hock 1991:73-77) that substrate influence must be held innocent until proven guilty. Indeed, most Atlantic Creoles display palatalisation phenomena and, for virtually all of them, there is no reason to expect these to be due to anything other than normal language development. For quite a few, it is even a rather obvious carry-over from the lexifier. The palatalisation that is found in most Atlantic FCs, for instance, is identical to what has been attested in both European and overseas French from the 13th century and onwards (Gueunier 1986; Gilléron & Edmont 1902-10). As pointed out in Parkvall (1995c:9) and McWhorter & Parkvall (1999), the fact that stops are palatalised even before vowels that are not front in the FCs, but are so in French, strongly suggests that palatalisation in FC represents a carryover from the lexifier.[42] A similar case can be made for palatalisation in English and ECs (Holm 1988:133-34).

I agree with Holm (1993:325) that, if substrate languages can be invoked as having caused palatalisation in any Atlantic Creoles, it is for the Gulf of Guinea PCs that this case can best be made.

The relevant basic facts regarding Gulf of Guinea PC palatalisation are as follow:[43] while Portuguese has all the four phonemes /s, z, ʃ, ʒ/, only the two former are phonemic in the core lexicon of the Creoles. Thus, instances of Portuguese /ʃ, ʒ/ have been depalatalised into /s, z/. On the phonetic level, however, [ʃ, ʒ] do appear, but only as allophones of /s, z/. To the naïve observer, this may suggest a rather non-systematic correspondence between Portuguese and the Gulf of Guinea PCs,[44] but the correspondence is in fact highly predictable, and can be accounted for through two different processes. In the figure below, the step from Portuguese to the phonemic level in the PCs involves depalatalisation, whereas the one from the PC phonemic level to the phonetic realisation involves palatalisation. The same four sounds provide both the input and the output, but are differently distributed, and therefore have different phonemic status.

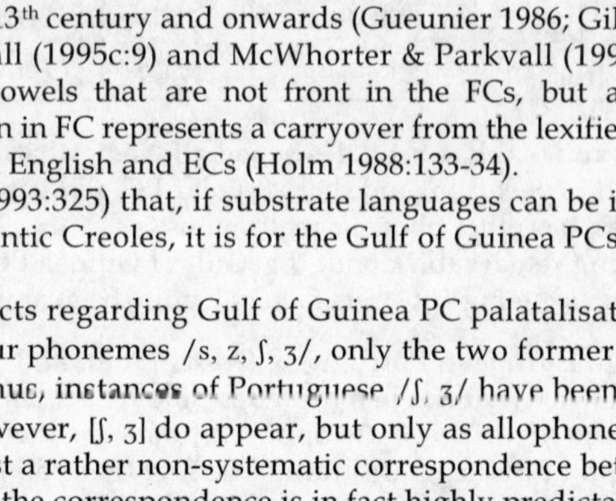

42 Examples include Guiana FC /t͡ʃum/ (< F *écume*), /t͡ʃɔ/ (< F *cœur*), Dominica FC /t͡ʃuji/ (< F *cueillir*), Trinidad FC /t͡ʃwi/ idem, St Lucia FC /zed͡ʒwi/ (< F *aiguille*), Haiti FC /d͡ʒɔl/ (< F *gueule*).

43 This section draws on data and analyses from Barrena (1957:19), Ferraz (1976:41, 1979:22), Granda (1994), Günther (1973:266-68), Lorenzino (1998:75) and Valkhoff (1966:90).

44 All the more so, since many of the sounds concerned – apart from all being phonemic – stand in allophonic relationships to each other in modern European Portuguese.

In addition to this, Portuguese (and underlying PC) /t, d/ are palatalised to /t͡ʃ/, d͡ʒ/ in the same environment, i.e. before high front vocoids. The following vocabulary items illustrate the outcomes of these processes.

LANGUAGE	WORD	ETYMOLOGY	GLOSS	SOURCE
Annobón PC	[basu]	(< P *baixo*)	'low'	Stolz (1986:73)
Annobón PC	[sulá]	(< P *chorar*)	'cry'	Stolz (1986:73)
Annobón PC	[kizu]	(< P *queijo*)	'cheese'	Stolz (1986:73)
Annobón PC	[t͡ʃigésu]	(< P *português*)	'European'	Granda (1994:435)
Annobón PC	[dãt͡ʃi]	(< P *doente*)	'ill'	Granda (1994:435)
Annobón PC	[ʃjolo]	(< P *senhor*)	'gentleman'	Ferraz (1976:41)
São Tomé PC	[(ŋ)gjãŋd͡ʒi]	(< P *grande*)	'big'	Carvalho (1984c:156)
Príncipe PC	[põt͡ʃi]	(< P *ponte*)	'bridge'	Ferraz (1975:156-57)
Príncipe PC	[ʃiku]	(< P *cinco*)	'five'	Ferraz (1975:156-57)
Príncipe PC	[palaʃju]	(< P *palácio*)	'palace'	Ferraz (1975:156-57)

The important exceptions to what has been described above is that Príncipe PC /d/ fails to palatalise where we would expect it to, and that Angolar PC, while operating within the same system as the other varieties, has other phonetic realisations.

This far, there is nothing remarkable about this Gulf of Guinea PC palatalisation, but there are in fact a few reasons for assuming substrate factors having been at work:

- Palatalisation is rare in European Portuguese (Atlas 1962), and palatalisation in Brazil – otherwise partly similar to what has just been described – is in all likelihood a 19th century innovation (Noll 1999:46-49, 196-97). As opposed to many other Creoles, there is thus no plausible lexifier origin of the palatalisation. The fact that palatalisation affects stops in positions before vowels that were etymologically schwa rather than /i/ further contributes to making a lexifier origin unlikely.
- As opposed to e.g. palatalisation in Cape Verde PC (Carvalho 1984c:155; Macedo 1979:123-24), the process is productive and (with the exception mainly of modern Portuguese loans) applies to all words. It even functions across word boundaries, as in Príncipe PC /kɔsa ig͡be/ → [kɔʃ ig͡be] {scratch body} 'to scratch oneself' and /baté/ 'to beat' + participle /-du/ → [bat͡ʃidu] 'beaten' (Ferraz 1975:157; Günther 1973:76).
- As noted above, palatalisation as such is exceedingly common among the world's languages. However, the precise strategy with regard to output forms and applicability is by no means identical everywhere. Among the Gulf of Guinea PCs, though, palatalisation does work in an almost identical manner in all four varieties (with the minor exceptions mentioned above).
- Most importantly, the similarities between the four varieties indicates that the process is of some age, since the four languages split up in the early 16th century. Again, although palatalisation is cross-linguistically frequent, it crucially does not happen overnight, but just like any other phonological change, it *takes time*. In many languages where the development of consistently applied palatalisation can be studied, the process often extends over centuries.[45] Substrate influence would explain the old age of the Gulf of Guinea PC palatalisation, since that could have made it appear instantaneously.
- As will be seen below, there are plausible prototypes in African languages, that from independent evidence can be inferred to have been present on the islands during the formative period of the PCs.

---

45 There are no early attestations of the Gulf of Guinea PCs, but the earliest evidence there is, from 1847, confirms that palatalisation was indeed present (Lorenzino 1998:232, 236). It is also worth noting that some attested sound changes, consisting in removing the high front vowels that triggered palatalisation in the first place (Ferraz 1979:23, 43) must have taken place later, proving beyond doubt that palatalisation is at least not recent.

Somewhat similar phenomena can of course be found in several African (and, for that matter, non-African) languages. But most do not fit the pattern just described perfectly. The languages discussed below are those in which palatalisation most strongly resembles that found in the Gulf of Guinea PCs.

In Akan and Isoko, it is velar rather than dental or alveolar stops that palatalise into [t͡ʃ, d͡ʒ], and in Nupe, it is /d͡z, t͡s/. In Jukun and Yoruba, non-high vowels may trigger palatalisation. Similar differences from palatalisation in Gulf of Guinea PCs can be found in most West African languages. However, I am aware of four West African languages which do seem to match the Gulf of Guinea PC pattern. All four lack phonemic /ʃ, ʒ/, and palatalise /s, z, t, d/ (but no other phonemes) into /ʃ, ʒ, t͡ʃ, d͡ʒ/, respectively, before front high vowels (but not otherwise). These languages are Ewe[46] (Kwa), Igbo, Etsako (Delto-Benuic) and Kikongo (Bantu) (Bentley 1887:518; Duthie 1996:13-15; Ferraz 1975:158, 1979:51; Lafage 1985:171; Laman 1912:4, 1936:lviii; Laver 1969:50; Williamson 1969a:86-87).

As mentioned above, Príncipe PC differs from its sister varieties in not palatalising /d/. Interestingly, this fits perfectly palatalisation patterns in Edo (Melzian 1937:xi cited in Lorenzino 1998:234), a language whose lexical imprint on the Gulf of Guinea PCs is well attested. This is in total agreement with the scenario outlined in Parkvall (1999d), where Príncipe PC is suggested to have a substrate with a stronger Lower Guinean and a weaker Bantu component in comparison to its sisters, due to having split off from Proto-Gulf of Guinea PC before the beginning of large-scale immigration of Bantus to São Tomé.

AREA	FEATURE	LANGUAGE	GROUP	SUGGESTED SUBSTRATE INFLUENCE
Phonology	Palatalisation	Gulf of Guinea PCs other than Príncipe PC	PC	+Ewe, +Igbo, +Etsako, +Kikongo
Phonology	Palatalisation	Príncipe PC	PC	+Edo

3.2.8 Labials

Characteristic of some Atlantic Creoles is the lack of the voiced labiodental /v/. Even in many Creoles where /v/ is indeed phonemic, a number of lexical items, presumably belonging to older layers, have the bilabial stop /b/ as a reflex of the labiodental fricative.

All the lexifier languages except Spanish have a phonemic opposition between /b/ and /v/. In Spanish too, /v/ once had phonemic status, and remained so for longer in southern Spain, which seems to have contributed the most to the peopling of Latin America. The two were merged in Castilian in the 17th century, but there still are dialects which preserve the older distinction (Munteanu 1996:161, 231; Stevens 1998).

On the other hand, a certain fluctuation between the two phonemes is attested for relevant older and regional varieties of English and Portuguese (Lalla & d'Costa 1990:56, 107; Ferraz 1979:35; Ferronha [ed.] n d:32; Cunha & Cintra 1985:7; Carvalho 1984c:153; Atlas 1962:17, 19, 29).

It does not seem to have been a general feature of any relevant variety of French, although isolated examples can be found in Acadian French (see e.g. Massignon 1962). Against the analysis of the stop in PCs as a retention of an archaic lexifier feature is the fact that 16th century Portuguese playwrights often used /b/ for black characters, where one would find /v/ in the mouth of whites (Raimundo 1933:20; Naro 1978:327; Tinhorão 1988:201), something that would rather point at it being a substrate effect.

/v/ is absent from the phonological inventories of basilectal Guinea-Bissau PC, Sranan EC, Ndyuka EC, and Gullah EC, in the latter of which /b/ and /v/ are merged to /β/.

Sporadic labial merger is attested for virtually all described English-lexicon varieties in the Americas and Africa, including highly acrolectal varieties such as Barbados EC, Trinidad EC, AAVE and Liberian English (Bilby 1983; Douglass 1882:118; Escure 1986; Fields 1995; Hancock

46 Not all dialects, though.

1969, 1987; Holm 1988:137; Jones 1971:69; Rickford & Handler 1994; Roberts 1988:103; Turner 1949:25; Washabaugh 1986; Wells 1982:634; Whitehead 1932:178; Winer 1993).

Because of this, Alleyne (1980:60-61) even suggests that an Atlantic proto-EC would have been /v/-less. He also points out that the English component of Saramaccan still is, although its Portuguese vocabulary does have /v/, indicating that early Sranan, from which Saramaccan got its English-derived vocabulary, must have lacked /v/ altogether - and indeed, so does modern Sranan.[47]

The merger of /b/ and /v/ is virtually unknown in French Creoles; the only work to mention anything similar is Poyen-Bellisle (1894:33, 53), according to whom /bini/ 'to come' (< F *venir*) and /bje/ 'old' (< F *vieux*) were used in (presumably a small area of) Guadeloupe.

Among the Portuguese Creoles, there is synchronically some fluctuation between the two sounds in modern Cape Verde PC (Macedo 1979:120-21; Carvalho 1984b:25). It has been suggested by both Carvalho (1984c:154) and Cardoso (1989:88) that the language originally lacked /v/, and that it has been re-established only through subsequent Portuguese influence. The same apparently applies to the sister language Guinea-Bissau PC (Holm 1988:136).

Among the Gulf of Guinea PCs, São Tomé PC and Annobón PC display a partial merger of the two phonemes (Carvalho 1984c:154; Ferraz & Valkhoff 1975:21; Ferraz 1979:35; Granda 1994:427, 434), whereas Príncipe PC - somewhat surprisingly - retains the fricative in etymologically motivated positions (Günther 1973:268; Stolz 1986:92).[48] The fact that the lexemes affected by the merger of labials are essentially overlapping constitutes a further piece of evidence that Annobón PC is an offshoot of São Tomé PC. It also allows us to conclude that the partial merger took place before the colonisation of Annobón, though apparently after the settling of Príncipe. In the scenario of Creole development in the Gulf of Guinea Islands proposed by Parkvall (1999d), this is another feature that suggests a stronger influence of Edo on Príncipe and of Bantu on São Tomé.

Brazilian Vernacular Portuguese also presents sporadic examples of this phenomenon, as did Negerhollands DC (Stolz 1986:69; Marroquim 1934:84-85).

In Papiamentu SC, both /b/ and /v/ have phonemic status (Munteanu 1996:231),[49] despite their merger in Spanish. This is mainly due to recent Dutch influence - in the Iberian part of the lexicon, the two are realised as a bilabial stop (Eva Eckkrammer, p c). Palenquero SC does not differentiate the two labials, but this might of course easily be ascribed to the lexifier.

Atlantic languages do not normally have /v/, and the phoneme is also absent from most potential Mande substrates, the main exceptions being Kpelle, Malinke, Mende and Vai. In European loans, however, the default substitute is /w/ rather than /b/ in Wolof and Mandinka (Peace Corps 1995a, 1995b), and the same goes for Diallo's (1998:118) Guinean informants.[50] Use of /b/ for etymological /v/ is attested in Wolof, though, as well as in Bullom languages and Fulfulde (all Atlantic), Mandinka (Mande) (Arnott 1969a:69; Delafosse 1929:90; Ndiaye 1996:109, 112; Peace Corps 1995b; Stolz 1986:109).

Kru, Kwa and Delto-Benuic languages are all heterogeneous groups in this respect. Within Kwa, however, one of the two most important subgroupings, Akan, is virtually altogether /v/-less, whereas the three major Gbe languages (Gẽ, Ewe, and Fon) all have phonemic /v/.

Delto-Benuic languages without /v/ include Efik, Igbo and Yoruba, as well as the geographically proximate Hausa, whereas Edo and Ijo have /v/, as do most relevant Bantu languages. Whenever substituted in European loan-words, /b/ seems to be the favoured option in both areas, as in e.g. Yoruba /dérébà/ (< E 'driver') (Banjọ 1986:539), Kimbundu /kirisobo/ 'Christopher' (< P *Cristóvão*) (Mendonça 1933:65), and Ntandu /nsábi/ 'key' (< P *chave*) and /pálába/ 'word' (< P *palavra*) (Stolz 1986:110). Within Bantu, however, there is a good deal of

---

47 Sranan has had an opposition between /b/ and /v/, thanks to borrowings from Portuguese and Dutch, though the latter has now merged with /f/. English-derived words - which arguably constitute the oldest part of the lexicon - consistently have /b/ for etymological /v/ (Norval Smith, p c).

48 Günther (1973:269) suggests that words in which Portuguese /v/ corresponds to Príncipe PC /b/ are later loans from São Tomé PC.

49 Considerable fluctuation is attested, however (Kouwenberg & Murray 1994:8; Munteanu 1996:230).

50 Diallo does not indicate the L_1 of his informants.

variation within small geographical areas. While Kikongo, for instance, has /v/, and shows few signs of substituting it for /b/ in the European-derived words in Swartenbroeckx (1973), the closely related Ntandu, as just seen, does precisely this.

In sum, then, the only clear thing about the substrate origins of v-lessness from a regional point of view, is that Akan is likely to have encouraged it, while a strong Gbe presence would presumably have contributed to the retention of /v/. In all other areas, both types of languages are spoken.

AREA	FEATURE	LANGUAGE	GROUP	SUGGESTED SUBSTRATE INFLUENCE
Phonology	Merger of /v/ and /b/	Guinea-Bissau PC	PC	+Akan, -Gbe, +various languages from all areas
Phonology	Merger of /v/ and /b/	Surinamese ECs[51]	EC	+Akan, -Gbe, +various languages from all areas
Phonology	Merger of /v/ and /b/	Gullah EC	EC	+Akan, -Gbe, +various languages from all areas
Phonology	Merger of /v/ and /b/	All other ECs	EC	(+Akan, -Gbe, +various languages from all areas)
Phonology	Merger of /v/ and /b/	Cape Verde PC	PC	(+Akan, -Gbe, +various languages from all areas)
Phonology	Merger of /v/ and /b/	Gulf of Guinea PCs other than Príncipe PC	PC	(+Akan, -Gbe, +various languages from all areas)
Phonology	Merger of /v/ and /b/	Negerhollands DC	DC	(+Akan, -Gbe, +various languages from all areas)
Phonology	Merger of /v/ and /b/	Papiamentu SC	SC	+Akan, -Gbe, +various languages from all areas

A use of /f/ for European /v/ sporadically occurs in at least Mandinka and Yoruba (Peace Corps 1995b; Alleyne 1980:175, 178; Banjọ 1986:539), but if this is more widespread in West Africa, it does not seem to have left any traces in any Atlantic Creole, except perhaps Angolar, for which Lorenzino (1998:76) documents some variation between /f/ and /v/.[52]

Scattered all over the Anglophone Caribbean (though mainly in the Leeward Islands) are cases of /w/ for etymological /v/. Despite it being attested for Upper Guinean languages as mentioned above, this seems to reflect dialectal English rather than substrate influence, for my impression is that the phenomenon is concentrated in particular to the areas with low rather than high black-to-white ratios. This geographical tendency may even be more pronounced in the francophone orbit, where the phenomenon is rarer, however.

Furthermore, older records of Jamaica EC display a sporadic use of /p/ for etymological /f/ (Lalla & d'Costa 1990:56, 119). The same tendency can be seen in a small number of lexical items in the Líbase dialect of Saramaccan EC and in Cameroon EC (Hancock 1969; Veenstra 1996:43; Dwyer 1966:513). African languages having /p/, but not /f/ include Asante and Lelemi (both Kwa) and Adamawa Fulfulde (Atlantic) (Clements 1985:56-57; Maddieson 1984:293; Ruhlen 1975:195). Izi (Delto-Benuic) has /p/, whereas /f/ is marginal (Meier, Meier & Bendor-Samuel 1975:77, 79).

AREA	FEATURE	LANGUAGE	GROUP	SUGGESTED SUBSTRATE INFLUENCE
Phonology	Merger of /p/ and /f/	Jamaica EC†	EC	(+Kwa, +Adamawa Fulfulde, +Izi)
Phonology	Merger of /p/ and /f/	Saramaccan EC (Líbase dialect)	EC	(+Kwa, +Adamawa Fulfulde, +Izi)
Phonology	Merger of /p/ and /f/	Cameroon EC	EC	(+Kwa, +Adamawa Fulfulde, +Izi)

51 English-derived lexical component only.

52 Both are phonemic, though.

Finally, Gullah EC has merged etymological /v/ and /b/ into /β/, while realising /f/ as /ɸ/. Turner (1949:242) suggests Twi, Wolof, Malinke, Kru, Yoruba or Gẽ as sources for this phenomenon. Although, for instance Ewe indeed has /β/ and /ɸ/, it also has /f/ and /v/, so that the use of bilabials for labiodentals is not an obvious result of Ewe influence. The only languages I have found which have /ɸ/, but not /f/ are Adamawa Fulfulde and Hausa, both spoken far from the Atlantic coast and the slave trading areas. No West African language known to me has /β/, but not /b/. An internal development in Gullah EC is therefore not unlikely.

3.3 Phonetics

3.3.1 Implosives

Reflexes of European plosives are implosive in all four Gulf of Guinea PC varieties (Ferraz 1975:155, 1979:21; Lorenzino 1998:71; Granda 1994:428). Implosives have furthermore been attested, although rarely, in Gullah EC (Salikoko Mufwene p c; though cf Turner 1949:240) and occasionally also in Haiti FC (Tinelli 1981:14).

Finally, Megenney (1993:157) claims that implosives occur in Caribbean Creoles in general, regardless of lexifier.[53] Since this is not to my knowledge supported by any other observer, some scepticism may be called for. According to Glenn Gilbert (p c), implosives are common in New World ECs in general, whereas Jeff Allen (p c) is not aware of them in St Lucia FC and Peter Patrick's (p c) thorough knowledge of Jamaica EC has not brought them to his attention.

10% of the languages in Maddieson's (1984:111) sample contain implosive stops, most (but by no means all) of which are spoken in Africa. Implosives were found in 29% of the Niger-Kordofanian languages in Ruhlen's (1976:158) sample. In other words, implosive stops are clearly over-represented in Africa.

African languages with phonemic implosive stops include Kisi, Adamawa Fulfulde (Atlantic), Dan, Kpelle, Vai (Mande), Bete, Godie (Kru), Efik, Gbari, Igbo, Ijo, Tarok (Delto-Benuic), Hausa (Afro-Asiatic), and the small north-western Bantu languages Mpongwe, Ngom, Fang, Benga, Duala, Njebi, Shira and Tsogo (Childs 1995:22, 27; Guthrie 1953; Maddieson 1984; Marchese 1984:127; Ruhlen 1975; Welmers 1976; Westermann & Ward 1933; Williamson 1969b:98). Most have parallel series of phonemic explosives, but in some languages, such as Kisi (Childs 1995:22), there is an implosive, but no explosive set of stops. In addition to these, Wolof stops have implosive allophones word-finally (Sauvageot 1965:18; Dumont 1990:111). Furthermore, Equatorial Guinean Spanish, with a north-western Bantu substrate, prefers implosive realisations of Spanish stops (Lipski 1985:34-35).

Since most of my phonological data concerns phonemes rather than actual phones, implosive stop allophones no doubt exist in other potential Atlantic Creole substrates than the ones mentioned here. Yet, it is potentially significant that no Kwa language, nor any of the major Western Bantu languages are included.

In sum, then, implosive realisations of stops, whenever occurring in Atlantic Creoles, is something that is in all likelihood substrate-induced. Unfortunately, though, data on neither the Creoles nor the potential substrates are sufficient to establish any precise relationships between Creoles and African languages.

3.3.2 Alveolar versus dental stops

Of the European lexifier Creoles, the two Germanic ones have alveolar stops, whereas stops in the three Romance ones are rather dental. Many Atlantic Creoles keep the realisations of the lexifier. In others, however, this is not the case. The /d/ of Cameroon EC is dental, whereas /t/ and /d/ has been reported to be alveolar in Dominica FC and Annobón PC (Dwyer 1966:5; Amastae 1979:87; Granda 1994:429).[54]

53 Megenney refers to William Stewart as cited in a 1974 publication by Gage, but neither occurs in his reference list

54 This is also the case of Dominican Spanish, as well as L_2 Spanish of Equatorial Guinea (Green 1997:5.4.4.2, 5.4.5; Lipski 1985:35).

The majority of West African languages in the UPSID database (well over 80%)[55] have alveolar stops – of the almost 40 relevant languages which have /t/ and/or /d/ phonemes for which I have details on the place of articulation, only a few have dental realisations. Malinke (Mande), Edo (Delto-Benuic) and Yaka (Bantu) have only dentals, whereas Temne (Atlantic), Ewe (Kwa) and Isoko (Delto-Benuic) permit both realisations. Gã, curiously, has a dental /t/, but an alveolar /d/. Other West African languages claimed by Turner (1949:23) and Ladefoged (1968:43-66) to have dental stops (not contrasting with other realisations) include Limba (Atlantic), Efutu, Anum, Nkonya, Fante, at least some dialects of Twi (all Kwa), Ora (Delto-Benuic), and Kikongo (Bantu).

Since most West African languages have alveolar stops, we may suspect that the realisation of stops in Dominica FC and Annobón PC is due to substrate influence (or possibly adstratal – in the form of English – for Dominica FC), but one that cannot be pinpointed.[56] The dental stops in Cameroon EC are also likely to be due to substrate influence, but since Cameroon EC is spoken mainly as an L_2, and is still in contact with African languages, this influence may well be post-formative. Thus, the place of articulation of plosives cannot be used to define the precise origin of substrate influences in Atlantic Creoles.

3.3.3 Aspiration

Aspiration is not always indicated in reference grammars, and moreover, since the phenomenon is gradient, it not impossible that aspiration of plosives is noted only to the extent that it differs from the native language of the observer. For instance, the voiceless plosives of Kisi are said by Childs (1995:28) to be aspirated, but less so than in English. In the UPSID database, aspiration is indicated, but a problem is that lack of such indication not necessarily implies that the voiceless plosives are unaspirated. My impression, though, is that unaspirated stops are the rule rather than the exception in West Africa.[57] Among the six languages in UPSID most of whose voiceless plosive explicitly are said to be aspirated, we find three out of the four Kwa languages included (Ewe, Gã and Akan). Other languages in which at least /p/ is aspirated include Susu (Mande) and Isekiri (Delto-Benuic; closely related to Yoruba) (Ladefoged 1968:14).

Apart from a couple of languages with both aspirated and unaspirated stops, the few West African languages other than the ones just mentioned that I have come across with aspirated stops are relatively small and rather distant from the coast, which would make them less likely substrates of Atlantic Creoles.

English is the only one of the five lexifier languages whose (voiceless) plosives are aspirated, and English Creoles are thus the ones where we would expect the lack of aspiraton of West African plosives to have an impact.[58] Such an impact has been attested in Gullah EC and Cameroon EC (Turner 1949:22-3; Dwyer 1966:5), which are said to have unaspirated voiceless plosives. Whatever the origin of the phenomenon, it obviously cannot be due to any of the African languages, which, just like English, has aspirated voiceless stops.

More interesting is the aspiration of at least word-final plosives in Cape Verde PC observed by both Nunes (1963) and Macedo (1979). The only Upper Guinean languages known to me which could have contributed to this – if it is indeed a result of substrate influence – are Kisi and Wolof (Childs 1995:28; Kevin Moore, p c), but again, data on aspiration are scarce, and it may well be that aspiration occurs more extensively in Upper Guinean languages.

AREA	FEATURE	LANGUAGE	GROUP	SUGGESTED SUBSTRATE INFLUENCE
Phonetics	Aspiration	Gullah EC	EC	-Kwa, -Susu, -Isekiri
Phonetics	Aspiration	Cameroon EC	EC	-Kwa, -Susu, -Isekiri
Phonetics	Aspiration	Cape Verde PC	PC	+Wolof, +Kisi

55 Additional data were taken from Ruhlen (1975).

56 It is noteworthy that the purportedly two major substrates of Annobón PC, Edo and Kikongo, both belong to the small group of African languages with dental stops, thus contrasting with Annobón PC itself.

57 In some few languages, notably Igbo, aspiration is phonemically contrastive.

58 Unaspirated plosives in e.g. Príncipe PC (Günther 1973:41) do not reveal any substrate influences, since Portuguese plosives themselves lack aspiration.

3.3.4 Retroflexion

At least two dialects of Cape Verde PC have also been reported to variably have retroflex plosives (Macedo 1979:96-97). Although several Kwa languages have retroflex stops (Ladefoged 1968:53, 56; Campbell 1991:27; Lefebvre 1998:402; UPSID), the only Upper Guinean language with such stops known to me is the Mande language Kpelle (Westermann 1924:1). As opposed to Cape Verde PC, however, retroflex stops in all these languages contrast phonemically with their non-retroflex counterparts. Again in contrast to Cape Verde PC, it is only /ɖ/ that has a retroflex articulation.

It should be noted in this context that only about a tenth of the languages featured in the UPSID database have phonemic retroflex stops, the vast majority of which are spoken in Australia (whose languages are notorious for consonant systems exceptionally well endowed in places of articulation) and India (where retroflex stops constitute an areal feature). The only West African language in UPSID with retroflex stops is Lelemi (Kwa). Given the cross-linguistic rarity of retroflex stops, internal development thereof in Cape Verde PC - a Creole which has remained in close contact with its lexifier throughout its history - would be somewhat unexpected.

3.4 Phonotactics

3.4.1 Syllable structures

It has often been noted that Atlantic Creoles, in comparison to their respective lexifiers, display a tendency towards CV syllable structure. A simple piece of evidence that there is indeed a difference is the fact that in a French dictionary (Pruvost-Beaurain [ed.] 1985, containing 51 200 words), 26% of the entries are vowel-initial. The corresponding number for Guadeloupe FC is 10%, and for Haiti FC 11% (Poullet, Telchid & Montbrand 1984; Bentolila 1976).

The drift towards canonic CV structure is something that need not be due to substrate influence, since a similar tendency may be observed in Pidgin and Creole languages all over the world, regardless of substratal input. Nevertheless, it could be that the *differences between* the various Creoles, as shown in e.g. Ericsson & Gustafson-Capková (1997), reflect difference in substrate composition. Atlantic Creole phonotactics are not equally strict, and nor are those of the West African substrates.

A word of caution is called for, however. As shown in Parkvall (1998), there is in Atlantic Creoles a correlation between syllable simplification and general typological distance from the lexifier. It is thus not only possible, but even plausible, that the proportion of CV syllables in comparison to more complex syllable types reflect a general departure from lexifier grammar and phonology, rather than the contribution of a specific substrate.

For some Atlantic Creoles, including Jamaica EC, Sranan EC, Krio EC, Cameroon EC, Príncipe PC and Negerhollands DC, it has been suggested or demonstrated that older varieties were closer to the ideal CV structure than their 20th-century descendants (Günther 1973:45; Lalla & d'Costa 1990:65; Stolz 1986:243; Holm 1988:112; Eersel 1984; Devonish 1989:27; Hancock 1969:24-25; Todd 1982:92).

While two of the lexifier languages, English and Dutch, manage quite complex syllables structures, Spanish and Portuguese syllables are closer to the canonic CV shape of West African languages, with French occupying an intermediate position.[59]

The proportion of CV syllables is rather similar in Palenquero SC and Spanish, the main difference being a higher proportion of CVC syllables in Spanish, and a higher proportion of V syllables in Palenquero, with non-nasal codas being very sparse (Ericsson & Gustafson-Capková 1997).

If Portuguese can be assumed to pattern with Spanish in this regard,[60] Guinea-Bissau PC (Couto 1999) aligns very well with the Ibero-Romance (it is in fact a lot closer to Spanish than is

59 Unfortunately, I have found detailed information on syllable structures and their distribution only for Spanish and Dutch (Ericsson & Gustafson-Capková 1997).

60 Phonologically speaking, that is. On the phonetic level, Portuguese syllable structures are more reminiscent of Slavonic than of Romance. Not surprisingly, however, 16th century Portuguese pronunciation was closer to today's underlying phonological level than the modern language is (Kihm 1994:16).

Palenquero). Data is lacking on Papiamentu SC, but I would assume it to be less like Spanish, because of the large amount of Dutch loan-words. Nor do I have any data on Cape Verde PC, but while its modern-day varieties abound with consonant clusters, I cannot help suspecting that most of these represent later developments, and that original Cape Verdean would have been rather more similar to Guinea-Bissau PC.

São Tomé PC has numerous complex onsets that would be impossible in any western European language (Ferraz 1979:26-27, 47), but there is reason to suppose that that this was not the case originally. For one thing, CV is still by far the most common syllable type, and almost all syllables are still open (Ferraz 1979:48). Secondly, the complex onsets are absent from its closest relatives (Lorenzino 1998:230). Thirdly, and most importantly, all four Gulf of Guinea PCs have taken rather radical measures (aphesis, syncope, apocope, prothesis, epenthesis, paragogue and metathesis are all abundantly attested) to make the Portuguese vocabulary conform to a CV pattern. This makes it possible to reconstruct an earlier stage of Gulf of Guinea PC looking rather like proto-Surinamese EC in basically having V and CV syllables only.

Despite a massive dominance of CV syllables (Sabino 1994:505), Negerhollands DC did allow CC onsets and CC codas[61] (Stolz 1986:100-01). What is noteworthy, however, is that while Negerhollands is unexpectedly tolerant when it comes to complex onsets, a surprisingly large amount of which survived creolisation, it was considerably less so with regard to codas, many of which have been considerably reduced or broken up by epenthesis (Stolz 1986:101). Sabino (1992:5) makes the same observation, and ascribes it to the Kwa languages Akan, Gã and Ewe.

Most striking, however, is the fact that ECs have taken more radical measures to achieve the unmarked CV shape than have FCs, and although English has more complex syllables than French, there are no Atlantic FCs with similarly strict constraints on syllable structures as the Surinamese ECs (Parkvall 1999c:32-33). Although this does not apply to less basilectal ECs of the insular Caribbean, even there, traces can be found of syllable restructurings unheard of among French Creoles. Although this does not prove beyond doubt an earlier stage where Caribbean ECs were as phonotactically rigid as the Surinamese ECs, it is highly suggestive of a less liberal ancestral form. In particular, even moderately basilectal ECs contain vocabulary items in which a paragogic vowel has been added in order to avoid even simple codas (Parkvall 1999c:32), just as is the rule in Surinam, where V and CV are basically the only available syllable types in Ndyuka EC and Saramaccan EC (Ericsson & Gustafson-Capková 1997), something that appears to earlier also have been the case in Sranan EC (Holm 1988:112; Eersel 1984; Devonish 1989:27). This is completely alien to FCs, which, although they often have reduced both onsets and codas, do not show any signs of ever having disallowed neither non-nasal codas nor complex onsets.[62]

In general, CV is by far the most common syllable type in West Africa, and a large number of languages allow nothing but V and CV syllables, that is, they have no codas, and no complex onsets. There are in fact even a few languages that disallow V syllables, or at least in which native vocabulary items may not be vowel-initial. There are, however, some differences within West Africa, both with regard to onsets and codas.[63]

Atlantic stands out as the one family were several types of codas are allowed; many languages of this group even tolerate syllable-final clusters. Bantu and Kru, on the other hand, typically accept no codas whatsoever. Kwa takes an intermediate position, in that these

---

61 Marginally, both onsets and codas could even contain three consonants.

62 Despite the opposite being true for the respective lexifiers, the total proportion of complex onsets and codas was higher, albeit marginally, in the FCs of Guadeloupe and St Lucia than for Jamaica EC in Ericsson & Gustafson-Capková's survey.

63 The claims regarding West African phonotactics in this section draw on evidence from Anon. (1961:5), Armstrong (1984:328), Arnott (1969a:64, 1969b:147-48), Bamgboṣe (1966:6, 168), Banjọ (1986:538), Bentley (1887:521), Blondé (1979:380), Childs (1995:33), Christaller (1875:13), Trutenau 1973), Cook (1969:41-42), Creissels (1989:64), David (1975:59), Delafosse (1929:86-89), Derive (1990:154), Duthie (1996:10-11), Elugbe (1984:296), Faraclas (1984:385), Ferraz (1979:48), United Nations (1999), Green & Igwe (1963:3), Guthrie (1953), Hoffmann & Schachter (1969:78-79), Houis (1963:37), Innes (1967:7), Jenewari (1984:112), Kelly (1969:157-58), Lafage (1985:161, 190), Laver (1969:52), Mafeni (1969:118-19, 123), Manfredi (1984:344), Marchese (1984:126), Meier, Meier & Bendor-Samuel (1975:55), Mendonça (1933:48), Migeod (1908:50), Ndiaye (1996:110), Niedzielski (1989:86), Opubor (1969: 129, 132), Plag & Uffman (1998:7), Rowlands (1959:16), Ruhlen (1975), Sabino (1994:506), Sauvageot (1965:48), Smith (1969:137-38), Spears (1967), Swartenbroeckx (1973), Valente (1964:27), Ward (1952:11), Welmers (1946:26, 1952:85, 1976:24), Westermann (1924), Westermann & Bryan (1952), S. Williams (1993:414), Williamson (1969b:107-08).

languages almost without exception admit codas, but only in the form of nasals and semivowels. The same applies to Mande and Delto-Benuic languages, though some few accept non-nasal consonant codas.

As for onsets, few West African languages tolerate any complex onsets where C2 is not a semivowel (S) or a liquid (L). Mande is the most strict group, in that only Malinke, Dan, and possibly Ivorian Mande languages (though cf Derive 1990:161) of the languages I have looked at permit any initial clusters whatsoever. Apart from this, I failed to observe any patterns, apart from a slight tendency of favouring CL rather than CS onsets in Kwa. In most other areas, though, languages tolerating CS and CL are spoken alongside those not allowing any complex onsets at all.

Thus, the most obvious observation regarding Atlantic Creole syllable structures is that a few varieties have or have had exceptionally rigid constrains, allowing basically only V and CV syllables.

Although this may not have been case had the substrate material been drawn from areas where most languages allow more complex structures, it is, however, not necessarily a substrate feature, since it could have been brought about by pidginisation tendencies alone. The fact that the Creoles which are most radical in this respect are the ones that are most typologically distant from their lexifiers in other regards would seem to support the notion that more drastic pidginisation rather than the "right" or "wrong" substrate might be what generates this phonotactical profile. Moreover, it would not point directly to any particular region in West Africa, since languages with only V or CV syllables are distributed all over that area.

It would seem, however, that something can be learnt from the differences between Atlantic Creoles in syllable structure simplification. Particularly striking is the difference between ECs and FCs, especially with regard to the use of paragogic vowels. A stronger representation of Atlantic languages in FC genesis is something that would account for this fact.

The fact that FCs are phonotactically more liberal than ECs has earlier been observed by Holm (1988:113) and Parkvall (1999c), both of whom suggest that it may point at a stronger Senegambian component in FC formation. Boretzky (1983:75) forwards the same suggestion with regard to Upper Guinea PCs.

Also noteworthy is the discrepancy in reduction between onsets and codas in Negerhollands DC – we might hypothesise this to have been caused by languages relatively tolerant regarding onsets, but considerably more strict with codas.

Three-consonant onsets are found in the Kwa (Gbe) language Aja and the Delto-Benuic language Isoko (Mafeni 1969:118-9; United Nations 1999), of which the former has only nasal codas, whereas the latter accepts no codas at all. Onsets consisting of two consonants, of which the second usually is a semi-vowel or a liquid, are found throughout West Africa, with a slight overrepresentation in the Kwa-speaking region. Sabino (1992:5) claims that Akan, Gã and Ewe, all Kwa languages, contain CLS onsets. This is not corroborated by my other sources, but if it is indeed true, that would suggest Kwa influence on Negerhollands syllable structure, since, as indicated above, Kwa languages in general – like most of the Negerhollands lexicon – do not admit codas other than semi-vowels or nasals.

AREA	FEATURE	LANGUAGE	GROUP	SUGGESTED SUBSTRATE INFLUENCE
Phonology	Syllable structure	ECs	EC	-Atlantic
Phonology	Syllable structure	FCs	FC	+Atlantic
Phonology	Syllable structure	Negerhollands DC	DC	+Kwa, +Isoko

3.4.2 Stop + liquid clusters in ECs

In at least Jamaica EC, /kl/ and /gl/ are substituted in at least word-final position for the clusters /tl/ and /dl/ of English (as in Jamaica EC /likl/ 'little' and /rigl/ 'riddle'). There has in other words been a tendency to replace alveolar stops with their velar counterparts before laterals. According to Cassidy & Le Page (1980:lix), the process is regular, and while /kl/ for /tl/ has been attested in a few locations Britain, the voiced counterpart has not.

Of the almost thirty African languages[64] in which I have searched for a similar distribution, most permit neither cluster, and few permit both. Yet another group of languages (the Upper Guinean languages Guinean Fulfulde and Kpelle) allow /tl/ and/or /dl/, but not /kl/ and /gl/. Neither of these languages can therefore be held responsible for the Jamaican development. There is another group of languages, however, in which velar, but not dental/alveolar plosives are found before laterals (in the material at my disposition). This group includes the Gur language Dagaari and the three Kwa languages Aja, Gẽ (both Gbe languages) and Baule. Of these, Dagaari and Baule are, as opposed to the Gbe languages, spoken in areas more peripheral to the slave trade.

AREA	FEATURE	LANGUAGE	GROUP	SUGGESTED SUBSTRATE INFLUENCE
phonology	stop+liquid clusters	Jamaica EC	EC	+Gbe (+Dagaari, +Baule)

3.4.3 Vowel harmony

Vowel harmony is often commented upon in studies on Atlantic Creole phonology. With the exception of Cape Verde PC, however (see below), no form of vowel harmony is productive in any Atlantic Creole, and show no signs of ever having been so either. There are slight *tendencies* towards vowel harmony, but these tendencies mainly manifest themselves in determining the quality of paragogic vowels (as in Sranan EC /bigi/ 'big' [< E *big*]) or of the etymological schwas (as in Trinidad FC /dubut/ 'to stand up' [< F *debout*]). To my knowledge, there exist no quantitative data, but my impression is that harmony tendencies are stronger in the Gulf of Guinea PCs than elsewhere, but even there, vowel harmony is neither generalised nor productive.

Vowel harmony is common in Africa, and 24% of the Niger-Kordofanian languages have some sort of vowel harmony, as opposed to 12% of the world's languages – only in Uralic and Altaic languages is the phenomenon more common (Ruhlen 1976:150). In contrast to the harmony systems of Uralic and Altaic, though, which operate with a front-back opposition, West African vowel harmony is typically based on aperture.

Its distribution is uneven in West Africa, though, apparently being relatively uncommon in Upper Guinea (Welmers 1973:39; Senghor 1963),[65] and among Bantu languages (though cf Ferraz 1979:50).[66] It is once again in Lower Guinea that the phenomenon is most widespread. It seems to be centred in the western parts, where Kru languages have fully developed harmony (Marchese 1984:121, 129; Innes 1966:16). Not unexpectedly then, Akan languages have stronger harmony requirements than the more eastern Gbe group (Bellon 1983:ix; Boretzky 1983:60; Christaller 1875:9, 192; Creissels 1989:81; Welmers 1973:35; Lafage 1985:150; Stewart 1971:198; Ultan 1973:40; Westermann & Bryan 1952:90), and in many Delto-Benuic languages, vowel harmony rules are no longer fully productive (Bamgboṣe 1969:168; Boretzky 1983:60; Campbell 1991:396; Creissels 1989:74; Green & Igwe 1963:1; Jenewari 1984:110; Kelly 1969:158; Meier, Meier & Bendor-Samuel 1975:50; Opubor 1969:127; Stewart 1971:198; Welmers 1973:34, 38-39; Westermann & Bryan 1952:90; Williamson 1969a:90, 1969b:107). In all these languages, vowel harmony systems are based on height rather than on frontness.

It is possible, but by no means certain, that the tendencies towards vowel harmony in Atlantic Creoles are due to the presence of harmonising vowel systems in West Africa, and yet, the only Atlantic Creoles known to me where a fully productive harmony rule operates is Cape Verde PC, whose substrate is arguably Upper Guinean.

In this language, unstressed etymological /e/ and /o/ are raised to /i/ and /u/ respectively when followed by these within the same word (Carvalho 1984b:40). Also, /a/ may occur in

64 The two dozen West African languages from United Nations (1999), and the dictionaries by Swartenbroeckx (1973) and Peace Corps (1995a, 1995b).

65 But cf Ndiaye (1996:108) for another view with regard to Atlantic languages. Also, Welmers (1973:39) points out that although Mande languages do not have vowel harmony proper, bisyllabic words with two identical vowels are remarkably frequent, something that may represent (although Welmers does not make any such claim) vestiges of a formerly productive harmony system.

66 Note for instance the following two European loans in Kikongo (Swartenbroeckx 1973), where a tendency *away from* harmonic vowels may be observed: /folona ~ folono/ (< P *forno*) 'oven', /buta / (< E *boat*) 'boat'.

pretonic syllables only if the stressed vowel is /a/ (Carvalho 1984b:41). This, Carvalho (1984b:42-43) claims, is a generalisation of a tendency present in embryonic form in southern Portugal. Other types of vowel harmony in various dialects of Cape Verde PC are described by Ferraz & Valkhoff (1975:26) and Carvalho (1984b:10). Apart from the existence of a similar tendency in Portugal, the absence of anything similar in the putative substrates makes it reasonable to suspect that these harmony rules developed after Creolisation, and independently of the substratal input.

Vowel harmony is thus an areal feature of West Africa, and in particular central and western Lower Guinea, which should surprise us by its absence rather than presence in Atlantic Creoles. This absence is all the more remarkable since non-harmonising loans in languages with vowel harmony are frequently adjusted to the phonological patterns of the host language (witness e.g. Swedish loans in Finnish). Also, vowel harmony as a productive process is readily borrowed, as exemplified by several Indo-European languages in Asia (Akhras 1998; Thomason & Kaufman 1988:218).

Chapter 4

Grammar

4.1 Reflexivisation

Since Van Name (1869-70:155), various scholars have pointed out that Atlantic Creoles have a preference for reflexive constructions involving the word for 'body' or the name of a body-part, as in the following examples:.

Haiti FC:	/m	ap	tuje	tɛt	mwẽ/			
	1sg	IMPERF	kill	head	1sg			'I will kill myself' (Lefebvre 1998:159).
Trinidad FC:	/mwẽ	te	ka	pale	baj	kɔ	mwẽ/	
	1sg	PAST	PROG	speak	give	body	1sg	
								'I was speaking to myself' (Thomas 1869:43)
Cape Verde PC:	/ɛl	mata	kabesa/					
	3sg	kill	head					'He killed himself' (Carvalho 1984c:162)

Quite often, parallels have also been drawn between this and a similar use in West African languages. This reflexivisation strategy, however, is not uncommon cross-linguistically,[1] and European lexifier languages are not completely alien to reflexive-like constructions involving 'body' or names of body-parts. As Holm (1988:205) points out, English has pronouns such as *anybody* as well as idiomatic expressions like *to save one's skin*.

Furthermore, although first brought into Creolist discourse by substratist Suzanne Sylvain (1936:65), superstratists rarely miss the opportunity to point out that medieval French texts, including the *Chanson de Roland* and the Villehardoin Chronicles, contain reflexive constructions involving *corps*. Goodman (1964:57-58) claims this strategy would have become rare as early as the 14th century, and would thus not have been likely to influence Atlantic Creole formation. Chaudenson (1974:734, 1979:77), who firmly believes that Creole reflexivisation has French origins, draws attention to modern-day attestations of *corps* reflexives in Saintonge in south-western France (Wartburg 1964:1212).[2]

Although European French is theoretically a possible source of body and body-part reflexivisation in FCs, and although the strategy as such is not uncommon world-wide, there are reasons for accepting an African prototype for the Atlantic Creole construction:

- Nothing suggests the *corps* construction was anything but marginal in European French, not least during the 17th and 18th centuries. In particular, no overseas variety of French has kept or developed reflexives involving 'body' or the name of body-parts.
- Corporal reflexivisation is not attested in the other lexifiers, and no variety of French would provide an explanation of this phenomenon in Creoles lexified by English, Portuguese or Spanish.
- On the other hand, many of the potential West African substrates have relevant reflexivisation patterns (see below).
- Despite the semantic transparency and cross-linguistic frequency of the construction, hardly any Creoles with non-African substrata make use of 'body' or the names of body-parts in reflexive constructions.[3]

---

1 See e.g. Carden (1993:106), Leslau (1952:71), MacKenzie (1990:142), Faltz (1977:32 cited in Fox 1981:332), Lefebvre (1998:160), Heine et al. (1993:31-32), Kemmer (1993:193), Lewis (1947:276-77), Munro (1976) and Abondolo (1998:25) for examples from a large number of languages from several different parts of the world.

2 For further details on French *corps* reflexivisation, see also Stein (1984:46), Einhorn (1974:69), Faine (1939:78), Munteanu (1996:348), Lefebvre (1998:168-69).

3 See e.g. Hancock (1980:20) and Baxter (1988:206), who nevertheless show Papia Kristang PC of Malaysia to be a notable exception – significantly, though, it is featured in its substrate Malay as well (Lewis 1947:276-77). Reflexives with /lekor/ (< F *le corps*) are found in the Indian Ocean FCs, which, however, did receive a West African

The following table illustrates the use of body (-part) reflexives in (West) African languages:

LANGUAGE	FAMILY	REFLEXIVE MORPHEME	SOURCE
Balanta	Atlantic	*body*	Rougé (1988:93)
Fulfulde	Atlantic	*head*	Houis (1980:20)
Mankanya	Atlantic	*body*	Rougé (1988:93)
Wolof	Atlantic	*head*	Goodman (1964:57-58)
Dogon	Dogon	*head*	Houis (1980:20)
Gurenne	Gur	*body*	Boretzky (1983:143)
Twi	Kwa	*body*	Martin Biko (p c)
Ewe	Kwa	*body?*	Bartens (1996:89)
Fon	Kwa	*body*	Muysken & Smith (1994:47)
Bassa-Nge Nupe	Delto-Benuic	*body*	Awoyale (1986:3)
Ebira	Delto-Benuic	*body*	Awoyale (1986:3)
Edo	Delto-Benuic	*body*	Thomas (1910:138)
Wano	Delto-Benuic	*body*	Thomas (1910:145)
Efik	Delto-Benuic	*body*	Carden (1993:105)
Igbo	Delto-Benuic	*buttocks*[4]	Holm (1988:205)
Igbo	Delto-Benuic	*body?*[5]	Awoyale (1986:2)
Urhobo	Delto-Benuic	*body*	Awoyale (1986:2)
Yoruba	Delto-Benuic	*body*	Taylor (1971:7-9)
Hausa	Afro-Asiatic	*head*	Houis (1980:20)
Margi	Afro-Asiatic	*head*	Houis (1980:20)

The most striking feature is the use of 'head' rather than 'body' in at least two Atlantic languages,[6] and the apparent absence of either in Mande and Bantu.[7]

'Head' seems to be a less common source for reflexives than 'body', although it is attested for Basque and Mordvin (Lefebvre 1998:160; Heine et al. 1993:120).

Among non-creolised varieties exposed to prolonged contact with African languages, body reflexives have also been attested in non-standard Dominican Spanish, as in *matar su cuerpo* 'to kill oneself' (cf standard Spanish *matarse*) (Green 1997:6.4.4.2).

An examination of the use of corporal reflexives in Atlantic Creoles provides the information set out in the table opposite. The following features merit special attention:

Corporal reflexives are absent from most ECs and, wherever they do exist, they marginally coexist with constructions directly reflecting English *-self*. This is in stark contrast to the FCs, presumably built on very much the same substrate material. Veenstra (1996:45) reports that body-part reflexivisation in Saramaccan EC is limited to physical actions, and that a literal reading is always possible, the normal reflexive morpheme being /seéi/, derived from English *self*. Given the relative absence of *body* from other ECs, its presence in Nigeria EC is likely to be an innovation patterned upon local substrates after the spread of Krio to Nigeria.

All major FCs, with the exception of Louisiana FC, use derivatives of *corps*. In addition, Haiti has constructions involving 'head' (likely to be an Upper Guinean feature) and 'buttocks'

---

input (Baker & Corne 1982). Regardless of this, Malagasy, another important input language in Indian Ocean FC genesis, uses a similar strategy (Carden & Stewart 1988:30; Carden 1993:106), and thus, body-part reflexives appear to remain confined to Creoles whose input components offered a model for it. For the record, Chaudenson (p c) sees corporal reflexivisation as a rather limited and lexicalised phenomenon in the Indian Ocean FCs.

4 This may be cross-linguistically rare, since Heine et al. (1993) make no mention of its existence.

5 Awoyale (1986:2) identifies the Igbo reflexive morpheme /ònwɛ/ with 'body', but then enigmatically adds on page 5 that the Igbo word for *"the* <u>*literal*</u> *human body"* [my emphasis] is /ahʊ/. Boretzky (1983:143) fails to see any similarity between /ònwe/ and the Igbo word for 'body'. In the closely related language Izi, the reflexive is expressed by /ònwó/ 'self' + pronoun or /óɲé/ 'person' + pronoun (Meier, Meier & Bendor-Samuel 1975:182), whereas body is /ɛ́hʊ́/ (Meier, Meier & Bendor-Samuel 1975:179).

6 Hausa, Margi and Dogon are spoken too far inland to have had any significant impact on Atlantic Creoles.

7 Mande languages mostly use a bare pronoun, whereas Bantu languages generally have a special reflexive form, insensitive to person and number distinctions.

(possibly due to Igbo). To be fair, though, corporal reflexives still admit a literal reading in at least Haiti FC (Lefebvre 1998:168), and in both this and several other FC varieties the *corps* construction alternates with bare pronouns or other reflexive constructions.

Upper Guinea PC have both 'body' and 'head' reflexives, the latter quite likely as result of Atlantic influence. Lower Guinea PCs all employ a 'body' construction, which leaves little doubt regarding its origin, since the very morpheme used is a loan from Edo (or possibly Igbo).[8]

No corporal reflexivisation has been attested in any DC – both Negerhollands DC and Berbice DC preferred constructions patterned on the lexifier.

Finally, Papiamentu SC also has 'body', whereas no corporal reflexives have been attested in Palenquero SC.

LANGUAGE	MORPHEME	ETYMOLOGY	SOURCE
Bahamas EC	/skin/[9]	*skin*	Holm & Shilling (1982:13)
Sranan EC	/skin/[10]	*skin*	Muysken & Smith (1994:56)
Sranan EC	/bere/[11]	*belly*	Muysken & Smith (1994:56)
Saramaccan EC	/sinkii/	*skin*	Muysken & Smith (1994:56)
Nigeria EC	/bòdi/	*body*	Holm (1988:204)
Louisiana FC	/kor/	*corps*	Corne (1999:120)[12]
Louisiana FC	/latɛt/	*la tête*	Corne (1999:120)[13]
Louisiana FC	/lapo/	*la peau*	Corne (1999:120)[14]
Northern Haiti FC	/kadav/	*cadavre*[15]	Goodman (1964:57-58)
Northern Haiti FC	/kɔ/	*corps*	Carden & Stewart (1988:19)
Haiti FC	/tɛt/	*tête*	Goodman (1964:57-58)
Haiti FC	/bũda/	[buttocks][16]	Holm (1988:205)
Guadeloupe FC	/kɔ/	*corps*	Maxette Févrin-Olsson (p c)[17]
Martinique FC	/kɔ/	*corps*	Maher (1993:412)
St Lucia FC	/kɔ/	*corps*	Carrington (1984:73)
Grenada FC	/kɔ/	*corps*	Phillip (1988:91)
Trinidad FC	/kɔ/	*corps*	Thomas (1869:43)
Guiana FC	/kɔ/	*corps*	Fauquenoy-Saint-Jacques (1972: 101)
Cape Verde PC	/kabesɒ/	*cabeça*	Meintel (1975:232; Carvalho (1984c:162)
Guinea-Bissau PC	/kabesa/	*cabeça*	Scantamburlo (1981:42)
Guinea-Bissau PC	/kurpu/	*corpo*	Rougé (1988:93)
Senegal PC	/korpu/	*corpo*	Rougé (1988:93)
São Tomé PC	/uɓwe/	Edo or Igbo 'body'	Lorenzino (1998:149)
Angolar PC	/oŋge/	Edo or Igbo 'body'	Lorenzino (1998:149)
Annobón PC	/oge/	Edo or Igbo 'body'	Barrena (1957:39)
Príncipe PC	/iɡ͡ɓe/?[18]	Edo or Igbo 'body'	Hancock (1980:20)
Papiamentu SC	/kurpa/	*cuerpo*	Munteanu (1996:346-47)

8 Though the realisations differ significantly in the four varieties (São Tomé PC /ubwe/, Príncipe PC /iɡ͡ɓe/, Annobón PC form /ogwe/, Angolar PC /oŋge/), comparative evidence (there are other Edoid loans where coarticulated stops in Edo and Príncipe PC correspond to labialised stops in Sãotomense) indicates that at least the Sãotomense and Principense forms are derivates of the same Edo etymon /eɡ͡ɓe/. Note, though, that the Annobonese and Angolar forms are closer to Awoyale's (1986:2) Igbo reflexive marker /ònwɛ/ than to that of Edo.

9 Of limited use.

10 Somewhat rare, but more frequently attested in older texts.

11 Somewhat rare, but more frequently attested in older texts. Heine & Reh (1984:272) and Heine et al. (1993:30) mention the existence of reflexives derived from 'belly' in Africa, but without indicating any specific language(s).

12 Attested in 19th century texts.

13 Only moderately grammaticalised.

14 Only moderately grammaticalised.

15 *Cadavre* is synonymous with *corps* in some dialects of north-western France.

16 Of African origin; a number of possible origins from languages all over West Africa have been suggested.

17 Bare pronouns are normally used, however (Corne 1999:132).

18 Hancock does not indicate the realisation of the morpheme in question, but only the gloss. However, /iɡ͡ɓe/ is the word for 'body' in Príncipe PC.

There are thus five different corporal origins for Atlantic Creole reflexives, viz. *head, buttocks, body, belly* and *skin.* Of these, I have found no plausible etymon at all for 'skin', used in the ECs of Surinam and the Bahamas, and in Louisiana FC – it may not even be African. *Belly*, found in Sranan EC, appears to be African but cannot be identified with any geographical or genetic entity in Africa. The other three do indeed correlate with specific African languages, resulting in the following schema:

AREA	FEATURE	LANGUAGE	GROUP	SUGGESTED SUBSTRATE INFLUENCE
Syntax	Reflexivisation	Nigeria EC	EC	+Kwa, +Delto-Benuic, +Atlantic
Syntax	Reflexivisation	Louisiana FC (body)	FC	+Kwa, +Delto-Benuic, +Atlantic
Syntax	Reflexivisation	Louisiana FC (head)	FC	+Atlantic
Syntax	Reflexivisation	Northern Haiti FC	FC	+Kwa, +Delto-Benuic, +Atlantic
Syntax	Reflexivisation	Haiti FC (buttocks)	FC	+Igbo
Syntax	Reflexivisation	Haiti FC (head)	FC	+Atlantic
Syntax	Reflexivisation	Lesser Antilles FC	FC	+Kwa, +Delto-Benuic, +Atlantic
Syntax	Reflexivisation	Guiana FC	FC	+Kwa, +Delto-Benuic, +Atlantic
Syntax	Reflexivisation	Cape Verde PC	PC	+Atlantic
Syntax	Reflexivisation	Guinea-Bissau PC (head)	PC	+Atlantic
Syntax	Reflexivisation	Guinea-Bissau PC (body)	PC	+Kwa, +Delto-Benuic, +Atlantic
Syntax	Reflexivisation	Gulf of Guinea PC	PC	+Kwa, +Delto-Benuic, +Atlantic
Syntax	Reflexivisation	Papiamentu SC	SC	+Kwa, +Delto-Benuic, +Atlantic

4.2 Negation

It has often been pointed out that African American language varieties use *negative concord,* i.e. what from the prescriptive point of view are superfluous negative elements of the type found in *I ain't done nothing*. For the present purposes, this kind of multiple negation is moderately interesting, in particular because it is even attested in varieties which have had no or only limited contact with African languages. Nor is it very surprising that many Creoles use a single invariant unbound monosyllabic morpheme (often derived from the lexifier's holophrastic negator, i.e. the word meaning 'no') in preverbal position as a sentence negator, since this is the most common negation pattern in at least European-lexified Pidgins, and also the least globally least marked option (Dahl 1979).[19]

Of interest, and potentially of great importance for the present discussion, however, is the fact that some of the Atlantic Creoles have either postverbal (often clause- or sentence-final) or circumverbal sentence negators. This cannot possibly be due to pidginisation universals, since, as Boretzky (1983) points out, we would not expect pidginisation to produce an output more complex than its input. Post- or circumverbal negation is likewise at odds with general trends observable among Pidgins. There is a possible pattern for postverbal negation in some European languages but, interestingly, it is absent from Creoles based on English and French, with at least partly postverbal negations,[20] and present mainly in varieties of Spanish and Portuguese lexicon despite negation being consistently preverbal in both these languages.[21] Furthermore, postverbal

19 It is likewise the most well-represented strategy among African languages (Heine 1976).

20 With the exception of the particularly acrolectal varieties of St Thomas (Valdman 1973:527) and Louisiana (Valdman & Klingler 1997:132), where /pa/ is postverbal, as in French. For Louisiana, this change seems to be recent (Neumann 1985), and due to pressure from Cajun French. Most FCs also have expressions such as /vepa/ 'to not want to', /pepa/ 'to not be able to', /sepa/ 'to not know', but these are better seen as lexicalised suppletives.

21 A lexifier origin for circumverbal negation has been proposed for Vernacular Brazilian Portuguese, but the *não* VP *não* construction is used only in a limited number of emphatic contexts in European Portuguese, and also appears to have been less common at the time of overseas expansion than it is now (Marroquim 1934:206; Perl 1998:422; Holm 1992:57; Schwegler 1996b; Mello 1996:146). Following Bernini & Ramat (1998), it seems reasonable to treat the second negation of this pragmatically marked construction as holistic, i.e. to translate it with 'no', rather than 'not'. As for Spanish, discontinuous sentence negation has never been attested in Spain (Schwegler 1993b:680, 1998a:235).

negation is uncommon in SVO languages (Bernini & Ramat 1998:4), and languages combining these two features are mainly found in western and central Africa and the Pacific (Dryer 1988:123 cited in Bernini & Ramat 1998:5). Substrate influence is therefore a very likely candidate for post- and circumverbal negation in Atlantic Creoles.[22]

In the Gulf of Guinea PCs, negation consists of a preverbal and a sentence-final element (the former optional in Príncipe PC and Annobón PC) as shown below:

LANGUAGE	NEG_1	NEG_2
São Tomé PC	na	fa
Angolar PC	na	wa ~ fo
Annobón PC	(na ~ ã ~ an ~ no)	f ~ fa ~ af
Príncipe PC	(na ~ nɔ)	fa ~ fã~ fo

Sources: Barrena (1957:49-50), Carvalho (1984a:162), Ferraz (1979:11), Günther (1973:78, 191), Lorenzino (1998:181), Post (1995:197), Valkhoff (1966:100).

This permits us to reconstruct proto-Gulf of Guinea PC sentence negation as /na … fa/, where NEG_1 is clearly derived from Portuguese *não*, but where NEG_2 is of obscure etymology (though see Boretzky 1983:102 and Stolz 1987b:14-15 for a suggestion).[23]

Negation involving both a preverbal and a postverbal element is also found in many varieties of Caribbean Spanish, though often archaic and stigmatised (Lipski 1994:215, 242; Megenney 1993:164; Schwegler 1993b:680). Double negatives are also possible in emphatic constructions in Papiamentu SC (Kouwenberg, p c), whereas Palenquero SC allows preverbal, circumverbal and postverbal negation, all three of which are common (Schwegler 1998a:263). All of the above varieties use the standard Spanish negator *no*, or phonetically marginally deviant varieties thereof. A similar situation is found in Vernacular Brazilian Portuguese, where *não* V *não* is commonly used (Marroquim 1934:196), and where a simple postverbal element is permitted (Mello 1996:147-48). Finally, Berbice DC has a sentence-final negation /ka(nɛ)/ (Kouwenberg 1995:237, 1994b:238).

For Berbice DC, the source is relatively obvious. We know that the substrate material of Berbice DC is less heterogeneous than that of other Creoles, with Eastern Ijo as the dominant component, and Eastern Ijo negates by means of a sentence-final /-ka/ (Kouwenberg 1994b:264). The second, optional, component of the Berbice negator may be Dutch *nee.*

As for the other varieties, the source of circum- or postverbal negation is less evident, since several West African languages display similar negation patterns. However, although some Atlantic and Kru languages such as Wolof, Kisi, and Abri (Samb 1983:103; Childs 1995:125; Westermann & Bryan 1952:54) make use of post- or circumverbal negators,[24] the vast majority of languages having this feature are concentrated to areas east of the Gold Coast, and in particular south of the equator. The westernmost of the important Lower Guinea languages having circumverbal negation is Ewe (Westermann 1939:7; Lafage 1985:358; Duthie 1996:37, 60), in which the second element (sentence-final) seems to be the most stable. In Delto-Benuic, postverbal negation is used in Idomoid, Igboid, Ijoid and Nupoid languages, and optionally also in Yoruba, which, however, normally negates preverbally (Boretzky 1983:102; Armstrong 1984:334; Givón 1975:79; Blench 1984:318; Gabriele Sommer, p c; Bamgboṣe 1966:71-72). A continuous area of unrelated or distantly related languages with clause-final negation is found east of Delto-Benuic (Bernini & Ramat 1998:5), although most of these are spoken too far from the coast to have had any impact on the Atlantic Creoles.

---

22 It should be noted, though, that sentence-final negation is found also in some European Romance varieties, e.g. Lombardian Italian (Bernini & Ramat 1998:3).

23 A postverbal negative element is marginally possible in Cape Verde PC (Cardoso 1989:68), but this construction seems to have more in common with the Portuguese emphatic negative than with negation in, say, São Tomé PC.

24 Note, however, that postverbal negation in Wolof and Abri is not clause-final. Also, my use of the terms *preverbal* and *postverbal* here refers to the position of the negator with respect to the verb stem, rather than to the verb unit as a whole, so that even a suffixed negator is considered postverbal.

Some Bantu languages, such as Yaka and Tiv (Guthrie 1967:52 cited in Ferraz 1975:163; Westermann & Bryan 1952:120) make do with a postverbal element only (clause-final in the case of Yaka, sentence-final in the case of Tiv), but most of the western Bantu languages, including Akwa, Bangi, Kikongo, Kimbundu, Umbundu, Ewondo, and Teke (Guthrie 1953:90; Ferraz 1979:11; Söderberg & Wikman 1966; Chatelain 1889:51ff, cited in Lorenzino 1998:182; Valente 1964:136; Boretzky 1983:103; Calloc'h 1911:58) negate by means of a circumposed morpheme consisting of a preverbal and a - usually - sentence-final element.[25] Strictly preverbal negators - the rule in the north-west - are thus the exception in Buntu.[26] This would allow us to hypothesise that post- or circumverbal negation in Atlantic Creoles and related languages varieties in the Americas can be ascribed to Bantu influence, although a few Upper or Lower Guinean languages could potentially have had the same effect.

Double discontinuous sentence negation has also been attested in Angolan Portuguese (Lipski 1994:48 cited in Mello 1996:148), but not in Upper Guinean Portuguese, something that appears to strengthen the hypothesis that Bantu influence was the decisive factor.[27]

Area	Feature	Language	Group	Possible substrate influence
Syntax	Negation	Gulf of Guinea PCs	PC	+Wolof, +Kisi, +Abri, +Ewe, +several Delto-Benuic languages, +almost any Bantu language
Syntax	Negation	Berbice DC	DC	+Ijo
Syntax	Negation	Papiamentu SC	SC	+Wolof, +Kisi, +Abri, +Ewe, +several Delto-Benuic languages, +almost any Bantu language
Syntax	Negation	Palenquero SC	SC	+Wolof, +Kisi, +Abri, +Ewe, +several Delto-Benuic languages, +almost any Bantu language

4.3 Postpositions

Like other functional categories, adposition inventories are usually severely reduced in pidginisation, and more radical Creoles therefore either have a restricted set of adpositions, or have grammaticalised a new set to compensate for the reduction associated with pidginisation.

Although postpositions may occasionally be found in western European languages, all lexifiers involved here are basically prepositional. The same applies to the vast majority of potential African substrates, and hence, not surprisingly, also to most Atlantic Creoles. European-based Creoles outside the Atlantic area are also generally prepositional, and this configuration is also what the Greenbergian universals would lead us to expect of an SVO language.

However, some few Atlantic Creoles do make use of postpositions. Although they all have prepositional elements as well, this is true for Berbice DC, and for the Surinamese ECs. Some of the Berbice DC postpositions are direct carryovers from the postpositional Eastern Ijo, as in the example below, where /aŋga/ 'side' has developed into a general locative marker:

Berbice DC: /eke mu koop brot ʃap aŋga/
1sg FUT buy bread shop LOC 'I will buy bread in the shop' (Robertson 1993:309)

However, Berbice DC nevertheless has placed Dutch prepositions postnominally:

Berbice DC: /eke habu ande bokap eke wari: ondro/
1sg havesomefowl 1sg houseunder
'I have some chickens under my house' (Robertson 1993:309)

25 There are also intermediate cases, such as the Cameroonian language Bafut, where the first particle is optional (Gabriele Sommer, p c).

26 The Congolese language Babole is one such exception (Gabriele Sommer, p c).

27 It is also attested (in the form of *não* V *não*) in the L_2 Portuguese of São Tomé (Mata 1988-89:161).

And the same is true for the Surinamese ECs:

Sranan EC (1781): /sinsi a kom na hoso ini/
since 3sg come LOC house in 'since she entered the house' (Bruyn 1996:34)

The tendency to use postpositions is greater in the more basilectal Saramaccan EC than in Sranan EC; thus, 'in the house' is /a di wosu dendu/ in Saramaccan EC (/dendu/ < P *dentro*), but /na ini a oso/ in modern Sranan (Sebba 1987:146). It is tempting to assume that this reflects a diachronic drift from post- to prepositions in Sranan, which has been in closer contact with Dutch than has Saramaccan.

It is difficult to suggest anything but substratal influence as responsible for this development. Interestingly, as mentioned above, most West African languages are prepositional. This applies to virtually all Atlantic and Bantu languages, and is also true of most major Delto-Benuic languages (Hawkins 1983:284; Campbell 1991: 399, 559, 1456; Bentley 1887:609; Leitch 1994:192; Westermann & Bryan 1952:28; Swift & Zola 1963:34; Migeod 1908:ix; Thomas 1910:140; Welmers 1973:311-12, 453).[28]

Postpositions, on the other hand, predominate in the Mande family (where in some languages they have developed into case suffixes), and in western Lower Guinea, that is in Gur, Kru and parts of the Kwa area (Campbell 1991:161, 915; Givón 1975:50-51, 73; Hawkins 1983:285, 287; Houis 1980:24; Innes 1966:42, 1967:63; Lafage 1985:241, 282; Migeod 1908:ix; Rowlands 1959:111; Spears 1967:143; Westermann 1924:12, 1939:3; Westermann & Bryan 1952:54).

The situation in Kwa appears complex, possibly reflecting the family's geographical location between Delto-Benuic and Kru. On the one hand, Hawkins (1983:284) depicts the group as mainly prepositional, but his "Kwa" refers to what is sometimes called "old Kwa", i.e. the older grouping that includes what is here referred to as "Delto-Benuic" languages (see § 1.3). Many, or perhaps most, of the Kwa languages proper (at least Ewe, Fante, Gã, Guang languages and Twi) clearly prefer postpositions (Hawkins 1983:285; Lafage 1985:241; Westermann 1939:3).

Although the Surinamese ECs show that appropriate conditions can generate postpositions in an Atlantic Creole, it is noteworthy that this has not happened elsewhere. Despite Dutch having some postpositions, and though solidly postpositional languages seem to have played a major role in the creation of e.g. Negerhollands, all the more than 20 adpositions in de Josselin de Jong's (1926) word list are prenominal.

AREA	FEATURE	LANGUAGE	GROUP	SUGGESTED SUBSTRATE INFLUENCE
Syntax	Postpositions	Surinamese ECs	EC	+Mande, +Gur, +Kru, +Kwa
Syntax	Postpositions	Berbice DC	DC	+Ijo

4.4 Complementation

Given the limited semantic content of complementisers, it is hardly surprising that they often disappear in pidginisation. Indeed, most Atlantic Creoles allow subordinate clauses to be introduced by zero forms, as in:

Belize EC: /wi no wɛjt fʊ ɪm Ø tɛl wi/
1pl NEG wait for 3sg tell 1pl 'We didn't wait for her to tell us' (Escure 1986:44)

Papiamentu SC: /e mira Ø e muhe ta bini/
3sg see DEF woman IMPERF come
'He sees that the woman is coming' (Munteanu 1996:395)

Other varieties have retained (or reintroduced) lexifier morphemes, as in:

28 In the agglutinating Bantu languages, case affixes do much of what adpositions do elsewhere, so the latter are less frequent in Buntu. Where they do occur, however, they are usually prenominal.

Jamaica EC:	/aj andastan dat dem ka:na him, im did get ʃat/	
	1sg understandCOMP 3pl corner3sg 3sg PAST PASS shoot:PAST-PARTICIPLE	
	'I understand that they cornered him and he got shot' (Denis 1998:13)	
São Tomé PC:	/inãse sebe k(w) a mataŋe mõci ɔme/	
	2pl know COMPIMPERS kill 3pl much man	
	'You know many people died' (Ferraz & Valkhoff 1975:30)	

In quite a number of Atlantic Creoles, though, a new complementiser has been generated through grammaticalisation of a *verbum dicendi*, i.e. a verb denoting a speech act. In the earliest stages of grammaticalisation, this verb introduces reported speech. Its use has then in some cases extended to verbs denoting cognition and perception, and finally to other contexts, as shown in Plag (1995:114-15). The first step was already taken in non-standard varieties of at least one lexifier, witness dialectal English forms such as *"I hear tell he'll come"*, and is reflected in moderately restructured varieties such as African American Vernacular English *"They told me say they couldn't get it"* (Todd 1982:52; Rickford 1977:212 cited in Holm 1988:185). More advanced stages are found in Jamaica EC: /mi bilib sɛ im a go kom/ 'I believe that he'll come' (Alleyne 1980:95). In the Surinamese and West African ECs, grammaticalisation has gone further than in any other Atlantic EC variety, so that derivatives of *say* or *talk* may correspond to almost all instances of the English complementiser *that*.

The issue whether the use of a *verbum dicendi* for complementation should be considered a case of verbal serialisation or not has been debated for some time. Mufwene (1991a:224), Holm (1988:185) and Bickerton (1981:117) regard *say* complementation as an instance of serialisation, whereas Boretzky (1983:176-7) and Sebba (1984a cited in Holm 1988:187) consider the verb in these contexts to have grammaticalised far enough to have lost its verbhood. Regardless of one's point of view, the construction must have started out as a case of serialisation, and it is certainly not a coincidence that it is currently used predominantly in serialising areas of the world.

Though somewhat limited cross-linguistically (Sebba 1984b cited in Holm 1988:188), the grammaticalisation of complementisers from a *verbum dicendi* is certainly not unknown outside the Atlantic and Africa, but Ebert (1991), Heine et al. (1993:191-94), Saxena (1995) and Lord (1993) indicate that the vast majority of languages having followed this grammaticalisation path are spoken in Africa and south-east Asia, i.e. in areas where serialising languages are spoken.

At least two non-Atlantic contact languages, viz. Tok Pisin and Pidgin Quechua, display similar phenomena (Faraclas 1990:14; Ebert 1991:77; Jansen, Koopman & Muysken 1978:125; Mühlhäusler 1997:173-74), but in both cases only to a limited extent. Note also that serialising languages provided input for both.

Although the Mande languages Mende, Malinke, Kpelle, Kuranko and Vai apparently have speech act complementisers (Ziegler 1981:206; Manessy 1989; Lord 1993:207; Heine et al. 1993:191-94), these are on the whole rare in Upper Guinea, and it is usually not clear from my sources whether or not they introduce clauses other than those containing reported speech.[29] In Lower Guinea, on the other hand, complementisers derived from verbs meaning 'to say' or 'to talk' – but introducing clauses not necessarily containing reported speech – abound. They have been attested in Godie, Dewoin (both Kru), Dagaari, Kusal, Moore (all Gur), Baule, Twi,[30] Asante, Fante, Ewe, Gã, Fon (all Kwa), Bekwarra, Edo, Efik, Ekpeye, Engenni, Gokana, Idoma, Idomoid languages in general, Igbo, Izi, Kalabari, Mbembe, Obolo and Yoruba (all Delto-Benuic) (Alleyne 1980:170; Armstrong 1984:334; Bamgboṣe 1966:77; Saxena 1995:359; Christaller 1875:91; Faraclas 1990:13; Heine et al. 1993:191-4; Lord 1993:207-08; McWhorter 1997b:158; Plag 1995:138). In the Bantu-speaking areas, Yemba – significantly spoken on the north-western rim of Buntu, where most languages present numerous structural similarities with the Delto-Benuic group – is the only language known to me which undoubtedly has *say* complementisers

[29] Heine et al.'s (1993:192) Vai example is an exception, though, where the subordinated clause is the complement of a verb meaning 'to know'.

[30] Lord (1993:151-79), however, suggests that the Twi complementiser /se/ (< 'to say') is only used to introduce citations, and that the more general complementiser /sɛ/ is in fact derived from a verb meaning 'to be like'. A similar development is reported from Idoma, and possibly also from Sanskrit, Akkadian, Lahu and Japanese (Lord 1993:209).

(Lord 1993:208; Heine et al. 1993:191-4).[31] Kimbundu's /kuma/ seems to be employed only to introduce reported speech, whereas Kikongo /vo/ might possibly be derived from the demonstrative /vo/ (cf English *that*) rather than the verb /vova/ 'to talk' (Plag 1995:137-8). Closer parallels with the Kwa and Delto-Benuic complementisers may be found in eastern Bantu languages (Gilman 1993:52-3; Lord 1993:207; Saxena 1995; Heine et al. 1993:191-94), none of which, however, provided substratal input for the Atlantic Creoles.

Since Turner (1949:201), the phonological proximity of the Akan complementisers /sɛ ~ se ~ sɪ/ and its EC counterpart /sɛ(j)/ has received a great deal of attention. Could it be that EC /sɛ/ is a direct loan from Akan rather than a calque? The presence of parallel complementation strategies in Creoles of non-English lexicon and the use of *talk* rather than *say* in Surinam proves that the surface similarity is not the whole story but it cannot, of course, be excluded as a reinforcing factor.

In the Atlantic Creoles, *say* or *talk* can introduce subordinated clauses containing material other than reported speech in most ECs, as can be seen in the table below.

VARIETY	SOURCE
Gullah EC	Rickford (1974:94)[32]
Jamaica EC	Bailey (1966:54, 112); Adams (1991:25).
Jamaica Maroon Spirit EC	Bilby (1983:48).
Miskito Coast EC	Holm (1986b:109).
San Andrés EC	Edwards (1974:19).
Providencia EC	Washabaugh (1986:164).
St Kitts EC	Roberts (1988:89).
Montserrat EC	Roberts (1988:89).
Antigua EC	Ziegler (1981:206).
Trinidad EC	Winer (1993:42, 262).
Guyana EC	Roberts (1988:89).
Sranan EC	Ziegler (1981:206)
Saramaccan EC	Alleyne (1980:95).
Krio EC	Fyle & Jones (1980:xliii).
Kru Pidgin English	Huber (1998a:17).
Ghana Pidgin English	Huber (1998a:17).
Nigeria EC	Agheyisi (1971:96).
Cameroon EC	Féral (1980:279).
Fernando Poo EC	Lipski (1992:46).

Conspicuously absent from the list is the notoriously English-like Barbados EC, and this despite there being a good deal of textual attestations from earlier stages of that language which have been examined by several Creolists. The presence in the list of Guyana and Trinidad, both of which were initially settled mainly from Barbados, may, however, be taken to suggest an earlier use of *say* complementation in the latter island. It is also of potential significance that, whereas all the other ECs use a reflex of English *say*, all the Surinamese varieties - and they alone - have derivatives of *talk*; in Saramaccan this is used alongside /faá/ (< P *falar*). This could be taken to suggest that *say* in this role developed after Surinam had been cut of from the rest of the Anglophone Caribbean, and in other words that it would have been absent from the proto-Pidgin.[33]

---

31 Heine et al. (1993:192) also document this phenomenon in Lingala. However, Lingala is a slightly restructured variety of Bobangi which is thought not to have existed until the late 19th century (Samarin 1990-91; Heine 1973:56).

32 This seems to be rare, though, since Cunningham's (1992) grammar does not provide any unequivocal examples. Turner's (1949) examples, too, tend to introduce other peoples' utterances.

33 The complementiser /taki/ is present in the first ever longer text in Sranan (from 1765), although some later 18th century texts show a variable use of it (Plag 1995:121).

Negerhollands DC makes a very similar use of /se/ (< D *seggen*) (Stolz 1986:229),[34] whereas Berbice DC has a construction where the *verbum dicendi* itself is a transfer from Ijo (Kouwenberg 1994c:337; Holm 1988:185-86), again revealing the extraordinarily heavy influence from a single substrate.

Papiamentu SC and Palenquero SC both retain complementisers based on superstratal *para* and *que* (Kouwenberg & Murray 1994:44-45; Porras 1992:200-01), and no *say* constructions have been recorded.

As for the Lower Guinean PCs, Post (1992:162) gives a satisfactory example from Annobón PC, whereas Lorenzino's (1998:127, 179) examples from Angolar PC all include reported speech. Jansen, Koopman & Muysken (1978:125) claim *verbum dicendi* complementisers exist in the sister dialect of Príncipe, but without giving an example.

In the remaining two groups of Creoles, the FCs and the Upper Guinea PCs, the situation is far less clear.

Guinea-Bissau PC has a complementiser /kuma/ – used mainly with speech act verbs and verbs denoting various mental processes – which is normally considered to be derived from Portuguese *como* 'how', but which may be influenced by a homophonous Malinke word meaning 'to say' which also functions as a complementiser (Chataigner 1963:47 cited in Manessy 1989).[35]

Verbum dicendi are not normally used for complementation in New World FCs, and are not reported in any reference grammar I have consulted on these languages.[36] However, Ludwig (1996) does provide a few interesting examples, where /di/ is in fact used in a way quite similar to that of other Atlantic Creoles:

Guadeloupe FC: /u te ka kɔ̃prã di ã pa te ke vin/
2sg PAST PROG understand **say** 1sg NEG PAST IRR come
'You thought I wasn't going to come' (Ludwig 1996:273).

Dominica FC: /kɔ̃pwã di u ka ãni vini fute timun -mwẽ kɔ̃sa?/
understand **say** 2sg IMPERF only come hit child 1sg like-that
'You think you can just come and hit my child like that?' (Ludwig 1996:287).

Many of the other examples he gives are less divergent from the lexifier, involving constructions apparently patterned on expressions such as *J'ai entendu dire*, etc., but notwithstanding its marginal status, the fact remains that at least some speakers of Guadeloupean and Dominican apparently do use *say* complementisers.

Holm (1988:186) mentions another, potentially interesting Haitian construction, in which /si/ seems to be semantically closer to EC or Akan /sɛ/ than to French *si*:

Haiti FC: /m pa te kɔ̃nẽ si papa -w te muri/
1sg NEG PAST know COMP father 2sg PAST die
'I didn't know that your father had died' (Holm 1988:186).

Despite this, the relative absence of *say* complementation in FCs is in stark contrast with the its widespread usage in ECs.

AREA	FEATURE	LANGUAGE	GROUP	SUGGESTED SUBSTRATE INFLUENCE
Syntax	*Verbum dicendi* complementation	ECs	EC	(+Mande), +Lower Guinea
Syntax	*Verbum dicendi* complementation	Negerhollands DC	DC	(+Mande), +Lower Guinea
Syntax	*Verbum dicendi* complementation	Berbice DC	DC	+Ijo
Syntax	*Verbum dicendi* complementation	Gulf of Guinea PCs	PC	(+Lower Guinea)
Syntax	*Verbum dicendi* complementation	Guinea-Bissau PC	PC	(+Mande)
Syntax	*Verbum dicendi* complementation	Lesser Antilles FCs	FC	(+Mande), +Lower Guinea

34 Given that Negerhollands DC was in close contact with neighbouring EC Varieties for much of its life, the possibility of /se/ being an EC calque cannot be excluded.

35 There is a possible cognate in the Vai complementiser /kèmú/ – Welmers (1976:100) does not indicate its etymology.

36 For this reason, I have erroneously suggested (Parkvall 1999c:41) that they are absent from FCs. This was, of course, before I came across the data in Ludwig (1996).

4.5 Conjunctions

Just like other highly grammatical categories, conjunctions are prone to disappear in restructuring, giving place to juxtaposition. This is evidenced in a large number of Pidgins, such as Chinese Pidgin English, Papua Pidgin English, Senegalese Tirailleur Pidgin French and Burundi Pidgin French, to mention but a few (Shi 1991:28; Mühlhäusler 1997:150-51; Manessy 1994:115; Niedzielski 1989:93).

In most Atlantic Creoles, however, the conjunction inventory has been increased to a size comparable to that of the lexifier,[37] either by reintroduction of lexifier morphemes, or by reallocation of other items to a conjunction role. Zero coordination seems to be most frequent in the Gulf of Guinea PCs (see e.g. Ferraz 1979:79; Lorenzino 1998:191; Ferraz & Valkhoff 1975:22).

Not unexpectedly, grammaticalisation strategies are frequently influenced by West African patterns, and that is, of course, what interests us here.

Two things in particular seem to characterise West African conjunctions. Firstly, in the vast majority of Niger-Congo languages, as opposed to European languages, the conjunction that co-ordinate NPs cannot join VPs or clauses (Welmers 1976:129). Secondly, the NP co-ordination is frequently derived from and/or homophonous with a comitative preposition, i.e. a word meaning 'with'.

It should come as no surprise, then, that both these phenomena are relatively frequent in Atlantic Creoles. Before continuing, we should note that neither is unique to West Africa and the Atlantic Creoles[38] - but being virtually unattested in overseas varieties of European languages and rare in European-lexicon Creoles outside the Atlantic,[39] it does seem fair to consider the phenomenon substrate-derived.

In the Atlantic Creoles, a conjunction synchronically or diachronically homophonous with a comitative preposition has been attested in the following varieties:

VARIETY	CONJUNCTION	ETYMON	SOURCE
Gullah EC	/lʌŋ(ə)/	*along*	Warantz (1986:87)
Miskito Coast EC	/wi/	*with*	Holm (1988:206)
St Kitts EC	<long>†	*along*	Baker & Bruyn (eds) (1999)
Sranan EC	/(n)aŋga/	*along*	Holm (1988:206)
Saramaccan EC	/ku/	*com*	McWhorter (1997b:46)
Cameroon EC	/weti ~ witi/	*with*	Todd (1982:70)
Louisiana FC	/avɛk ~ ave/	*avec*	Valdman & Klingler (1997:137)
Haiti FC	/ak ~ akɛ ~ avek ~ ave/	*avec*	Orjala (1970:36)
St Lucia FC	/ɛk ~ ɛvɛk/	*avec*	Carrington (1984:125-26)
Guiana FC	/kɛ/	*avec*	St-Jacques-Fauquenoy (1972)
Cape Verde PC[40]	/ku/	*com*	Almada (1961:136)
Guinea-Bissau PC	/ku/	*com*	Bartens (1996:125)
São Tomé PC	/ku/	*com*	Lorenzino (1998:191)
Príncipe PC	/ki/	*com*	Günther (1973:80)
Angolar PC	/ki/	*com*	Lorenzino (1998:192)
Annobón PC	/ku/	*com*	Stolz (1986:238)
Negerhollands DC	/mi/	*met*	Stolz (1986:237)
Berbice DC	/mɛtɛ/	*met*	Kouwenberg (1994c:163)
Papiamentu SC	/ku/	*con*	Holm (1988:206)

37 For instance, Stolz (1986:237) enumerates no less than twenty different conjunctions in Negerhollands DC, and Carrington (1984:125ff, 140ff) mentions several dozen in St Lucia FC.

38 In Stolz's (1998:108) global sample, 19% of the languages have conjunctions homophonous with comitative adpositions.

39 The phenomenon is not exclusive to Creoles of the Atlantic, and in e.g. Papia Kristang PC, /ku/ (< P *com*) may translate either as 'with' or 'and' (Baxter 1988:114, 199-200), but it is far more common in the Atlantic area than in restructured languages elsewhere.

40 Sotavento varieties only. Barlovento dialects instead use /ma/ (< P *mais*).

This homophony between 'with' and 'and' is even more widespread in Niger-Congo, and has been attested along the entire West African coast in languages such as Wolof, Fulfulde, Manjaku, Mandinka, Dogon, Moore, Ewe, Fon, Fante, Twi, Awutu, Gã, Yoruba, Engenni, Edo, Igbo, Hausa, Teke, Ngbaka and a large number of Bantu languages (Calloc'h 1911:59; Carreira & Marques 1947:70-2; Christaller 1875:90; Goodman 1964:94-95; Heine et al. 1993:53-54; Holm 1988:206; Lord 1993:47-59; Lumsden 1994; Peace Corps 1995b; Thomas 1910:140; Welmers 1946:63; Westermann 1939:8; Jouni Maho, p c; Tore Jansson, p c).

Even more interesting is the fact that an African word meaning 'with' does not correspond to *all* instances of European 'and', but only to some of them. Between VPs and phrases, another morpheme is generally used, as schematically illustrated below:

	COMITATIVE ADPOSITION	MORPHEME USED TO JOIN NPS	MORPHEME USED TO JOIN VPS OR CLAUSES
European languages	**with**	**and**	
Niger-Congo languages	**with**		**and**

The use of a comitative adposition to join nouns and a conjunction proper between other constituents is reported from all the most relevant geographical West African regions concerned here.

Languages displaying this dichotomy include Wolof, Vai, Bambara, Mandinka, Mende, Dogon, Moore, Ewe, Asante, Twi, Fante, Gã, Yoruba, Edo, Izi, Igbo and Hausa (Bamgboṣe 1966:98; Baudet 1981:113-114; Bellon 1983:40; Boretzky 1983:216; Duthie 1996:92; Heine et al. 1993:53-4; Lafage 1985:384; Meier, Meier & Bendor-Samuel 1975:170, 179; Migeod 1908:123; Peace Corps 1995b; Samb 1983:123; Thomas 1910:140; Ward 1952:153; Welmers 1946:53, 1976:129; Westermann 1939:8). Again, absent from this list are Bantu and Kru languages. At least for the Bantu languages, this is due to many of them relying on juxtaposition for clausal conjunction

In some Atlantic Creoles, this partition is neatly reflected. Thus, Sranan EC and Saramaccan EC use /(n)aŋga/ (< E *along*) and /ku/ (< P *com*) respectively to join NPs, but /(h)ɛn/ between clauses (Adrienne Bruyn, p c). In the same way, Cameroon EC apparently uses /witi/ (< E *with*) between NPs, but /an/ (< E *and*) between clauses (Dwyer 1966:245, 388). Similarly, Angolar PC /ki/ (< P *com*) conjoins NPs, but not clauses, for which /i/ (< P *e*) is used (Lorenzino 1998:192). Negerhollands DC /en/ (< D *en*) is found interclausally, whereas /mi/ (< D *met*) joins individual words (Stolz 1986:237). Berbice DC has /mɛtɛ/ between NPs, but uses /an/ to join clauses (Kouwenberg 1994c:137). Similarly, Papiamentu SC /ku/ (< S *con*), which joins NPs, is in complementary distribution with /i/ (< S *y*), used between adjectives, verbs and sentences (Baudet 1981:113).

Particularly conspicuous by their absence here are most English-based Creoles.

As for the FCs, they present a relatively complex picture. Haiti FC seems to largely conform to the substratal pattern in that nouns are typically conjoined by /ak/ (< F *avec* ? [see below]), leaving /e(pi)/ (< F *et (puis)*) to join adjectives, VPs and clauses (Baudet 1981:113). This is reminiscent of the situation in Mauritius FC, where Baker says with regard to older texts that "**et** *is at all times far more often employed to conjoin sentences than nouns, whereas the forms deriving from* **avec** *and* **ensemble** *are hardly ever attested as conjunctions between sentences*" (Baker 1996:52).

A similar picture obtains in Louisiana FC, in which /e(pi)/ can be used both within and between clauses, whereas /avɛk ~ ave/ is only used to join phrases (Valdman & Klingler 1997:137). Neumann's (1985:344) 20th century data from the highly decreolised St Martin variety, however, shows use of the more French-like /e(pi)/ to the complete exclusion of /avɛk ~ ave/.

In Lesser Antillean and Guianese FCs varieties, the erstwhile (?) distinction between the two conjunctions has been blurred to the extent that one can find both in positions where the other would be expected. This is amply illustrated in the following sentence in Carriacou FC:

misje ʃat se te jɔ̃ sakwi bug epi sakwi bɛl mustaʃ
mistercat COP PAST INDEF devilish guy with devilish beautiful moustache
'Cat was a hell of a guy with an incredibly beautiful moustache,...'

avɛk misje tɔti te ni jɔ̃ sakwi bɛk
CONJ misterturtle PAST have INDEF devilish beak '...and Turtle had a devilish beak' (Kephart 1991:87)

From other reference grammars and collections of folk stories in Lesser Antillean and Guianese FCs that I have examined, a similar picture emerges. The two conjunctions /epi/ and /ɛk ~ kɛ ~ ɛvɛk ~ avɛk/ appear to have become synonymous, and either can be used as a comitative (or, for that matter, instrumental) preposition. A look at the system in other Atlantic Creoles suggests that this may not always have been the case, but admittedly, there is no actual proof that they ever were distinct.

In Príncipe PC, as in the FCs, the conjunctions /ki/ (< P *com*) and /i/ (< P *e*) may both join NPs (Günther 1973:80).

Most West African languages could thus have imposed an NP conjoiner derived from 'with'. The Bantu languages are unlikely to have directly contributed to the division of labour between this and a separate VP or clause conjoiner. However, it would still be hazardous to see this configuration in the Creoles as evidence of lack of Bantu influence, since once the NP linker is in place, the clausal conjoiner could have been taken over from the lexifier. Though I regard it as appropriate to see the data discussed above as an example of substrate influence, it cannot be associated with one particular area in West Africa.

A few more details regarding Atlantic Creole conjunctions may be worth noting. First, Boretzky (1983:110-11) points out that Saramaccan EC, Príncipe PC, Ewe and Yoruba all present the peculiarity of having a conjunction homophonous with the 3sg pronoun. In all four languages, this morpheme is monosyllabic, but all nevertheless contain three phonemes (/hɛ́n/, /eli/, /éjè/ and /òun/ respectively), which reduces the possibility of ascribing this to a mere coincidence. This may be widespread in Lower Guinea, since one could *possibly* add the Kwa languages Twi (3sg non-human nominative /ɛno/, 3sg possessive /ne/, conjunctions /ɛne, ɛ́nna, nè, nà/) and Fante (3sg object form /na/, conjunction /nà/) – but I am unfortunately not in a position to determine whether these actually are cognates or not. I would not suspect it to be cross-linguistically common, or even particularly widespread in Africa, however, since Ewe is the only such language cited by Heine et al. (1993:171-72).[41]

Although subordinations/complementisers are known to grammaticalise from demonstratives, which in turn may double as 3sg personal pronouns, grammaticalisation of conjunctions from personal pronouns seems not to be very common cross-linguistically.

AREA	FEATURE	LANGUAGE	GROUP	SUGGESTED SUBSTRATE INFLUENCE
Syntax	conjunction from 3sg	Saramaccan EC	EC	(+Lower Guinea)
Syntax	conjunction from 3sg	Príncipe PC	PC	(+Lower Guinea)

A word of caution may be required, though, for although I have not come across this in Western Bantu, it is attested in Bantu languages outside the scope of this study (John McWhorter, p c; Jouni Maho, p c), and may be more widespread. The evidence of this feature being of Lower Guinean origin must therefore be considered as weak.

Secondly, Bruyn (1996:35) draws a parallel between the use of a verb meaning 'to finish' as a consecutive conjunction in both Sranan EC (/kaba/ < P *acabar*) and Ewe (/vɔ/). However, Ewe is not necessarily responsible for this development since Cape Verde PC and Guinea-Bissau PC (neither of which is known to have been influenced by Ewe) have, in fact, precisely the same feature (Stolz 1986:188; Heine et al. 1993:89), which is also found in areas outside of West Africa, e.g. in Western Nilotic (Bavin 1983:160). The relative semantic closeness between the two concepts also makes me somewhat reluctant to see this as a substrate transfer.

Finally, the phonetic realisation of conjunctions in some Atlantic Creoles is close to that of some West African languages. Caution is certainly called for here, though, since such similarities will turn up if only one takes a large enough number of potential substrates into account. Also,

41 A number of other ECs (including Gullah, Sranan, Ndyuka, and Krio) have a conjunction /ɛn/, presumably derived from English *and*, which is phonetically close to the 3sg pronoun, presumably derived from English *him*. In these cases, coincidence should not, of course, be excluded.

as is to be expected given the highly grammatical nature of conjunctions, very little phonetic material is typically used to express them. Nevertheless, the form /na/ commonly found in ECs, and the forms /ke ~ ak ~ ake ~ ɛk/, found in several FCs, though not impossible to derive from *and* and *avec* respectively, represent somewhat unexpected reflexes of these two lexifier items. It cannot therefore be excluded that West African conjunctions such as Fante /nà/, Twi /na/, Igbo /nà/ or some cognate of Kituba /ná/ (Welmers 1946:46; Christaller 1875:90; Green & Igwe 1963:46; Swift & Zola 1963:34) played a role in determining the phonetic shape of EC conjunctions, and similarly, Wolof /ak/, Balanta /ke/,[42] Mende /ke/[43] or Edo /ke/ (Thomas 1910:227; Migeod 1908:123; Innes 1967:69; Quintino 1951:26; Samb 1983:123) could have done the same for FCs.

4.6 Verbal serialisation

For a long time, verbal serialisation has occupied a place at the very centre of Creole studies. The phenomenon has been used by both substratists and universalists to argue in favour of their respective positions. As explained in chapter 1 and in McWhorter & Parkvall (1999), I see the fact that serial verbs occur in precisely those Creoles with serialising substrates as strong support for a substrate derivation.

Though no definition of serialisation has been accepted by all or even most scholars,[44] serialisation encompasses structures used to express a wide range of functions. In this section, however, I will concentrate exclusively on the five main types of serial verb constructions more commonly found in Atlantic Creoles, viz. *benefactive, lative, dative, instrumental* and *comparative* serialisations. As Sebba (1987:174) points out, it is often difficult to distinguish between benefactive and dative constructions. Should, for instance, the interpretation of the Sranan EC sentence /a kisi den fisi gi mi/ {3sg catch DEF:PL give 1sg} be 'He caught the fish for me' (i.e. on my behalf) or 'He caught the fish (and then gave it to me)? In this particular case, both readings happen to be possible (Huttar 1981:297), but this may not always be the case and, like Sebba, I will therefore here subsume both benefactive and dative serialisation under the same heading.[45] As *verbum dicendi* complementation will treated separately (§4.2.6.1 below), that leaves us with four serialisation types.

When examining serial structures in Atlantic Creoles, one must beware of the degree of lexicalisation or grammaticalisation. Several constructions are not only lexicalised in the Creoles, but were often so even in the lexifier (Alleyne 1996:168; Kouwenberg & Muysken 1995:215; Post 1992; Sebba 1997:196; Seuren 1990a:15; Valdman 1978:167, 228). Also, serial verb constructions may be more or less transparent, and more or less central to the grammar, depending on their degree of grammaticalisation. A strongly grammaticalised, and thus less transparent, construction would of course be less likely to transfer into an emerging Creole - all the more so since tightly grammaticalised serialisations are often unstable, tending towards prepositional constructions. Moreover, a serial construction may be *the* way of expressing some syntactic relationships in a language, but merely *one of several* alternative ways to express others. Thus, a substrate with serial verbs might well yield a Creole without them, if it also offers an adpositional option.

Just as European languages have constructions that would qualify as serialisation under some definitions, some Creoles that are not normally regarded as serialising display phenomena that present similarities with serial verbs. Thus, the Brava dialect of Cape Verde PC may use

42 Means 'with', but cannot be used as a conjunction.

43 Rarely used.

44 Definitions vary greatly with regard to their inclusiveness; the interested reader may compare, for instance, the definitions provided by Collins (1997:462), Creissels (1991:324), Jansen, Koopman & Muysken (1978:125), Kouwenberg & Murray (1994:47-48), Lorenzino (1998:176), McWhorter (1997b:22), Muysken & Veenstra (1995:290), Porras (1992:198), Veenstra (1996:74), Williamson (1984:30), Winer (1993:41-42) and Wittmann & Fournier (1983:193). For more on verb serialisation in general, see for example Joseph & Zwicky (eds) (1990), Sebba (1987) and Lefebvre (ed.) (1991).

45 Both Heine et al. (1993:99) and Östen Dahl (p c) see the dative construction as a later development of the benefactive one. Although there may be syntactic and historical reasons for this, I would personally not exclude the possibility of the development having gone in the opposite direction - after all, the dative 'give' preserves more of the original semantics than does its benefactive counterpart.

/tɔrnɒ/ 'turn' in the sense of 'again', as in /bu tɔrnɒ baj/ {2sg turn go} 'You go away again' and /bu tɔrnɒ bɛŋ/ {2sg turn come} 'You come back again' (Meintel 1975:222). Similarly, Wilson (1962:24-6 cited in Stolz 1986:216) demonstrates that the sister dialect Guinea-Bissau PC has serial-like constructions involving motion verbs such as /baː/ 'to go' and /biŋ/ 'to come'.

In West Africa, serial verb constructions are limited to a relatively well-defined area stretching from Liberia in the west to Cameroon in the east, including the Kru, Gur, Kwa and Delto-Benuic languages. Many Creoles, such as Gullah EC, Krio EC, the Surinamese ECs, Haiti FC, Lesser Antillean FC, Guiana FC and the Gulf of Guinea PCs have all four serialising constructions discussed here. Others, such as Leeward Lesser Antillean EC and Negerhollands DC lack only the comparative serialisation in my data. Yet others, including Barbados EC, Louisiana FC, Upper Guinea PC, Papiamentu SC and Palenquero SC have few serials or lack them altogether, either because of a non-serialising substrate, or because of extensive decreolisation.

4.6.1 Lative serialisation

Lative serialisation involves a verb of movement which specifies the direction of the action expressed by the other verb, as in the following examples:

Annobón PC:	/nameneʃi	t͡ʃiku	kompaɲi	bi	iai/
	2pl	boy	accompany	come	here

'You are the boys who accompanied me here' (Post 1992:156)

Negerhollands DC:	/mi	ka	briŋ	di	koː/
	1sg	CPLTV	bring	3sg:INANIM	come

'I have brought it hither' (Diggelen 1978:77)

This type of serial construction is attested in all major Atlantic ECs varieties.[46]

Lative serials are common in Haiti FC and Lesser Antilles FC dialects, but rare in Louisiana FC (Ludwig 1996:253; Lefebvre 1993:269; Taylor 1977:7-9; Phillip 1988:111; Neumann 1985:268-70, Valdman & Klingler 1997:131). Their status in Guiana FC is not clear. Fauquenoy-St-Jacques (1972:104) and Green (1988:454) give a number of examples which might be considered serial, but in none of their examples, does an object or other element occur between the two verbs, which might mean that they should be seen as lexicalised units. Curiously, the only unambiguous example I have come across is the first ever recorded sentence of Guiana FC (cited in Saint-Quentin 1872:194-95):

Guiana FC (1744):	*Anglai*	*pran*	*Yapoc,*	*yé*	*méné*	*mon père*	*allé,*
	English	take	Oyapock	3pl	take	priest	go
	toute	*blang*	*foulkan*	*maron*	*dan bois*		
	all	white	run away		woods		

'The English conquered Oyapock, they took the priest, all the whites have fled into the woods'

In the Gulf of Guinea, the use of lative serials may be somewhat limited in Angolar and Príncipe PCs, but is apparently both productive and common in the languages of São Tomé and Annobón (Jansen, Koopman & Muysken 1978:131; Lorenzino 1998:177; Boretzky 1993:84; Ferraz & Valkhoff 1975:22; Hagemeijer 1999; Post 1992:154-56, 1995:201).

Negerhollands DC lative serialisation is documented by, among others, Diggelen (1978:76-7), Stolz (1986:157, 216), Rossem & van der Voort (1996:15), and similar constructions are found in Berbice DC (Kouwenberg 1994c).

Of the SCs, Papiamentu SC has lative serialisations (although some constructions are lexicalised; Kouwenberg & Muysken 1995:214-15), whereas Palenquero SC does not.

---

46 Gullah EC (Turner 1949:210-1; Mufwene 1990:92), Belize EC (Escure 1991), Jamaica EC (Alleyne 1980:91), Jamaica Maroon Spirit EC (Bilby 1992:9), St Kitts EC (Vincent Cooper, p c), Trinidad EC (Winer 1993:263), Barbados EC (Roberts 1988:129), Guyana EC (Alleyne 1980:91), Sranan EC (Sebba 1987:24, 46), Ndyuka EC (Huttar 1981:294-95, 303, 307), Saramaccan EC (Veenstra 1996:93; Byrne 1987:204), Krio EC (Denis 1998:13-14), Nigeria EC (Faraclas 1990:98-99), Cameroon EC (Todd 1982:109).

In West Africa, lative serials are not to be found in Atlantic or Mande families, and seemingly not in Kru languages either.

Among Bantu languages, serialisation occurs mostly in the north-western corner of the Bantu-speaking area, where languages such as Bamileke (Givón 1975:68) may well have acquired this feature through contact with the geographically proximate Delto-Benuic languages.

The area where lative serialisation truly abounds, is that in which Kwa, Delto-Benuic and Gur are spoken, where it is rather hard to find languages lacking lative serials.[47]

The findings of this and the following subsections will be summarised at the end of the section on serial verbs.

4.6.2 Benefactive/dative serialisation

The benefactive/dative serialisation involves the verb 'give', marking either the semantic role RECIPIENT or BENEFICIARY.

Nigeria EC: /à báj njám gív dém/
1sg buy yam give 3pl — 'I bought them the yam' (Faraclas 1990:98).

Martinique FC: /jo ka travaj ba mwẽ/
3pl IMPERF work give 1sg — 'They were working for me' (Alleyne 1996:172)

In this role, *give* might be analysed as a preposition rather than a verb, and this has indeed be done. In the Lesser Antillean FCs, the full verb 'to give', /baj/ (< Old F *bailler*), is phonologically distinct from the case marker /ba/. Furthermore, the case marker cannot be fronted without the object following it, nor is any copy left at the extraction site (cf §4.11 below), which suggests preposition rather than verb status (Alleyne 1996:172). From a semantic point of view, *give*-constructions have also in some varieties evolved beyond the dative or benefactive function, as in the following example, where it rather marks the semantic role of GOAL.

St Lucia FC: /ɛs u kaj mene i baj dɔktɛ?/
Q 2sg IRR lead 3sg give doctor
'Will you take him to the doctor?' (Carrington 1984:158)

It is thus possible to view serial *give* as a preposition, and this is what Taylor (1971), working mainly on Dominica FC, did. Hall (1966), on the other hand, argued that it must be a verb, since it takes TMA marking. Holm (1988:185) takes an intermediate position, seeing dative *give* as a serial verb, while considering its benefactive (near-)homonym a preposition. Fortunately, this issue is for the present purposes of limited relevance, since even under the preposition analysis, the grammaticalisation of dative/benefactive *give* must have started from a serial verb construction.

Dative/benefactive serials exist in Gullah EC, and formerly also existed in Bahamas EC (Jansen, Koopman & Muysken 1978:131; Baudet 1981:112; Parsons 1918:53 cited in Hancock 1987:281). Although marginal in Jamaica EC and absent in Belize EC, they have been attested in the Maroon Spirit Language EC (Alleyne 1996:175, 1998; Hellinger 1979:322). Lesser Antillean EC varieties having dative/benefactive serialisation include not only Antigua EC and St Kitts EC, but also upper mesolects, such as Carriacou EC, Grenada EC, Trinidad EC and Tobago EC (Hancock 1987:281; Manessy 1995:177; Vincent Cooper, p c; Allsopp [ed.] 1996:256; Winer 1993:25, 42).

The construction has not been attested in Barbados EC, but is present in all Surinamese varieties (Alleyne 1980:94; Byrne 1987:180; Fagerli 1995:103-4; Healy 1993:286; Huttar 1981:297; Jansen, Koopman & Muysken 1978:145; Sebba 1987:50; Seuren 1990a:16), and seems to have existed also in late 19th century Guyana EC (Hancock 1987:281). In West Africa, Krio EC,

---

47 Examples include: Twi, Fante, Aja, Gã, Gẽ, Ewe, Fon (all Kwa), Bekwarra, Edo, Efik, Ekpeye, Engenni, Gbari, Ibibio, Igbo, Ijo, Izi, Jukun, Ekpari, Kalabari, Kolokuma, Mbembe, Nupe, Obolo, Oron, Yoruba (all Delto-Benuic) and Vagla (Gur) (Bellon 1983:23; Christaller 1875:131; Faraclas 1990:99; Givón 1975:67-68, 1979:15; Huttar 1981:295-96; Lafage 1985:41, 281, 354; Lefebvre 1991:40, 1993:269; Lord 1993:11; Manessy 1995:177, 215; McWhorter 1997b:25, 28; Rowlands 1969:21; Sebba 1987:149, 184; Seuren 1990a:19; Thomas 1910:139; Ward 1952:107-09; Welmers 1973:369, 373, 377).

Ghanaian Pidgin English and Nigeria EC all make use of dative/benefactive serials (Denis 1998:13; Huber 1996:55; Faraclas 1990:98).

All New World FCs except Louisiana FC have dative/benefactive 'give' (Taylor 1971:294-95; Ludwig 1996:283; Alleyne 1996:172; Jansen, Koopman & Muysken 1978:131; Hall 1966:78; Manessy 1995:177-78; Damoiseau 1984:78; Carrington 1984:123-24; Thomas 1869:109), which, as we saw above, is quite strongly grammaticalised.[48]

Upper Guinea PCs present no constructions of this kind, but they are represented in all four Gulf of Guinea varieties (Lorenzino 1998:177, 192; Post 1992:158, 1995:200; Hancock 1980:20; Barrena 1957:27; Jansen, Koopman & Muysken 1978:131; Muysken 1988:298; Ferraz 1987:341; Valkhoff 1966:93), although Hagemeijer (1999) argues that dative/benefactive 'give' in São Tomé PC has grammaticalised beyond verbhood.

Negerhollands DC, too, had dative/benefactive serialisation, as does Berbice DC (Diggelen 1978:76; Stolz 1986:216; Sabino 1992:8; Rossem & van der Voort 1996:15; Kouwenberg 1994c), while both Atlantic SCs lack them altogether.

The pattern among the West African substrates comes as no surprise. Kwa in general marks dative/benefactive serially,[49] as do most Delto-Benuic languages.[50] Some Kru and Gur languages,[51] and the north-western Bantu periphery,[52] align with this group.

The Atlantic, Mande, and, so far as I am able to tell, Kru families do not use dative/benefactive 'give'.

4.6.3 Comparative serialisation

Comparative serialisations normally involve a verb meaning 'to surpass' or 'to exceed', as in:

Gullah EC:	/i tɒl pas mi/	
	3sg tall pass 1sg	'He is taller than I' (Turner 1949:215)
Jamaica EC:	/olu bin it pas in padi/	
	Olu PAST eat pass 3sg friend	'Olu ate more than his friend' (Denis 1998:14)

They occur in a wide variety of Atlantic Creoles and their potential substrates, but not in Asian or Pacific Creoles. As can be seen, the predicate may be either adjectival or verbal in many languages, adjectives and verbs being closely related, although usually distinct,[53] categories in most Atlantic Creoles

True *pass*-comparatives seem somewhat rare in the ECs, though they are attested in many of the major varieties, such as Gullah EC, Jamaica EC, Sranan EC, Ndyuka EC,[54] Saramaccan EC, Krio EC, Kru Pidgin English, Liberian English, Ghana EC, Nigeria EC, Fernando Poo EC, Cameroon EC (Agheyisi 1971:113; Denis 1998:14; Dwyer 1966:110, 216, 329; Fyle & Jones 1980:xliii; Hancock 1975:258; Huber 1998a:17; Huttar 1981:315-57; Sebba 1987:52, 197; Turner 1949:214-5; Veenstra 1996:98). The most important absentees from this list are the Leeward Islands ECs where the construction is indeed not used (Vincent Cooper, p c).

48 Only a couple of days before completing this manuscript did I realise that a case of dative-marking /done/ has indeed been attested in Louisiana (Klingler 2000:26). This single 19th century example is, however, the only one known.

49 Twi, Fante, Asante, Awutu, Baule, Gã, Fon and Ewe (Sebba 1987:149, 175; Welmers 1973:374; Redden et al. 1963:67; Lord 1993:40; Creissels 1991:324; Lafage 1985:279; McWhorter 1997b:26; Westermann 1939:5; Holm 1988:185).

50 Bekwarra, Edo, Efik, Ekpeye, Engenni, Ibibio, Gbari, Igbo, Ijo, Izi, Jukun, Kalabari, Kolokuma, Mbembe, Nupe, Obolo, Oron and Yoruba (Bamgboṣe 1966:77; Faraclas 1990:99; Givón 1975:70; Baudet 1981:112; McWhorter 1997b:28-9; Givón 1975:75; Huttar 1981:300; Rowlands 1969:83; Lord 1993:38-9). I might add that Faraclas's (1990:99) claim that Izi would have dative/benefactive serials is not corroborated by Meier, Meier & Bendor-Samuel's (1975:153) reference grammar, which instead mentions a benefactive suffix /-rú/.

51 Dagaari, Vagla, Moore and several Senufo languages (Fagerli 1995:103, 112; Huttar 1981:299-300; Givón 1975:59; Heine et al. 1993:97-99). Others, such as Grebo, use a verbal vowel suffix (Innes 1966:33).

52 Bamileke and Suga (Fagerli 1995:114; Givón 1975:69, 1979:15).

53 The dividing line between them, however, need not necessarily correspond to that of the lexifier, of course.

54 Huttar (1981:317) labels this "marginally acceptable", though.

The Surinamese Creoles possess an alternative comparative construction with /moro/ or /mɔ́ɔ/ (< E *more*), as in Sranan EC /kofi bigi moro asaw/ 'Kofi is bigger than an elephant' (Sebba 1987:23). Although etymologically different, this strategy is syntactically equivalent to the *pass*-comparative construction, since /moro ~ mɔ́ɔ/ also functions as a main verb with the approximate meaning of 'to surpass'.

Among the FCs, *pass*-comparatives are used in riverine Louisiana FC (but not in the more decreolised prairie dialects),[55] in Haiti FC, in all major varieties of Lesser Antillean FC, and in Guiana FC – thus in all reasonably basilectal Atlantic FCs (Carrington 1984:72; Fauquenoy-St-Jacques 1972:103; Green 1988:454; Hall 1966:82; Holm 1999:109; Klingler 1997:6, 2000:27; Ludwig 1996:281; Taylor 1951:58; Thomas 1869:33).

Like other serial constructions, the *pass*-comparatives are absent from Upper Guinea PCs (where the lexifier strategy is used), but found on the Gulf of Guinea islands. The comparative use of 'pass' is recorded for the two major varieties, São Tomé PC and Príncipe PC (Valkhoff 1966:102; Lorenzino 1998:179; Ferraz & Valkhoff 1975:23). An apparently more common reading of the *pass*-serial in the Lower Guinea PCs is 'a lot' rather than 'more than'.[56] This is the only one that has been documented in the two other Gulf of Guinea Creoles, Angolar PC and Annobón PC (Barrena 1957:29; Post 1992:159; Maurer 1995:51; Lorenzino 1998:179), and it is also more frequently mentioned than the comparative reading for São Tomé PC; it is even the only one given by Hagemeijer (1999) and Ferraz (1979:109). This use may be related to Yoruba /d͡ʒù/ 'pass', which expresses both the comparative and the excessive (Manessy 1995:174).

Serial comparatives have to my knowledge not been found in any DC or SC.

Wittmann & Fournier (1983:195) argue that the *pass*-comparatives in Haiti FC are of French origin, on the grounds that they *"ne sont nullement caractéristiques de l'ensemble des langues nigéro-congolaises"*. The important thing, of course, is not whether they are characteristic of Niger-Congo languages as a whole, but whether they were present in those Niger-Congo languages that provided the substratal input of Haitian.

In West Africa, *pass*-comparatives (using *(sur)pass, exceed* or similar verbs) are used even outside the serialising area of Lower Guinea. Non-serial *pass*-comparatives (something like *He surpasses me in wealth* rather than a serial *He is rich surpass me*) are found in the Atlantic languages Wolof, Kisi and Fulfulde, the Mande languages Bambara, Mende, Mandinka, Susu, Vai and Kpelle, in some Chadic languages, and in several Bantu languages, such as Babole, Teke, Kikongo, Kimbundu, and Umbundu (Bentley 1887:561; Boretzky 1983:106; Calloc'h 1911:73; Childs 1995:20; Turner 1949:215; Heine et al. 1993:77-79, 210-11; Holm 1988:189; Huttar 1981:319, 1993:53; Innes 1967:126; Laman 1912:98; Leitch 1994:192; Spears 1967:130-31; Söderberg & Wikman 1966:16; Valente 1964:119). These, together with the inherent semantic transparency of the construction, may have had a reinforcing effect on the comparative serials in Atlantic Creoles.

The only languages having true serial *pass*-comparatives are those of Lower Guinea, including the Kwa languages Asante, Fante, Twi, Gã, Ewe and Fon, and the Delto-Benuic languages Edo, Efik, Ekpeye, Engenni, Ibibio, Igbo, Ijo, Izi, Kalabari, Kolokuma, Mbembe, Nupe, Obolo, Wano and Yoruba (Bellon 1983:32; Christaller 1875:48; Duthie 1996:36; Faraclas 1990:99; Lafage 1985:273, 277; McWhorter 1997b:26, 29; Meier, Meier & Bendor-Samuel 1975:149; Redden et al. 1963:50; Rowlands 1969:124; Sebba 1987:206; Thomas 1910:135, 144; Welmers 1946:66, 1973:372, 375; Westermann 1939:25). To this list could be added languages of the north-western fringe of the Bantu-speaking area, such as Lam-nso (Todd 1982:22).

4.6.4 Instrumental serialisation

Instrumental serialisation in Atlantic Creoles and their substrates involves a verb meaning 'take' to mark instrumental case, as in the following example:

---

55 It was also rejected by Klingler's (p c) informant from New Orleans, one of the last remaining speakers of the New Orleans dialect of Louisiana FC.

56 For the record, Hagemeijer (1999) gives a number of arguments against a synchronic analysis of the *pass*-comparative constructions as serials. Convincing though they are, they are, for present purposes, of lesser importance since the current non-serial construction must be grammaticalisation of a former serialisation.

Sranan EC: /no teki baskita t͡ʃari watra/
NEG take basket carry water 'Don't carry water with a basket' (Sebba 1987:59)

In many languages dealt with here, the instrumental construction differs from other serialisations in that it is less grammaticalised. In several varieties, 'take' may only be used when the taking is literal, and the event is thus perceived rather as two consecutive actions. Theoretically, whether the semantics required for this to be a truly serial construction are present or not might be verified by testing the grammaticality of sentences where the instrument is inalienably possessed, and hence cannot literally be taken. However, I do not have access to informants for most of the languages concerned, and secondly, even in languages only involving the consecutive-action type of construction, the inalienably possessed objects such as body-parts may for the pragmatic effect be 'taken'.

This construction is attested in virtually all major EC varieties in the Atlantic.[57]

In the francophone orbit, instrumental serialisation is recorded in all New World varieties except Louisiana FC (Alleyne 1996:170; Ludwig 1996:61, 248, 284; Dalphinis 1985:9; Corne, p c). Just like Barbados EC, Louisiana FC is remarkably close to its lexifier, and it could be that this, rather than the "wrong" substrate, is responsible for the absence of the construction.

Instrumental serialisation is further attested in São Tomé PC (Tjerk Hagemeijer, p c),[58] Negerhollands DC and Papiamentu SC (Sabino 1992:7; Rossem & van der Voort 1996:15; Sebba 1987:171; Huttar 1981:300), but is clearly absent from Berbice DC and Upper Guinea PCs as well as from Palenquero SC (Jansen, Koopman & Muysken 1978:128; Lorenzino 1998; Kouwenberg 1994c; Porras 1992:198; Post 1995:200).

African languages having an instrumental 'take' include most important Lower Guinean languages.[59] This group also contains the Gur languages Vagla and Dagbani,[60] the peripheral Bantu language Bamileke,[61] and – somewhat surprisingly – also Kikongo (Mufwene 1996:116, 1997a:181; Huttar 1981:301; Lord 1993:128; Givón 1975:68).

A similar phenomenon, the instrumental serialisation involving 'use' rather than 'take', is documented in the Kru family (Givón 1975:74). It does not embrace all Kru languages, though, and Grebo, for instance, uses an instrumental suffix (Innes 1966:22).

That leaves Atlantic and Mande as the only families entirely without instrumental serialisation.

4.6.5 TMA marking of serial constructions

Inherent in many definitions of serial verbs is the inability of the two verbs to take different TMA marking, since they would, if they were able to do so, belong to two different clauses. This criterion would disqualify some serial-like structures in for instance Ewe and Izi from the domain of serialisation (Huber 1996:56).

57 In the North American ECs Gullah and Bahamian, in the western Caribbean varieties, in both Leeward and Windward dialects of the eastern Caribbean (though not Barbados EC), in Guyana EC, and in all varieties of Surinam and West Africa (Agheyisi 1971:103; Arends, Kouwenberg & Smith 1995:107; Bailey 1966:134; Byrne 1987:160; Escure 1986:45; Givón 1979:17; Hancock 1987:270, 318; Huttar 1981:301; Jansen, Koopman & Muysken 1978:130, 146; McWhorter 1997b:98; Sebba 1987:59, 170; Seuren 1990a:15; Turner 1949:211; Veenstra 1996:100).

58 The existence of this construction has been explicitly denied by Jansen, Koopman & Muysken (1978:128) for São Tomé and Príncipe PCs, and by Post (1995:200) for Annobón PC, and is conspicuously absent from Lorenzino's (1998) description of Angolar PC. Hagemeijer's attestation of it in his corpus may suggest that it is also to be found in the other varieties, though one suspects it to be marginal.

59 Anyin, Asante, Awutu, Fante, Gã, Twi, Ewe, Fon (all Kwa) and Bekwarra, Edo, Efik, Ekpeye, Engenni, Ibibio, Igbo, Izi, Kolokuma, Mbembe, Nupe, Obolo, Oron, Ekpari, Yoruba and Ijo (all Delto-Benuic) (Bellon 1983:23; Collins 1997:466; Faraclas 1990:99; Givón 1975:67-68, 75, 1979:14-15; McWhorter 1997b:27; Lefebvre 1991:39; Lord 1993:117, 127, 132; Manfredi 1984:353; Redden et al. 1963:149; Sebba 1987:166, 169; Ward 1952:3, 108-09; Welmers 1946:41, 1973:369). Manessy (1995:170) cites the same Igbo sentence as does Givón (1975:68), but includes an 'and' in his morphemic translation, and does not consider the construction serial.

60 At least one other Gur language, Moore, uses 'take' non-serially to encode the instrumental case (Schiller 1990:38; Givón 1975:59).

61 Again, Manessy (1995:170), citing the same sentence as Givón, includes an 'and' in his morphemic translation, and does thus not consider the construction serial.

In most serialising languages, modification of the commanding verb has scope over the entire series.[62] Therefore, a sentence such as Papiamentu SC /mi a hibe dret͡ʃa/ {1sg CPLTV take:3sg repair} 'I took it to have it repaired' would be impossible unless the mending was actually carried out, because of the completive marker that precedes the first verb.

Almost all Atlantic Creoles permit TMA marking only on the first verb in a series, but for Saramaccan EC and Negerhollands DC, double TMA marking is attested (McWhorter 1992; Sabino 1992:5-6), and the former even allows TMA marking on the last verb only (Seuren 1990a:17). V2 marking alone seems to be typical of Akan languages (Seuren 1990a:17), whereas overt marking on both verbs is common in many a Kwa language (Akan, Gã, Ewe, Gẽ), but only sporadically attested in Delto-Benuic (Ijo, Ekpari) (Seuren 1990a:17; McWhorter 1997b:47-48).

Most Delto-Benuic languages normally seem to mark overtly only the first verb in the series (Edo, Gbari, Igbo, Nupe, Yoruba; McWhorter 1997b:48; Kós-Dienes 1984:122), just like the majority of Atlantic Creoles.

It should be noted, however, that languages having double TMA marking seems to form a subset of the group of languages allowing TMA on the first verb only of a serial construction. Thus, while double marking in a Creole may be taken as indicative of a Kwa (or Ijo or Ekpari) substratal contribution, single marking in no way excludes a Kwa substratal impact.

The data discussed above can thus be summarised as follows:

		LATIVE	BENEFACTIVE/ DATIVE	COMPARATIVE	INSTRUMENTAL	TMA MARKING ON V2
Gullah	EC	+	+	+	+	
Western Caribbean	EC	+	~	+	+	
Leeward islands	EC	+	+	-	+	
Windward islands	EC	+	+	-?	+	
Guyana	EC	+	†	-	+	
Surinam	EC	+	+	+	+	+
West Africa	EC	+	+	+	+	
Louisiana	FC	*rare*	-	+	-	
Haiti	FC	+	+	+	+	
Lesser Antilles	FC	+	+	+	+	
Guiana	FC	+	+	+	+	
Upper Guinea	PC	-	-	-	-	
Gulf of Guinea	PC	+	+	+	+	
Negerhollands	DC	+	+	-	-	+
Berbice	DC	+	+	-	-	
Papiamentu	SC	+	-	-	+	
Palenquero	SC	-	-	-	-	
Atlantic in general	Atlantic	-	-	- / *non-serial*	-	
Mande in general	Mande	-	-	*non-serial*	-	
Kru in general	Kru	-	-	-	*'use'*	
Gur in general	Gur	+	+	-	+/*non-serial*	
Kwa in general	Kwa	+	+	+	+	+
Delto-Benuic in general	Delto-Benuic	+	+	+	+	-
NW Bantu in general	Bantu (NW)	+	+	+	?	
Bantu in general	Bantu	-	-	*non-serial*	-	
Kikongo	Bantu	-	-	*non-serial*	+	

As can be seen, all four types of serialisation are confined to the same area in West Africa, with the exception of the lack of comparative construction in Gur and the presence of the instrumental construction in an important Bantu language (Kikongo). The former fact can be disregarded since Gur languages are spoken too far from the major slaving areas to have had any significant impact on Atlantic Creole genesis. The second should also be considered of limited importance, since the

62 The first verb in SVO languages; the last verb in SOV languages.

given that, in general, the Creoles have more than one of the four serialising constructions, while no Creole patterns with Kikongo in having only the instrumental. We can therefore assume that the presence of serialisation is due to influence from a single area of Africa, namely Lower Guinea, where Kwa, Delto-Benuic and peripheral north-western Bantu languages are spoken. The comparative construction might have been reinforced by the presence of *(sur)pass/exceed* comparatives elsewhere, but since these are found all over the coast, they are of no use in pinpointing the precise African origin of the Creole comparatives. (As it happens, this is also the least well-represented type of serialisation among Atlantic Creoles, which further suggests that the influence from non-serialising languages must have been negligible).

What the division of serialisation into these four constructions could help us understand, however, is the *extent* of Lower Guinean influence on a given Creole. If we award each Creole one point for each construction in the table below, we arrive at the following picture:

LANGUAGE		NUMBER OF SERIALISING CONSTRUCTIONS (MAX=4)
Gullah	EC	4
Western Caribbean	EC	3,5
Leeward Islands	EC	3
Windward Islands	EC	3
Guyana	EC	3
Surinam	EC	4
West Africa	EC	4
Louisiana	FC	1,5
Haiti	FC	4
Lesser Antilles	FC	4
Guiana	FC	4
Upper Guinea	PC	0
Gulf of Guinea	PC	4
Negerhollands	DC	2
Berbice	DC	2
Papiamentu	SC	2
Palenquero	SC	0

This, of course, ignores the frequency of the constructions within the language. As mentioned above, many constructions are marginal in the Gulf of Guinea PCs. Also, as in many of the cases already discussed, lack of observable Africanisms might point at close contact with the lexifier rather than at the Creole having had the "wrong" substrate. It is nevertheless worth noting that serialisation abounds in several Creoles while it is poorly represented in others.

While serialisation as such is clearly linked to Lower Guinea, the V2 TMA marking in Surinamese ECs and Negerhollands DC helps us narrow the focus from Lower Guinea in general to Kwa in particular for these languages. We can thus schematically illustrate the substratal impact as follows (where <++> indicates a stronger influence than <+>).

LANGUAGES	SUGGESTED SUBSTRATE INFLUENCE
Gullah EC, Western Caribbean ECs, Leeward Islands ECs, Windward Islands ECs, Guyana EC, West Africa ECs	++Lower Guinea
Surinam ECs	++Kwa
Louisiana FC	+Lower Guinea
Haiti FC, Lesser Antilles FCs, Guiana FC	++Lower Guinea
Upper Guinea PC	-Lower Guinea
Gulf of Guinea PC	++Lower Guinea
Negerhollands DC	+Kwa
Berbice DC	+Lower Guinea
Papiamentu SC	+Lower Guinea
Palenquero SC	-Lower Guinea

4.7 Determiner systems

An interesting piece of evidence suggesting that substratal composition indeed does influence determiner placement is provided by the fact that the Tirailleur Pidgin French, once used among the French Army's African recruits, had DEM N order in its Senegalese variety, just like Mandinka (and optionally Wolof and Bambara), but N DEM, just like Kikongo, when spoken by Congolese soldiers (cf Queffelec & Niangouna 1990:17-18; Manessy 1994:113).

Most varieties of the European lexifier languages have preposed demonstratives, whereas the vast majority of substrate demonstratives are postnominal, the main exceptions being Mandinka, and optionally also Wolof and Bambara, all situated in the geographic periphery of the slave-exporting area.[63]

The vast majority of Atlantic Creoles here conform to the typically European (DEM N)[64] rather than the typically West African (N DEM) word order pattern, but there are a few exceptions, in that some Creoles place demonstratives after the NP head.[65]

These include most FCs except some varieties in Louisiana and French Guiana, the Surinam ECs, and the Gulf of Guinea PCs.[66] (Ferraz 1976:43, 1979:73, 81; Stolz 1986:133; Carvalho 1984c:160); Lorenzino 1998:140; Taylor 1977:174; Parkvall 1995c:21; Fauquenoy-St-Jacques 1979; Klingler 1992:113; Valdman & Klingler 1997: 118). Since this is a general West African feature, it can safely be regarded as substrate-induced, but it cannot be claimed to be caused by any specific languages. We could use it as evidence for lack of influence from the few African languages that have DEM N order, but some of these (Wolof, Bambara) also permit N DEM, while others are so insignificant in this context that we would not expect them to have had any influence in any case (Teke, Supyire). Yet others (Mandinka and Wano) would seem to be more interesting, but they remain aberrant in a wider context, as both Mande languages in general, as well as other Edo dialects, prefer N DEM. Again, these languages having left their mark on Atlantic Creoles would be more surprising than them not having done so.

As for articles, all Atlantic Creoles that overtly mark of indefiniteness do so prenominally. Definite articles too (where such occur), are placed before the NP head, with the important exception of FCs.[67] This, however, could be said to follow from their etymology. New World FCs have an enclitic /-la/ as a marker of definiteness, which is presumably derived from the similarly placed French demonstrative *-là*.[68] In much the same way, while some authors have remarked on the tendency among French Creoles to allow material to intrude between the NP head and the phrase-final determiner, this is could be said to follow from the pragmatic use of *-là* in many varieties of colloquial French (see e.g. Fournier 1996; Demers 1992; Dolbec & Demers 1992; Forget 1989; Vincent 1994).

---

63 Data on demonstrative placement in African languages in this section were drawn from Bamgboṣe (1966:98), Calloc'h (1911:63), Campbell (1991), Carreira & Marques (1947:50ff), Cérol (1991:85-86), Childs (1995:247), Duthie (1996:56), Dwyer (1984:58), Ferraz (1976:43, 1979:81), Givón (1975:55-56, 60), Huttar (1981:319), Innes (1967:45, 55), Lafage (1985:260), Marchese (1984:133), Marques (1947a:86), Migeod (1908:72), Quintino (1951:10), Rowlands (1959:65), Samb (1983:46), Smith (1967:18), Söderberg & Wikman (1966:19), Taylor (1977:7-9), Thomas (1910:144), Ward (1952:57), Welmers (1976:71) and Westermann & Bryan (1952).

64 Although French can be considered having offered a model for postposed demonstratives in FCs, it is quite obvious that this cannot be the whole story, given constructions in several FCs such as Trinidad FC /tab sla la/ 'this/that table'. To my knowledge, nothing like **Table cela-là* has ever been recorded in any French dialect, and it does seem reasonable to assume that the West African substrate is responsible for the generalisation of the postnominal position of determiners. So although the French demonstrative adjective *-là* is indeed postnominal, this has in FCs in general developed into a determiner that is more anaphoric than deictic, and in the example just cited, the French demonstrative pronoun *cela* has taken over the determiner role.

65 I am disregarding here Creoles where the demonstrative is derived from a European adverbial, rather than directly inherited, since *thing-here* or *thing-that* would be derivable from the word order of the lexifier.

66 Príncipe PC, however, permits both orders.

67 Exceptions to the exception being mesolects in Louisiana and on St Thomas (Neumann 1985:132; Valdman 1973:527), where article placement follow the French pattern.

68 Support for this is found in the fact that the determiner is often said to be semantically intermediate between a definite article and a demonstrative (e.g. Valdman 1978:191; Valdman & Klingler 1997:117; Neumann 1985:132; St-Jacques-Fauquenoy 1972:106, 1974:33-34, 1979). Also, such an etymology is, of course, supported by the fact that the development of definite articles from demonstratives is cross-linguistically exceedingly common.

There is thus little to say regarding substrate influence so far as articles are concerned – all the more so since both West African languages and the European lexifiers tend to have prenominal articles.

4.8 Reduplication

Several types of reduplication strategies are used in Atlantic Creoles, but my having dealt with these in some detail in Parkvall (*forthcoming*), allows the following section to be kept rather short. Also, it was claimed in that paper that most of the attested reduplication strategies found in Creoles cannot with certainty be ascribed to substrate influence.

The most obviously substrate-derived reduplication pattern in the Atlantic is undoubtedly that found in mostly the Surinamese ECs according to which a reduplicated verb yields a predicative element rather similar to a European past participle. The following examples illustrate this:

Ndyuka EC:	/a	fensee	fika	opo	-opo/	
	DEF	window	remain	open	open	
						'The window was left open' (Huttar & Huttar 1997:405)
Saramaccan EC:	/ɗí	náki	-náki	wómi/		
	DEF	beat	beat	man		'the beaten man' (Veenstra 1996:81)

The process is basically productive, although limited to affecting transitives (/m͡bói-m͡bói/ 'cooked') and "unaccusative" intransitives (/kaí-kaí/'fallen'), and excludes non-affecting transitives (*/sí-sí/ 'seen'), stative transitives (*/sábi-sábi/ 'known'), "unergative" intransitives (*/wáka-wáka/ 'walked') and ditransitives (*/dá-dá/ 'given') (Kramer 1998, with reference to Saramaccan). The result of this reduplication functions as an adjective, and is less verb-like not only in that it can be used attributively and predicatively with a copula, but also in that it does not take TMA marking and fails to leave a copy at the extraction site when fronted (Bakker, Smith & Veenstra 1995:172).

This type of construction has also been attested in Nigeria EC (Agheyisi 1971:63; Faraclas 1990:121), a descendant (albeit indirect) of the Surinamese ECs.[69] In Jamaica EC, also in part descended from Surinam, this deverbal reduplication is applicable to a limited number of forms, including /katakata/ 'scattered' (< /kata/ 'scatter'), /la:fila:fi/ 'inclined to laughter' (< /la:f/ 'to laugh') and /t͡ʃatɪt͡ʃatɪ/ 'talkative' (< /t͡ʃat/ 'to chatter') (Kouwenberg & La Charité 1998:6-7; Gooden 1998:8).

For once, the substratal prototype is relatively obvious, for reduplication of verbs results in adjectives in a great many Lower Guinean languages (Westermann & Bryan 1952:91). It is documented for the Kwa languages Twi, Akpose, Fon and Ewe as well as the Delto-Benuic languages Bekwarra, Engenni, Ibibio, Efik, Igbo, Mbembe, Obolo and Yoruba (Campbell 1991:1475; Christaller 1875:46; Creissels 1991:187; Duthie 1996:52; Faraclas 1990:121; Lafage 1985:191, 270; Lefebvre 1998:319-20; Ward 1952:17, 173; Westermann 1939:22). Possibly related is the reduplication of verbs in Izi, which seems to yield something akin to European gerunds (Meier, Meier & Bendor-Samuel 1975:160).

Faraclas (1990:125) claims that this construction also exists in Tok Pisin, and Dixon (1980:73) mentions a similar phenomenon in Roper River Kriol of Australia, which he explicitly ascribes to substrate influence. Although it no doubt exists elsewhere, I have not come across other cases in older languages, with the exception of Sentani of New Guinea (Bernhard Wälchli, p c, citing Cowan 1965). It thus seems less common than the other types discussed in this Parkvall (*forthcoming*).

Because of its distribution, it is therefore reasonable to assume that the adjectivising deverbal reduplication entered proto-Sranan as a transfer from Lower Guinean languages, and that it subsequently spread via Jamaica back to West Africa – the migrations required for this diffusion are all well attested.

---

69 See e.g. Baker (1999b) and McWhorter (1995) for details on the genetic relationship between the Surinamese and West African ECs.

Several instances of other deverbal reduplications are attested in the literature. Examples of reduplicated verbs resulting in adverbs or nouns are to be found in Jamaica EC, Trinidad EC, Sranan EC, Ndyuka EC, Saramaccan EC, Nigeria EC, Berbice DC and Papiamentu SC (Agheyisi 1971:63, 107; Allsopp [ed.] 1996:180; Boretzky 1983:147; Cassidy & Le Page 1967:324, 446; Huttar & Huttar 1997:396; Kouwenberg & La Charité 1998:5-6; Kouwenberg & Murray 1994:21; Sebba 1997:199), but it is difficult to avoid the impression that many or even most of these are lexicalised. For Negerhollands DC, for instance, Kouwenberg & La Charité admit that their example is the only one they have come across. Similarly, I have only found one single example in Guadeloupe FC.[70] The claim that *"The general lack of transparency of deverbal noun reduplications in all the pertinent languages, and the fact that they are invariably restricted to a small number of cases, suggests that these represent vestiges of what may once have been a more productive morphological relationship"* (Kouwenberg & La Charité 1998:5) is definitely not unreasonable, but not necessarily true. Rather, it seems to me that many a language with a well-documented history has some idiosyncratic reduplication which need not represent a once productive strategy.

In many Atlantic Creoles, reduplication is no longer productive, and one can only speculate whether or not what must etymologically been seen as reduplicative structures are synchronically opaque fossilised remnants of a former morphological process (see e.g. Kouwenberg & Murray 1994:21, Maurer 1998:182 and Sebba 1997:200 for a large number of examples from Papiamentu SC). Some of these may potentially be formed on substratal patterns, but if so, these seem not to have been identified.

In some Creoles, however, we find a number of more or less lexicalised idiosyncracies which are directly patterned on non-productive or at least completely opaque sub- or adstratal structures. Numerous good examples are found in Rougé's (1988) dictionary of Guinea-Bissau PC, some of which are reproduced in Parkvall (*forthcoming*). For most of these, Rougé provides exact parallels in local Atlantic languages. The substrate influence in this case is perhaps more adequately classified as lexical rather than structural, but obvious substrate influence it is.

Another reduplication strategy discussed in Parkvall (*forthcoming*) which stands out as possibly substrate-induced is the attenuating one, as in Haiti FC /blãʃblãʃ/ {white-white} 'whitish' and /dudu/ {sweet-sweet} 'rather sweet' (Valdman 1978:157). In the Atlantic area, there is some evidence of the same process in Jamaica EC, Guyana EC, Sranan EC, Ndyuka EC, Saramaccan EC, Haiti FC, Annobón PC and Negerhollands DC (Huttar & Huttar 1997:404; Long 1775 vol. 2:426-27; Alleyne 1980:106; Carter 1987:226; Adamson & Smith 1995:223; Bakker, p c; Post 1992:159; Stein 1998).

As explained in Parkvall (*forthcoming*), I suspect there to have been a substrate model for this, but my attempts at identifying it have been in vain, for the only West African languages in which I have come across similar constructions are spoken in Northern Nigeria (Smith 1967:46; Al-Hassan 1997; Frajzyngier 1965; Ronald Cosper, p c; Shuji Matsushita, p c), that is at some distance from the area where slaves were drawn for the European plantation colonies. It seems in general to be common mainly in south-east Asia and the Pacific, and in eastern Africa, and its occurrence in northern Nigeria appears to represent an extension of the east African linguistic area.

A final observation of potential significance, but which is difficult to evaluate in this particular context (since the difference cannot be linked to any particular part of West Africa) is that reduplication in general seems to be more widespread in Atlantic ECs than in Atlantic FCs (for further details, see Parkvall *forthcoming*).

AREA	FEATURE	LANGUAGE	GROUP	SUGGESTED SUBSTRATE INFLUENCE
Syntax	Reduplication	Surinamese ECs	EC	+Kwa, +Delto-Benuic
Syntax	Reduplication	Nigeria EC	EC	+Kwa, +Delto-Benuic
Syntax	Reduplication	Jamaica EC	EC	+Kwa, +Delto-Benuic
Syntax	Reduplication	Guinea-Bissau PC	PC	+Atlantic

70 /reglo-reglo/ 'ponctuellement' (< /reglo/ 'ponctuel') (Ludwig et al. 1990:277).

4.9 Reinterpretation of morpheme and lexical category boundaries

In many Creoles, both within and outside the Atlantic area, a certain number of nouns include what is etymologically - but not synchronically! - a specifier or modifier, or even a complement. Thus, while the NP *la porte* 'the door' consists of a noun and a determiner in French, its reflex /lapɔːt/ 'door' in e.g. Martinique FC is monomorphemic. In Creolist literature, this is normally referred to as *agglutination*, which, of course, should not be taken to suggest that is in any way a morphological process.

Reinterpretation of morpheme boundaries is fairly common in language restructuring, and incorporation of definite articles, pluralisers, class markers, prepositions and other material into nouns and other phrasal heads is attested in a large number of contact languages, as can be seen from the examples below:

LANGUAGE	ITEM	GLOSS	ETYMON	SOURCE
Papia Kristang PC	/anoti/	'night'	(< P *à noite* 'at night')	Baxter (1988:45)
Bislama EC	/lasup/	'soup'	(< F *la soupe* 'the soup')	Mühlhäusler (1997:155)
Guinea-Bissau PC	/manduku/	'club'	(< Biafada *ma* 'plural prefix' + *ndoko* 'club')	Rougé (1994:99)
Kenyan Kinubi	/sabí/	'friend'	(< Arabic *sahib í* 'my friend')	Owens (1996:157)
Skepi DC	/skun/	'shoe'	(< D *schoen* 'shoes')	Robertson (1989)
Tok Pisin EC	/tudir/	'expensive'	(< E *too dear*)	Mühlhäusler (1997:155)
Papiamentu SC	/larejna/	'queen'	(< S *la reina*)	Munteanu (1996:259)
Sranan EC	/jesi/	'ear'	(< E *ears*)	Hancock (1969:52-3)
Nigeria EC	/kɔmɔt/	'leave'	(< E *come out*)	Agheyisi (1971:53)

Other contact languages where similar phenomena have been attested include, among others, Delaware Jargon, Ivory Coast Popular French, Pitcairn EC, Eritrean Pidgin Italian, Kituba, Mobilian Jargon, Pidgin Eskimo, KiSetla Pidgin Swahili, Manchurian Pidgin Russian, Pidgin Fijian and Samoan Pidgin English (Drechsel 1996:255; Holm 1989:603, 610; Corne 1999:206; Mufwene 1997a:179; Vitale 1980:51; Ross & Moverly 1964:162-3; Mühlhäusler 1997:148, 154; van der Voort 1997:376-77; Jabłonska 1969:143).

There is thus nothing remarkable about morpheme boundary reinterpretation in contact languages as such - on the contrary, it is precisely what we would expect from non-native parsing of utterances produced by speakers of another language.

What is interesting, though, is the distribution of agglutinated items between the various Creole languages. The first observation to be made is that agglutination is far more common in FCs than in other Creoles. This might be explained by the tendency of English, Portuguese, Dutch and Spanish nouns to occur without a definite article more often than their counterparts in French due to the frequent marking of partitive articles in French. In addition to this, French word-stress being considerably weaker than that of the other four languages examined, this may have made it more difficult to adequately perceive the boundary between noun and article.

The English definite articles may possibly also have been easier to assimilate as such because of their limited allomorphy (partly due to the lack of a gender distinction, and partly because of the articles' failure to merge with other morphemes into portmanteau morphs), and indeed, ECs have consistently retained the lexifier DEF, as opposed to other Atlantic Creoles.

One might also expect that Portuguese definite articles, the Spanish masculine article, and the Dutch neuter DEF would be less likely to merge with the head noun, since they alone among lexifier definite articles are not consonant-initial - agglutination of a Portuguese DEF would thus lead to a departure from the favoured CV syllable structure. Agglutinating an elided French article, by contrast, would make a vowel-initial word conform to the preferred CV structure.

Nevertheless, there are instances of agglutination in PCs too (as well as isolated examples in SCs, as we just saw). Although the phenomenon is marginal in the Upper Guinea varieties,[71] there are quite a few agglutinated items in the Gulf of Guinea Creoles. There is a great deal of variation between the three islands, though. Combining the data found in Boretzky (1983:58-59),

71 But see Almada (1961:89) and Silva (1957:129).

Ferraz & Valkhoff (1975:25), Ferraz (1975:160, 1979:27), Granda (1994:433), Green (1988:466), Günther (1973), Barrena (1957:21) and Valkhoff (1966:92, 133), we find that while there are, in the basic word stock, about 14 relevant items in São Tomé PC, and 15 in Annobón PC, there are no less 66 in Príncipe PC.[72] The words in the sister varieties basically form a subset of those found in Príncipe PC.

Among the French Creoles, no variety approaches Mauritius FC and its daughter dialects in the Indian Ocean in terms of numbers of agglutinated items (Baker 1984; Grant 1995a, 1995b; Parkvall 1995c:14, 16-17). In the New World, there are also some differences between the various FCs. The enormous difference between the Indoceanic and Atlantic FCs suggests that substratal factors may have something to do with agglutination patterns. This is indeed what Baker (1984) and Grant (1995b:169) propose – they suggest that agglutination in Mauritian and its daughter dialects would reflect the distribution (and perhaps to some extent also the semantics) of Bantu class prefixes in that speakers of Bantu languages would not find it odd that a great many nouns has the same initial syllable. While this may be true for Mauritius FC, whose substratal input was eastern rather than western Bantu, it does not seem to hold for the Atlantic languages. Louisiana FC, for instance, received less Bantu slaves than perhaps any other plantation colony in the Americas, and nevertheless has a higher number of agglutinated items than any other American FC (the other American FCs being rather similar to one another in this respect [Grant 1995b:153]). Also, there seems to be no agglutination of definite articles at all in Palenquero SC, which appears to be built on a solidly Bantu foundation.

Could, then, Bantu influence be responsible for the incorporation of etymological definite articles into nouns in the Gulf of Guinea PCs? It would seem not. Both language-internal evidence suggests that Upper Guinean influence predated Bantu influence in São Tomé (Parkvall 1999d), and given that agglutination only affects the basic vocabulary, and given that it is far more common in Príncipe PC, which split off from São Tomé PC at an early date, and then received less Bantu influence, we should instead focus on Upper Guinea.

Interestingly, in many Kwa and Delto-Benuic languages, verbs tend to be vowel-initial, whereas virtually all nouns begin with a vowel, this being due to a noun class prefix consisting of a vowel having fossilised as part of the noun (Welmers 1973:40). Languages for which this has been claimed to hold (apart from Welmer's generalisation) include Akpose and Fante (both Kwa) and Edo (Delto-Benuic) (Westermann & Bryan 1952:100; Welmers 1946:44; Omoruyi 1986:66). The case of Edo is particularly interesting, given that a large part of non-Bantu lexical contribution to the Gulf of Guinea lexicon has been identified as Edo (Ferraz 1979). This may well be the source of agglutination patterns in the Gulf of Guinea Creoles in general, and in Príncipe PC in particular. Note, furthermore, that while many nouns thus have been made vowel-initial in the Gulf of Guinea Creoles, São Tomé PC *verbs* never begin with a vowel (Ferraz 1979:27).

A similar suggestion has been made with regard to the Surinamese Creoles by Alleyne (1980:61-2, 156-58, 1996:137-38, 1998) and Stolz (1986:115, 120), where initial prothetic vowels would be fossilised class markers in the words shown below.

LANGUAGE	ITEM	GLOSS	ETYMON	SOURCE
Sranan EC	/alata/	'rat'	(< E *rat*, S *la rata*, P *o rato*?)	Alleyne (1980:61-62)
	/alen/	'rain'	(< E *rain*)	Alleyne (1980:157)
	/alesi/	'rice'	(< E *rice*)	Alleyne (1980:61-62)
Saramaccan EC	/abíti/	'a little bit'	(< E *a bit*, D *een beetje*)	Stolz (1986:120)
	/abosúkee/	'cricket'	(< D *boskrekel*)	Stolz (1986:120)
	/ad͡ʒínd͡ʒa/	'ginger'	(< E *ginger*)	Alleyne (1980:156)
	/ahó/	'hoe'	(< E *hoe*)	Alleyne (1980:156)
	/alísi/	'rice'	(< E *rice*)	Alleyne (1980:156)
	/aláta/	'rat'	(< E *rat*, S *la rata*, P *o rato*?)	Alleyne (1980:156)

72 This includes only cases involving the agglutination of an entire definite article. It must be emphasised that although the total number may not be impressive even in Príncipe PC, a majority of these words are such that they belong in the Swadesh list, and examples include items such as *rain, ashes, knife, leaf, moon, night, earth, field, iron, fire, cloth, wind, bread, sea, tree,* and the names of several body parts.

To support his claim, Alleyne adduces the following arguments:

- While, as seen above there are numerous nouns in the Surinam ECs beginning with /a/, even in cases where it is not etymologically motivated, Donicie & Voorhoeve's (1963) Saramaccan dictionary contains only one single *verb* with an initial /a/, viz. /ákisi/ 'to ask', and this is vowel-initial even in the lexifier, and furthermore has a consonant-initial allomorph /hákisi/ 'to ask' (Alleyne 1980:158). It thus seems that the agglutination process only affects nouns.
- The occurrence of intervocalic /l/ in Sranan is normally restricted to recent Dutch loans, but could be explained in the items above if a former morpheme boundary is postulated between the initial vowel and the liquid (Alleyne 1980:61-62).
- Prothesis of /a/ goes against the general tendency to modify word structure in the direction of CV-syllables (Alleyne 1980:156). Unstressed initial vowels are normally deleted (as in Sranan EC/gri/ 'agree'), and occasionally a prothetic consonant is added in order to obtain CV-structure (as in the above-mentioned /hákisi/). Moreover, the Surinamese Creoles have gone further in the direction of CV syllables than most other Atlantic Creoles (Ericsson & Gustafson-Capková 1997).
- With the exception of /arata ~ alata/ 'rat', where the initial vowel might derive from Spanish *la rata*,[73] prothetic vowels do not occur in other Atlantic Creoles.[74]

Similar developments can be seen in European loan-words in West Africa, such as Fante /akóntàá/ 'account, calculation, reckoning' (< P *(a) conta*).

Just as in the case of the prothetic vowels in the Gulf of Guinea PCs, it is not a question of class markers being transferred as such – rather, a class system in a state attrition has made the category of nouns depart from the otherwise preferred CV pattern in certain substrates, and it is the tendency towards vowel-initial nouns that may have crossed the Atlantic.

More-or-less fossilised class markers consisting of a vowel only are mostly found in Lower Guinean languages, whereas Bantu languages generally have fully functional class markers, usually of CV structure. Upper Guinean languages variably preserve the noun class system, but there are in any case no important differences between nouns and verbs, vowel-initial items being relatively rare in both categories.[75]

Given that the vocalic prothesis described above affects only nouns, and not verbs, and taking into account Alleyne's claims above, it does seem likely that the Lower Guinean tendency towards vowel-initial nouns and consonant-initial verbs, ultimately traceable to a fossilisation of the dying noun-class system influenced the structure of verbs and nouns in the Atlantic Creoles of Surinam and the Gulf of Guinea islands. Even if the French Creole agglutination strategy as such has nothing to do with substrate influences (since it is attested in all French-related Pidgins and Creoles, regardless of substrate), its very different frequency in various FCs (which does not correlate with overall typological distance from French) might suggest that substrate factors were somehow at work. I have not been able to identify these, however.

AREA	FEATURE	LANGUAGE	GROUP	SUGGESTED SUBSTRATE INFLUENCE
Syntax/Phonology	Agglutination	Surinam ECs	EC	+Kwa, +Delto-Benuic
Syntax/Phonology	Agglutination	Gulf of Guinea PCs (especially Príncipe PC)	PC	+Kwa, +Delto-Benuic

73 This etymon is not unlikely, given that rats were introduced into the Caribbean by the Spanish (Philip Baker, p c).

74 Many FCs have a few items beginning with /es/ + stop, where standard French (and the Latin etyma) have /s/ + stop. This, however, seems to reflect dialectal French pronunciations.

75 An examination of 7 305 words in Wolof and Mandinka (Peace Corps 1995a, b), for instance, reveals a proportion of consonant-initial words well above 90% for both nouns and verbs in both languages. Somewhat similar figures were found in the Bantu dictionaries examined (Whitehead 1899; Dzokange 1979).

4.10 Tense, mood and aspect marking

The area of tense, mood and aspect marking has long occupied a position at the centre of Creolistics, in particular since Bickerton's (e.g. 1981, 1984) far-reaching claims regarding the innate language faculty as the ultimate source of most Creole structures. Although most Creolists agree that Bickerton exaggerated the similarities between the TMA systems of various Creoles, even many of those who strongly disagree with his Language Bioprogram Hypothesis admit that similarities in TMA systems among Creole languages world-wide are indeed striking and not obviously explained by other factors.

Of course, one possible such factor is substrate influence, but even the most ambitious attempts at describing Creole TMA systems as partial or total relexifications of substratal patterns, such as Lefebvre (1998) and Winford (1999) are far from convincing. Nevertheless, even if the general outline of the TMA system cannot be ascribed to substratal influence, it might well be that parts of it could be said to bear witness of African influence. I believe that the secondary use of progressives to encode the future is one such feature.

4.10.1 Progressive is also used for future

One of the interesting observations made by Bybee, Perkins & Pagliuca (1994:275-77) is that while the extension of presents and imperfectives into the domain of the future are not particularly remarkable, the similar expansion of progressive morphemes is. In other words, while older and more tightly grammaticalised morphemes of the imperfective domain - such as imperfectives and presents - may spill over into encoding the future (as in most European languages), the purportedly younger (Bybee, Perkins & Pagliuca 1994:172) progressives rarely do since, by virtue of being less grammaticalised and generalised, they preserve more of their original semantic content. Interestingly, however, the use of progressives to encode future actions is precisely what we find in several Atlantic Creoles.

To be sure, progressives being drafted for service as future markers is not unknown among the world's languages.[76] Nevertheless, apart from Bybee, Perkins & Pagliuca (1994), both Bertinetto (2000; p c) and Östen Dahl (p c) assure me that this phenomenon is indeed rather rare cross-linguistically.

Several ECs[77] have been claimed to use the progressive marker /(d)e ~ (d)a/ to encode future/irrealis, including Gullah EC, St Thomas EC, St Kitts EC, Sranan EC, Saramaccan EC, Guyana EC and Krio EC (Hancock 1987; Turner 1949:213; Boretzky 1983:120-1; Cooper 1979:84). In all of these, however, with the possible exception of Saramaccan EC and St Thomas EC, the same morpheme is also used for habitual. Nevertheless, it seems like the Western Caribbean ECs, i.e. Jamaica EC and its daughter languages (e.g. Hancock 1987; Holm 1989:407) for the most part favour zero-marking of habituals, making /(d)e ~ (d)a/ more of a true progressive (with a possibly somewhat marginal function as habitual), rather than a general imperfective marker.

Among the FCs, /ka/ is the normal marker of both habitual and progressive, although it also has a marginal function as future marker in both the Lesser Antilles varieties and in Guiana FC (Valdman 1978:219; Amastae 1975:40; Thomas 1869:99; St-Jacques-Fauquenoy 1972:78; Jadfard 1997:17).[78]

---

76 Bertinetto (1995, 2000, p c), Bybee, Perkins & Pagliuca (1994:277), Campbell (1991:114) and Léger (1999) document it in the following languages from all over the world: Albanian, Alyawarra, Arabic (to some extent), English, Finnish (historically), Icelandic, Kinyarwanda (possibly), Ladino, Nepali, Pangasinam, Persian, several Athabaskan languages, several languages of the Dhegiha branch of Mississippi Valley Siouan (Omaha-Ponca, Osage, Kansa and Quapaw), Somali, some dialects in south-eastern Norway, some varieties of Latin American Spanish, and southern Italian dialects.

77 Since English also allows *-ing* with future readings, mesolects having a reflex of this morpheme (which could be a direct influence from the lexifier) are not included in this discussion, but only ECs which have an etymologically distinct progressive marker (usually /(d)a/ ~ /(n)a/).

78 The Eastern Caribbean FC future/irrealis marker /kɛ/ (with allomorphs) has repeatedly been suggested to derive from a combination of the imperfective and the main verb /ale/ 'to go'. This is supported by the existence of virtually all the forms along the developmental path (/ka ale/ > /kale/ > */kae/ > /kaj/ > /kɛj/ > /kɛ/), and by the plausibility

Haiti FC and Louisiana FC, just like the ECs of the same area, normally zero-mark habituals, and /ap/ (and its allomorphs) may thus be seen as essentially a progressive, with a secondary function as a future marker (Valdman & Klingler 1997:125; Neumann 1985:213; Valdman 1978:217).

In the Gulf of Guinea PCs, as in the Lesser Antilles FCs, the progressive, habitual and future/irrealis markers appear to be historically related, but nowhere does a progressive marker seem to be used as such as with future reading. This, however, is the case in Guinea-Bissau PC (Scantamburlo 1981:55).

In Cape Verde PC, the morpheme /(s)ta/ is a true imperfective rather than a progressive (Lang 1993; Pereira 1999:10). The same seems to apply to the /ta/ of Papiamentu SC, which Munteanu (1996) and Maurer (1987, 1998) even label PRESENT.

Palenquero SC has separate morphemes for future and progressive (Schwegler 1998a:256), although Holm (1988:164) speculates that they may be historically related.

Negerhollands presents a complex picture, with its three future/irrealis markers /sa(l)/, /le/ and /lo/ and its three progressives /ka(n)/, /le/ and /lo/. Due to the almost unparalleled wealth of historical documentation on Negerhollands, the relative frequency of these can be studied over time, from which a number of interesting semantic shifts can be inferred. Both /le/ and /lo/, the interesting morphemes in this context, are described as DURATIVE by most authors.[79] While /le/ clearly had habitual functions (Rossem & van der Voort 1996:14), and was even described as PRESENT by Diggelen (1978:75), /lo/ only marginally functions as habitual in the texts in Josselin de Jong (1926) (see Stolz 1986:179), and seems to have taken over futural functions mainly in the 18th and 19th centuries (suggested by Diggelen 1978:76 to have happened under the influence of Papiamentu SC). In any case, neither form was originally unequivocally progressive.

Both Skepi DC and Berbice DC, finally, have separate markers for progressive and future/irrealis.

Thus, what is entirely or at least essentially a progressive can be said to function as a future marker in the following languages:

LANGUAGE	GROUP	SOURCE
(Jamaica EC)	EC	Peter Patrick (p c)
(Belize EC)	EC	Holm (1988:164)
Louisiana FC	FC	Valdman & Klingler (1997:125), Neumann (1985:213)
Haiti FC	FC	Valdman (1978:217)
Guinea-Bissau PC	PC	Scantamburlo (1981:55)

The grammaticalisation path is not known in detail, but one possibility is that a combination of the progressive + a verb meaning 'to go', possible with a future reading in e.g. Sranan EC (Boretzky 1983:121) could have been eroded, with the result of this combination becoming similar in its surface realisation to the progressive.[80] This, however, has resulted in a separate phonetic form in Eastern Caribbean FCs (as we have already seen), and also in the Lower Guinea PCs (Günther 1973:248).

I would prefer to suggest that the grammaticalisation path would have gone from progressive, via inceptive to future – clearly, being about to do something and actually doing something are semantically close, and both result in a state where this something has been done. Note also that with verbs denoting a change of state, progressives (*Il est en train de s'endormir*) and (proximate) futures (*Il va s'endormir*) may result in near-synonymous sentences. As we would expect, then, several observers (Valdman 1970:116; Ans 1968; Sylvain 1936; Corne 1999:145; Alleyne 1996:126; Boretzky 1983:121; Diggelen 1978:75-76; Bull 1975:20 cited in Stolz

of the phonological changes involved. Yet, the new future/irrealis is in any case a form phonetically separate from the imperfective.

79 Compare the various characterisations in Stolz (1986:179), Bruyn & Veenstra (1993:34, 38), Holm (1988:149), Markey (1979:131), Muysken & Meijer (1979:xvi), Diggelen (1978:75, 95), Rossem & van der Voort (1996:14).

80 This is also how Spears (1990:138) explains a third use of /ap/ in Haitian, that of marking conditionals (/te + ap/ > /ap/).

1986:169)[81] have remarked that the use of the progressive in languages such as Haiti FC, Martinique FC (historically), Guinea-Bissau PC, Negerhollands DC indicates a more proximate and/or more certain future than the use of the future/irrealis morpheme. The same goes for the combination of PROGRESSIVE and 'to go' in Ndyuka EC vis-à-vis the use of /go/ alone (Holm 1988:165).

Although a local development for the Haitian pattern has been suggested by Lefebvre (1998:126-27), [82] the relative cross-linguistic rarity of this feature, coupled with the fact that it goes against documented grammaticalisation theory (where the functions of a morpheme expand gradually without skipping anything on its way, in this case the general imperfective/present) makes this less likely.

The Guinea-Bissau PC case can easily be explained by postulating a more recent habitual gram /ta/ – possibly borrowed from the dialects of the Cape Verdes – intruding into what was initially the exclusive domain of a general imperfective /na/, whereby the latter gets reduced to marking progressive and future/irrealis alone (in both cases sharing the duty with /ta/). Adopting this scenario, Guinea-Bissau PC would thus once have shared the pattern of its sister varieties of the Cape Verdes, only with a different imperfective morpheme.

Since zero marking as such does not normally actively partake in grammaticalisation, but is rather defined by what is left over after the expansion of other morphemes, we would have expected the progressives of the Western Caribbean to have covered the habitual space as well, before expanding into the future/irrealis domain. Yet, this is not the case.

Since the Creoles concerned share African substrate languages, the obvious place to look for a source is in the latter.

The following African languages have been reported to allow the expression of the future with the same morpheme as the progressive:

LANGUAGE	GROUP	SOURCE
Kisi	Atlantic	Childs (1995:117)
Maukakan	Mande	Léger (1999)
Fante	Kwa	Welmers (1946:39)
Gã	Kwa	Boretzky (1983:125)
Igbo	Delto-Benuic	Boretzky (1983:136), Léger (1999)
Tiene	Bantu	Guthrie (1953:83)

Of the above languages, Maukakan and Tiene must be regarded as marginal, as they are spoken in areas which were hardly touched by the transatlantic slave trade.

In a number of other languages from all over West Africa, a more general imperfective or present may be used to mark future actions but, as noted above, this is less remarkable from a cross-linguistic perspective.

AREA	FEATURE	LANGUAGE	GROUP	SUGGESTED SUBSTRATE INFLUENCE
Syntax	PROG as FUT	(Jamaica EC)	EC	+Kisi, +Fante, +Gã, +Igbo
Syntax	PROG as FUT	(Belize EC)	EC	+Kisi, +Fante, +Gã, +Igbo
Syntax	PROG as FUT	Louisiana FC	FC	+Kisi, +Fante, +Gã, +Igbo
Syntax	PROG as FUT	Haiti FC	FC	+Kisi, +Fante, +Gã, +Igbo
Syntax	PROG as FUT	Guinea-Bissau PC	PC	+Kisi, +Fante, +Gã, +Igbo

81 Chataigner (1963:45-7 cited in Stolz 1986:161), however, takes the diametrically opposite view with regard to the same language (Guinea-Bissau PC)! Of potential interest is that Bull is a native speaker of the language in question.

82 Lefebvre's suggestion is that future /ap/ is a local development of the preposition /apre/ (< F *après*), and thus not directly related to the progressive /ap/. Apart from the problems already mentioned, this does not account for why two TMA markers of different age would both have eroded phonetically to precisely the same extent and in precisely the same unexpected way (/pe/ would be the expected form, but, although attested in the Indian Ocean and in Louisiana, it is in Haiti confined to the south [Orjala 1970:35]). Also, temporal (as opposed to spatial) prepositions do not constitute a common source for progressives (Bybee, Perkins & Pagliuca 1994).

There are a few other peculiarities about Atlantic Creole TMA systems, which I have not studied but which, once examined, might yield further substrate correspondences. A brief discussion of two of these follows.

4.10.2 Absolute versus relative tense

Bakker, Post & van der Voort (1995:250), among others (see also Lefebvre 1998:115), point out that Atlantic Creoles tend to have a TMA system based on relative rather than absolute tense, i.e. tense is marked not necessarily in relation to the time of speech, but in relation to a point of reference determined by discourse factors. Whether this, or simply a weak grammaticalisation of past markers (or a combination of both), is responsible for the widespread phenomenon that they (p 253) label *proleptic marking* (the non-marking of tense once the time frame has been discursively established) is unclear. In any case, I do not have enough data from either Creoles or African languages to further develop this subject, although it might reveal interesting parallels.

4.10.3 Aspect prominence

A somewhat related phenomenon is that of aspect prominence. It has often been claimed, in rather general terms, that Atlantic Creoles, in comparison to their European lexifiers, display this feature, as illustrated by the following quotes:

- "*Most* [Romance] *Creole verb systems give precedence to aspectual over strictly temporal relations. Few recognise more than one time opposition, [±PAST], and some indeed could be argued to function entirely on aspectual distinctions*" (Green 1988:451).
- "*Der Grad der Grammatikalisierung* [of aspect in Creoles] *ist dabei viel höher als bei vergleichbaren Strukturen in den europäischen Basissprachen*" (Stolz 1986:177).
- "*Instead of the European conjugation, which is based upon tenses and moods, the Creoles introduced into Portuguese or French the verbal system of the African languages, in which the aspects of the action are the dominating element, not so much the tenses*" (Valkhoff 1966:104).

It is not clear exactly what is meant by "aspect prominence", but a reasonable interpretation of the term in the Atlantic Creole context might be that TMA markers of the imperfective domain show a higher degree of grammaticalisation than do the various markers whose primary semantic contribution is +PAST.

Aspect prominence has been claimed to characterise at least the following Atlantic Creoles:

LANGUAGE	SOURCE
Gullah EC	Turner (1949:225)
Nigeria EC	Faraclas (1990:105)
FCs in general	Valdman (1983:217)
Dominica FC	Amastae (1975:39)
St Lucia FC	Carrington (1984:117)
Guinea-Bissau PC	Wilson (1962:21-3)
Gulf of Guinea PCs	Valkhoff (1966:108), Ferraz & Valkhoff (1975:18-20)

For some others, including Nigeria EC and Príncipe PC, explicit claims to the contrary have been forwarded (Poplack & Tagliamonte 1996:91; Maurer 1997:425). Yet others such as Sranan EC and Cape Verde PC are suggested to have been aspect-prominent, but are now on their way to conforming more to the European pattern (Healy 1993:287-88; Morais Barbosa 1975:146, 1992:179-80).

In African languages, aspect has been claimed to predominate over tense in the languages listed in the table overleaf.

For a few West African languages, however, other TMA categories have been suggested to be more important. For Rask (1828:22), temporal distinctions were more central to the Gã verbal system than aspect, and mood has been claimed to be the most important category in Grebo

(Kru) and in southern Delto-Benuic languages in general (De Bose & Faraclas 1993:377).[83] Of possible importance here is the absence of claims regarding aspect prominence in Bantu languages. Indeed, my impression from the various reference grammars I have gone through is that Bantu favours temporal rather than aspectual distinctions. All in all, however, for want of detailed data, as well as of a better definition of the very concept of "aspect prominence", it is difficult to draw any conclusions from this, and I include a discussion here mainly as a "suggestion for further research". I do suspect, however, that it is no coincidence that a number of authors have drawn attention to what they see as aspect prominence in both West African languages and in Atlantic Creoles.

LANGUAGE	GROUP	SOURCE
Wolof	Atlantic	Samb (1983:83)
Fulfulde	Atlantic	Westermann & Bryan (1952:29)
Mandinka	Mande	Rowlands (1959:74)
Kpelle	Mande	Westermann (1924:18)
Bariba	Gur	Welmers (1952:93)
Dogon	Dogon	Plungian (1997)
Ewe	Kwa	Lafage (1985:319)
Gẽ	Kwa	Winford (1999:4)
Yoruba	Delto-Benuic	Ward (1952:77)
Bekwarra	Delto-Benuic	Faraclas (1990:105)
Efik	Delto-Benuic	Faraclas (1990:105)
Ekpeye	Delto-Benuic	Faraclas (1990:105)
Engenni	Delto-Benuic	Faraclas (1990:105)
Ibibio	Delto-Benuic	Faraclas (1990:105)
Kalabari	Delto-Benuic	Faraclas (1990:105)
Kolokuma	Delto-Benuic	Faraclas (1990:105)
Mbembe	Delto-Benuic	Faraclas (1990:105)
Obolo	Delto-Benuic	Faraclas (1990:105)
Oron	Delto-Benuic	Faraclas (1990:105)
Hausa	Afro-Asiatic	Kirk-Greene (1971:135)
Margi	Afro-Asiatic	Campbell (1991:900)

4.11 Predicate cleft (verb fronting)

Atlantic Creoles have a number of syntactic, phonological and lexical devices for emphasising a sentence constituent. These include cross-linguistically common options such as repetition, reduplication, lengthening of phonetic segments, pitch raising, left dislocation and lack of vowel elision.

Many of the Atlantic Creoles also have a focusing or topicalising strategy involving fronting and a copula to introduce the fronted element as in Negerhollands DC /da wat mi sa du/ {COP what 1sg FUT do} 'What shall I do?' (Stolz 1986:219). Apart from the fact that the fronted constituent happens to be an interrogative in the example just cited, this is not particularly different from fronting in European languages. Also, Harries (1973:89) points out that many languages which normally lack an equative copula, such as Tagalog and colloquial Arabic, require a copula-like element to introduce fronted elements.

Most focusing strategies used in Atlantic Creoles are thus not particularly remarkable. However, many varieties, as first pointed out by Schuchardt (1914), also have a construction commonly referred to as *predicate cleft*, but also variably labelled *double predication* or simply *verb fronting*. Some examples of this phenomenon are given below:

Gullah EC: /də to:k i də to:k/
COP talk 3sg PROG talk 'He's really *talking*' (Mufwene 1987:71).

83 This is certainly the feeling that Green & Igwe's (1963) grammar of Igbo conveys.

Jamaica EC: /a ti:f d͡ʒan ti:f di mango/
COP steal John steal DEF mango
'John *stole* the mango (he didn't buy it)' (Bailey 1966:86)

Sranan EC: /da skrifi mi de skrifi/
COP write 1sg PROG write
'I am actually writing' (Allsopp 1976:14)

Louisiana FC: /se malad mo malad/
COP ill 1sg ill
'What I am is really ill' (Valdman & Klingler 1997:134)

Martinique FC: /se aʃte ʒɔzjan aʃte wɔb -ta -la ãvil/
COP buy Josianne buy dress DEM DEF in-town
'J. *bought* this dress in town (it wasn't just given to her)' (Damoiseau 1984:58)

Negerhollands DC: /da sla:p mi ka sla:p/
EMPH sleep 1sg PERF sleep
'I have really slept' (Rossem & van der Voort 1996:17)

Papiamentu SC: /ta duna m' a duna -bu e buki/
COP give 1sg PAST give 2sg DEF book
'I *gave* you the book' (Kouwenberg & Muysken 1995:212)

As can be seen, the function is not only emphatic, but often also contrastive, in that the verb is contrasted to other verbs that, had the circumstances been different, might potentially have taken its place.

Predicate cleft in Atlantic Creoles thus typically consists in fronting the VP head while leaving a copy at the extraction site, and using a copula to introduce the verb copy,[84] which also receives additional stress. The following characteristics and peculiarities of predicate cleft in Atlantic Creoles may be noted:

- The copula is optional in many varieties, but the verb copying is not. Thus, to emphasise the verb in the Haiti FC sentence /kabrit baj ʃẽ liv la/ {goat give dog book DET} 'The goat gave the book to the dog', the only option is /(se) baj kabrit baj ʃẽ liv la/ {(COP) give goat give dog book DET}, whereas simple fronting without copying, as in */(se) baj kabrit Ø ʃẽ liv la/ would be ungrammatical (Valdman 1978:260).
- This contrasts with other categories, such as nouns, which do not normally leave copies at the extraction site when fronted (though see below).
- Haiti FC /li malad/ {3sg ill} 'He is ill'[85] cannot undergo fronting with the clause-final copula normally used in cleft constructions involving non-predicates (as for instance when WH-words are fronted), so the more European-like */se malad li je/ {COP ill 3sg COP} 'It is ill he is' is similarly ungrammatical (Alleyne 1996:95).
- Most Atlantic Creoles do not allow overt TMA marking on fronted verbs, though Manfredi (1993:17) gives the following example from Haiti FC: /se te aʃte mari te aʃte flɛ-a/ {COP PAST buy Mary buy flower DET} 'Mary *bought* these flowers'.

With the reservations already mentioned, the strategy is virtually identical in all the Creoles listed in the table overleaf.

---

84 Holm (1988:179) labels this a *highlighter*. For most varieties, the term *copula* is appropriate in the sense that the same morpheme is also used in copular constructions, but in some languages such as Negerhollands DC, the highlighter morpheme is at least not synchronically identifiable with a copula. It is possible, and maybe even likely, however, that the Negerhollands DC highlighter was borrowed from neighbouring ECs, where it does fulfil copulative functions.

85 In many varieties, adjectives, which to a great extent behave syntactically like stative verbs, may also be fronted. In fact, Manfredi (1993:31) even gives an example of a clefted predicative noun in Haiti FC: /se dɔktɛ ʒak dɔktɛ/ 'A doctor is what Jacques is'. This is the only example of this kind that I have seen, though.

LANGUAGE	SOURCE
Gullah EC	Mufwene (1987:71)
Bahamas EC	Hancock (1987:317)
Jamaica EC	Bailey (1966:86)
Providence EC	Hancock (1987:317)
Belize EC	Hancock (1987:317)
St Kitts EC	Cooper (1980:45)
Montserrat EC	Roberts (1988:89)
Antigua EC	Roberts (1988:89)
Dominica EC	Roberts (1988:89)
St Lucia EC	Roberts (1988:89)
Carriacou EC	Hancock (1987:317)
Grenada EC	Hancock (1987:317)
St Vincent EC	Roberts (1988:89)
Trinidad EC	Winer (1993:41)
Tobago EC	Hancock (1987:317)
Guyana EC	Allsopp (1976:14)
Sranan EC	Voorhoeve (1971:313)
Ndyuka EC	Huttar (1981:307)
Saramaccan EC	Veenstra (1996:19)
Krio EC	Denis (1998:3)
Nigeria EC	Agheyisi (1971:119)
Cameroon EC	Mufwene & Gilman (1987:126)
Louisiana FC	Valdman & Klingler (1997:134)
Haiti FC	Lefebvre (1993:264)
Guadeloupe FC	Cérol (1991:83-4)
Dominica FC	Amastae (1975:52)
Martinique FC	Damoiseau (1984:58)
St Lucia FC	Carrington (1984:147
Trinidad FC	Thomas (1869:105)
Guiana FC	Fauquenoy-St-Jacques (1972:72)
Karipuna FC	Corne (1999:152)
Negerhollands DC	Stolz (1986:207)
Berbice DC	Kouwenberg (1994c:437)
Papiamentu SC	Maurer (1998:175), Kouwenberg & Muysken (1995:212)

Though verb fronting is attested for the Gulf of Guinea PCs (Lorenzino 1998:180; Post 1995:200), none of these languages to my knowledge makes use of verb copying in combination with a highlighter morpheme.

Emphatic or contrastive verb constructions involving two instances of the same verb are not unknown in European languages, as is illustrated by the following Romance examples:

Piedmontese: *Mange' a lo mangia*
(NW Italy): eat:INF 3sg:SUBJ 3sg:OBJ eat:PRES:3sg 'He really ate it!' (Masja Koptjevskaja-Tamm, p c)

Italian *Per esser ci, c' era ma era chiuso*
for COP:INF there there COP:PAST but COP:PAST closed
'It was there all right, but it was closed' (Masja Koptjevskaja-Tamm, p c)

Brazilian Vernacular Portuguese: *Falar ele falou*
speak:INF 3sg:M speak:3sg:PAST 'He certainly talked' (Holm 1988:179, 1992:58)

Spanish: *Hablar Habló*
speak:INF speak:3sg:PAST 'He certainly talked' (Laura Álvarez, p c)

Magoua French:[86] *Màlàd yé té màlàd, yon pa té kàpàb lsové*
ill 3sg COP:IMPERF ill 3pl:AUX NEG COP:PERF capable 3pl:OBJ-rescue
'He was so ill that he could not be saved' (Wittmann 1996)

86 Spoken around Trois-Rivières, Canada.

Similar constructions are also attested in Yiddish and Hungarian (Masja Koptjevskaja-Tamm, p c). In this European-type clefting, the first verb is generally in the infinitive, whereas the second one is fully tensed. This is reflected in Vernacular Brazilian Portuguese, whose clefting is thus probably of a European rather than an African, or even Creole type.[87]

Apart from the verb marking, the European predicate cleft as illustrated above differs from the Creole one mainly through the absence of a highlighter copula. Note also that a potential European prototype is attested only for some of the Atlantic Creole lexifiers, but not for English (**[It] is talk I am talking*) or Dutch (**Het is praat ik praat*[88]) (its existence in Portuguese is of less importance, since no PC has the construction sketched above in any case). The absence of a perfect model in Europe, as well as the lack of similar clefting in Indian Ocean, Asian and Pacific Creoles (see e.g. Muysken 1988:299; Corne 1999:23; Seuren 1993:57), leads to the suspicion that predicate cleft as discussed here may be of African origin.

Given the striking similarities between predicate cleft constructions in Atlantic Creoles, one might expect whatever African prototype it may have to closely follow the Creole pattern. However, although predicate cleft is indeed common in West African languages, no single potential substrate seems to match the Creole construction perfectly. Although focal, topicalising, emphatic or contrastive strategies involving predicate cleft are used in a large number of West African languages, several features set them apart from the typical Atlantic Creole clefting.

For one thing, the focus marker, or highlighter (which is often, but not necessarily, homophonous with a copula) is frequently not clause-initial, but introduces the occurrence of the second verb, or is even clause-final. This appears to be the case in e.g. Kisi, Wolof, Mende, Twi, Fon, Gun, Yoruba and Izi (Aboh 1998:13; Alleyne 1980:170, 172; Allsopp 1976:15; Childs 1995:125, 271; Holm 1988:179; Lefebvre 1993:265; Meier, Meier & Bendor-Samuel 1975:160; Seuren 1993:63; Taylor 1977:7-9).

Secondly, the verb is not in clause-initial position in some languages, since the subject is left-dislocated together with the verb, which results in a SVOV word order in the case of Igbo and its close relative Izi (Manfredi 1993:10; Meier, Meier & Bendor-Samuel 1975:160). Fronting of both subject and verb is apparently also a possibility in Twi (Allsopp 1976:15). In Fon, on the other hand, it is not the subject that is fronted with the verb, but the entire VP (Lefebvre 1993:265).

A third, even more striking feature is that deverbal morphology (nominalisation or gerundive) is affixed to one of the verb occurrences in many of the potential substrates. It is a central feature of verbal cleft in at least Kisi, Mende, Tepo, Vata, Fon, Igbo, Izi and Yoruba (Alleyne 1980:172; Allsopp 1976:15; Childs 1995:125, 271; Holm 1988:179; Lefebvre 1993:265; Manfredi 1993:10-5; McWhorter, p c, Meier, Meier & Bendor-Samuel 1975:160; Taylor 1977:7-9). It does not seem to occur in Bantu languages.

As for the placement of the focus marker, it should be noted that two of the Atlantic Creoles, namely Cape Verde PC[89] and Palenquero SC, place it after the fronted element, rather than before it (Alleyne 1980:103; Marlyse Baptista, p c). This would make Palenquero and Cape Verdean predicate cleft somewhat similar to strategies employed in Mende, Wolof, Gun, Twi or Yoruba (Aboh 1998:13; Alleyne 1980:170-2; Allsopp 1976:15; Holm 1988:179; Seuren 1993:63; Taylor 1977:7-9).

The nominalisation of the verbs is seemingly a major difference between the Atlantic Creoles and many of their potential substrates. It might be invoked that the nominal status of the fronted predicate is not overtly marked only because of the relative absence of morphology in Creoles. Thus, Faraclas (1990:131) claims that the clefted verb is in fact nominalised in Nigeria EC, but that the nominalisation is zero-marked. For at least some Creoles, though, there is indeed overt marking of nominalisation, as exemplified by, for instance, the use of the Haiti FC DEF illustrated in the following sentence from Baudet (1981:109-10):

---

87 For potential French prototypes of Creole predicate cleft, see also Corne (1999:193-5). Note also that the examples above contradict Holm's (1992:58) claim that Brazilian Vernacular Portuguese and Afrikaans are the only European languages to display predicate cleft.

88 Hancock (1980:230) attests a construction *Sit die kinders sit speel* 'The children are sitting and playing' in Afrikaans, but to my knowledge, no variety of European Dutch would allow **Zitten de kinderen zitten te spelen.*

89 It is not obvious how this "focus marker" should be interpreted in Cape Verde PC. It is homophonous with the complementiser, and it would therefore seem that a sentence such as /e kore k el kore/ {it ran that he ran} 'He ran as fast as he could' (Baptista, p c) should be interpreted as consisting of two clauses rather than one.

Haiti FC: /pãdã m malad -la/
while 1sg ill DET 'during the time I was ill'

And still, */di-a li di m sa/ 'He really told me that' is ungrammatical in this language. Note also that Haitian, as pointed out above, is a language that permits TMA marking on the fronted element (Manfredi 1993:17), providing further evidence that it is indeed a verb rather than a noun. Finally, the transfer of this structure into L_2 French by FC speakers results in fronted predicates having French verbal rather than nominal morphology (Manessy 1995:218; Mufwene 1987:81; Françoise Loe-Mie, p c), suggesting that native speakers themselves analyse the element in the fronted position as a verb rather than as a noun. Nevertheless, there is at least one Atlantic Creole in which nominalisation does seem to be involved in the fronting process. Consider the following sentence in Saramaccan EC:

Saramaccan EC: /dí woóko mi woóko tidé/
DEF work 1sg work today 'I really worked today!' (Sebba 1987:85)

As opposed to other Atlantic ECs, the highlighter morpheme here is not a copula, but rather the definite article, something that suggests that the fronted verb is nominalised. Note that not even in its close relative Sranan EC, does the clefted verb show any signs of having nominal status.

The following table summarises some of the differences between the West African and the prototypical Atlantic Creole (as described above) predicate cleft strategy and other topicalisation methods:

LANGUAGE	FAMILY	DIFFERENCE	SOURCE
Wolof	Atlantic	Fronted element a noun rather than a verb. Copula follows fronted verb.	Allsopp (1976:14)
Kisi	Atlantic	Fronted verb nominalised. Focus marker sentence-final	Childs (1995:125, 271)
Mende	Mande	Fronted element nominalised. Second rather than first element introduced by a copula, both followed by an emphatic marker	Allsopp (1976:15)
Tepo	Kru	Fronted verb nominalised. No highlighter.	Manfredi (1993:15)
Vata	Kru	Fronted verb nominalised. No highlighter. Nominalisation not evident in the sample sentence given by Lumsden & Lefebvre.	Manfredi (1993:15), Lumsden & Lefebvre (1990:762)
Fon	Kwa	Entire VP fronted, leaving only a pronominal trace at the extraction site. Fronted predicate nominalised.	Lefebvre (1993:265)
Gun	Kwa	Focus marker follows first verb. No highlighter.	Aboh (1998:13, p c).
Twi	Kwa	Highlighter follows first verb.	Seuren (1993:63), Alleyne (1980:170)
Twi	Kwa	Complementiser introduces second verb occurrence, indicating two clauses rather than one	Seuren (1993:64)
Twi	Kwa	Subject follows the verb when the verb is fronted. No copula used	Allsopp (1976:15).
Igbo	Delto-Benuic	SVOV. TMA on first verb, second verb nominalised.	Manfredi (1993:10)
Izi	Delto-Benuic	SVOV. Second verb in gerund form.	Meier, Meier & Bendor-Samuel (1975:160)
Yoruba	Delto-Benuic	First element nominalised. Copula-like element placed between the two occurrences of the fronted element (which may be non-verbal).	Rowlands (1969:189)
Kikongo	Bantu	No highlighter copula. Used interchangeably with non-clefted sentences by some speakers.	Allsopp (1976:15), Charles Harvey (p c).

There may, of course, be other differences that are not evident in the data I have examined.

In addition to the above table, there are data for a few languages that are difficult to evaluate. Faraclas (1990:133) enumerates a number of Delto-Benuic languages having predicate cleft (Bekwarra, Efik, Ibibio, Igbo, Izi, Mbembe, Obolo, Oron), but does not give enough details to make a comparison between these and the Atlantic Creoles possible. In addition, Sebba (1997:188) and Bynoe-Andriolo & Yillah (1975:234) both give the same example from Temne (Atlantic), /kɨbulɔ kɔmɔ bulɔ (jaŋ)/, which Sebba glosses as {it is work he works} and Bynoe-Andriolo & Yillah translate as 'He's really working', but the lack of a detailed morphemic translation hinders a definitive judgement of the sentence.

Mande languages such as Kpelle and Vai can be excluded from consideration, since verbs cannot be topicalised at all in these languages (Welmers 1973:321, 1976:114). Innes (1967:176) states that fronting is uncommon in colloquial Mende, and his examples include no instances of fronted verbs. Predicate cleft may also be absent from Ewe. Duthie's (1996:39) description of Ewe does not provide interlinear morphemic translations of his sentences illustrating verb topicalisation, but so far as I can see, a focus marker is used instead of verb fronting.

There are certainly some similarities between the Atlantic Creole clefting and verb focus strategies in a variety of West African languages, but the almost identical structures of the Atlantic Creoles would lead one to expect closer correspondences than I have been able to find. If a structure paralleling the typical Creole cleft indeed exists in West Africa, it can hardly be widespread.

The presentative copula is optional in many Atlantic Creole predicate cleft constructions, but whenever it occurs it does so clause-initially (except in Palenquero SC, as noted above). This is striking partly because it instead precedes the second verb occurrence in many West African languages, but also because other types of cleft sentences require other copular morphemes in many of the languages. Most FCs, for instance, use a clause-final /je/ in other types of clefts. Speculatively, one possibility would be that the predicate cleft construction was assimilated in the Atlantic Creoles before there was a copula. By the time one had been introduced, this was placed in initial position in analogy with presentative constructions, which often have an emphatic nuance.

In sum, there are a few features of Atlantic Creole predicate cleft which make an African derivation likely. For one thing, similar strategies not only exist in most West African languages, but are so very conspicuous that Pulleybank (1990a, b) mentions them as the most noteworthy feature of Kwa and Delto-Benuic languages. Furthermore, predicate cleft is generally absent in Creoles with no West African substrate material (Holm 1999:113). On the other hand, some European languages offered constructions not unlike the ones found in the Creoles. More generally, the fact that verbs, as opposed to other categories, are fronted only after leaving a copy behind may be a general tendency among the world's languages because the predicate seems too semantically and/or syntactically important to the matrix sentence to be extracted from it. After all, even European languages other than the ones referred to above require a dummy verb in this position, as in colloquial German *Laufen* ***tut*** *er*, whereas other contituents fail to leave such a copy (cf *Peter habe ich Ø gestern getroffen*). Most importantly, however, no African language that I know of parallels the Creole cleft constructions more than vaguely.

4.12 Number marking

In many Atlantic Creoles, as well as in several of their potential substrates, the 3pl pronoun serves as a nominal pluraliser. The similarity between a Creole (Negerhollands DC) and West African languages in this respect was, I believe, first pointed out by Rask (1828:18).

Despite its apparent semantic transparency, this use of the 3pl pronoun is cross-linguistically rare (Greville Corbett, p c; Holm 1988:193). Furthermore, no Asian or Pacific Creoles have this feature (see e.g. Hancock 1980:20), except for Tok Pisin and its closest relatives, many of whose substrates, incidentally, also have a plural marker homophonous with the 3pl pronoun (Goulden 1990).

The fact that nothing similar is attested for any of the European lexifiers except (marginally) English,[90] coupled with the global rarity of the construction in question, is a strong case for substratal derivation and, indeed, many West African languages do pluralise NPs by adding the 3pl. The PL=3pl pluralisation strategy is used in the following Atlantic Creoles:

LANGUAGE	GROUP	PRENOMINAL	POSTNOMINAL
Gullah	EC	+	+
Afro-Seminole	EC	+	+
Bahamas	EC		+
Jamaica	EC		+
Cayman Islands	EC		+
Belize	EC	+	+
Miskito Coast	EC		+
Providence	EC		+
Costa Rica	EC		+
St Thomas	EC		+
St Kitts/Nevis	EC	+	+
Antigua	EC		+
Carriacou	EC		+
St Vincent	EC		+
Barbados	EC	†[91]	
Trinidad	EC		+
Tobago	EC	+	+
Guyana	EC	+	+
Sranan	EC	+	
Saramaccan	EC	+	
Kru Pidgin English	EC	+	
Krio	EC	+	+
Liberian English	EC		+
Nigeria	EC	+	+
Fernando Poo	EC		+
Cameroon	EC	+	+
Louisiana	FC	†[92]	+
Haiti	FC		+
Grenada[93]	FC		+
Guiana	FC		+
São Tomé	PC	+	
Angolar	PC	+	
Príncipe	PC	+	
Annobón	PC	+	+
Negerhollands	DC		+
Papiamentu	SC		+

The preposed position of the plural morpheme in English Creoles might be due to colloquial English influence, but as can be seen, many ECs place their pluralising 3pl morpheme

90 Cf non-standard English *them books*. Note, though, that this would not explain the presence of the construction in Creoles of non-English lexicon, and would furthermore not be a satisfactory model for the construction involving a *postposed* 3pl; to my knowledge, anything like **books them* has never been attested on the British Isles.

91 Attested in 1834 (Fields 1995:95).

92 Attested in 19th century texts (Hall 1992:234-35).

93 It is surprising that Grenada FC, but no other dialect of Lesser Antillean FC has this feature (see discussion in Parkvall 1995c:90-1). According to Valdman (1983:216, referring to Turiault 1875-76:77), Martinique FC would formerly have had it as well. However, the only example Valdman gives is /se bɛf la jo mɔ/ 'These cows are dead', which would in modern Martinican be rendered as /se bɛf la mɔ/. It is not clear, however, why the 3pl /jo/ might not be a resumptive pronoun rather than an NP determiner, all the more so since the 1874 sentence contains the current plural marker /se/.

postnominally, which can hardly be derived directly from the lexifier. This, together with the sharing of the same feature with neighbouring Creoles of other lexical affiliations suggests a non-European origin.

As mentioned above, several West African languages employ 3pl as a nominal pluraliser. Boretzky (1983:89) discusses several instances of this phenomenon, but many of the morphemes he treats are just one of many plural markers in a given language, and given the tendency for both these and the 3pl pronouns to be monosyllabic, it may well be that chance resemblances are responsible for many of the apparent cases of PL=3pl usage. Indeed, Manessy (1985:135) concludes that the phenomenon is less common in West Africa than has often been assumed by substratophile Creolists.

To begin with, the Atlantic, Mande, and Kru languages of Upper Guinea do not display any phonetic similarity between their 3pl pronouns and nominal pluralisers,[94] with the exception of Fulfulde (Arensdorff 1913:24, 107).

The Bantu languages too seem to show a complete lack of PL=3pl constructions; in other words, the phenomenon is virtually confined to Lower Guinea, where it has been attested in Twi, Fante, Gã, Aja, Gẽ, Ewe, Hausa, Ebira, Yoruba, Igbo, and possibly also the Edo dialect Epie (Rask 1828:17-8, 20; Welmers 1946:42; Westermann 1930:47; Westermann & Bryan 1952:92; Lafage 1985:252-3; Manessy 1985:133-34; Goodman 1964:45-6; Boretzky 1983:88; Bamgboṣe 1966:99; Duthie 1996:57; Alleyne 1980:151).[95] In several of these, however, the pluralising use of the 3pl is subject to various restrictions. For instance, Fante, Gã, Yoruba, and Igbo apparently use 3pl as a pluraliser mainly with animates (Welmers 1946:42; Rask 1828:17-18, 20; Manessy 1985:134; Boretzky 1983:88), and at least in Yoruba, plural marking is always optional (Bamgboṣe 1966:109).

Assuming, then, that the extended use of 3pl as a nominal pluraliser in Atlantic Creoles springs from the similar use in these or closely related West African languages, we still need to account for the position of the 3pl morpheme in the Creoles.

In the Kwa languages mentioned above, the pluraliser derived from 3pl precedes the noun it determines, with the exception of Ewe, where both positions are allowed, and Twi, in which it is postposed. As for the Delto-Benuic languages, Yoruba normally preposes its plural marker, whereas Igbo places it after the noun. Note, though, that with demonstratives, Yoruba also allows the order N PL DEM, as in /igi awɔn ni/ 'those trees' (Alleyne 1980:151).

Interestingly, the postnominal version of the Ewe pluraliser (/-wó/) not only follows the head noun, but indeed the entire NP including determiners (Lafage 1985:254; Westermann 1939:2; Duthie 1996:56), and the resulting word order N DEF PL thereby closely reflects that of French Creoles such as riverine dialects of Louisiana FC, Haiti FC, and Guiana FC. Therefore, Ewe or Twi, or possibly Igbo or Fulfulde would seem to be the most likely sources of the FC 3pl pluraliser.

In Papiamentu SC too, the pluraliser and 3pl /naŋ/ follows the noun, as well as its adjectival attributes, but precedes other non-head material in the NP (Kouwenberg & Murray 1994:49). Again, Twi, or possibly Ewe, Fulfulde or Igbo, seem to be the most plausible sources of this

---

94 Goodman (1964:46), Hancock (1986:94), and Dalphinis (1985:9) all claim that the Mandinka 3pl pronoun functions as a pluraliser, and Heine et al. (1993:170-1) and Westermann (1947:7 cited in Günther 1973:25) add five other Mande languages. However, the pronominal system set out in Rowlands (1959:55) rather suggests the opposite, viz. that plural pronouns in Mandinka consist of the corresponding singular pronoun and a plural affix, a state of affairs which also obtains in Mandarin and in some languages of New Guinea (Corbett 2000), among others. This appears also to be the case of other Mande languages (cf e.g. Derive 1990:200-01; Welmers 1976:46 – Welmers explicitly claims this with regard to Vai, one of the languages mentioned by Westermann). In general, Mande languages do not mark number at all, at least not on {-HUMAN} nouns (Welmers 1971:131). Boretzky (1983:88) and Heine et al. (1993:170-71) also adduce Bambara, in which language both the plural suffix and the 3pl pronoun are indeed /-u/. This might of course be a coincidence, and even if that is not the case, evidence from other Mande languages just cited rather suggests that causality would go in the opposite direction, i.e. that the pronoun derives in part from the plural marker rather than vice versa. Similarly, Westermann's (1947:7 cited in Günther 1973:25) claim that Efik would be a language where PL=3pl is suggested to be due to a misreading by Manessy (1985:133).

95 Heine et al. (1993:170-1) add three Bantu languages, which, however, are spoken outside the area from which slaves were drawn. Similarly, Westermann (1947:7 cited in Günther 1973:25) mention two other African languages, one Khoisan and one Nilo-Saharan, both spoken outside the relevant area.

construction; as opposed to the FCs, Yoruba is also a possible option, given that the internal structure of the Papiamentu NP is N PL DEM (Kouwenberg & Murray 1994:48).

The Negerhollands plural clitic /sinu ~ sender/ (< West Flemish *zijnder*) is interesting since it seems to have been less grammaticalised than its counterparts in other Creoles. For one thing, it is rare in Negerhollands texts from before about 1750 (Stein 1995:50). Secondly, it remained optional until the death of the language, and inanimates were often left unspecified for number (Stolz 1986:122; Rossem & van der Voort 1996:17), and this may be taken to suggest that the pluralising function was introduced relatively late (or, of course, that the grammaticalisation process proceeded more slowly than elsewhere). In any case, the morpheme was postnominal, and once again, Twi, Ewe, Fulfulde, or Igbo seem like the most plausible donors.

The Gulf of Guinea PCs all pluralise by preposing 3pl to the noun.[96] Boretzky (1983:35) traces the pronoun itself (/iné/, with various allomorphs such as /ne ~ nẽ ~ anɛ ~ ɛnɛ ~ inɛ ~ ina ~ na ~ nã/, etc.) to Edo /ina ~ ana/, which may suggest that the construction itself is of Edo origin. Most varieties of Edo, however, do not use 3pl as a generic pluraliser, although Manessy (1985:133) draws attention to the morpheme /íg͡bani/ in the Epie dialect, which has some pluralising functions, and which he suggests may be related to the 3pl /g͡bánɪjɛ/. Edo and the related Wano (Thomas 1910:135, 144) mark plural optionally through change of the initial vowel, or through preposing of a pluraliser /ávbé/ (Omoruyi 1986:68), which bears no resemblance to the 3pl pronoun. This would rather suggest that Yoruba any of the Kwa languages having PL=3pl except Twi would be syntactically likely candidates, unless 15th century Edo behaved differently from the modern language in this respect.

As for the ECs, the placement of the pluraliser varies, as could be seen in the table above, and some have only a preposed variety of *them*. These include Barbados EC† (attested in 1834), the Surinamese ECs, and Kru Pidgin English. This construction is similar enough to colloquial English *them books* not to require any substratal explanation. For virtually all other varieties, though, postnominal *them* is attested. Fulfulde, Twi, Ewe, or Igbo influence seems once more plausible. It is noteworthy that the Surinamese ECs lack postposed 3pl, given that these languages in general are more distant from their lexifier, and display more parallels with African languages than most other Atlantic Creoles.

Note, finally, that the use of 3pl as a nominal pluraliser is conspicuously absent from Upper Guinea PC and Palenquero SC, presumably bearing witness of the lack of impact of Lower Guinean languages on these Creoles.

AREA	FEATURE	LANGUAGE	GROUP	SUGGESTED SUBSTRATE INFLUENCE
Syntax	3pl=pl	Gullah EC	EC	+Ewe, +Twi, +Igbo, +Fulfulde
Syntax	3pl=pl	Bahamas EC	EC	+Ewe, +Twi, +Igbo, +Fulfulde
Syntax	3pl=pl	Western Caribbean EC	EC	+Ewe, +Twi, +Igbo, +Fulfulde
Syntax	3pl=pl	Leeward Islands EC	EC	+Ewe, +Twi, +Igbo, +Fulfulde
Syntax	3pl=pl	Windward Islands EC	EC	+Ewe, +Twi, +Igbo, +Fulfulde
Syntax	3pl=pl	Guyana EC	EC	+Ewe, +Twi, +Igbo, +Fulfulde
Syntax	3pl=pl	West Africa EC	EC	+Ewe, +Twi, +Igbo, +Fulfulde
Syntax	3pl=pl	Louisiana FC	FC	+Ewe, +Twi, +Igbo, +Fulfulde, +Fante, +Gã, +Aja, +Gẽ, +Yoruba
Syntax	3pl=pl	Haiti FC	FC	+Ewe, +Twi, +Igbo, +Fulfulde
Syntax	3pl=pl	Guiana FC	FC	+Ewe, +Twi, +Igbo, +Fulfulde
Syntax	3pl=pl	Gulf of Guinea PC	PC	+Yoruba, +Ewe, +Fante, +Gã, +Aja, +Gẽ, (+Edo?)
Syntax	3pl=pl	Negerhollands DC	DC	+Ewe, +Twi, +Igbo, +Fulfulde
Syntax	3pl=pl	Papiamentu SC	SC	+Ewe, +Twi, +Igbo, +Fulfulde, +Yoruba

96 Post (1995:202) includes the phrase /mina kit͡ʃi teʃ nen saj/ {child small three PL DEM} 'the three small children', which shows that both positions apparently are possible in Annobón PC. This, however, is the only such example I have come across.

4.13 Miscellaneous word order issues

Surprisingly few of the Atlantic Creoles display any far-reaching differences in word order in comparison to their lexifiers. To be sure, Romance Creoles have generalised SVO order to the benefit of the SOV order used with pronominal subjects, but this is an extension that would seem to follow from restructuring rather than from substrate influence. Similarly, postposition of pronominal possessors could also be seen as an extension of a pattern offered by the lexifier.

Some striking examples of the relative fidelity to lexifier word order is offered by the fact that Romance-based Creoles in general not only retain the N ADJ order, but even the exceptions to this order (corresponding to French *une pomme verte* versus *une bonne pomme*), including the cases where both orders are possible, but yield different readings.[97]

Similarly noteworthy is the retention of Germanic ADJ N in the ECs of Surinam, despite the vast majority of West African languages being N ADJ. This is paralleled in the Pacific, where the Melanesian ECs are ADJ N, despite their speakers being from predominantly N ADJ language backgrounds.

The Gulf of Guinea PCs, however, provide an interesting exception – although São Tomé PC and Angolar PC follow the European order (Ferraz & Valkhoff 1975:22; Lorenzino 1998:135), both Príncipe PC and Annobón PC have generalised the tendency for nominal modifiers to follow the head, and extended this even to numerals (Post 1995:201; Ferraz 1976:43-44; Bartens 1996:122). This cannot be said to have a prototype in Portuguese. Note the spectacularly un-European structure of the following Annobón PC examples (from Ferraz 1976:44 and Barrena 1957:33):

Annobón PC:	/ojo	mu	dos/			
	eye	1sg	two			'my two eyes'
Annobón PC:	/omã	di	neŋi	dos	limpi/	
	hand	of	3pl	two	clean	'their two clean hands'
Annobón PC:	/lávulu	dos	mensaj/			
	book	two	this			'these two books'

Numerals following rather than preceding nouns seems to be rule rather than the exception in West Africa,[98] and while Annobón PC could be said to owe its NP syntax to its substrates, again, the precise origin of this influence cannot be determined.

Ferraz (1976:44) draws attention to the fact that Annobón PC numerals not only follow the nouns, but also that the order in NPs involving more than one modifier is N POSS NUM ADJ, and that this ordering, while being unlike Portuguese, is identical to that of Kikongo. Unfortunately, I am not able to say to what extent this occurs in other parts of West Africa.

Ferraz (1976:44) further points out that adverbs in Annobón PC, as opposed to Portuguese, follow the adjectives they determine, as in /fumozu mujtu/ 'very pretty', and draws a parallel between this and Kimbundu. Again, this is something that I did not collect enough data on when examining reference grammars of African languages, but Ferraz usually mentioned other potential (Delto-Benuic) substrates in his works so, in the absence of more data, I am inclined to consider the feature Bantu.

AREA	FEATURE	LANGUAGE	GROUP	SUGGESTED SUBSTRATE INFLUENCE
Syntax	Internal NP syntax	Annobón PC	PC	+Bantu

97 See e.g. Goodman (1964:22f), Bollée (1977:42), Neumann (1985:138), Valdman & Klingler (1997:120), Carrington (1984:75-6), St-Jacques-Fauquenoy (1972:104), Kouwenberg & Murray (1994:48), Munteanu (1996:286-87). This also applies even to non-Atlantic Pidgins and Creoles, such as the Pidgin French of Burundi and the Tayo FC of New Caledonia (Niedzielski 1989:90; Ehrhart 1993:144; Corne 1999:23).

98 Bella (1946:734), Bentley (1887:567), Campbell (1991:398), Duthie (1996:83), Innes (1966:88), Leitch (1994:192), Maia (1964:26-27), Marchese (1984:133), Samb (1983:70), Smith (1967:18), Spears (1967:279), Swift & Zola (1963:51), Welmers (1973:297), Westermann & Bryan (1952).

Chapter 5

Lexicosemantics

Although there is quite a lot of controversy regarding which areas of a language are most easily affected by contact (see e.g. Weinreich 1953:34-37, 67 for discussion and references), there seems to be a general consensus that open-class lexical items are normally borrowed before any phonological, syntactical or morphological (i.e. more structure-dependent) features of the donor language are accepted. Thus, although we cannot say whether phonological or syntactic features tell us most about the true origins of a Creole, we should de-emphasise the importance of the lexicon. Unfortunately, the lexicon is precisely that part of language which presents the most idiosyncrasy – there are more possible ways of saying 'book' than there are possible ways of syntactically or morphologically expressing, say, a possessive relationship between 'John' and 'book'. Therefore, a word with a satisfactory etymology is normally far easier to relate to a specific substrate language than is a grammatical construction but, while more reliably explored, lexical affinities are less indicative of the genetic origins of a language, given the lesser stability in the open-class part of the lexicon compared to the grammar.

5.1 Lexicon

Unless otherwise noted, all data in this section are based on Parkvall (1999f), henceforth referred to as *Afrolex*, which the reader may consult for further references.[1] Before proceeding, I would like to point out a few problems inherent in Atlantic Creole etymologising.

Notoriously difficult items include several more-or-less pan-Creole words which also appear to be more-or-less pan-African. These include, among others, /bumba/, meaning 'buttocks, anus', /t͡ʃubum/ 'falling into water', /fufu/ 'mashed yam, etc., /d͡ʒuk/ 'to stab', /ɲamɲam/ 'to eat'. With minor differences in meaning and/or pronunciation, all of these exist in a large number of Creoles and, for all of them, plausible etymologies have been suggested in languages from both Upper and Lower Guinea and from Buntu (see *Afrolex* for details). Two examples will illustrate this:

- /bubu/ is attested in Gullah EC, Bahamas EC and Jamaica EC with the sense of 'noxious flying insect'. Three etymologies proposed for this are (i) Fulfulde /mbubu/ 'a fly', (ii) Fon /bũbu/ 'insect', and (iii) Kikongo /mbu/ 'mosquito' (Holm 1983:311; Cassidy & Le Page 1967:74). It can thus plausibly be related to all three major areas of slave exportation from West Africa.
- The word /asunu/ 'elephant' is found in the ECs of Jamaica and Guyana, and corresponds to somewhat similar forms in Sranan (/asaw/) and Saramaccan (/zaun/), with the same meaning. These forms might perhaps be related to /zãba/, found in Guadeloupe FC and Dominica FC, and to /zamba/ and /θamɓa/ of São Tomé PC and Angolar PC, respectively, all with the same meaning. The use of the elephant as a character in folklore points to a Bantu origin (Tchang 1990:152), and thereby possible etyma such as Kikongo /nzau/ (Laman 1912:59) or /n-zamba/,

[1] An electronic copy of this document is available upon request to Creolists willing to provide constructive comment and/or additional data. *Afrolex* 1.15 contains etymological information about 3 000 words of presumed African origin in Atlantic Creoles. In all, it contains more than 2 600 references to ECs, 900 each to FCs and PCs, 350 to SCs, and about 70 to DCs. The etymologies are derived from about 200 different sources, but in particular Alleyne (1980, 1996), Allsopp (ed.) (1996), Anglade (1998), Aub-Büscher (1984), Baker (1993), Cassidy (1964), Cassidy & Le Page (1967), Cérol (1991), Dalphinis (1985), Emanuel (1972), Ferraz (1979), Ferraz & Valkhoff (1975), Fyle & Jones (1980), Günther (1973), Hall-Alleyne (1990), Hancock (1969, 1987), Holloway & Vass (1993), Holm (1988), Holm & Shilling (1982), Hurault (1983), Huttar (1985), Arends, Kouwenberg & Smith (1995), Lipski (1989, 1994), Lorenzino (1998), Lumsden (1994), Macedo (1979), Mafeni (1971), Manigat (1998), Maurer (1992), Megenney (1989, 1992), Mendonça (1933), Mühlhäusler (1997), Patrick (1995), Quint-Abrial (1998), Rougé (1994), Silva (1957), Smith (1987a, 1997), Taylor (1977) and Turner (1949).

a form found not only in Kikongo, but also in Kimbundu and Mbangala (Ferraz 1979:91). However, Cassidy (1964:274) proposes Twi /e-sóno/, which seems reasonable, at least so far as Jamaica and Guyana EC are concerned. To further complicate matters, Malinke has a form /samba, sãba/ (Delafosse 1929:101), while Gambian Mandinka has /samo:/ (Peace Corps 1995b), and so this word, like /bubu/, might also owe its presence in these Creoles to languages of Buntu, Lower or Upper Guinea - the three principal slave exporting areas of Africa.

Nevertheless, cases like the above are the exception rather than the rule; for most words in *Afrolex*, one or several reasonably plausible etyma are proposed from one geographical area only. However, the above explains certain apparent anomalies in what follows, such as Mande words in São Tomé PC and Bantu words in Cape Verde PC.

Please note that the summaries of the following subsections will be found at the end of the chapter rather than at the end of each subsection.

5.1.1 Origins of closed-class items

Since there is a general consensus that items belonging to closed classes (whence the name, of course) are more resistant to borrowing than others, substratal origins for such words may be particularly revealing. Some of the cases of closed-class items of African origin below have already been mentioned.

One category which has attracted particular attention is that of the Creole TMA markers, but the reader will notice that they are excluded here. This is because I do not find the accounts of substratal derivation of these very convincing. A case in point is the imperfective marker /ka/, used in the Lesser Antilles and Guiana FCs. In the creolistics literature, no less than 13 different sources from 11 different substrate languages, ranging from Wolof to Hausa, have been suggested (see Parkvall 1995c:3), but none of these is necessarily more plausible than the four or so French etyma which have also been proposed.[2]

Similarly, it has also been suggested that the imperfective marker of the Gulf of Guinea PCs, which, as it happens, is also realised /ka/, may derive from languages such as Edo, Twi, Nupe, Ewe, Ewondo and even Upper Guinea PC (Ferraz 1979:85; Green 1988:450; Bartens 1996:88; Rougé 1999) but, again, I see no reason why potential Portuguese sources such as *ficar, cá* or *capaz* should be less likely.

Although African etyma have at one time or another been proposed for most Atlantic Creole TMA morphemes, the vast majority are not only more satisfactorily accounted for by assuming an origin from various lexifier auxiliaries, but such a derivation is also preferable in that it entails less recourse to the *Cafeteria Principle*.

The same applies to elements such as copulas; although African etyma are certainly possible (see e.g. Holm 1988:177), it is by no means obvious that such a derivation is preferable to a European origin (cf McWhorter 1997b:103-15).

5.1.1.1 Palenquero SC and Berbice DC pluralisers

Palenquero SC is one of the few Atlantic Creoles to have a pluraliser neither homophonous with the 3pl (§4.12) nor with that of the lexifier. Instead, a preposed /ma/ is used.[3] This morpheme is identified as a Bantu pluraliser by e.g. Schwegler (1998a:259). Holm (1988:194) adds that /ma/ is homophonous with the plural marker of class 6 inanimate nouns, but without revealing to which language(s) he refers (/ma-/ being found in a large number of geographically disparate Bantu languages).

Berbice, too, has an obviously substrate-derived pluraliser. Its plural suffix /-apu/ is clearly a reflex of Eastern Ijo /-apu/, plural marker used with {+HUMAN} nouns (Robertson 1993:304).

---

2 *Qu'à, capable, quand, qui* (Gérmain 1976:107; Boretzky 1983:131; Goodman 1987; Jennings 1993b:146; Van Name 1869-70; Maher 1994). It is of course also possible that /ka/ results from convergence of items from several sources.

3 This morpheme has sometimes been referred to as a prefix but, although certainly etymologically true, the pluraliser can be separated from its noun by a free morpheme, as in /ma ndo mano/ {PL two hand} 'the two hands' or /ma uto tankero/ {PL other drunkard} 'the other drunkards' (Lorenzino 1993:401; Lewis 1997:3).

5.1.1.2 Interrogatives in Saramaccan EC, Angolar PC and Berbice DC

The Atlantic Creoles, just like a large number of Pidgins and Creoles world-wide (and, for that matter, also a fair number of older languages), have interrogatives based on an invariable WH-element and a nominal part specifying what is being questioned. Thus, 'who' is realised as *what person*, 'where' as *what place*, 'when' as *what time*, etc. The fact that this trait is shared by some languages of West Africa has led some authors to suggest a causal relationship. However, apart from appearing in several parts of the world, bimorphemic interrogatives of this type are – for reasons of semantic transparency – particularly common in Pidgins and Creoles, regardless of lexifier or substrate. Also, having one or two bimorphemic interrogatives corresponding to what in English is one word is not necessarily more remarkable than the fact that English lacks a single word corresponding to French *combien*, and the use of the bimorphemic 'how many' in its place. Therefore, we cannot with certainty invoke a substratal origin for Atlantic Creoles bimorphemic interrogatives. Muysken & Smith (1990:893) also make the point that it is precisely the *opaque* forms in Saramaccan EC which are demonstrably African transfers, and it is this which makes the substrate hypothesis untenable so far as bimorphemic interrogatives are concerned. They say this with reference to the two Saramaccan items /a͡mbɛ́/ 'who' and /a͡ndí/ 'what', which are derived from Fon /me ~ mɛ̌/ 'who'[4] and /ani/ 'what' respectively (Muysken & Smith 1990:892).

In addition to this, Berbice DC also has a partly substrate-derived interrogative – the nominal part of /wa aŋga/ 'where' can be related to Kalabari,[5] an Ijo dialect (Muysken & Smith 1990:892).

The Gulf of Guinea PCs contain a number of interrogative elements whose origins are unclear.[6] The only form which has definitively been demonstrated to be African is Angolar PC /kút͡ʃi/ 'which' (also used in /dia kut͡ʃi/ and /ola kut͡ʃi/, both meaning 'when' [cf P *dia* and *hora* respectively]), which Maurer (1992:166) identifies as being derived from Kimbundu /kuʃi/ 'which one'.

5.1.1.3 Pronouns

Given the fact that pronouns, as high-frequency items, are typically monosyllabic and not infrequently monophonemic, almost any given pronoun in any Creole is bound to be phonetically reminiscent of forms in some West African languages. The creative adherent of the *Cafeteria Principle* could easily assemble an entire Atlantic Creole pronoun paradigm from material picked from substrates only, provided that his language sample is large enough (or else that his requirements on phonetic and semantic similarities are lax enough) – and, sadly, this has also been done by less serious authors. Each member of the pronoun paradigm of Haiti FC is paralleled by more or less homophonous pronouns with the same meaning in Edo, Kikongo, Umbundu, Wolof and Ewe,[7] but, of course, this is not how language contact works. A pronoun paradigm is simply not assembled from bits and pieces in five different languages. There is, of course, even less reason for assuming this, because the vast majority of Creole pronouns can easily be traced to a lexifier item. Furthermore, the forms that are not immediately evident reflexes of lexifier forms are usually realised /i/, /a/ or /u/, which makes substratal comparisons more difficult. In most of the cases presented below, however, the alternative explanation – development from lexifier forms – would require a considerable stretch of imagination.

5.1.1.3.1 2sg /i/ in ECs

A 2sg form /i/ is found in Jamaican Maroon Spirit language EC, Sranan EC, Ndyuka EC and Saramaccan EC (Bilby 1983:53; Hancock 1969:61-63, 1987:277), and according to Veenstra (1994:109-10 cited in McWhorter 1997b:18) also in earlier Jamaica EC.[8] Although mono-

---

4 This word probably once had an initial /a/, as its cognates in the neighbouring languages Ewe and Gẽ still do.

5 Kalabari /anga/ 'side' (cf §5.1.1.6).

6 Bartens (1995:121) suspects several of these forms to be African, but does not attempt to identify any Niger-Congo cognates.

7 The corpus here consists of the complete set of personal pronouns from about 60 West African languages taken from a similar number of reference grammars. In addition to this, some further forms are provided in the creolistics literature.

8 I write "according to" since I have some doubts regarding the accuracy of this claim.

phonemic, and therefore difficult to relate to any specific African source, the phonological distance from English *you* is after all considerable, and would seem to call for an alternative derivation.

African languages having /i/ as a 2sg form include the Mande languages Mandinka, Ivorian Mande languages, Vai and Bambara, the Kwa language Fante, and the Delto-Benuic Igbo (Campbell 1991:160; Derive 1990:200; Rowlands 1959:55; Welmers 1946:28, 1976:43; Green & Igwe 1963:32).

5.1.1.3.2 1pl /u/ in Surinamese ECs

Sranan EC, Ndyuka EC and Saramaccan EC have a 1pl pronoun /u/. Since this is not obviously related to English *we*, nor to any substratal form */u/, I believe it to be related to /unu/ (see §5.1.1.3.4 below), with which it coexists in Sranan and Ndyuka, both of which also have the intermediate forms /ũ ~ un/ (Alleyne 1980:111; Holm 1988:204; Hancock 1969:60-62).

5.1.1.3.3 3sg /a/ in ECs

A 3sg form /a/ is attested in all Surinamese ECs, as well as in Jamaican Maroon Spirit EC (Hancock 1969:60-62; Hancock 1987:293; Bilby 1983:53) and, according to Veenstra (1994:109-10 cited in McWhorter 1997b:18), also in older Jamaica EC. The Maroon Spirit Language also has an alternate 3sg form /o/ (Bilby 1983:53). Belize EC, finally, may use /a/ as both 3sg:OBJ and 3pl:OBJ (Escure 1986:52).

West African languages having a 3sg pronoun realised /a/ include the Atlantic languages Kasanga, Kobiana, Manjaku and Serer, the Mande languages Bambara, Ivorian Mande languages, Mandinka and Vai, the Delto-Benuic Efik (Marques 1947a:85, 1947b:892; Carreira & Marques 1947:47; Senghor 1963:289; Rowlands 1959:55; Welmers 1976:43; Campbell 1991:160, 397; Derive 1990:200), and more than a dozen Bantu languages from Cameroon and Gabon (Guthrie 1953), from where very little slave exportation took place. A 3sg pronoun /o/ or /ɔ/ is found in the Atlantic languages Fulfulde and Kisi, the Kwa languages Fante and Twi, the Delto-Benuic languages Igbo and Yoruba, and the Bantu languages Kimbundu and Umbundu (Westermann & Bryan 1952:28, 92; Childs 1995:104; Welmers 1946:28; Green & Igwe 1963:32; Ward 1952:78; Bamgboṣe 1966:105; Maia 1964:37; Valente 1964:177), but the marginal existence of such a form in ECs alongside /a/ makes me suspect that the Maroon Spirit form is a mere phonetic variant thereof. In addition to these languages, Igbo has an impersonal pronoun (corresponding to French *on* or German *man*), which might be a source. It does not, however – contrary to McWhorter (1997a:80) – have a 3sg proper which is realised /a/. One 3sg which does exist in Igbo, though, is the /o ~ ɔ/, which matches the Maroon Spirit allomorph (Green & Igwe 1963:32; Campbell 1991:600; Westermann & Bryan 1952:92).

5.1.1.3.4 2pl /unu/ in ECs

Among the ECs, 2pl is the form that deviates most from the corresponding lexifier form. *A posteriori*, we may note that the original form was sensitive to restructuring, since – perhaps because of homophony with the 2sg form – *you* (plural) has not survived in any basilectal variety. Two basic strategies have been used to replace it. The Leeward islands in the north-eastern Caribbean use a combination of *all* and *you* (typically realised /a:jʊ/), also found in St Vincent, Trinidad and Guyana, and marginally also in Jamaica, presumably reflecting Kittitian emigration to these territories (Hancock 1969:61-63; Roberts 1988:96; Winer 1993:43; Cassidy & Le Page 1967:8; Baker, p c). This alternates with *you all* in Guyana (Hancock 1969:61-3), which also occurs in Gullah (Cunningham 1992:18), and generally in southern American English.

The other alternative is more interesting: various realisations of /unu/[9] are found in Gullah and on the Bahamas, in Jamaica and the western Caribbean (Bay Islands English, Cayman Islands English, Belize EC, Costa Rica EC, Miskito Coast EC, Providencia EC, San Andrés EC), in Barbados, in all the Surinamese and West African Creoles (Adams 1991:20; Agheyisi 1971:122;

9 Including /ína ~ ɔ́na ~ áno ~ ánu ~ ʌnə ~ hə́nə ~ jínə ~ júna ~ ona ~ u ~ ũ ~ ún ~ únə ~ úna ~ úno ~ únu ~ únú ~ ú:nu ~ wúnə/.

Alleyne 1980:111; Cunningham 1992:18; Edwards 1974:14; Fields 1995:99-100; Hancock 1969:61-3, 1987; Herzfeld 1986; Warantz 1986:85; Washabaugh 1986:166).

Here, a partial match is provided by the Atlantic Mankanya (/ane/), and a number of Bantu languages[10] (Valente 1964:177; Eynde 1960:91; Guthrie 1953:38, 65; Marques 1947a:85; Laman 1912:118, 125; Bentley 1887:576). The only *perfectly* matching language, however, is Igbo, whose 2pl pronoun is /unù/ (Westermann & Bryan 1952:92; Campbell 1991:600). This in turn, helps us in determining the origins of the pronouns discussed in the preceding sections with greater precision. As already noted, languages do not normally assemble their pronominal paradigms from a large number of different sources. Let us therefore recapitulate the suggested sources from the two preceding sections:

2sg /i/	3sg /a/	2pl /unu/
	Kasanga	
	Kobiana	
	Manjaku	
	Serer	
	Efik	
Mandinka	Mandinka	
Ivorian Mande	Ivorian Mande	
Vai	Vai	
Bambara	Bambara	
Fante		
Igbo	(Igbo)	Igbo
	several Bantu lgs	

Combining the evidence, we thus have reason to assume that no less than two pronoun forms in certain ECs, and one form in most ECs, were taken over from Igbo. The support lent from /unu/, the phonetically most complex form, makes the case for /i/ considerably stronger than it would otherwise be, had the pronouns been considered in isolation. As opposed to McWhorter (1997a:80), I prefer not to count 3sg /a/ as a certain transfer from Igbo, but I would not want to exclude the possibility of a relation between /a/ in Igbo and in the ECs.[11]

5.1.1.3.5 Various forms in Berbice DC

Berbice DC has 1sg, 2sg and 2pl forms of Dutch origin. Of the remaining forms, 3sg /ori ~ o ~ a/ and 3pl /eni ~ ini/ are both of Eastern Ijo origin (Robertson 1993:307-08). Kouwenberg (1994c:591) acknowledges that the origin of the 1pl form /enʃi ~ iʃi ~ içi/ remains a mystery.

5.1.1.3.6 Skepi DC 2sg

Skepi DC has a 2sg /aʃu/ (Robertson 1989:15, 20), which does not appear to be Dutch. I have not found a plausible African etymon for this item, which would seem to suggest an Amerindian origin. However, to the best of my knowledge, no Amerindian language in the area has a 2sg which is even remotely similar to /aʃu/, so the derivation of this pronoun in Skepi DC remains enigmatic.

---

10 Kikongo (/eno ~ jeno ~ lu ~ nu), Kimbundu /jenu/, Umbundu (/(h)ene/), Chokwe (/enu/), Tsogo (/no/) and Yambasa (/nʊ/), all of which ultimately derive from a proto-Bantu form **nu* (Holm 1988:204). See also Goodman (1964:41) and Hancock (1987:274) for suggestions regarding more African languages providing potential etyma.

11 Embarrassingly, I realised shortly before submitting the final version of the manuscript (thanks to Philip Baker, p c) that I had overlooked the possibility of /i/ and /u/ (see §5.1.1.3.2 above) resulting from vocalisation of the initial semi-vowels of *you* and *we* respectively. Unfortunately, time constraints allowed me neither to discuss this possibility more fully, nor to work out its repercussions in the concluding chapter. Admittedly, the absence of 3sg /a/ in Igbo, together with the possibility to after all deriving /i/ from English reduces the value of the above observations.

5.1.1.3.7 Plural pronouns in Palenquero SC

Palenquero SC has the somewhat old fashioned 2pl form /enú/, and the 3pl pronoun /ané ~ enu/ (the last allomorph of which is also archaic; Schwegler 1991:63, 1993a), which Porras (1992:200) relates to Kimbundu /enu/ and /ene/ respectively. Schwegler (1998b) suggests the alternative Kikongo etymons /éenu ~ éeno/ and /a/ '3pl' + /né/ 'demonstrative particle', whereas Schwegler (1998a:260) proposes the Kimbundu 3pl /enu/. Also of interest is that Eynde (1960:91) gives /enu/ as the 2pl form in Chokwe.

Palenquero has also taken over the Kikongo 2pl:IMPERATIVE suffix /-eno/, as in e.g. /ableno/ 'talk!' (Schwegler 1999).

5.1.1.3.8 3pl /naŋ/ in Papiamentu SC

Papiamentu SC has a 3pl morpheme /naŋ/ which also constitutes a pluraliser (see §4.12), and as such is optionally suffixed to the 2pl /boso(naŋ) ~ bosnaŋ/ (Munteanu 1996:295; Kouwenberg & Muysken 1995:217). I have not found any West African pronoun form which resembles this more than the Wolof 3rd and 4th series subject pronoun /naɲ/ (Samb 1983:59). The fact that the velarisation of the final nasal in Papiamentu is phonetic rather than phonemic - word-final nasals are always velar in the language - makes the similarity somewhat greater. In attempts to demonstrate the interrelatedness of Papiamentu and the Gulf of Guinea PC, parallels have often been drawn (e.g. by Valkhoff 1966:96) between their respective 3pl pronouns; if there is any truth in this hypothesis, this would ultimately trace the Papiamentu 3pl to Edo /ina ~ ana/[12] (cf §5.1.1.3.11).

5.1.1.3.9 Generic /a/ in Gulf of Guinea PCs

The Gulf of Guinea PCs have a generic pronoun /a/ unmarked for person and number (corresponding to French *on* or German *man*, and to reflexive or passive constructions in the lexifier) (Ferraz 1979:66; Lorenzino 1998:144). Ferraz (1979:66) and Lorenzino (1998:154, 184) claim the etymon to be the Edo impersonal pronoun /à/, also found in the related Wano (Thomas 1910:145). However, Igbo and its close relative Izi also have an impersonal pronoun form /a/ (Green & Igwe 1963:32; Meier, Meier & Bendor-Samuel 1975:236), which is not *a priori* a less likely candidate. Hausa, which has a similar form (Günther 1973:178) must, however, be considered too geographically distant from the slave-exporting areas to have had an impact. Another Delto-Benuic language, Yoruba, uses /a/ 'someone' as an impersonal pronoun in constructions corresponding to European passives (Turner 1949:209).

5.1.1.3.10 1sg /n/ in African PCs

In both Upper and Lower Guinea PC varieties, the 1sg pronoun may be reduced to a nasal consonant, homorganic with the following segment (Cardoso 1989:25; Silva 1957:132; Ferraz & Valkhoff 1975:22; Ferraz 1979:62; Green 1988:447; Lorenzino 1998:144; Meintel 1975:212; Scantamburlo 1981:49; Valkhoff 1966:96). African influence has been suggested (Valkhoff 1966:96; Baptista, p c), and indeed, almost all Niger-Congo 1sg pronouns contain a nasal consonant (as do their counterparts in most European languages), and about one West African language in six has a 1sg allomorph consisting only of a nasal consonant. This is relatively uncommon in the Upper Guinean languages (i.e. the potential substrates of the Upper Guinea PCs), but is found in Balanta and Mandinka (Quintino 1951:11; Rowlands 1959:55). In Lower Guinea and among the Bantu languages, i.e. the substrates of the Gulf of Guinea PCs, nasal consonant 1sg forms are found in Ewe, Gã, Efik, Igbo, Tiv, Yoruba and Kikongo (Anon. 1961; Campbell 1991:397; Duthie 1996:52; Green & Igwe 1963:32; Laman 1912:118; Rask 1828; Söderberg & Wikman 1966:17; Ward 1952:78; Westermann & Bryan 1952:92, 119). However, derivation from Portuguese *mim* can by no means be excluded.

12 Presumably, then, through the following development: /ana/ > /na/ > /nã/ > /nan/ > [naŋ].

5.1.1.3.11 Various forms in Gulf of Guinea PCs

The Gulf of Guinea PCs have several peculiar forms. To begin with, São Tomé PC has a 2pl /(i)nãse/ (Valkhoff 1966:96; Ferraz 1979:65), cognate with Príncipe PC /ína ~ ínɛ ~ ínɛ̃/ (Boretzky 1983:35).[13] Valkhoff (1966:96) claims a Bantu origin, without giving any details whatsoever. Boretzky (1983:35) instead suggests Edo 3pl (sic) /ina ~ ana/. The 3pl form suggested by Boretzky is indeed phonetically close, but semantically less so. The closest potential candidates I have come across are Bantu 2pl forms such as Umbundu /ene/ and Kimbundu /eɲe/ (Valente 1964:177; Maia 1964:35-36), which also have the advantage of being able to be used in isolation, as opposed to most other pronominal forms in those languages.

The above, however, would not account for the 2pl forms in the closely related Angolar PC (/eθe ~ θe/; Lorenzino 1998:144) and Annobón PC (/namaseʒi/;[14] Valkhoff 1966:96), which do not seem to be Edo, and the origins of which remain enigmatic to me.

Finally, Príncipe PC has a 2pl form /ɔ́wo/ which is not attested in the other Gulf of Guinea PCs. The closest match I have been able to find in West Africa is Edo /ùwà/ (Omoruyi 1986:65).

The Gulf of Guinea PCs also have 3pl pronouns which appear not to originate in the lexifier. They come in several related shapes: São Tomé has /inẽ/, Angolar PC has /anɛ ~ enɛ/, Príncipe PC has /ína ~ ínɛ̃/, and Annobón PC has a 3pl /ineɲi/ (Ferraz 1979:65; Valkhoff 1966:96; Günther 1973:65; Lorenzino 1998:144). Note that the São Tomé form is similar to, but not identical with, the 2pl pronoun in the same language. Again, Valkhoff (1966:96) proposes a Bantu etymon, without indicating what the donor language would be, whereas Boretzky (1983:35) once more invokes Edo, which has a 3pl /ina ~ ana/. At least for Angolar, a case could also easily be made for derivation from the same Bantu sources as the Palenquero forms mentioned above. The Kimbundu 3pl /ene/, suggested by Maurer (1992:165), is also about as close to the São Tomé form as is the proposed Edo etymon.[15]

5.1.1.3.12 Reduction of pronominal paradigms

Given the drastic reduction of both the lexicon and the grammatical machinery associated with pidginisation, the pronoun system usually suffers some severe losses. In a language having a pronoun system distinguishing three persons, two numbers, two genders of the 3sg and three cases, as do many European languages, twenty-one forms would be required to avoid homophony. In many Pidgins and basilectal Creoles, only number and person distinctions are generally upheld, reducing the number of forms used to six.

Some rudimentary Pidgins have rationalised even further, and in e.g. Russenorsk, Taimyr Pidgin Russian and Alamblak Pidgin Yimas (Belikov, n d; Wurm 1996:83; Shi 1991:17; J. Williams 1993:359), there are no plural forms of pronouns. In other Pidgins, such as Samoa Pidgin English and Naga Pidgin (Mühlhäusler 1997:148; Wangkheimayum & Sinha 1997:2), plurals are generated through the addition of the nominal pluraliser to the singular forms. This analyticity can be seen even in older languages, such as Quechua, Dakota, Mandarin and a number of Mande and Papuan languages (Creissels 1991:155; Derive 1990:200; Welmers 1976:46; Campbell 1991:369; Corbett 2000).

Curiously, neither of these paradigmatic reductions are attested in the Atlantic, not even in the varieties furthest from their respective lexifiers.[16] Despite partial or total abandonment of gender and case distinctions, Atlantic Creole pronoun systems generally retain two numbers and three persons. Interestingly, this is contrary to some of the lexifiers. Apart from the formal use of

---

13 The final syllable /se/ in São Tomé PC might perhaps be the demonstrative /se/ (< P *esse*).

14 Used alongside /bútulu/ (< P *vós outros*).

15 Should the Gulf of Guinea PC 3pl be of Bantu origin, it may have interesting implications for the settlement history of São Tomé. As mentioned in §4.12 above, there is little reason to doubt that the use of 3pl as a nominal pluraliser is of Lower Guinean origin. *If* the 3pl itself is of Bantu origin, that might be taken to suggest that the first slaves on São Tomé were Bantu, and that they introduced the 3pl into the original Pidgin, which would then, like most Pidgins, have lacked overt number marking. Later batches of speakers of Lower Guinean languages would then have introduced the pluralising function of the pronoun. The evidence in Parkvall (1999d) argues that this was not the case, and thus that the pronoun is Edo rather than Bantu.

16 With the possible exception of Mendonça's (1933:67) attestation of 3pl *osêle* (< P *os* + *ele*) in Brazilian Vernacular Portuguese. This form does not seem to have been recorded by anybody else.

2pl as 2sg in many European languages, English does not even have a distinction between 2sg and 2pl, and in spoken French, 3sg and 3pl are homophonous.[17] Yet, these forms are distinguished in most corresponding Atlantic Creoles.

There are a few exceptions, however, all of which involve the reduction of plural forms to two rather than three. For some languages, such as the Indian Ocean FCs and Northern Haiti FC, this might well be due to mere phonetic erosion,[18] but in other cases, this explanation can be excluded. The other varieties concerned are:

- Palenquero SC /enú/ can function both as 2pl and 3pl, though being somewhat archaic in the former role (Porras 1992:199; Schwegler 1991:63). Palenquero SC 3sg /ele/ also "occasionally has a third-person plural function" (Schwegler 1999:5.2.3.1).
- The Surinamese ECs may use /unu/ (or derivates thereof, such as /u ~ ũ ~ un/) both as 1pl and as 2pl (Alleyne 1980:111; Hancock 1969:60-62, 1987).
- In many varieties of Haiti FC, especially in the central parts of the country, /nũ ~ n/ does service as both 1pl and 2pl pronoun (Valdman 1978:290).

Alleyne (1980:111) uses Igbo, arguably the source of the very morpheme /unu/ to explain the Surinamese usage; according to him /unu/ may be used in both the 1pl and 2pl role in Igbo, something that is not corroborated by my sources.

As for Haiti FC, 1pl /nũ/ is of course from French *nous*. The homophonous 2pl has often been suggested to be the same Igbo /unu/ as we have already seen in several ECs. One wonders, though, why the only non-French pronoun in any Atlantic FC would be precisely the same African form that is found in so many ECs. This is certainly not impossible, but would be a quite remarkable coincidence, in particular since the adoption of this Igbo item in ECs is usually claimed to be an attempt at avoiding the homophony between 2sg and 2pl of English – homophony is precisely what borrowing of /unu/ (and subsequent reduction to /nũ/) into Haitian would create! One possibility, of course, would be that the Igbo/EC form was introduced in Haiti from Jamaica.[19] Interestingly, though, in the areas where Jamaican influence is greatest, that is in southern Haiti (Reinecke 1937:297 cited in Holm 1989:383), distinct forms for 1pl and 2pl are used (Chaudenson, Mougeon & Béniak 1993:122).

So far as I can see, the merger of the pronoun forms must therefore be due to other factors. This would be either independent development caused by reasons lost to history, or substrate influence, which in this case would mean West African languages having homophonous 1pl and 2pl forms (for the Surinam ECs and Haiti FC) or 2pl and 3pl forms (for Palenquero SC).

Languages that fit into the first category include four small Kru languages referred to by Goodman (1964:41), and the three minor Bantu languages Njebi, Mbere and Teke (Guthrie 1953:72, 75, 80).

The second category (matching Palenquero's 2pl/3pl merger) would comprise Ivorian Mande languages (Derive 1990:200) and the Wolof object and possessive forms (Sauvageot 1965:91; Gamble 1963:141). Clitic forms of 2pl and 3pl in Efik are distinguished only by tonal means (Campbell 1991:397).

To the best of my knowledge, no major West African language uses the same form for 3sg and 3pl other than marginally.

These mergers between plural pronoun forms, and the languages they appear in, both seem too marginal to claim a substrate origin for the reduction of the plural pronoun set in any Atlantic Creole.

One possibility, though, is that Ewe played a role in the shaping of the Haiti FC pronominal system. 1pl and 2pl in Ewe and Grebo are distinguished by tone, according to most descriptions

---

17 Some French dialects also use *je* for 1pl, though there seems to be no reason to suppose that such varieties were involved in Creole formation. In any case, while e.g. *je parlons* is attested, this construction seems not to cooccur with disjunctive pronominals such as *moi*, which are the only ones to have reflexes in FCs.

18 These varieties all have /zot/ for both 2pl and 3pl, derived from non-standard French *vous autres* and *eux autres* respectively.

19 A large number of slaves were taken from Jamaica to Haiti in the 17th and 18th centuries (Parkvall 1995c:83-84 and §6.3.2 below).

(Agbedor 1996:20; Duthie 1996:52; Innes 1966:13, 50-51). However, Lefebvre (1998:142) argues that although the tonal distinction is featured in most Ewe reference grammars (1pl /mǐ/ vs. 2pl /mī/), many speakers do in fact use /mí/ in both functions. Nevertheless, an argument in favour of independent development is the fact that 2pl /nu/ is unattested in Haitian prior to the 20th century (Corne 1999:144).

5.1.1.4 Numerals

Numeral systems in Atlantic Creoles present surprisingly little deviance from lexifier models, the differences in most cases being purely phonological. In the vast majority of Creoles, numerals differ only in phonetic realisation from their respective etyma, and it is rather the absence of substrate influence that strikes the observer. Features common in West Africa, such as the use of *hand* for 'five', *two hands* for 'ten', *whole person* or *person finished* for 'twenty' or Western Bantu vigesimal counting systems, are nowhere to be found and, instead, lexifier influence goes right down to the level of morphophonemic alteration, as in FCs, where French *liaison* vowels surface only when etymologically vowel-initial words follow, as in /dɛ/ 'two' ~ /dɛze/ 'two o'clock'.

Among the few exceptions are Saramaccan EC, Cameroon EC, Papiamentu SC, and conservative varieties of Guinea-Bissau PC and Gulf of Guinea PC,[20] all of which have more analytical systems where 'eleven' is something like *ten and one*, 'twelve' *ten and two*, and so on. All the above except Papiamentu SC also have similar ways of expressing tens from 20 to 90.

Although many West African languages have similar systems, this is not remarkable, since it is both cross-linguistically common,[21] and also represents precisely the tendency towards analyticity that one would expect of pidginisation.

The only spectacularly divergent exception is Angolar PC. Although its sister languages of São Tomé, Príncipe and Annobón use Portuguese numerals up to ten, and thereafter numerals based on Portuguese material, Angolar has only assimilated the Portuguese terms for 1-3, 50, 100 and 1000 (Lorenzino 1998:107).[22] As can be seen from the following table, Angolar numerals from three and onwards match those of Kimbundu so closely, that derivation from anything but Kimbundu is out of the question.

	ANGOLAR	PORTUGUESE	KIMBUNDU[23]
1	ũá	um ~ uma	moxi
2	do:θú	dois ~ duas	iari
3	te:sí	três	tatu
4	kúaná	quatro	uana
5	tanɔ́	cinco	tanu

	ANGOLAR	PORTUGUESE	KIMBUNDU
6	θámánɔ	seis	samanu
7	θambári	sete	sambuari
8	náke	oito	nake
9	úvwa	nove	ivua
10	kwín	dez	kuinii

Sources: Maurer (1992:167), Rosenfelder (n d)

Higher numerals also follow the Kimbundu pattern, with 11-19 being constructed by means of a connective /ne/ joining the units and the ten (Kimbundu has /ni/ in the same function; Lorenzino 1998:107). Up to 100, /ma/ is prefixed to the tens, just as in Kimbundu (Maia 1964:25).

5.1.1.5 Intensifying morpheme in Saramaccan EC

Saramaccan EC has an intensifying morpheme /wɛ/, which is used (a) to *"lend contrastive focus to a fronted element"*, (b) *"On the clausal level* [to] *delineate the proposition as novel information"*, and which (c) *"can replace the copula"* (McWhorter 1997b:92). While this marker has traditionally been assumed to be derived from English *well*, McWhorter (1997b:92, 139) argues that it is instead of Fon origin, given the existence of a Fon morpheme with not only the pragmatic and syntactic properties above, but also precisely the same phonetic realisation.

---

20 Sranan EC apparently once had a similar system as well (Koefoed & Tarenskeen 1996:131).

21 Note that this is historically the case for both Germanic and Romance.

22 However, this basilectal system is now being replaced by its Portuguese counterpart (Maurer 1995:47-48 cited in Bartens 1998:184).

23 For typographical reasons, the diacritics of the Kimbundu numerals were left out in the original source.

5.1.1.6 Prepositions

Thompson (1961:111) was the first to point out that a great many Creoles around the world had a preposition /na/ with a wider semantic range than most European prepositions. Prepositions phonetically close to this are found in most Atlantic ECs, PCs, in Negerhollands DC and Papiamentu SC. FCs have potentially related forms /nã/. While normally believed to ultimately stem from Portuguese *na* (< *em* + *a* 'in the [feminine]'), several substratist writers (e.g. Taylor 1971; Alleyne 1980:111; Holm 1988:207-08) have drawn attention to phonetically and semantically similar forms in West African languages. Indeed, locatives such as Bambara /-na/, Yoruba /ní/, Igbo /ní ~ nà/ and Kituba /ná/ (Houis 1980:24; Holm 1987:420; Welmers 1973:311-12, 314; Green & Igwe 1963:45; Swift & Zola 1963:34) are phonologically and semantically close, but this does not exclude other explanations. For one thing, /na/ is phonologically unmarked, and derivation from European prepositions such as English *in* (Gullah EC has the intermediate form /inə/), French *dans* or *en*, Portuguese *na* mentioned above, or Dutch *naar* are certainly not out of the question. Also, similar locatives can be found in completely unrelated languages such as Tibetan (Lyovin 1997:156).

As for the semantics, Creole /na/ cannot be said to precisely mirror any particular African language, and the semantic extension may rather be due to pidginisation - a number of representative Pidgins and Creoles outside the Atlantic group hardly use more than one single adposition, including Lower Guinean Tirailleur Pidgin French, Lingua Franca, Tok Pisin EC, several Asian PCs, Philippine SCs, Chinook Jargon and Sango (Hancock 1980:20; Koefoed 1979:50-1; Thompson 1961:112; Manessy 1994:112; Faraclas 1990:128). Nor is West Africa the only area where older languages make do with a minuscule set of locative adpositions; this also applies to languages such as Tagalog and Buginese (Campbell 1991:233, 1305).

For these reasons, Atlantic Creole /na/ cannot with any certainty be claimed to be of substratal origin.

Other prepositions may nevertheless be of African origin. Sebba (1987:50) suggests that Sranan EC /doro/, glossed as 'reach, arrive' or 'through' is derived from Twi /doro/, of which he gives no translation. Dutch *door* 'through' might also be a possible etymon, though.

A remarkably large number of Atlantic Creoles (including all FCs,[24] many ECs, Negerhollands DC and Berbice DC) have locative adpositions derived from a word meaning 'side' (*côté* in the case of FCs, *kant* in the case of DCs). Possible parallels in West Africa are Twi, in which /ŋkjéŋ/ 'side' is *"used to indicate position, location"* (Cassidy & Le Page 1967:408), and Kpelle, for which Westermann (1924:12) glosses /daː/ as both 'Rand, Ende' and 'an, bei, vor'. However, I have insufficient data to determine how widespread this multifunctionality may be.

Finally, Turner (1949:210) adduces the Gullah EC preposition /də/ 'to', and somewhat implicitly suggests Ewe /ɖə́/ 'to reach' (as used in serial verb constructions) as its etymon.

Altogether, some of the suggested African etyma of Atlantic Creole prepositions are suggestive, but none is really conclusive. I therefore abstain from drawing any conclusions from this section.

5.1.1.7 Negation in African PCs

Both mainland and insular varieties of Upper Guinea PC have a sentence negator /ka/, which has usually been thought to derive from Portuguese *nunca.* Support for this derivation is lent by the fact that Papia Kristang PC of Malaysia uses the same form although, according to Stolz (1987b:13), this is a rather late development. He instead proposes the Mandinka negative verb /ka/, and various forms thereof as the source of the Upper Guinea PC negator (pp 13-15).

The Lower Guinea PCs have, as mentioned in §4.2, a circumverbal negation strategy involving a sentence-final /fa/. The origin of this is by no means clear, but Schuchardt (1888:217) suggested derivation from P *fugir* 'to flee', in turn a calque on the optional Yoruba postverbal negative element /rárá/, said to be related to /rá/ 'to vanish'. Although this view is supported by both Boretzky (1983:102) and Stolz (1987b:14-15), I regard it as overly speculative unless alternative possibilities have been seriously considered.

---

24 As well as those spoken in the Indian Ocean.

5.1.1.8 Bound morphemes in Berbice DC

As would be expected in languages derived from Pidgins, the Atlantic Creoles are extremely poor in affixal morphology, and the few bound morphemes there are, are directly or indirectly derived from the lexifier (via grammaticalisation of erstwhile free morphemes). The exception to this rule is Berbice DC, which is not only morphologically richer endowed than other Atlantic Creoles, but in which *all* bound morphemes are derived from a single substrate language, Eastern Ijo (Kouwenberg 1994c, 1996:1351).

5.1.2 Origin of open-class items

Before going into the intricate details and problems of Atlantic Creole etymologising, it is convenient to note that two languages are exceptional as far as their vocabulary is concerned. Whereas the African lexical contribution is normally well below a tenth of the total recorded vocabulary,[25] 15-20% of the Angolar PC lexicon (23% of the Swadesh 100-item list) is estimated to be of African origin, whereas the Berbice DC lexicon is at least 20% African (Lorenzino 1998:100, 225-26; Kouwenberg 1996:1351).[26] These two varieties stand out not only through the size of the African contribution, but also by it being derived largely from one single substrate in each case – Kimbundu for Angolar PC, and Eastern Ijo for Berbice DC.

The Kimbundu impact on Angolar was first noticed and identified by Negreiros (1895).[27] Of a total of 1112 words with established etymologies, 13% are claimed to be Kimbundu by Lorenzino (1998:113).[28] As for Berbice DC, Kouwenberg (1996:1351) identifies 38% of the words on Swadesh's 100-item list as coming from Ijo (as opposed to 57% Dutch). In all, more than 180 Ijo words have been identified in Berbice DC (Anthony Grant, p c), most of which belong to relatively basic semantic domains.[29]

In the other Atlantic Creoles, however, the situation is less clear-cut. With the exception of those spoken along the African coast, every Creole-speaking territory received at least some demographic input from more or less every slave-exporting area in West Africa.

As is so often the case in substratist studies, there is a tendency for authors to find what they want to find. Cassidy & Le Page's (1967) etymological dictionary of Jamaica EC, for instance, is a milestone in Creole studies, and yet, it is clear that its authors emphasise the Akan component in its lexicon. For one thing, while Akan sources are frequently cited, almost all non-Akan etymologies in the dictionary are taken from Turner's (1949) work on Gullah EC. Furthermore, when comparing Cassidy & Le Page's proposed etymologies with suggestions advanced in other studies, the Akan bias is noticeably less.[30] Hopefully, this problem is less serious here, given the large number of sources – about 200 – used in compiling *Afrolex*. While many of these sources have their particular 'pet substrate', the combining of the data makes reliability judgements easier.

The following tables show the *approximate* distribution of Atlantic Creoles lexical Africanisms in the *Afrolex* database. To highlight the differing contributions of the major African languages,

---

25 Some estimations of the African component of various Atlantic Creoles lexicons include: Sranan EC: 2% (Voorhoeve 1973:138 cited in Holm 1989:443), Saramaccan EC: 4% (Bartens 1995:244), Nigeria EC: 12% (Mafeni 1971:105), São Tomé PC: 7% (Ferraz 1979:8) or 10% (Lorenzino 1998:225), Negerhollands DC: 5% (Josselin de Jong 1926 cited in Holm 1989:327), Papiamentu SC: 0,9% Maduro (1953:43-134 cited in Munteanu 1996:410), Palenquero SC: 3% (Bartens 1995:277, 1996:128) or 10% (Bickerton & Escalante 1970:260).

26 Robertson (1989:9) gives the even higher figure of 27,5%.

27 An even earlier observer, Greeff (1882 cited in Ferraz 1974:178) even mistook Angolar for Kimbundu.

28 As opposed to 84% Portuguese; however, given the large number of words of unknown etymology (10,8% of the total sample), the actual Portuguese contribution is smaller than this suggests. In fact, Maurer (1992:163 cited in Lorenzino 1998:15) suggests the Angolar lexicon to be only 65% Portuguese.

29 It is remarkable that the Ijo versus Dutch ratio is higher in the core than in the peripheral parts of the Berbice DC lexicon – this is quite unlike the distribution in other Creoles, and even in Angolar is Kimbundu better represented outside the Swadesh list than within it. It is similarly noteworthy that the language contains more Ijo verbs than nouns (Anthony Grant, p c). Although it is unclear what implications this has for theories of Berbice DC genesis, these two facts may indicate that the Ijo component somehow predates the Dutch one. In any case, it seems likely that the processes behind the formation of Berbice DC are in many respects fundamentally different from those that led to most other Atlantic Creoles.

30 Philip Baker (p c) suggests that this reliance on Akan may have been because Christaller's (1881) Twi dictionary was about the best there was for any West African language at the time.

the category 'other' has been deleted in the tables below. The latter category mainly includes words from Kru, Gur and Chadic, the total of which does not surpass 5% in any Creole. Major contributors are outlined in black.

English-lexicon Creoles

Sources	Leeward Islands ECs	Jamaica EC	Central American ECs	Surinam ECs	Gullah EC	Gullah EC[31]	Barbados+ Trinidad+ Guyana ECs[32]
Atlantic	8%	5%	9%	5%	13%	17%	12%
Mande	11%	9%	9%	6%	**40%**	23%	15%
Kwa	**40%**	**53%**	**41%**	**47%**	9%	12%	**27%**
Delto-Benuic	22%	17%	16%	13%	8%	10%	25%
Bantu	20%	15%	23%	28%	31%	**39%**	21%
n=	57	237	36	341	330	245	82

French-lexicon Creoles

Sources	Haiti FC	Lesser Antilles FCs	Louisiana FC	Guiana FC
Atlantic	6%	14%	17%	10%
Mande	10%	8%	28%	17%
Kwa	**45%**	22%	6%	**33%**
Delto-Benuic	11%	11%	6%	23%
Bantu	27%	**43%**	**44%**	17%
n=	203	135	13	21

Portuguese-lexicon Creoles

Sources	Annobón PC	São Tomé PC	Príncipe PC	Guinea-Bissau PC	Cape Verde PC
Atlantic	0%	3%	0%	**56%**	28%
Mande	0%	0%	2%	36%	**60%**
Kwa	0%	3%	5%	2%	2%
Delto-Benuic	**56%**	36%	**52%**	4%	2%
Bantu	39%	**56%**	40%	2%	8%
n=	16	104	51	131	86

Dutch- and Spanish-lexicon Creoles

Sources	Negerhollands DC	Papiamentu SC	Palenquero SC
Atlantic	0%	11%	2%
Mande	0%	6%	1%
Kwa	31%	**44%**	2%
Delto-Benuic	13%	6%	3%
Bantu	**52%**	33%	**92%**
n=	21	15	190

31 Excluding items used only in stories, songs and prayers, which are for the most part of Mande origin.

32 These were merged, since *Afrolex* contains so few items from Barbados EC despite this variety being central to any scenario of Creole genesis. EC appears to have been imported to Guyana and Trinidad mainly from Barbados.

5.1.2.1 Identifying the oldest stratum of African lexicon

As mentioned above, there is a general consensus on vocabulary, and in particular non-core lexicon, that it is easier to borrow than material central to the linguistic system. When examining lexical Africanisms in Atlantic Creoles, we should therefore take care not to uncritically assign major importance to a potential substrate just because it has contributed the largest number of substrate-derived vocabulary items to the Creole in question – that influence could well be post-formative. We should, however, ask ourselves if a diachronic layering can be observed. The oldest stratum (if any) should be more indicative of sub- rather than adstratal influence than would what might be more recent loans.

Given the relative scarcity of early written material on Creole languages, and the virtual non-existence of truly early documentation, it is difficult to establish which African words are the oldest. There is, however, one way in which this could be done, and that is through distributional evidence. As has already been mentioned (§1.2.2, see also chapter 6), Creoles were not necessarily born in the locations where they are presently spoken, and at least for some groups of Creoles, family trees could be established. Thus, the Gulf of Guinea PCs constitute a group of genetically related languages, as do the Upper Guinea PCs. Similarly, the Atlantic ECs and FCs seem to be related within each lexical group (for further discussion of this, see Parkvall 1999c; Baker 1987, 1999a; McWhorter 1995). Thus, words shared by several Creole within a genetic grouping may be presumed to be older than the ones which are not shared, since it would require more of a chance factor that one and the same item was borrowed independently by two different languages.

5.1.2.1.1 Portuguese-lexicon Creoles

Let us begin by having a look at the origin and distribution of the African vocabulary items in Upper Guinea PCs:[33]

Source	In any Upper Guinea PC	In Cape Verde only	On the mainland only	Shared
Mande	47%	65%	38%	54%
Atlantic	50%	28%	61%	42%
Other	3%	7%	1%	4%
n=	*210*	*74*	*116*	*20*

As can be seen, the mainland varieties (spoken in Guinea-Bissau and in the Senegalese province of Casamance) are considerably more Atlantic than are the insular varieties. This is unsurprising, given that they are still in contact with Atlantic languages, and still have the possibility of borrowing from these.

Guinea-Bissau is massively Atlantic-speaking (only about 10% of the population speak Mande languages), so we would expect the Mande component to have been imported from elsewhere (i.e. the Cape Verdes), whereas Atlantic adstrate influences would have boosted the already existing Atlantic share of the African-derived lexicon.

Moreover, the Atlantic component found in Guinea-Bissau PC, but not on the Cape Verdes consists mainly of words derived from languages such as Diola, Banyun and Manjaku, all spoken in Guinea-Bissau. The shared Atlantic component, on the other hand, derives more from geographically more distant languages, such as Wolof.

The shared items (the rightmost column) are considerably more equally distributed between the two major donor branches, and even show a slight overrepresentation of Mande. This suggests that proto-Upper Guinea PC did not arise in what is today Guinea-Bissau, *pace* Scantamburlo (1981:12), Santos (1979:22) and Naro (1978:317).

The Mande words concerned are all from languages spoken in Senegambia rather than further to the south, whereas the Atlantic influence is equally divided between the Bak, East Seneguinea and Senegambian subgroups, i.e. can be traced to Senegambia and what is today Guinea-Bissau (with the exception of one single item from Temne, spoken mainly in Sierra Leone).

---

33 Again, the etymological data used here is from the *Afrolex* database.

For the Lower Guinea PCs, this approach also proves useful, as the following table demonstrates.

African vocabulary items in the Gulf of Guinea PCs

SOURCE	IN ANY OF GULF OF GUINEA PC[34]	OCCURING IN MORE THAN ONE VARIETY
Bantu	59%	44%
Edoid	28%	33%
Yoruboid	6%	9%
Igboid	2%	7%
Others (mainly Kwa)	6%	8%
n=	102	50

While Bantu dominates in the group as a whole, Delto-Benuic languages (in particular Edo, but also Yoruba and Igbo and their respective relatives) contributed more extensively to what is assumed to be the oldest layer of Africanisms, and in fact surpass Bantu in this part of the lexicon. This could be taken to suggest that some of the Bantu influence in the Gulf of Guinea PCs is post-formative.

5.1.2.1.2 English-lexicon Creoles

Just over 80 words with relatively reliable etymologies in *Afrolex* are attested in both Surinam, the only EC-speaking territory to be cut off from contact with the others at an early date, and in at least one other Atlantic EC, something that once more suggests a certain antiquity. The origins of these items are distributed as follows:

GROUP	SHARE
Atlantic	10%
Mande	8%
Kwa	43%
Delto-Benuic	21%
Bantu	17%
n=	81

5.1.2.1.3 French-lexicon Creoles

In the Francophone Caribbean, a smaller amount of African words are shared – as commented on in Parkvall (1999c:45-46), the case for a genetic link between New World FCs is weaker than it is for New World ECs, in particular from the lexical point of view. In all, 41 African items for which reasonably plausible etymologies have been proposed are shared between Haiti FC and any of the Lesser Antilles FCs.[35] The distribution differs strikingly from that set out above for ECs:

GROUP	SHARE
Atlantic	15%
Mande	7%
Kwa	20%
Delto-Benuic	13%
Bantu	44%
n=	41

---

34 Angolar is excluded here, since it is believed to constitute a post-crystallisation partial relexification of Sãotomense (see §6.4.2). Words found only in Angolar are, not unexpectedly, Bantu..

35 The number of documented Africanisms in Louisiana FC and Guiana FC are too small to be taken into account

As can be seen, the proportion of shared Bantu items by far exceeds that found in ECs.[36] Another striking difference here is that although the Kwa component dominates the Lower Guinean share, it is Gbe languages rather than Akan languages (as opposed to the ECs) which are most prominent.[37]

The above attempt at identifying the oldest layer of lexical Africanisms cannot be carried out for the SCs and DCs, since they are not demonstrably related to anything else.[38]

5.2 Semantics

The Atlantic Creoles contain a fair number of idiomatic calques and semantic remappings of apparent African origin. Substrate influences in semantics remain a severely underexploited area of study, and the seemingly most useful paper on this subject, Huttar (1975), is unfortunately not available to me. Holm (1987) contains some interesting examples and, from descriptions of individual languages,[39] more material can be found. The most striking conclusion, from the little material I have been able to gather, is that semantic restructurings and remappings of potential relevance here appear to be of three main types.

First, the severe reduction of the Pidgin lexicon has necessitated expansion partly through the lexicalisation of semantically transparent compounds,[40] of which traces may often still be detected in since long nativised Creoles. Much of what may look African in Creole semantics may therefore well be but an indirect manifestation of former Pidginhood, which may coincide with the semantics of the input languages. Thus, the concept of 'toe' is expressed as *foot-finger* or *finger-foot* in Cameroon EC, and formerly also in Trinidad EC and Berbice DC (Winer 1993:77, 78-80; Robertson 1994:70; Todd 1982:16), but although this is also the case of an African language such as Gã (Rask 1828:30), and undoubtedly others as well, *foot-finger* is also a way of saying 'toe' that could predictably be invented on the spot by anybody not knowing any other word. The same applies to the compounds *mouth water* 'saliva' and *eye water* 'tears' (both extremely common both in Atlantic Creoles and in West African languages), and perhaps also to the charming *caca nez* 'snot', *caca yeux* 'rheum, dirt in the eyes', *caca z'oreilles* 'ear wax' and *caca les dents* 'food stuck between the teeth after a meal', found in several FCs. Of course, when both a Creole and its potential substrates display fewer divisions of a particular semantic field than does the lexifier, it is impossible to tell whether this is a reflex of pidginisation or of substrate influence. For instance, many West African languages have fewer basic colour terms than Average Western European, and although this is or has been true for some Atlantic Creoles as well, it is impossible to tell whether we are dealing with Africanisms or universals of pidginisation.

Secondly, in some cases where there is reason to suspect a true semantic Africanism, one quickly discovers that it is common to African languages throughout the once slave-exporting area. For instance, in the majority of the Atlantic Creoles, the lexifier items meaning *foot* and *hand* are extended to refer to the limbs up to the elbow and knee respectively, and sometimes even include the entire arm or leg. However, a rapid perusal of some dictionaries of West African languages quickly reveals that literally dozens of them in all the relevant areas share the same feature. Even semantic features that to the European eye seem more exotic and idiosyncratic often yield similar results. 'Ankle' is expressed as *eye of foot* not only in Haiti FC, but also in African languages ranging from Manjaku, Mankanya and Balanta to Kikongo, thus covering

36 This was also noted by Corne (1999:135), who remarked that while Martinique FC and Guadeloupe FC share 65% of the Bantu words found on either of the islands, the same is true only for a third of the African lexicon derived from other sources.

37 While the proportions of Gbe vis-à-vis Akan is relatively similar in Lesser Antilles FCs as in the lexicon shared by these varieties and Haiti FC, the Kwa component in Haiti FC is massively Gbe. This, I believe, suggests that the Gbe material in Haiti FC is later than the Akan material.

38 Though relatedness within these two groups has been suggested as well (Bickerton & Escalante 1970:263; Parkvall 1999c:51-2).

39 Alleyne (1980:115-6), Bartens (1996:129-130), Cassidy & Le Page (1967), Dalphinis (1985:108), Ferraz (1979:101-02), Hancock (1980:81), Holm & Shilling (1982), Todd (1982), Meintel (1975:239-41), Boretzky (1983:288-89) and Taylor (1977:159) may be mentioned as particularly useful sources.

40 On this subject, see for instance Cassidy (1971:215-16), Hancock (1996:24-25), Holm (1989:574), Mühlhäusler (1997:137), van der Voort (1997:385).

much of the entire West African coast.[41] Similarly, the compound *day clean* for 'dawn', found in most Atlantic ECs, and at least Lesser Antillean FC, may seem odd to a European, but is paralleled in at least Wolof, Malinke, Yoruba and Bantu languages such as Luba, together representing almost the entire stretch of coast from which Africans were transported to the New World. As in so many other cases, it is difficult to avoid the feeling that many a researcher who knows beforehand what substratal influences he wants to find, is content when having found a pan-African feature in his pet substrate, disregarding the fact that the feature in question is an areal one.

Finally, in the few cases where a truly idiosyncratic calque can be identified with reasonable certainty, it is usually confined to the Creoles still in contact with African languages, such as Krio EC, Cameroon EC, Nigeria EC or Guinea-Bissau PC (see e.g. Fyle & Jones 1980 and Rougé 1988 for copious examples).

In addition, there are the cases where a European word with little relevance in Africa or in the Americas gets remapped on the semantics of a phenomenon unknown in Europe. Thus, the reflex of Portuguese *lobo* in Guinea-Bissau PC means 'hyena' rather than 'wolf'. This, too, must be regarded as rather trivial.

Although semantics and idiomatic expressions might be a promising area in which to look for specific substrate influences, examining the material available to me was not particularly rewarding. To be sure, probable substrate retentions can be detected, but can usually not be associated with any particular area. I therefore abstain from drawing any conclusions from the semantic evidence.

41 Incidentally also in Asian PC and their substrates (Hancock 1980:81; Clements 1996:11).

Summary of chapter 5

AREA	FEATURE	LANGUAGE	GROUP	SUGGESTED SUBSTRATE INFLUENCE
Core lexicon	1sg	Upper Guinea PC	PC	(+Balanta, +Mandinka)
Core lexicon	1sg	Lower Guinea PC	PC	(+Ewe, +Gã, +Efik, +Igbo, +Tiv, +Yoruba, +Kikongo)
Core lexicon	2pl	Gullah EC	EC	+Igbo
Core lexicon	2pl	Western Caribbean ECs	EC	+Igbo
Core lexicon	2pl	Barbados EC	EC	+Igbo
Core lexicon	2pl	Surinamese ECs	EC	+Igbo
Core lexicon	2pl	West Africa EC	EC	+Igbo
Core lexicon	2pl	São Tomé PC, Príncipe PC	PC	+Umbundu, +Kimbundu
Core lexicon	2pl	Príncipe PC	PC	+Edo
Core lexicon	2pl:IMPERATIVE	Palenquero SC	SC	+Kikongo
Core lexicon	2pl=1pl	Haiti FC (central dialect)[42]	FC	+Ewe
Core lexicon	2sg	Western Caribbean ECs	EC	+Igbo
Core lexicon	2sg	Surinamese ECs	EC	+Igbo
Core lexicon	3pl	São Tomé PC, Príncipe PC, Annobón PC	PC	+Edo, +Kimbundu
Core lexicon	3pl	Angolar PC	PC	+Kikongo, +Kimbundu
Core lexicon	3pl	Berbice DC	DC	+Ijo
Core lexicon	3pl	Papiamentu SC	SC	+Wolof, +Edo
Core lexicon	3pl	Palenquero SC	SC	+Kikongo, +Kimbundu, +Chokwe
Core lexicon	3sg	Berbice DC	DC	+Ijo
Core lexicon	All bound morphemes	Berbice DC	DC	+Ijo
Core lexicon	Generic/impersonal pronoun	Gulf of Guinea PCs	PC	+Edo, +Wano, +Igbo, +Izi, +Yoruba
Core lexicon	Intensifying morpheme	Saramaccan EC	EC	+Fon
Core lexicon	Interrogatives	Saramaccan EC	EC	+Fon
Core lexicon	Interrogatives	Angolar PC	PC	+Kimbundu
Core lexicon	Interrogatives	Berbice DC	DC	+Ijo
Core lexicon	Most numerals	Angolar PC	PC	+Kimbundu
Core lexicon	Pluraliser	Berbice DC	DC	+Ijo
Core lexicon	Pluraliser	Palenquero SC	SC	+Bantu
Core lexicon	Sentence negation	Upper Guinea PCs	PC	(+Mandinka)
Lexicon	Exceptionally high number of basic vocabulary items	Angolar PC	PC	+Kimbundu
Lexicon	Exceptionally high number of basic vocabulary items	Berbice DC	DC	+Ijo
Lexicon	Lexicon (in descending order)	Gullah EC	EC	Mande/Bantu[43], Atlantic
Lexicon	Lexicon (in descending order)	Western Caribbean ECs	EC	Kwa, Delto-Benuic, Bantu
Lexicon	Lexicon (in descending order)	Leewards Islands ECs	EC	Kwa, Delto-Benuic, Bantu
Lexicon	Lexicon (in descending order)	Barbados EC	EC	Kwa/Delto-Benuic, Bantu
Lexicon	Lexicon (in descending order)	Surinam ECs	EC	Kwa, Bantu, Delto-Benuic
Lexicon	Lexicon (in descending order)	Negerhollands DC	DC	Bantu, Kwa, Delto-Benuic
Lexicon	Lexicon (in descending order)	Louisiana FC	FC	Bantu, Mande, Atlantic
Lexicon	Lexicon (in descending order)	Haiti FC	FC	Kwa (mostly Gbe), Bantu, Delto-Benuic
Lexicon	Lexicon (in descending order)	Lesser Antilles FCs	FC	Bantu, Kwa, Atlantic
Lexicon	Lexicon (in descending order)	Guiana FC	FC	Kwa, Delto-Benuic, Bantu/Mande
Lexicon	Lexicon (in descending order)	Cape Verde PC	PC	Mande, Atlantic
Lexicon	Lexicon (in descending order)	Guinea-Bissau PC	PC	Atlantic, Mande
Lexicon	Lexicon (in descending order)	São Tomé PC	PC	Bantu, Delto-Benuic
Lexicon	Lexicon (in descending order)	Príncipe PC	PC	Delto-Benuic, Bantu
Lexicon	Lexicon (in descending order)	Annobón PC	PC	Delto-Benuic, Bantu
Lexicon	Lexicon (in descending order)	Papiamentu SC	SC	Kwa, Bantu, Atlantic
Lexicon	Lexicon (in descending order)	Palenquero SC	SC	Bantu
Lexicon	Oldest lexical stratum	ECs	EC	10% Atlantic, 8% Mande, 43% Kwa (mostly Akan), 21% Delto-Benuic, 17% Bantu
Lexicon	Oldest lexical stratum	FCs	FC	15% Atlantic, 7% Mande, 20% Kwa (mostly Gbe), 13% Delto-Benuic, 44% Bantu
Lexicon	Oldest lexical stratum	Upper Guinea PC	PC	54% Mande, 42% Atlantic
Lexicon	Oldest lexical stratum	Gulf of Guinea PC	PC	49% Delto-Benuic, 44% Bantu

42 While all varieties of Haiti FC have 2pl /nu/, the extension of this to the 3pl seems to be an innovation of the central dialect area, both the northern and southern dialects having /zot/ in this role (Valdman 1978:205; Corne 1999:144).

43 Depending on whether the (mainly Mande) words "used only in stories, songs and prayers" are included or not.

Chapter 6

Demographic data

I will refrain from going into much detail here, but in Parkvall (1999c) I gave some reasons for seeing many of the Atlantic Creoles not as local developments, arguing that the number of Creole geneses in the Atlantic was more limited than is often – implicitly or explicitly – claimed, and that many varieties are just offshoots of other Creoles (or their Pidgin ancestors). Similar claims have been made for Atlantic ECs by McWhorter (1995) and Baker (1999a).

Genetic relationships between languages are often subject to debate, but are even more difficult to define when it comes to Creoles; traditional *Stammbaum* theories deal with mother-daughter relations between languages, but an emerging Pidgin is not yet a language. Given that whatever was transported from one location to another may have been relatively unstable, genetic relationships might still be controversial even if we had a complete historical record of population movements and ideal linguistic data.

As a consequence of this, I have chosen to not to attempt to account for slave importations in every single Creole-speaking area but, rather, to limit myself to those which were the centres of diffusion into other colonies.

For all the colonies considered here, I have only taken imports prior to 1750 into consideration, since I believe that all Atlantic plantation Creoles had basically crystallised by then. The oldest colonies had by then been settled for more than 250 years, and many of those in the Caribbean for well over a century, and there must have been considerable numbers of native speakers likely to keep the language relatively stable despite the influx of new arrivals from Africa.[1]

Shortly before the completion of this thesis, the long awaited Eltis et al. (1999) was finally published. Intended to be the definitive resource of slave trade data, it unfortunately proved to be somewhat disappointing for present purposes for a variety of reasons. Not only is there an emphasis on 18th and 19th century voyages – which is understandable, given that the quality of historical documentation improves the closer one gets to present time – but there is also a focus on trade conducted by the country which "owned" the colony into which slaves were importated. Regardless of the data presented in Eltis et al. (1999), where importation to e.g. English colonies was undertaken almost exclusively by English slavers, slave trade historians seem to agree that the Portuguese and the Dutch (as repeatedly pointed out in the following) were in fact the major suppliers to St Kitts and Barbados in the early days. Even more serious is the fact that shipments documented in other sources that I have consulted are simply mysteriously missing from Eltis et al.'s CD-ROM.[2] Despite its obvious usefulness, Eltis et al. (1999) thus nevertheless needs to be complemented by other sources.

6.1 The Transatlantic slave trade

The slave trade followed as a natural consequence of Portuguese overseas expansion, which in turn was a direct continuation of the reconquest of their home country from the Moors. Portuguese expeditions gradually ventured further and further down the African coast, until they

1 Children made up well over a third of the slave population on many of the Lesser Antilles long before the end of the 17th century (Ly 1955:49, 51; Peytraud 1897:137; Beckles 1990:51), and even in colonies with exceptionally high levels of slave exploitation and mortality (something that usually coincides with lower birth rates), such as Haiti and the Guyanas, there was nevertheless already quite a substantial proportion of children by the early 1700s (Peytraud 1897:137; Singler 1993c:250, 1994; Bickerton 1993; Postma 1990:185).

2 This is even more noteworthy, given that I drew the attention of the editors to some of these sources prior to its publication, but without receiving any reply.

eventually rounded the Cape of Good Hope and reached India. By this time, they had established several trading posts along the African coast, as well as colonies on the various islands off its coast that they had discovered along the way. African slave labour was used extensively on Madeira as well as on the Azores, the Canary Islands and in Portugal itself, but there is no evidence for any Creole languages ever having developed there. As we know, however, the more southerly Cape Verde and Gulf of Guinea islands became, and still are, Creole-speaking, and Pidgin Portuguese was used all along the African coast (as well as in Asia).

The Transatlantic slave trade began almost immediately after Columbus' voyages to the Americas. In the early days, however, only one nation was involved, namely Portugal. In the treaty of Tordesillas of 1493, a papal bull divided the world into a western (New World minus Brazil) and an eastern (Old World) zone, and proclaimed the former to be Spain's sphere of influence and the latter to be Portugal's. For this reason, Spain was not allowed to procure slaves in Africa, and had to rely on Portuguese shipping for her needs. At this time, Upper Guinea was the prime supplier of slaves, but the trade in Lower Guinea and in Bantu-speaking areas developed quickly, and the dominance of Upper Guinea was rather abruptly followed by an equally near-total dominance of Buntu from about 1615 (Curtin 1969:104).

By the eve of the 17th century, the Netherlands had broken loose from a considerably weakened Spain, and began to engage in colonial expansion. This expansion, however, did not so much involve overseas settlement (which in part explains the scarcity of Dutch-based Creoles) as trade. Since Portugal was part of the Spanish realm between 1580 and 1640, the Dutch interfered not only with Spanish shipping, but also attacked Portuguese trading posts in Africa and Asia with considerable success. They even conquered and briefly held some of the Portuguese plantation colonies in Brazil. Thus, for a brief but, from our point of view, exceptionally important period, the Netherlands was the world's major slaving nation.

At about the same time, at the beginning of the 17th century, the two countries that were to become the dominant powers in the Atlantic area, England and France, entered the scene. They both established their first plantation colonies in the 1620s, and after having bought or stolen slaves from the Portuguese, Spanish or Dutch, they gradually started to develop trades of their own.

For all Creoles under discussion here, with the exception of the African PCs and Palenquero SC which are likely to have developed (or at least *may* have developed) in the 16th century, it is the period from the 1620s that is of interest to us. While the slave trade of the 18th and 19th centuries is rather well documented, there is a major problem in that any account of the 17th century slave trade will have to rely heavily on guesstimates. What we do have from the earliest days is evidence of tendencies rather than concrete data. As mentioned above, we know that the Portuguese slave trade shifted from Upper Guinea to Buntu around 1615. We also know that the Dutch conquered most of the Portuguese installations in Lower Guinea and some of those in Buntu in the 1630s, but that the latter were later reconquered. Other crucial events (as will be seen) include the conquest of Brazil by the Dutch (which forced the latter to develop their own slave trade), and its recapture by the Portuguese (which forced the Dutch to seek other markets).

As noted above, the Spanish conducted no slaving (until the late 18th century). The Dutch, on the other hand, being more interested in trade than in colonisation, had a constant over-capacity. The British and the Portuguese were largely self-sufficient, but often had a surplus to offer others,[3] while the French usually only managed to supply part of the number of slaves needed in their own colonies. Regardless of this, all nations bought or stole slaves from one another, so that there is absolutely no guarantee that a batch of slaves bought and transported by one nation ended up in plantation colonies controlled by that same nation. This is a major problem since the trade, despite all the lacking data, is in general far better documented than the ethnolinguistic composition of the plantation workforces themselves.

Although we have some idea of who bought from whom, two other conduits are far more difficult to explore, namely theft and smuggling. The mercantilist European governments usually issued concessions on colonial trade to various trading companies which monopolised trade with

3 This also applied to other slave-trading nations with few or no plantation colonies, mainly Denmark, Sweden, Brandenburg and Courland, but the impact of these countries on the formation of Creole languages (with the exception of the Danish and Brandenburgian deliveries to the Virgin Islands) must have been negligible.

specific colonies. It goes without saying that this created a paradise for smugglers, particularly since taxes were high and demand almost constantly outstripped supplies.

Some extreme cases of this include the Spanish Caribbean, into which two thirds of all slaves had been taken illicitly in the 1540s (Rout 1976:63). During the boom years towards the end of the 18th century, a third of the slaves imported into the British West Indies is believed to have ended up in Haiti (Spears 1993:164; Sheridan 1974:319). Even in the early days, 29% of the British West Indian imports are said to have entered the colonies illegally (Curtin 1969:54).

6.1.1 Theft and conquest of slaves

Since an almost constant state of war reigned between the European colonisers, islands were frequently attacked by hostile forces, which sometimes conquered the entire island and/or carried off significant numbers of slaves.

Large numbers of slaves, sometimes several thousand, were thus taken from one island to another and, in some cases, these made up a significant proportion of the slave population in their new country. Wherever appropriate, reference to documented thefts of slaves will be made below.

There are thus severe difficulties in estimating the ethnolinguistic composition of the slaves in the colonies where Creole languages are believed to have arisen. Nevertheless, what follows is an attempt at doing this.

6.1.2 Trading areas in Africa

The first important thing to note is that the geographical distribution of languages in West Africa is not radically different today from the 17th century situation. Hair (1967:247) talks about *"a striking continuity"* and concludes that *"the ethnolinguistic units of the Guinea coast have remained very much the same for three, four or five centuries"*. Similarly, Manning (1982:24) points out that *"the geographic location of the population has been extremely stable"*.

Although all languages change through time, there is no reason to assume that the relevant West African languages have changed more during these centuries than have the West European ones. Comparative evidence, as well as the few textual sources that exist, confirm this.

Both from the typological and the geolinguistic point of view, we can thus accept the ethnolinguistic distribution of the population in West Africa today as a reasonable approximation of the situation in 17th century West Africa when it supplied slaves to plantations in the Caribbean.

As the slave trade developed, its victims were drawn from areas further and further inland, so that Loango in the 18th century delivered slaves from as far away as 600 km. In the early days, however, a radius of about 80 km would seem to cover all the ethnic groups represented on the American plantations. For the period that interests us the most, i.e. the 17th century, most observers seem to agree that slaves rarely originated from places more distant from the coast than 200 km, and only occasionally from as far away as 300 km inland (Curtin 1969:102, 201-02; Manning 1982:32, 1990:62-70; Morton-Williams 1964; Patterson 1967:126; Peukert 1978:61-70, 289-99).

This map shows the extent of the 200 and 300 km zones referred to above. Note that this is a simplifying generalisation – areas such as the Ivory Coast and Cameroon were less affected by slave trade than most other parts of the West African coast Also, along major rivers – in particular the Senegal and the Congo, trade reached further inland than it did elsewhere.

For reasons of graphic reproduction, the map is compressed along the Y-axis.

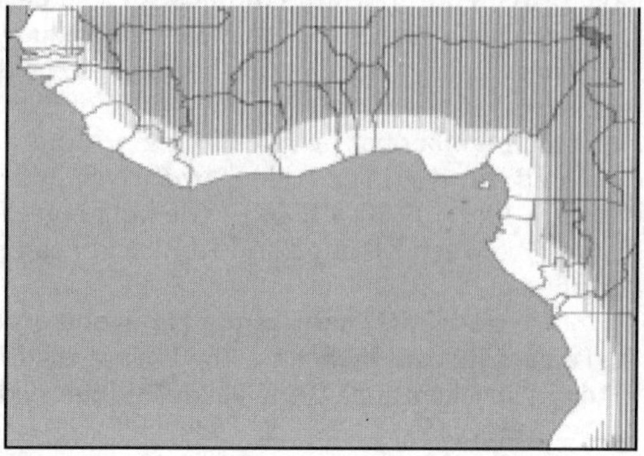

Most of those sold into servitude were prisoners of war, or (more rarely) political prisoners and criminals. For this reason, of course, the ethnolinguistic composition of New World slaves depended heavily of political conditions in, and warfare between, West African nations.

We do have some knowledge of the conditions in the African trading posts, but unfortunately not enough to determine the extent of exposure to European languages there prior to shipment. It has been suggested, however, that this is indeed where Caribbean Creoles began to form (see Parkvall 1995c and McWhorter 1995 and the references cited therein). Regardless of this, it is of potential importance that some slaves might have had some command of Pidgin Portuguese, the common trade language along the coast prior to departure from Africa. Some may also have spoken an indigenous lingua franca apart from their native tongue. Such means of interethnic communication may have included Wolof for the Senegalese, Yoruba or some Gbe language for people from the Slave Coast, and Kikongo or Kimbundu for Bantus. The impact of such linguistic skills, however, can hardly be determined.

Six areas of exportation supplied the bulk of all slaves in the relevant period. ***Senegambia*** was the first part of sub-Saharan Africa to come into contact with Europeans. Shipped from here were speakers of Atlantic languages, such as Wolof, Fulfulde, Temne, Limba, Serer, Kisi, Sherbro and Manjaku, and Mande languages such as Bambara, Malinke, Mandinka, Dyula and Kpelle, most of the latter group being closely related almost to the point of inter-intelligibility. It could be also be significant that Mande and Atlantic are in many ways the typological mirror images of one another. Purely speculatively, this may have neutralised some of the potential for Senegambian languages to leave their mark on embryonic Creoles.

South of Senegambia are the ***Rivers of Guinea*** and ***Sierra Leone***, whose inhabitants also spoke languages of the Atlantic and Mande families.

Between Upper Guinea proper and Lower Guinea is the ***Windward Coast*** (also known as the ***Pepper Coast*** or ***Malguetta Coast***), from which relatively few slaves were sold. For this reason, we would not expect the languages spoken here – mostly belonging to the Kru group – to have had much of an impact on Atlantic Creole formation.

While the ***Ivory Coast*** was virtually unexploited by slave traders, the ***Gold Coast*** was for some years the prime supplier to Transatlantic plantations. Here, Kwa languages/dialects of the Akan cluster (Asante, Twi, Fante) dominate.

Slightly further to the east, the aptly named ***Slave Coast*** or ***Bight of Benin*** area furnished slaves speaking, on the one hand, Kwa languages of the Gbe group (Ewe and Fon being major representatives) and, on the other, Delto-Benuic languages such as Yoruba. Before 1730, Slave Coast exports were almost all Ajas, i.e. speakers of Gbe languages. Interestingly, Yorubas, whose language is often used as evidence in substratist discussions, were hardly represented at all before the 1740s.[4] The presence of Nupe-speakers began to be reported at about the same time, followed by that of non-Delto-Benuic languages such as Hausa towards the end of the 18th century (Manning 1982:9, 335-37, 1990:67, 250). Although related to Kwa (and indeed formerly included in this group), the Delto-Benuic languages are not anywhere near mutually intelligible with these, but there are a great many typological similarities.

To the east again of the Slave Coast is ***Biafra***, including the delta of the Niger. Biafra seems to have been less important a supplier than most in terms of volume, but nevertheless appears to have provided important colonies such as Berbice, St Kitts and São Tomé with crucial early contingents of speakers of Delto-Benuic languages such as Igbo, Ijo and Edo.

Buntu, finally, chiefly supplied slaves speaking the closely related Kikongo and Kimbundu languages. In the vicinity of the mouth of the Congo, the Portuguese in the early 1500s mainly exported members of peoples living around the Malembo Pool, but from the 1530s, the trade expanded further inland along the river and southward towards the area around Luanda (Thomas 1997:109-10, 130-32). The languages concerned are relatively closely related, and the distance between Kikongo and Kimbundu can be said to be similar to that between Spanish and Portuguese.

Slave trade historians Linda Heywood and John Thornton (p c) estimate that exports from this area between 1615 and 1640 were made up of roughly 45% Kimbundu-speakers, 25% Kikongo-speakers and 30% speakers of intermediate languages.

---

4 Many of the Ewe, however, spoke Yoruba as a second language (Speedy 1994:83).

6.2 English Creoles

Until the beginning of the 1660s, the majority of slaves in Barbados, the most important English plantation colony, were supplied by Dutch traders (Handler & Lange 1978:25; Watts 1987:203; Emmer 1991:85). The reason for this was the fall of Dutch Brazil, which deprived the Dutch of much of their slave market. Since they still controlled much of the trade on the West African coast, the Dutch were forced to sell their slaves at a loss to other colonial powers (Batie 1991:47). In addition, they were at the time the only European power with a well-developed commercial infrastructure in West Africa. Later on, however, the English became not only self-sufficient, but also supplied the French and Spanish colonies with numerous slaves.

6.2.1 Gullah

Curtin (1969:157) provides a regional breakdown for slaves imported into the Carolinas between 1733 and 1807. However, the latter post-dates the initial settlement by almost a century and a half, and Curtin's numbers also exclude imports from the Caribbean, whereas a majority of the slaves in the 17th century were from Barbados alone (Rickford 1997:3; Holm 1986a:9, 1989:492; Mufwene & Gilman 1987:123). In addition to these settlers, and immigration from Virginia and Bermuda (Wilkinson 1933:334-35; Holm 1989:492) – where no Creole has ever been attested – Baker (1999a:340) documents settlers from the Leeward Islands, and he furthermore demonstrates that Gullah has strong similarities to both of these varieties. Since the Leewards and Barbados appear to have provided the main demographic (and presumably also linguistic) input to Gullah in the early years, and for want of detailed import figures from Africa, it seems likely that early Gullah must essentially have been an offshoot of Eastern Caribbean EC.

Curtin's figures thus refer only to the period during which Africa was the main source of slaves, and although most of the structure of Gullah must have been fixed by the time of their arrival, the regional origins of these slaves may lie behind some of the subsequent divergence between Gullah and Eastern Caribbean EC.

Imports to the Gullah-speaking area, 1733-1807

Senegambia	20%
Sierra Leone	7%
Windward Coast	16%
Gold Coast	13%
Slave Coast	2%
Biafra	2%
Angola	40%
Mozambique and Madagascar	1%

Source: Curtin 1969:157

Eltis et al. (1999) give details for about 85 ships delivering slaves to the Carolinas and Georgia, though unfortunately none from before 1710. As we shall see, the ethnic distribution is noticeably different from that of other colonies in the high reliance on Senegambia and the minor contribution from the Gold and Slave Coasts.

	Senegambia	Windward Coast	Gold Coast	Slave Coast	Biafra	Buntu
1710s	28%	0%	44%	0%	28%	0%
1720s	100%	0%	0%	0%	0%	0%
1730s	20%	2%	4%	0%	10%	65%
1740s	33%	2%	9%	0%	33%	22%

6.2.2 Jamaica and the Western Caribbean

It would seem that the Western Caribbean ECs (Belize EC and Miskito Coast EC) are in essence offshoots of early Jamaica EC (or 19th century Jamaican in the case of the varieties spoken in Costa Rica and Panama).[5]

Jamaica was conquered by the English in 1655. The force included 1 000 Leeward islanders and 2 811 Barbadians, many of whom afterwards settled permanently on Jamaica, and they were followed by more settlers from Barbados, Nevis and Bermuda (Le Page 1960:10; Sheridan 1974:93, 95, 211; Holm 1986a:9). Since most of these early immigrants, many of whom in any case died shortly after arrival, were unemployed and landless whites, it is unlikely that they would have brought many slaves.

About 400 slaves (possibly making up as much as half of the Jamaican slave population at the time) were captured on the Dutch Leeward islands of St Eustatius and Saba in 1665 and taken to Jamaica (Goslinga 1971:390, 1979:39).[6]

After the Dutch take-over of Surinam, several hundred English and Jewish planters emigrated from there to Jamaica between 1668 and 1680 (mainly 1671-75). In all, they were accompanied by at least 1 000, and perhaps as many as 1 500 slaves (Hancock 1969:14; Sheridan 1974:211, 367; Arends 1995:236; Cassidy 1971:220; Le Page 1960:17). Surinamese slaves would thus have made up a tenth of the total slave population in the island. Baker (1999a:337) allows one to conclude that they left a clear linguistic imprint, particularly on the Maroon Spirit Language (Bilby 1983, 1992) which, although now reserved for ritual purposes, may have been the everyday language of at least some segments of the Jamaican rural population. Despite the Surinamese slaves only having made up 10% of the island total, it is remarkable that they apparently had an disproportionate linguistic impact on the local speech forms - Jamaican is far closer to the Surinamese ECs than to Barbadian according to Baker's (1999a:337) calculations. A possible explanation is that whereas Barbadians, Kittitians and Bermudians settling in Jamaica emigrated precisely because they lacked the means (including slaves) to subsist in their home islands, the Surinamese planters - who emigrated for political reasons - were major slaveowners. It could also be that the English-lexicon contact language of Surinam had developed more rapidly than those of St Kitts or Barbados because of the higher proportion of slaves the former.

The 1670s also saw an increase in slave imports from Africa; about 1 000 a year arrived in the 1670s (at a time when the total slave population was about 10 000), and annual imports rose to 3 674 in the following decade (Sheridan 1974:211). From about 1670, slaves made up a majority of the Jamaican population, and the number of slaves doubled between 1680 and 1690 (from 15 000 to 30 000; Dunn 1972:312).

Until 1674, Barbados is estimated to have delivered a third of all Jamaican slaves, and for the rest of the 17th century about a fourth (Curtin 1969:58).[7] Most of the remainder must be presumed to have arrived from Africa, most of whom would probably have been supplied by the Royal African Company (Le Page 1960:61).

The following table is Curtin's (1969:160) "speculative approximation" of Jamaican slave imports during the first century of settlement.

---

5 A possible exception is the EC of San Andrés and Providencia, which presents some peculiarities that may have a local origin (such as frequent denasalisation, habitual marker *study*, past marker *went*). This, together with the fact that the two islands were the first English settlements in the Western Caribbean (and indeed, colonisation post-dated that of St Kitts and Barbados by only a few years) suggests that role of San Andrés and Providencia as a centre of diffusion of EC may be seriously underestimated, and this is clearly a matter that calls for further research. I have no data on slave imports to San Andrés and Providencia, and it is likely that most of their slaves were brought in from elsewhere in the Caribbean. Immigration of Englishmen (with or without slaves) is attested from Bermuda, Jamaica, St Kitts, the Miskito Coast (Holm 1986a:6; Batie 1991:43; Washabaugh 1986:157).

6 There has been speculation (e.g. Goodman 1985) that a DC was spoken on St Eustatius and Saba at the time, but the absence of Dutch influences in Jamaica EC makes this less likely.

7 This would have led to less (but still significant) Biafran dominance in the 1660s than is suggested by the table derived from Eltis et al. (1999) below and, for the 1670s, a more even balance between the Gold and Slave Coasts.

	1655-1701	1702-25	1726-50	1764-88[8]
Senegambia	5%	11%	7%	2%
Sierra Leone	1%	7%	7%	0%
Windward Coast	13%	8%	9%	8%
Gold Coast	6%	35%	27%	42%
Slave Coast	28%	31%	13%	12%
Biafra	8%	2%	22%	30%
Buntu	40%	8%	14%	6%
Unknown & other	0%	0%	1%	0%

After the English conquest of Jamaica in 1655, slaves were almost exclusively taken there on board English ships, apart from some deliveries by the Dutch in the 17th century, and the occasional arrivals of French slavers in the 18th century. Although maroons are said to have been left behind by the Spanish, there is nothing to suggest that the English "inherited" plantation slaves from the island's former owners.

Only one shipment is documented for the 1650s. That decade is therefore excluded in the table below, which – based on Eltis et al. (1999) – shows slave deliveries to Jamaica by decade.

	SENE-GAMBIA	SIERRA LEONE	WINDWARD COAST	GOLD COAST	SLAVE COAST	BIAFRA	BUNTU	EAST AFRICA
1660s	0%	0%	0%	0%	18%	71%	10%	0%
1670s	5%	0%	0%	43%	14%	25%	10%	5%
1680s	4%	1%	0%	4%	41%	15%	32%	2%
1690s	22%	6%	0%	4%	23%	15%	30%	0%
1700s	6%	0%	0%	51%	25%	7%	10%	0%
1710s	1%	1%	1%	58%	33%	1%	3%	1%
1720s	15%	1%	4%	37%	22%	5%	17%	0%
1730s	5%	16%	5%	19%	5%	21%	29%	0%
1740s	5%	2%	4%	28%	2%	39%	20%	0%

It has repeatedly been pointed out in the linguistic literature (e.g. Alleyne 1993) that Twi was the dominant substrate component in the genesis of Jamaican. As can be seen in the figures above, Gold Coast slaves were indeed the biggest single group through parts of the island's history, although there can hardly have been an absolute dominance of Akan people at any time. Many an observer has therefore suggested that the Akan dominance would have been more cultural than numerical. Patterson (1973:30-31) does not support this however – he characterises the Akan in Jamaica as keeping to themselves, and not being very popular among their colleagues in misfortune.

6.2.3 Leeward Islands

St Kitts was not only the first English colony in the Leeward group, but also in the entire Caribbean, and most of the other Leewards were settled from there, with the partial exception being Antigua, which, although initially settled from St Kitts, received a great number of immigrants from Barbados and Surinam (Sheridan 1974:185, 191; Watts 1987:216, 376).[9] The only estimate of the geographic origins of early slaves on St Kitts is Parkvall (1999b:70), reproduced overleaf in slightly modified form.

8 The last column is based on a sample of 34 010 slaves, taken from *African origins of some Jamaican slaves (1764-88): Regional origins of slaves bought by four Jamaican brokerage firms, 1764-88*, (Downloaded 1998-02-16 from <www.whc.neu.edu/prototype/Dbases/br3e1_2d.html .>.)

9 In Baker's (1999a:337) quantitative measurements, Antiguan is about as similar to Kittitian as to Barbadian, but rather unlike the Surinamese ECs.

PERIOD	SENEGAMBIA + SIERRA LEONE	WINDWARD COAST	GOLD COAST	SLAVE COAST	BIAFRA	BUNTU
1620s	1%	0%	1%	1%	1%	96%
1630s	3%	0%	3%	18%	6%	71%
1640s	5%	0%	5%	35%	10%	45%
1650s	5%	0%	20%	30%	10%	35%
1660s	3%	0%	13%	25%	55%	5%
1670s	3%	0%	34%	21%	34%	8%
1680s	11%	14%	15%	27%	11%	21%
1690s	13%	19%	20%	25%	8%	14%
1700s	4%	2%	68%	18%	9%	0%
1710s	17%	0%	23%	13%	37%	10%
1720s	3%	0%	36%	50%	11%	0%
1730s	0%	0%	22%	0%	61%	17%
1740s	0%	0%	6%	9%	53%	32%

The method used in calculating the above consisted of assuming Portugal to have delivered all the slaves to St Kitts during the 1620s and half of those imported in the 1630s. The Dutch were credited with having provided half of all slaves arriving in the 1630s, and all those who came in the 1640s and 1650s, after which the English trade became dominant (see Parkvall 1999b for details). Combining these assumptions with data on the Dutch and Portuguese trading habits (Postma 1990:112, 298; Curtin 1969:104) permits a speculative reconstruction of slave ethnicities on St Kitts.

The changes here with regard to the table in Parkvall (1999b) consist in replacing Le Page's (1960:75) rough estimate for the 1660s and 1670s English trade with data on documented expeditions in Eltis et al. (1999). For the English trade of the following two decades, there is a great discrepancy between the estimate of Curtin (1969:121, 129) and the data in Eltis et al. (1999). I do not know why this is so, and I have here simply used average figures intermediate between those of Curtin and Eltis et al. Linda Heywood & John Thornton's (p c) comment that virtually all Dutch exports from Lower Guinea 1637-55 consisted of Gbe-speakers (and that Gold Coast slaves became numerous only thereafter) has also been taken into account. For the 18th century, finally, I have relied on actual shipping figures, based on Eltis et al. (1999). Only for the 1740s is the number of ships therein enough to draw any conclusions for St Kitts alone. For the 1700s to the 1730s, shipping to all the English Leeward islands[10] is therefore used as an approximation.

Eltis et al. (1999) is only moderately useful for the early days, since it includes a mere handful of deliveries to St Kitts from before 1700. If we again combine the numbers for all the English Leeward Islands, we get a picture which is relatively similar to the one just presented, with the exception that the figures for Lower Guinea are consistently somewhat higher, at the expense of those for Upper Guinea. This source also enables differentiation between the various sources within Lower Guinea. Somewhat surprisingly, Biafra was the dominant supplier for most of the time (suggesting languages such as Ijo, Igbo, Efik and Edo), mainly interrupted by a Gold Coast dominance in the 1690s and 1700s.

6.2.4 Barbados and the Windward islands

For Barbados, too, demographic data are scarce, and for the early years, only a reconstruction similar to that for St Kitts above can be made.

The number of ships documented before 1660 by Eltis et al. (1999) is so small, and many of them in any case lack information on the African origin of the slaves, that this source cannot be used for the early deliveries. Since nothing indicates that St Kitts and Barbados had different trading practices, I have combined an estimate of the kind presented for St Kitts above for the years before 1660 with the data from Eltis et al. (1999) for the years thereafter. The few mentions there are of the ethnic compositions of the servile work force in Barbados (Handler & Lange 1978:26; Beckles 1990:32) are compatible with this reconstruction.

10 St Kitts, Nevis, Montserrat, the British Virgin Islands, Antigua and Anguilla.

PERIOD	SENEGAMBIA + SIERRA LEONE	WINDWARD COAST	GOLD COAST	SLAVE COAST	BIAFRA	BUNTU
1620s	1%	0%	1%	1%	1%	96%
1630s	3%	0%	3%	18%	6%	71%
1640s	5%	0%	5%	35%	10%	45%
1650s	5%	0%	20%	30%	10%	35%
1660s	3%	0%	18%	29%	48%	3%
1670s	0%	0%	0%	46%	37%	17%
1680s	9%	0%	12%	40%	10%	29%
1690s	8%	1%	35%	40%	11%	5%
1700s	3%	1%	47%	36%	4%	9%
1710s	8%	0%	52%	25%	7%	8%
1720s	2%	0%	32%	39%	21%	6%
1730s	8%	0%	26%	23%	10%	33%
1740s	9%	0%	21%	3%	57%	10%

The ECs of the Windward islands proper – Dominica, St Lucia, Grenada, St Vincent, Trinidad and Tobago – are all late developments (late 18th century onwards), and all seem to represent koinés with varying proportions of Barbadian and Leeward influences, and/or to be the outcomes of the encounter between standard English and local FCs.

6.2.5 Guyana

Just like the Windward ECs, Guyana EC is a late development (second half of the 18th century) that represents nothing but a continuation and levelling of pre-existing ECs – mainly Barbadian and various Leeward varieties – with subsequent influences from standard English and the two Guyanese DCs (i.e. Skepi DC and Berbice DC). Slave demographics are in other words more or less irrelevant, since Guyana EC is not the result of a local creolisation. This is also the conclusion drawn by Baker (1999a).

6.2.6 Surinam

Surinam was first permanently settled in 1650 by settlers from both Barbados and the Leeward Islands (Baker 1999a:339; Lier 1971:19; Williamson 1923:153). Given that the Dutch delivered most slaves to the English planters until the Second Dutch War (as a result of which Surinam was transferred to the Dutch), only Dutch slave trade needs to be taken into account as far as Sranan EC and its daughter languages are concerned. Trade figures are also all that we have; I have seen no early ethnicity data from the plantations themselves.

Saramaccan EC (just like the other Maroon Creoles of Surinam) is quite obviously an offshoot of early Sranan partly relexified by the mysterious PC referred to by Ladhams (1999a) as Djutongo.[11] Although Bickerton (e.g. 1998:255) persists in claiming that Sranan and Saramaccan developed independently of one another, it is relatively easy to convincingly demonstrate the opposite (for a concise example, see e.g. McWhorter 1997b:13-19).

With the exception of one single ship from 1675, Postma (1990: 82, 308-19) only presents data of specific relevance to Surinam from the 1680s and onwards.[12] For the preceding decades, the only relevant data are Postma's (1990:112, 115, 298) estimates of the Dutch slave trade in general.[13] The combination of these is set out in the table overleaf.[14]

11 I use this term the same way Ladhams does, i.e. to denote a hypothesised but unattested PC once spoken on Jewish-owned plantations in Surinam, and from which Saramaccan EC drew its Portuguese lexicon. However, note that some (e.g. Holm 1989:439) equate it with Saramaccan itself, and others (e.g. Bakker, Smith & Veenstra 1995:169) with proto-Sranan.

12 Excluding ships for which no African source of slaves is indicated.

13 Eltis et al. (1999) note only three ships for the 1660s, and two for the 1670s.

14 The data from before the 1650s refer to the Lesser Antilles, from which a progenitor of Sranan is believed to have been brought. "Mixed Guiana/Surinam" cargoes are divided equally between Guyana and Surinam.

PERIOD	UPPER GUINEA	GOLD COAST	SLAVE COAST	BIAFRA	BUNTU
1620s	1%	1%	1%	1%	96%
1630s	3%	3%	18%	6%	71%
1640s	5%	5%	35%	10%	45%
1650s	3%	32%	25%	5%	35%
1660s	5%	18%	41%	9%	25%
1670s	2%	7%	51%	5%	36%
1680s	0%	3%	38%	0%	58%
1690s	0%	0%	51%	0%	49%
1700s	0%	8%	77%	0%	16%
1710s	0%	0%	76%	0%	24%
1720s	0%	68%	29%	0%	3%
1730s	0%	58%	34%	0%	7%

Thus, Slave Coast peoples would have been the most stable presence in Surinam for most of the relevant period. Bantus were also numerous until the early 18th century, whereas any Gold Coast influence in the Surinamese ECs must have entered the languages relatively early or rather late in their formative periods.

Of potential importance is the fact that Surinam was remarkable for the slow rate of nativisation of the slave population. In the third quarter of the 18th century, 71% of all slaves were still African-born (Arends 1995:263).

6.2.7 West Africa

The question of whether Krio emerged locally or is an import from the Americas has been debated for a long time. The former position has been advocated by, among others, Devonish (1997), Corcoran (1998), and in particular Hancock (1969, 1981, 1986, 1987), but has been challenged – to my mind very convincingly – by McWhorter (1995, 1996), Baker (1999a) and Huber (1998a, 1998b, 1998c).[15] Evidence in favour of the New World origins of Krio includes a multitude of linguistic features, but also extra-linguistic ones such as the Jamaican, Sranan and Krio all being currently or formerly referred to by their speakers as *taki-taki*.

Sierra Leone was settled mainly by Maroons and Free Blacks ultimately from Jamaica and the USA, and Krio shows important similarities to both Jamaican, the Maroon Spirit Language (and thereby also to its ancestor Sranan) and Gullah. Although the impact of Jamaican Maroons has usually been emphasised, Baker (1999a) shows that Krio in fact has more in common with Gullah than with Jamaican. There seems to be more of a consensus on the other varieties of West African EC being descendants of Krio.

6.3 French Creoles

The settlement histories of many FC-speaking countries are somewhat better documented than those of the Anglophone Caribbean. This is fortunate, because the French slave trade was less successful than the English in meeting the needs of the nation's own planters, and the study of the French slave trade is thus less rewarding. As was the case with the English colonies, the French relied almost exclusively on Dutch shipping until the 1660s (Emmer 1991:85), to the extent that slaves were not captured from the Portuguese and Spanish. But as opposed to the English, France never became completely self-sufficient, and continued to import from other nations throughout most of the history of slavery in the French Caribbean.

Mettas (1978, 1984) provides detailed information for the 18th century French trade, but plantation ethnicity data are relatively scarce, as are early trading data. It may therefore be of some value to try to reconstruct the relevant data through some indirect pieces of evidence. For one thing, we know that the slaves arriving in the French colonies around the mid-17th century were in general captured from the Iberians (Debien 1974:250-51). We further know that Dutch trade developed as a consequence of their capture of Brazil, and that the Dutch desperately had

15 Of course, some features that set Krio apart from the American ECs are local developments. Huber (1998a) mentions 12 linguistic features that are likely to have developed on the African coast rather than in the Americas, and several others that may have done so. Most Krio structures, however, are clearly of New World origin.

to find new markets for their slaves following their loss of Brazil, leading to their becoming major suppliers to the English and the French before these nations had developed their own trade (Emmer 1991:83; Batie 1991:47). The Dutch supplied most of the slaves to France's American colonies between about 1640 and 1664 (Emmer 1991:85; Linda Heywood & John Thornton, p c).

Organised French trade finally took off only in about 1670 (Gaston-Martin 1948:8) and yet, according to Curtin (1969:121), the French never delivered more than 40% at most of all slaves imported to their own colonies during the 17th century. Taken together, this leads me to propose the following pattern of French 17th century slave acquisitions according to supplier:

	PORTUGUESE	DUTCH	ENGLISH	FRENCH
1620s	100%	0%	0%	0%
1630s	100%	0%	0%	0%
1640s	0%	100%	0%	0%
1650s	0%	100%	0%	0%
1660s	0%	50%	25%	25%
1670s	0%	40%	25%	35%
1680s	0%	40%	25%	35%
1690s	0%	40%	25%	35%

A picture of the 17th century French trade can be calculated from the 38 individual voyages whose African places of trade are mentioned in Eltis et al. (1999), Karam (1986:70), Cultru (1913:xxxviii), Jennings (1995a:29), Singler (1993c) and Ly (1955). However approximate these numbers are (numbers of slaves must in most cases be inferred by me from the tonnages of the ships), this shows a greater proportion of Senegambian slaves than in the trade data for any other nation during this period. It is remarkable there are no documented reports of Bantu-speakers being transported by French shipping at this time, with the exception of two small batches of Mozambicans taken to Martinique in 1670.

PERIOD	SENEGAMBIA	GOLD COAST	SLAVE COAST	BIAFRA
1660s	46%	0%	30%	23%
1670s	41%	10%	36%	13%
1680s	57%	0%	43%	0%
1690s	66%	0%	34%	0%

A speculative reconstruction of the origins of African slaves in French plantation colonies can be made by combining the two tables above with details on 17th century Portuguese, Dutch, British and French slave trade derived from Curtin (1969), Postma (1990:112, 298), Richardson (1989), Mettas (1978, 1984), Linda Heywood and John Thornton (p c), and Eltis et al. (1999), as was done for the English Lesser Antilles above. The results, in theory applicable to any French colony, are presented below.[16]

PERIOD	UPPER GUINEA	GOLD COAST	SLAVE COAST	BIAFRA	BUNTU
1620s	1%	1%	1%	1%	96%
1630s	1%	1%	1%	1%	96%
1640s	5%	0%	50%	0%	45%
1650s	5%	15%	45%	0%	35%
1660s	16%	13%	35%	25%	14%
1670s	17%	18%	36%	16%	15%
1680s	28%	6%	43%	4%	21%
1690s	32%	7%	39%	3%	20%

16 A problem here, as mentioned in §6.2.3, is that I found an astonishing discrepancy between Curtin's (1969:121, 129) numbers for the English slave trade in 1680s and 1690s, and the shipping documented by Eltis et al. (1999). While Curtin estimates the Windward Coast to have been (by quite some margin) the greatest exporting region, no such traffic at all is recorded by Eltis et al.! I must admit that I have no idea why this should be so, and I have simply made a compromise between the two datasets. The inevitable error resulting from this ought to be lesser here, however, since English trade is only postulated to have been responsible for a fourth of the total imports during the two decades concerned.

With the exception of the 1650s (whose trade we would expect to be reflected in the 1664 Guadeloupean census), the correspondence with the three censuses of 1664, 1680 and 1690 from Guadeloupe, Martinique and French Guiana respectively is striking and indeed quite encouraging (see below).

6.3.1 Louisiana

The attestation of a dialect of Louisiana FC in Alabama (Marshall 1991), cut off from Louisiana in 1763, suggests that the language existed pretty much in its current form before the massive immigration of planters and slaves from Haiti.[17] No significant immigration from the other French Caribbean islands is documented (though cf Hall 1992:58, 179-180, 382-397; Neumann 1985:190 and Debien 1974:454), but cannot be ruled out. Although influenced by Haiti FC, the Creole of Louisiana must at least in part be a local creation, rather than an import from Haiti (cf Neumann 1985; Hall 1992; Speedy 1994).

Compared to the Caribbean islands, the slave population nativised at an exceptionally rapid rate in Louisiana (Hall 1992:175) and, after only a couple of decades of settlement, a majority of all slaves in Louisiana were locally born.

Slaves were first imported to what is today Louisiana in 1719 (Hall 1992:10), but the colony also included parts of Mississippi, Alabama and Florida, where the French kept slaves even before the first imports into Louisiana proper. Unfortunately, the origins of these slaves are not known, nor is their impact - if any - on Louisiana FC genesis.

In the very beginning of French colonisation of Louisiana, Africans from the Slave Coast dominated, but as early as the mid 1720s, Senegalese were more numerous (Hall 1992:35). In all, about two thirds of the slaves imported under the French were from Senegambia, most of the remainder being from the Slave Coast (Hall 1992; see also Mettas 1978, 1984 and McWilliams 1953). Out of a total of 23 slavers destined to Louisiana before 1758, sixteen were from Senegal, six from the Slave Coast, and one from Angola (Hall 1992:59). To this, it should be added that, immediately upon arrival, the 200 slaves aboard the first ship from the Slave Coast, *l'Aurore,* were taken to Pensacola (now in western Florida) to help fortify the town which was threatened by the Spanish. As Pensacola nevertheless fell to Spain shortly afterwards, all these slaves were lost (Speedy 1994:94), thus making Senegalese dominance among slaves actually involved in Creole formation in Louisiana even more marked.

Speakers of Kwa languages were also relatively numerous in colonial Louisiana, whereas the proportion of those speaking Bantu languages was virtually negligible. Hall (1992:289) also provides an ethno-linguistic breakdown of the Senegambian slaves in Louisiana: 29% would have been Malinke or Maninka, 25% Bambara (both Mande), 22% Wolof and 10% Fulfulde (both Atlantic). In all, approximately two thirds were Mande while the remaining third were speakers of Atlantic languages (Hall 1992:32).

Practically all the slaves who arrived in French-ruled Louisiana did so between 1719 and 1729, so there is thus little point in giving the regional distribution for different decades. For all documented slave imports, the approximate distribution is as follows (Mettas 1978, 1984; Hall 1992; McWilliams 1953:251):

Region	Share
Senegambia	66%
Windward Coast	4%
Slave Coast	25%
Buntu	6%

From the last three centuries of the 18th century, some documentation exists on slave ethnicities in Louisiana. Of the 81 African-born slaves mentioned by Klingler (1997:2), 11% were from Upper

[17] In the first decade of the 19th century, planters fleeing the revolution in Haiti would have made up something like a sixth of all whites, with their slaves constituting about the same proportion of Louisiana's servile population. If only taking Francophones into account, the proportion of Haitians would have come close to 30% of all whites. It has been suggested that it was this immigration that brought FC to Louisiana in the first place. If that were the case, it would have had to subsequently diverge from Haiti FC at a rather amazing pace.

Guinea, 50% from Lower Guinea, and 25% from Bantu-speaking areas.[18] From the same period (1770s-1790s), Hall (1992:403-06) gives the ethnic composition of African-born slaves in the Pointe-Coupée district as 33% Upper Guineans, 41% Lower Guineans and 26% Bantus. It must be borne in mind, however, that by this time, the majority of all slaves in Louisiana was in any case locally born, and thus probably L_1-speakers of Louisiana FC.

6.3.2 Haiti

Haiti[19] was settled in part from the Lesser Antilles (Cornevin 1982:23; Crouse 1940:82; Hornot 1776:490; Houdaille 1973; Larsen 1928:12; Parkvall 1995c:83-84). Both English and French buccaneers from the Lesser Antilles established themselves on the island of Tortuga (La Tortue) as early as in 1629, and this population soon spilled over to the Haitian mainland. The first evidence of black slaves that I have come across refers to 1634 (Crouse 1940:82), but there is no way of knowing whether an early form of Haiti FC was spoken at the time. Strictly speaking, the settlement of Haiti is thus roughly simultaneous with that of the Lesser Antilles, but Haiti initially developed more slowly. At the time of the first census, in 1681, whites still made up about two thirds of the total population, and the non-white population did not form a majority of the total until just before the turn of the century (Parkvall 1998; Watts 1987:320; Rogozinski 1992:76; Singler 1993a:240, 1993c, 1994).

As opposed to Louisiana, the slave population of Haiti nativised very slowly. As late as the 1790s, when slave importation ceased, two-thirds of all slaves were still born in Africa (James 1991:133; Cornevin 1982:39). This low reproduction rate – a consequence of the higher degree of labour exploitation in Haiti than Louisiana – may have protracted stabilisation of the language somewhat. Therefore, African arrivals after the initial settlement may have played a greater role in Haiti than in Louisiana.

According to Fouchard (1979:273), the first Africans in Haiti came from St-Louis and Gorée in Senegal, whereas later arrivals, who came after Creole had become established, were mostly from Lower Guinea. Six ships are documented from before the 1690s (Mettas 1978, 1984; Ly 1955; Eltis et al. 1999), all of which came from Senegambia. No shipping is attested for the following decade, and the only three vessels recorded from between 1700 and 1710 were all from the Slave Coast

A large number of Haitian slaves were taken to Haiti from the Caribbean colonies of other nations as a result of French raiding, but many were also bought from the English on Jamaica (Parkvall 1995c:83-84; Rogozinski 1992:91). Large-scale imports from the British began in 1713 (Rogozinski 1992:91), but even in the late 18th century, demand for labour in Haiti was so great that planters had to import slaves from Jamaica. In the boom years towards the end of the 18th century, 4 000-5 000 slaves a year were smuggled from Jamaica to Haiti (Sheridan 1974:319), which is a number far higher than what the French trade could provide. Indeed, according to Raynal (1784:227), Jamaica furnished almost four times as many slaves to Haitian planters as did the French African trade. It is noteworthy that a successful French raiding of Jamaica in 1694 yielded somewhere between 1 200 and 3 000 slaves, which must have corresponded to somewhere between a fourth and half of all slaves in Haiti at the time, and thus an even larger proportion of the forced immigration for that decade (Parkvall 1995c:83). This has potential importance for Haitian dialectology, as Jamaican slaves – for reasons of geography – tended to be over-represented in the south-west, and EC influence is indeed stronger there than elsewhere in the country (Holm 1989:382-83). The low number of Upper Guineans among the English slave imports may thus have emphasised a trend already evident in the French trade, namely an over-representation of Upper Guineans in northern Haiti as compared to the country as a whole for at least the first decade for which it is possible to make a regional breakdown of the documented imports (30% Upper Guineans in the north, as compared to 16% in the centre and 0% in the south during the 1710s).

---

18 5% belonged to ethnicities that I was unable to identify, and a further 10% were Cangas, i.e. Kru speakers from today's Liberia and the Ivory Coast Of the Lower Guineans, Gẽ speakers alone made up 22%, followed by Yorubas (10%) and Igbos (9%).

19 The country has been known as *Haiti* only after independence, and as *Saint-Domingue* during the French era. To avoid confusion, I consistently use the former name regardless of the historical period to which I refer.

The available shipping data (Mettas 1978, 1984; Eltis et al. 1999) provide numbers for the 1680s and for the 1710s and onwards, the number of recorded ships from other decades being too small to allow any conclusions. For the period before 1680, as well as for the 1690s and 1700s, the best we can do is to make a reconstruction similar to the one presented above for French imports in general. This is set out of below.

PERIOD	UPPER GUINEA	GOLD COAST	SLAVE COAST	BIAFRA	BUNTU
1620s	1%	1%	1%	1%	96%
1630s	1%	1%	1%	1%	96%
1640s	5%	0%	50%	0%	45%
1650s	5%	15%	45%	0%	35%
1660s	16%	13%	35%	25%	14%
1670s	17%	18%	36%	16%	15%
1680s	100%	0%	0%	0%	0%
1690s	32%	7%	39%	3%	20%
1700s[20]	29%	4%	48%	4%	17%
1710s	25%	0%	57%	4%	13%
1720s	15%	1%	70%	0%	15%
1730s	21%	9%	45%	1%	25%
1740s	33%	17%	21%	1%	39%

English deliveries have already been taken into account in the general reconstruction of 17th century French slave imports, but it is clear that Jamaican slaves played a special role in the peopling of Haiti. If we compare the above table with the statistics for Jamaica (§6.2.2), it becomes clear that the most important difference is the important role of Gold Coast slaves in early 18th century Jamaica in comparison to Haiti. I will not attempt at revising the numbers for Haiti, however, since we do not know how large a proportion of the Haitian slaves was furnished by Jamaican traders, but the reader should be aware that Gold Coasters are in all likelihood under-represented in the table above in comparison to their actual share of the slave population in colonial Haiti.

Singler (1994), based mainly on Richardson (1989), suggests that the Gbe share of the Haitian slave population became dominant in the 1690s, and rose further to above 60% during the three first decades of the 18th century. Such a statement is true of French shipments only. It is not true if imports from Jamaica are taken into account.

6.3.3 The Lesser Antilles

The first permanent French settlement in the Lesser Antilles (and in the Caribbean as a whole) was that of St Kitts, and St Kitts provided input to Martinican and other Lesser Antillean FCs (Jennings 1995b; Parkvall 1995a, b; Tertre 1667-1671; Petitjean-Roget 1980:138; Chauleau 1966:112). French Kittitians also settled in Guadeloupe, and many of the French inhabitants of St Croix - initially peopled from St Kitts - were resettled on Guadeloupe (Rennard 1954:36; Hanotaux & Martineau 1929:399; Dookhan 1975:10; Petersen 1855:10).

No details are known of the origins of slaves in French St Kitts, but since the French essentially acquired their slaves from the same sources as the English,[21] the table in §6.2.3 above provides the best estimate for the first decades of colonisation.

Throughout the history of French colonisation of the Lesser Antilles, Martinique has had more influence on neighbouring islands than Guadeloupe. All of the Windward FC varieties derive from Martinique FC, and even St Barthélemy FC has been shown to be more closely related to Windward FC than to Guadeloupean (Calvet & Chaudenson 1998:60, 68; Maher 1993). Thus, for want of detailed figures on slaves in French St Kitts, the ethnic composition of Martinican slaves, and to a lesser extent those of Guadeloupe, will have to represent the substrate of Lesser Antillean FC.

20 The row for the 1700s here represents an average between the preceding and the following decade.

21 At the end of the 17th century, the French still acquired most of its slaves from other nations (Chauleau 1966:103), and it was only in the 18th century that French slave trade was able to supply at least more than half of the demand in the French New World colonies.

In Martinique, slaves from the Gold Coast and elsewhere in Lower Guinea dominated in the earliest period, with Mandes being completely absent, but locally-born slaves seem to have formed the majority quite early on (Singler 1993c, 1994; Debien 1974). Bouton (1640:98) claimed that the first slaves came from Senegal, but in Singler's 1680 figures, these form only about 20% of the servile population, the rest being from Lower Guinea or from the Bantu-speaking Congo/Angola region (Singler 1993c, 1994).

Singler (1993c, 1994) lists the origins of 82 African-born slaves in the 1664 census of Guadeloupe, and 277 African-born slaves in the 1680 Martinican census, and claims that the differences between the two censuses is due to separation in time rather than in space. Although I was originally sceptical about this (Parkvall 1995c:82), I am now prepared to accept it. At least officially, Guadeloupe imported most of its slaves by way of Martinique, and I now believe that the differences that can be observed between the two censuses do reflect changes in the slave trade noted above (cf the table in §6.2.3 above). The following table shows the differences in plantation ethnicity data between the two censuses:

GROUP	1664 (GUADELOUPE)	1680 (MARTINIQUE)
Atlantic	11%	21%
Mande	2%	0%
Kwa	22%	39%
Gur	5%	0%
Delto-Benuic	14%	20%
Bantu	45%	19%

The only other local ethnicity data of which I am aware are those of Debien (1974) who gives the ethnic composition of 55 African-born Maroons in Guadeloupe. Upper Guineans account for slightly less than a third, Lower Guineans for almost two thirds, whereas Bantus make up only 7%. These data, however, relate to the late 18th century, and are thus too late to have had any major significance.

The following table shows imports before and after the censuses studied by Singler. Unfortunately, neither Eltis et al. (1999), nor the additional works consulted, permit a reliable estimate of imports before 1710, the number of ships recorded being too small. For this reason, I have again combined the data derived from these sources with an estimate of the kind already set out for St Kitts and Barbados above, adopted to French trading practices as shown in §6.3.

PERIOD	UPPER GUINEA	GOLD COAST	SLAVE COAST	BIAFRA	BUNTU
1630s	2%	6%	22%	1%	71%
1640s	2%	10%	43%	0%	45%
1650s	5%	20%	31%	10%	35%
1660s	3%	18%	29%	45%	8%
1670s	1%	35%	33%	25%	7%
1680s	9%	10%	42%	10%	29%
1690s	9%	34%	44%	11%	4%
1700s	4%	47%	38%	4%	9%
1710s	4%	2%	70%	10%	13%
1720s	11%	2%	63%	1%	23%
1730s	10%	10%	55%	1%	25%
1740s	17%	21%	29%	2%	31%

6.3.4 French Guiana

A permanent French settlement in Guiana was established in 1664, thus a couple of decades after the colonisation of the Lesser Antilles. Large-scale immigration from the Antilles is attested, but is mainly a recent phenomenon.[22] Nevertheless, given the similarities between Guiana FC and the Lesser Antillean FCs, many of which are attested well before the 19th century immigration

22 See e.g. Chérubini (1985:98), Dorion-Sébeloue (1985), Dupont-Gonin (1970), Gorgeon (1985), Honychurch (1975:155), Lasserre (ed.) (1979) and Papy (1955:220-21).

(Fauquenoy [ed.] 1989; Parkvall 1999c), I consider it likely that an Antillean FC was taken to French Guiana at an early date.

The 17th century French slave trade to Guiana is documented in Jennings (1995a:27, 29), Karam (1986:70) and Singler (1993c:219-220, 222).[23] In all, these authors mention 20 shiploads of known geographical origin. Assuming that the cargoes whose size is not given consisted of about 150 slaves,[24] we arrive at the following very approximate figures:

PLACES OF TRADE	SHARE
Senegambia	35%
Gold Coast	10%
Slave Coast	35%
Biafra	20%

The last documented arrival of Senegambians took place in 1699, and the 1700-1730 deliveries show a total reliance on Lower Guinea. Speakers of Bantu languages would seem to be conspicuous by their absence throughout most of the colony's early history; the first documented arrival of Bantus is only in 1730 (but cf the plantation ethnicity data below). Disregarding inputs from other French New World colonies (of which we know nothing), it would thus seem that Senegambian influences predate 1700, whereas traces of Bantu languages would post-date 1730.

Jennings (1993a:33) points out that a large number of Lower Guinean slaves had lived in the colony for thirteen years before the first Senegalese arrived, and concludes that the original Pidgin was created by Frenchmen and Gbe speakers alone. Between 1660 and 1673, *all* slaves on the Rémire plantation (see below) were Gbe (Jennings 1999:6).

During the 18th century, 61 French ships brought about 3 200 slaves to Cayenne (Mettas 1978, 1984). Until the 1740s, virtually all slaves were from Lower Guinea, and it was not until 1771 that a slaver again arrived from Senegal. After this date, however, Senegambians became the dominant group among newly imported slaves, and quite likely among the African-born population as a whole. Between 1785 and 1792, all 11 slavers came from Gorée or St-Louis in Senegal, but there can be little doubt that Guiana FC existed as a separate language by this date.

French Guiana is unusual in that not only the trade itself is reasonably well recorded, but the ethnic composition of slaves on one of the largest plantations is also documented. The 1690 slave inventory of the Rémire plantation (listing ethnicities of 104 slaves, or about a twelfth of the colony's slave population at the time) has been published by Debien (1965), and its linguistic value has later been exploited by Singler (1993b, 1993c, 1994) and Jennings (1995a, 1997, 1999). Singler (1994) summarises the linguistic affiliations of the African-born slaves as follows:

GROUP	PROPORTION
Atlantic	11%
Mande	8%
Kwa	54%
Delto-Benuic	11%
Bantu	17%

Like the shipping data above, the Rémire census suggests a dominance of Lower Guineans (in particular speakers of Gbe languages), and a small proportion of Bantus. The main difference lies on the one hand in the relatively limited number of Upper Guineans in the Rémire inventory, which is explained by the arrival of many Senegalese only in the 1690s, and on the other hand in the presence of Bantus on Rémire, despite their absence in any shipping records from this period. In any case, even on Rémire, the number of Bantus is lower than in most other New World colonies at the time.

23 Surprisingly, almost all shipping to French Guiana documented by these sources is ignored by Eltis et al. (1999).

24 Cf Stein (1979:210). The actual average number of slaves delivered by slavers documented as selling slaves in French Guiana before 1750 is 143. For ships buying slaves in more than one region, the number has been equally divided between these two.

Just like Jennings (1995a), Singler (1994) emphasises that the Gbe speakers were dominant in the initial phase of settlement, and Gbe speakers alone would have made up an absolute majority of all African-born slaves on the Rémire plantation from the beginning until the 1690 census was taken.

6.4 Portuguese Creoles

6.4.1 Upper Guinea

There is considerable controversy regarding whether Upper Guinea PC emerged on the mainland, and was later taken to the Cape Verde Islands, or whether it arose on the islands, only later to be taken to today's Guinea-Bissau and Casamance. Silva (1957:31), Silva (1985:32, 47) and Carreira (1972:337-38) advocate an insular origin, whereas Scantamburlo (1981:12) and Santos (1979:22) are equally convinced that Cape Verde PC was taken to the islands from the mainland. However, the Cape Verdes would in any case have drawn its slaves from Senegal and Guinea-Bissau (Albuquerque & Santos [eds.] 1991:154-55), and regardless of where the common ancestor of Cape Verde PC and its mainland sister language emerged, the substrate material would be Atlantic and Mande languages.[25]

The major African languages of Guinea-Bissau are Balanta, Fulfulde, Manjaku and Papel (all Atlantic) and Mandinka (Mande). When the Portuguese first arrived, Mandinka is said to have been more widespread than it is today, and in addition, Temne (Atlantic) was used as a lingua franca (Rougé 1994:142).

As one would expect, the ethnolinguistic make-up of the Cape Verdean founder population seems to have been relatively similar. Barros (n d:38) mentions Balanta, Ejamat, Papel, Wolof and Bijago (all Atlantic) as the most important African languages in the early days of settlement of the Cape Verdes. Meintel (1984:23) adduces that 16th century archival evidence, blood group similarities, and onomastics all provide proof of the early presence of speakers of Wolof, Lebu, Fulfulde (Atlantic), Mandinka and Bambara (Mande). Lang (1994:3) suggests that the Atlantic-speakers dominated at first, but that the proportion of Mandes increased through time.

For geographical reasons, it is hardly surprising that speakers of Lower Guinean or Bantu languages are not relevant substrates of Upper Guinea PCs (although isolated individuals may have arrived from these areas).

6.4.2 Lower Guinea

Annobón and Príncipe were both settled from São Tomé between 1500 and 1503 (Sundiata 1990:18; Hodges & Newitt 1988:18; Lorenzino 1998:43; Ferraz 1983:120; Liniger-Goumaz 1988:21). Ferraz (1979:9), Holm (1989:278) and Maurer (1997:431) all claim that in comparison to São Tomé, the substrate material of Príncipe PC is more Delto-Benuic and less Bantu. This is apparently mainly based on lexical evidence, but their account also fit the phonological facts (see Parkvall 1999d).

From a purely structural point of view, the maroon Creole Angolar PC, spoken in the southern parts of São Tomé, is clearly a dialect of São Tomé PC;[26] it is distinguished mainly by a different lexicon, and some relatively minor – albeit conspicuous – phonological peculiarities. Of the core lexicon, about two thirds is cognate with São Tomé PC (Ferraz 1979:9), the remainder being mainly of Kimbundu origin. Linguistic and historical evidence leave little doubt that Angolar is a partially relexified variety of Sãotomense. It is not clear, though, what this implies regarding the Sãotomense input in Angolar formation. Ferraz (1983:122) believes that Angolar without its Kimbundu component corresponds broadly to mid-16th century Sãotomense, and infers from this that numerals higher than three (which are of Kimbundu origin in Angolar) were lacking in early Sãotomense. Holm (1989:280) suggests that the Kimbundu words would have been present in early Sãotomense, but that they were later replaced by items of Portuguese origin and only retained in Angolar. This however, would not explain why the Sãotomense speakers

25 As mentioned in §5.1.2.1, there is at least lexical evidence suggesting that the islands were the true birthplace of Cape Verde PC.

26 This is more evident in the description offered by Lorenzino (1998) than in the one given by Maurer (1995).

consistently discarded words of Kimbundu origin, but kept those of Edo and Kikongo origin.[27] The very glossonym Angolar, as well as studies of physical anthropology (Paulo 1959; Almeida 1956), all suggest that Angolar developed from the partial adoption of Sãotomense by a wholly Bantu population.

Since the grammatical and phonological discrepancies between Sãotomense and Angolar are relatively minor, they can be regarded as a single language in everything but the lexicon. Insofar as the adoption of Kimbundu vocabulary does not appear to have anything to do with creolisation as such - but rather is a result of language shift with heavy substratal lexical retentions, which I see as something fundamentally different from pidginisation/creolisation - Angolar has limited importance for the discussion of substrate transfer in pidginisation/creolisation.

For present purposes, then, the main significance of Angolar is that it *may* shed light on (i) the nature of Sãotomense when the first Maroons escaped, and (ii) the ethnolinguistic composition of the island's slaves at the time. Unfortunately, it is not clear precisely when the Maroon population was founded. Archival sources first mention runaway slaves in 1499, and the number of fugitive slaves increased during the 1510s and 1520s, so that in 1535, the Maroon problem seriously threatened the prosperity of the colony (Sousa 1990:298; Neves 1989:18; Lorenzino 1998:54).

So, on the one hand, the Angolar population may have existed as early as in 1499 when the first slaves escaped, but on the other, Hodges & Newitt (1988:60) believe that there was no Angolar ethnicity prior to the early 18th century, when these people are first mentioned in official Portuguese documentation. There is thus a span of at least 200 years during which the Angolar language may have emerged.

Lorenzino (1998:44) suggests 1550 as the starting date. If this is correct, Angolar less its Kimbundu component might correspond to the state of development of Sãotomense in 1550 (although Angolar has of course not been completely cut off from its mother language since then), which implies that São Tomé PC had largely acquired its modern shape by that time. A second possible inference is that the slave population in 1550 was numerically and/or socially dominated by Kimbundus (although it cannot be excluded that Kimbundus were over-represented among the fugitives).

Given the high proportion of shared structures, it thus seems that the common ancestor of all four Gulf of Guinea PCs can be traced back to São Tomé, the first Portuguese colony on the islands.

Portuguese colonisation on São Tomé first began in 1485, although the first large number of settlers and slaves did not arrive until the 1490s (Neves 1989:16; Ballong-Wen-Mewuda 1988:124; Tenreiro 1961:59).

All sources agree that only Gbe, Delto-Benuic and Bantu languages are potentially important substrates of Sãotomense.[28] The relative proportions, however, and the time at which the different groups arrived, are more difficult to determine.

According to the orders from the Portuguese king issued in 1485, the planters of São Tomé were allowed to import slaves from the Niger delta (Sousa 1990:196; Garfield 1992:45), and Ferraz (1979:13) confirms that speakers of Delto-Benuic did indeed arrive in the late 15th century.

In the 1490s, when the booming economy required more slaves, imports were also authorised from Bantu-speaking areas (Albuquerque 1989:184; Tenreiro 1961:60; Sousa 1990:223). Sousa's (1990:483-93) figures for 1499-1553 includes *only* Bantus, and the 4 307 slaves taken to the island in 1516 were all Kongos (Garfield 1992:39). Slave trade with Benin was prohibited in 1538 (Thiele 1987:83), which would have made Kongo an even more important supplier.

---

27 The Edo and Kikongo lexical material in Angolar is also present in Sãotomense, but not vice versa. Despite a higher overall proportion of African words, Angolar thus has fewer retentions from all substrate languages except Kimbundu (Lorenzino 1998:116). In other words, if one subtracts the Kimbundu element, lexical Africanisms in Angolar basically form a subset of those in Sãotomense.

28 Neves (1989:17) claims that many of the first slaves were from Elmina on the Gold Coast (an Akan-speaking area), but though some slaves may have come from Elmina (see below), it is unlikely that their number was particularly high. Many of the slaves imported during the first decade were in fact re-exported to Elmina (Garfield 1992:21-22, 29), partly for local use, and partly in order to be sold to the Spanish in the New World. Elmina was thus a net importer *from* rather than a net exporter *to* São Tomé.

Speakers of Kimbundu began arriving in larger numbers from the 1560s, and then replaced the Kongos as the dominant Bantu group in the 17th century (Rawley 1981:25, 33).

Neves (1989:149-50) and Garfield (1992:16) believe that the first slaves taken to São Tomé were Bantus, and that imports from Lower Guinea only commenced in the 17th century. As we have seen, Lower Guineans were present early on, so it may be that Neves and Garfield, ignoring this, refer to a later wave of Lower Guineans. However, the similarities between the four PC varieties in the area suggest that the language was already crystallised by that time.

My speculative interpretation of the few pieces of evidence that there are (for more details, see Parkvall 1999d) is that Delto-Benuic languages (in particular Edo, according to Ferraz 1979:12, 1983:120) represent the oldest layer of substrate material in Sãotomense, but that their dominance was a very short-lived one, and that the slaves soon were overwhelmingly Bantu-speaking. If this assumption is correct, it would basically imply that anything of Delto-Benuic origin in Sãotomense dates to the first few decades of colonisation. It also suggests that the formation of the Angolar group and its language post-dates 1560, when speakers of Kimbundu became numerous on the island.

As in the case of the Upper Guinea PCs, another possibility is that Gulf of Guinea PCs emerged on the mainland rather than on São Tomé. Although older sources frequently mention the existence of restructured Portuguese on the Lower Guinea coast, actual citations are scarce.[29] One interesting piece of evidence, however, is Barbot's (1746:361) sentence *Vos sa Dios* 'You are Gods', recorded in Benin in 1682. The copula here, *sa*, is identical to that of the insular Lower Guinean PCs. I suspect that *sa*, < P *são* – a rather idiosyncratic choice,[30] indicates a genetic relationship between the Guinea Islands PCs and the now extinct Pidgin Portuguese of the mainland, but unless more evidence is found, there is no way of knowing in which direction transfer took place. The Portuguese reached the area in the second half of the 15th century, and set up a number of important establishments on the Gold and Slave Coasts, starting with Elmina in 1471. There would thus be enough time for a Pidgin to develop on the coast, and for it to be taken to São Tomé by the slaves accompanying the first settlers.

6.5 Dutch Creoles

6.5.1 Negerhollands

The first slaves on St Thomas were speakers of Twi, and Akan slaves continued to be the most numerous until at least the 1730s (Stolz & Stein 1986:16; Feldbæk & Justesen 1980). Relatively large numbers of slaves were also imported from the Slave Coast (Jones 1985), and Sabino (1988, 1992:3-4) considers Ewe a major substrate of Negerhollands alongside Akan and Gã. Although the presence of Bantus and Upper Guineans is indeed attested on St Thomas (e.g. Oldendorp 1777:244), the substrate of Negerhollands seems to be thoroughly Kwa.

Nativisation was relatively rapid, and in 1692, a fifth of the slaves were locally born (van Rossem & van der Voort 1996:7). Note that this diminishes the importance of the Gold Coast deliveries somewhat, in favour of Slave Coast imports.

Early deliveries to the Danish West Indies were provided by English and Brandenburgian slavers, but from the beginning of the 18th century, the Danes themselves transported most of the slaves required on the islands. Since the only Danish footholds in Africa were located on the Gold Coast, this eventually led to an exceptionally heavy Kwa bias in the workforce of the Danish West Indies. The following table combines data found in Eltis et al. (1999) and Postma (1990).[31]

29 But cf Barbot (1732), Dapper (1675:107), Hemmerson (1674:21), Müller (1676:193), Naro (1978) and Perl (1982, 1994).

30 Magnus Huber (p c), however, suggests *sois* as the source. *São* and *sois* are 3pl and 2pl forms, respectively, of the copula *ser*.

31 The 1700s Buntu proportion is greatly affected by the inclusion of *De Vliegende Hart* from Postma (1990:82), which delivered 420 slaves from Loango in 1707. The ship is missing from Eltis et al.'s data.

PERIOD	SENEGAMBIA	WINDWARD COAST	GOLD COAST	SLAVE COAST	BIAFRA	BUNTU
1690s	0%	0%	55%	45%	0%	0%
1700s	5%	0%	42%	18%	7%	28%
1710s	0%	0%	67%	0%	0%	33%
1720s	0%	0%	100%	0%	0%	0%
1730s	0%	0%	100%	0%	0%	0%
1740s	0%	5%	93%	2%	0%	0%

6.5.2 Skepi

The first documented slave deliveries were from Senegambia, but the Gold Coast soon became the prime supplier. Shortly afterwards, the Slave Coast became dominant, and remained so until the late 18th century (Postma 1990). Bantu slaves never seem to have been very numerous. Several contingents were also purchased from Curaçao (Postma 1990), from Surinam and various English colonies (Smith 1962:17; Storm van's Gravesande 1911 vol. 1:632; Netscher 1888:128; Postma 1990:189, 217).

6.5.3 Berbice

Postma (1990:193-94, 309-47) and Netscher (1888:194) give the geographical origins of 24 shiploads of slaves arriving in Berbice between 1714 and 1791. Nine of these, however, were from the "Guinea Coast", which could mean any part of the West African coast The other deliveries were distributed as follows:

ORIGIN	PROPORTION
Gold Coast	41%
Slave Coast	15%
Buntu	42%
Curaçao	2%

The first attested importation of Bantu slaves, however, took place in 1763, at a time when there is little reason to doubt that the Berbice language already existed (see e.g. Robertson 1994). The attested imports thus indicate a massive Gold Coast dominance in the first half of the 18th century. The documented imports of which the African origins are given, however, are from 1714, whereas slaveholding in Berbice is attested from the very start of the colony in 1627 (Robertson 1993:298).

There were plans in the 17th century to import slaves in large numbers from Arguin (present-day Mauretania) and from Lower Guinea (Goslinga 1971:343; Jones 1985:19), but there is no evidence that it actually took place. Until 1720, it seems like Berbice planters acquired most of their slaves from Surinam (Postma 1990:189, 217).

Berbice DC is thus unusual in that the linguistic evidence clearly displays an Ijo influence so massive that no one contests it, whereas the slave trade records do not mention even a single shipment from an Ijo-speaking area.

6.6 Spanish Creoles

6.6.1 Papiamentu

Of the 363 slavers documented in Postma (1990:82, 308-19), 111 went to Curaçao. 60 of these arrived prior to 1700, when most (e.g. Munteanu 1996:43; Maurer 1985:42 cited in Bartens 1996:138; Rens 1953:54 cited in Bartens 1996:138) seem to agree that Papiamentu had already emerged. Here is the geographical breakdown for the early imports given by Postma (based on 15 964 slaves whose origins are known):

REGION	% OF THOSE OF KNOWN ORIGIN
Senegambia	1%
Gold Coast	7%
Slave Coast	56%
Buntu	36%

Unfortunately, there are no data for pre-1674 arrivals. Since there seems to be no systematic deviances between the Curaçao imports and the Dutch slave trade as a whole, we will have to make do with Postma's (1990:112) estimated figures for the earlier period. Curiously, Postma (1990) and Eltis et al. (1999) give radically different numbers for the 1680s.

	1660s	1670s	1680s[32]	1690s	1700s	1710s	1720s
Senegambia	5%	8%	0%	0%	0%	0%	0%
Ivory Coast	2%	0%	0%	0%	0%	0%	0%
Gold Coast	18%	19%	15%	0%	17%	9%	57%
Slave Coast	41%	19%	63%	60%	41%	66%	29%
Biafra[33]	9%	0%	0%	0%	0%	1%	0%
Congo/Angola	25%	54%	22%	40%	42%	24%	14%

The number of ships documented from the 1730s-1740s is too small to provide any reliable regional breakdown.

Overall, there is thus a relatively strong Slave Coast dominance, with a substantial Bantu contribution. A cumulative reconstruction for the first 70 years of colonisation based on available data yields similar results – the slave population in Curaçao at the time was predominantly from the Slave Coast, with a strong Bantu representation, a small Gold Coast contingent, contributions from elsewhere being virtually negligible.

It may be, however, that Papiamentu was imported to the Netherlands Antilles from elsewhere – the strong Portuguese lexical component suggests that it may in fact be a relexification of a PC, possibly imported from Africa (Lenz 1928; Navarro Tomás 1953; Granda 1974; Megenney 1984, 1985; Maurer 1998:201) or from Brazil (Goodman 1987; Holm 1989:300-01, 1992:40; McWhorter 1999b). Relexification from an African PC does not strike me as particularly likely, simply because the shared features are rather limited in number (see also Parkvall 1999e). The Brazil hypothesis is difficult to maintain, not only because no PC has ever been documented in Brazil, but there is also historical evidence that speaks against it (Arends 1999; Ladhams 1999a, 1999b; Parkvall 1999e).

6.6.2 Palenquero

Historical evidence suggests that the maroons who founded El Palenque de San Basilio (and presumably created the Palenquero language) fled the Colombian plantations in about 1600 (Rout 1976:110; Holm 1989:310).

Imports to Colombia were dominated by Yolofs[34] until about 1580, whereas late 16th and early 17th century arrivals were predominantly Bantu (Vila Vilar 1977; Del Castillo 1982, 1984). In Eltis et al. (1999), the proportion of Bantu-speakers is above 95% for all decades between 1590 and 1650, except for the 1610s, when it drops to 70% due to arrivals from several other areas (none of which alone surpassed 10%). From the 1650s onwards, data is only sporadically available in Eltis et al. (1999) – only eight ships for the entire century following 1650 – but what little there is, suggests a reliance on the Slave Coast, rather than on Bantu-speaking areas. These imports may in any case be too late to have influenced the formation of Palenquero.

The presence of some apparently Portuguese-derived features (Megenney 1982; Schwegler 1991, 1993b; Porras 1992:200), together with the oft-cited contemporary witness of the Jesuit missionary Sandoval,[35] has made many an observer suggest that Palenquero is a relexification of

32 The column for the 1680s represents my attempt at combining the data found in Postma (1990) and in Eltis et al. (1999) while trying to evaluate the reliability of the two sources in each case. They differ greatly for this particular decade with respect to the relative proportions of the Gold and the Slave Coast (the former representing 9% in Postma and 39% in Eltis et al.). The differences are not only numerical, but there are also ships found in one source that are mysteriously missing in the other, which is surprising, since Postma is Eltis et al.'s main source so far as the Dutch slave trade is concerned. The numbers presented here are closer to those of Postma than Eltis et al.

33 Coded "BB" by Postma. Since this code does not figure in his list of abbreviations, the interpretation as "Bight of Biafra" (elsewhere "GB") represents a guess on my part. "Bight of Benin" (=Slave Coast), the other possible interpretation, figures correctly abbreviated in the same table.

34 Yolof refers to a speaker of the Wolof language.

35 *"[L]os que llamamos criollos y naturales de San Thomé, con la communicación que con tan bárbaras naciones han tenido el tiempo que han residido en San Thomé, las entienden casi todas con un género de lenguaje muy corrupto y reversado de*

São Tomé PC. However, as was the case with Papiamentu, the linguistic evidence in favour of this, while suggestive, is not especially strong, and the Sandoval quote may in any case post-date the creation of Palenquero.

6.7 Identifying substratal origins on non-linguistic grounds

It should also be possible to use extra-linguistic elements of popular culture to determine the substratal origin of Afro-American communities. I will only give a brief overview of such parallels, mainly in order to highlight the possibilities that such studies could provide as a complement to what historical evidence has to offer. Thus, Price's claim (1976:33-35 cited in Seuren 1990a:19) that the Saramaccan descend from Slave Coast peoples is based partly on cultural similarities.

In a similar way, Bastide (1971) claims Akan to be the dominant African component in the cultures of Surinam, Barbados, the Carolinas, Jamaica, San Andrés and St Lucia. For Haiti, he identifies Fon as having been dominant, whereas cultural Bantuisms are to be found in Colombia.[36]

6.7.1 Oral traditions

Some of the peoples in question identify with a particular African ethnicity. In the Gullah-speaking areas, there is a tradition of claiming Sierra Leonean ancestry which, however, seems to be of dubious authenticity.[37] On Carriacou too, various segments of the population also identify with certain African peoples (Sunshine et al. 1982; Hill 1974:53). Similar identifications can no doubt be found among at least some people in virtually every creolophone territory.

Although this may potentially be of great significance, my feeling is that 20th century developments in Black self-awareness in the Americas has among many descendants of African slaves led to an urge to identify with an African ethnic group that has been stronger than the desire for historical accuracy, and that this reduces the scientific potential of self-identification.

Mention should be made, however, of El Palenque de San Basilio – In the opening lines of one of the best-preserved ancestral songs in El Palenque, speakers of Palenquero claim that "*Chi ma nkongo, chi ma ri loango ...*", which Schwegler (1996a:524ff) translates as 'From the Kongo (people) [we come], from those of Loango ...'

Glossonyms are also suggestive. In both Surinam and Jamaica, there are special cryptolectal registers called *Kromanti* or *Kumenti* (cf Kormantin, toponym in Akan-speaking territory), and the Ndyuka-speakers also have a *Papa* (cf Popo, a toponym of the Gbe-speaking area) register (Hurault 1983; Alleyne 1980:157; Voorhoeve 1971:314). The lexicons of these registers seem to come mainly from languages of the areas from which they take their names.

6.7.2 Oral literature

One kind of oral literature, the use of proverbs and parables, has particularly often been said to be characteristic of both Africa and African American societies in comparison to Europe (e.g. Roberts 1988:157-58). The proverbs themselves are often similar from one Creole-speaking area to another (cf e.g. Roberts 1988:156-59; Jones 1971:85ff; Poullet, Telchid & Montbrand 1984;

---

la portuguesa que llaman lengua de San Thomé, al modo que ahora nosostros hablamos con todo género de negros y naciones con nuestra lengua española corrupta, como comúnmente la hablan todos los negros" (Sandoval 1627:94). [My translation: Those that we call Creoles of São Tomé, because of having been in contact with barbarians there, for the most part make themselves understood in a sort of very corrupt and backwards version of Portuguese called 'the language of São Tomé', for which reason we too now speak to blacks of different ethnicities in a corrupt Spanish, as the blacks themselves commonly do].

36 Note, however, that Bastide (1971:11) explicitly claims that there is no connexion between the dominance of a certain African culture in a New World territory and the number of slaves imported from the corresponding area of Africa.

37 In e-mail correspondence with Gullah-speakers, I have been repeatedly been assured that every single Gullah can trace his or her ancestry to Sierra Leone, and that demographic input from other areas was negligible. My questioning of this "truth" offended some correspondents.

Jadfard 1997:57ff; Thomas 1869:116-24; Shillingford 1970:31).[38] Widespread proverbs such as *In front of the hen, the cockroach is never right* have been attested in at least Barbados, Jamaica, Louisiana, Haiti, Guadeloupe, Dominica, Martinique, St Lucia, Grenada, Trinidad, French Guiana and Curaçao (David & Jardel 1971 cited in Prudent 1980:98; Hall 1966:40). David & Jardel also mention the saying *If you can't suck your mummy, then suck your granny* ('One must make the best of what there is if nothing better is available') in several FCs, which also exists in a number of ECs (e.g. Allsopp 1976:17; Mathews 1822:77). I have not taken the time to investigate the potentially African origin of these proverbs but, if they are indeed African, they too might contribute to the knowledge of the precise geographical origins of today's African American populations.

The same applies to the use of riddles, which may also be a more integrated part of Afro-American than European culture. Riddles of the type *Standing water? Sugar cane!* and *Hanging water? Coconut!* (or *orange*) exist in a number of Creole-speaking areas, including Sierra Leone, Guadeloupe and Dominica, but also Mauritius (Fyle & Jones 1980:388-89; Poullet, Telchid & Montbrand 1984:92; Shillingford 1970:31; Baissac 1880; see also Roberts 1988:155-56).

Opening and closing formulas used in story telling could potentially provide some information on the origins of the peoples participating in the formation of Atlantic Creoles. The Sranan folktale opening formulas containing /tin tin tin/ and /kri kra/ are strikingly similar to /tim tim/ and /krik krak/, used with similar function in most American FCs (Bartens 1996:152), and may be of African origin. The latter is also documented for Belize EC (Escure 1986:46-7), and the former for Virgin Islands EC (Emanuel 1972).

Similarly, the very themes of the stories (see Chaudenson 1992:270-71; Bartens 1996:153-55; Parsons 1933, 1936 and 1943) are likely to contain elements of African origin which may shed further light on the origins of the Creole speakers.

The characters figuring in the traditional folktales would also seem to be able to tell us something about the origins of the Creole creators,[39] but my data are too limited to allow any firm conclusions.

The most well-known character is undoubtedly the spider, usually known under his Akan name Anansi. The spider, unknown as a folktale hero in Europe, is well known in most of Lower Guinea, and also in most Atlantic Creoles. He is known as Anansi in Gullah EC, Bahamas EC, Jamaica EC, Belize EC, Miskito Coast EC, Antigua EC, Nevis EC, St Vincent EC, Guyana EC, Sranan EC, Ndyuka EC, Saramaccan EC, Haiti FC, Dominica FC, Carriacou FC, Guiana FC, Negerhollands DC, Papiamentu SC and in Chocó Black Spanish of Colombia (see e.g. Baker 1993:146, 1999a:318; Josselin de Jong 1926:28; Hall 1966:95; Escure 1986:46; Anglade 1998:58-59; Smith 1997; Bartens 1996:150; Adamson & van Rossem 1995:79; Roberts 1988:147-48). Not only is the name of the spider of Akan origin, but the very use of a spider as a folktale hero points at Lower Guinean influence, although this feature apparently extends into the southern part of Upper Guinea (Tchang 1990).

In the FC-speaking Commonwealth Antilles, the spider is also known in folktales, but usually as /kɔ̃pɛ zajẽ/ (< F *Compère Araignée*) rather than as Anansi (Allsopp [ed.] 1996:29).[40]

The absence of the spider is most conspicuous in Louisiana and in the African PCs, but Louisiana FC and Upper Guinea PC folktales, as well as those of Haiti, feature the hyena in the trickster role. Not only is the hyena typical of Upper Guinean oral literature (Tchang 1990:152), but the character is known as /buki/ in Louisiana and Haiti, as in Wolof (Hall 1992:96; Bartens

38 However, just as is the case with conventionalised greetings, some caution may be required, since proverbs often represent manifestations of common human wisdom independent of cultural affiliation. For instance, the Yoruba saying *When the cat is gone, the house is taken over by the mice* (Ward 1952:253) is close to proverbs of several European languages (cf English *When the cat's away, the mice will play*, French *Quand le chat dort, les souris dansent*, German *Wenn die Katze außer dem Haus ist, tanzen die Mäuse*, Swedish *När katten är borta, dansar råttorna på bordet* and Irish *Nuair atá an cat amuigh bíonn na luch ag damhsa*), but this presumably does not indicate cultural diffusion.

39 Lichtveld (1931), said to provide detailed information on this subject, was unfortunately unavailable to me.

40 In Dominica FC, the Rabbit (/kɔ̃pɛ lapẽ/) often has the role of the spider, but it is interesting to note that even so, his speech shares some of the peculiarities of Anansi's. Just like Anansi (at least in Cuba, Jamaica, Surinam, Sierra Leone, Liberia and Nigeria), *Compère Lapin* palatalises /s/ into /ʃ/ in Dominica (Shillingford 1970). Anansi's speech is otherwise characterised by lisping and nasality (Roberts 1988:152; Carrington 1984:21), among other things (see also Cassidy & Le Page 1967:483).

1996:151).[41] The presence of the hyena must thus be taken as an indication of Upper Guinean influence. To my knowledge, it is not attested in the oral literature of areas where ECs, DCs, Lower Guinean PCs or SCs are spoken.

The Elephant occurs in folktales of Guadeloupe and Martinique (Bartens 1996:151), as well as in a large number of African cultures, mostly in Buntu (Tchang 1990:152). The fact that the Elephant is referred to as /zãba/ in Lesser Antillean FC (a word probably related to western Bantu forms, cf. Baker 1993:146 and Ferraz 1979:91) strengthens the hypothesis that the folktale character is a Bantu legacy.

The two remaining major tricksters of Atlantic Creole folktales, the Hare (or Rabbit) and the Turtle are somewhat less useful for the present purposes, since they occur in this role not only in Atlantic Creole cultures, but also in Europe, as well as in most of sub-Saharan Africa (Tchang 1990:152-53).

We may also note the presence of a Bantu character in Haitian folklore, the werewolf /bizɔ̃go/ who eats people through a hole in his back, is apparently based on Bantu traditions (Bastide 1971:110).

One final characteristic aspect of Creole (in this case Gullah) storytelling ascribed to African influence by Turner (1949:220-21) is frequent repetition, as exemplified in the extract below:

Gullah EC: /ɒj jɛdɪ di hɐws krakɪn, ju no, at dɪ bak; jɛdi dɪ haws krakɪn, krakɪn; an ɒj lɪsn, kipa lɪsnɪn/
'I heard the house cracking, you know, at the back; heard the house cracking, cracking; and I listened; kept listening' (Turner 1949:221).

6.7.3 Pragmatics

Pragmatic factors such as greetings and responses to greetings may also provide an fruitful field of research, although these seem to a great extent to be universal, in that many cultures independently of one another use greetings consisting of inquiries about the health of the interlocutor or his relatives, or requests for news in general. The fact that speakers of many or even most Atlantic ECs respond to the greeting *What's happening?* with /mi de/, which may be interpreted as either 'I exist' or 'I'm there' seems somewhat less expected, though, and may be of African origin.

6.7.3.1 Use of ideophones

The use of ideophones in Atlantic Creoles could be seen as a case of substrate influence intermediate between pragmatics and language structure. Their frequency in both West African languages and Atlantic Creoles, as well as their relative absence in Pidgins and Creoles elsewhere (Bartens 1996:132) makes it plausible that they are substrate-induced. They are also more numerous in Atlantic Creoles still in contact with African languages, i.e. the West African ECs and Guinea-Bissau PC (Bartens 2000). It is difficult, however, to relate specific ideophones to specific substrates. Rather, it seems that most Creole ideophones are coined locally.[42] So while there could be an African impetus behind the very presence of this lexical category virtually alien to or at least marginal in European languages, it is in general not possible to relate this to any specific West African substrate.[43]

6.7.4 Popular/religious beliefs

Many religious and supernatural beliefs are clearly African. In Haiti, where voodoo worship is particularly prevalent – a commonly repeated cliché is that while 90% of all Haitians are Catholics, 100% are voodoo practitioners – four different cults can be distinguished, three of

---

41 In Cape Verde PC, the same trickster is known as /lobu/ (< P *lobo*) (e.g. Meintel 1975:247), but despite what the etymology would lead one to expect, /lobu/ means 'hyena' rather than 'wolf'.

42 This is explicitly claimed for Guinea-Bissau PC by Scantamburlo (1981:66).

43 Ideophones for which this is indeed possible are included in the lexical study in §5.1.2. I have the impression (shared by Armin Schwegler, p c) that ideophones are less common in Bantu languages than they are in Upper and Lower Guinea, and should this be true, their frequency in the Creoles could provide some further clues regarding the substratal foundation of various Atlantic Creoles. For want of more detailed data, however, no firm conclusions can be drawn.

which correspond to slave-exporting areas in Africa, viz. *rada* (from the western Slave Coast, i.e. Gbe-speaking areas), *nago* (from Yoruba-speaking areas), and *kongo* (from Kikongo-speaking areas) (Hurbon 1993:71-72).[44] Most observers seem to agree that Gbe-speakers have left the most conspicuous imprint on the religious life of Haiti.

Voodoo traditions were formerly also present on the French Lesser Antilles and in Louisiana, but at least in the latter case, they can easily be coupled to the early 19th century immigration of Haitians (Bastide 1971:147; Tallant 1946).

As for other areas, Bastide (1971:59) gives examples of Boni (a Ndyuka-speaking group) deities of Akan, Gbe and Bantu origin. Note the absence of influence from Upper Guinea and Nigeria, much of which is and was dominated by Islam.

Bastide (1971:105-06) expresses some surprise at the small amount of Bantu influence on African American religious life, and suggests this to be due to Bantus having been more adaptive than Lower Guineans.

One might suppose that religious practices crystallise at a rather early stage, but the case of some Afro-American cultures shows that this evidence must be treated with some caution. For instance, Yoruba seems to have played a decisive role in the formation of Afro-Brazilian cults, reflected in the number of Yoruba-derived lexical items in Brazilian Vernacular Portuguese pertaining to this sphere (Castro & Castro 1977). However, although some Yorubas were sold to the Americas in the early 18th century, their share of the total volume exported from this region exceeded 10% only in the 1740s - if all African exports taken into account, this number would of course be far smaller – and became truly important only in the 19th century (Manning 1982:250, 335-37). Of course, by this time, Creole languages (and, one would imagine, Creole religions) had long been established. Judging only from historical and demographic evidence, we would thus expect the Yoruba impact on the New World African communities to be minimal. And yet – at least in terms of religious beliefs – this seems not to be the case.

6.7.5 Onomastics

Onomastics might provide further clues, but toponyms of African origin are rare – by the time African slaves became numerous in the plantation colonies, Europeans had already named most localities, and African names were in any case unlikely to gain official recognition.

A few place-names of African origin can nevertheless be found in Creole-speaking areas of the New World and off the African coast These include *Accompong* and *Bayacoota* in Jamaica, *Nago Town* and *Congo Town* in the Bahamas, *Bambarra* in the Turks and Caicos islands, the river names *Cassewina* and *Cormatijn* of Surinam, *Mayoumbé* on Marie-Galante, *Moudong* in Guadeloupe, *Pico do Mocambo* in São Tomé, *Matamba*, *Casingi*, *Casingito* and *Masinga* in the vicinity of El Palenque,[45] and *Engombe* in the Dominican Republic.

Personal names of African origin are also relatively rare – the Kwa habit of naming children for the weekday on which they were born has been recorded mostly in EC-speaking areas – in particular Jamaica, but also in Surinam and the Carolinas (Russell 1868; Cassidy & Le Page 1967; Patterson 1973:37; Sebba 1987:209; Mühlhäusler 1997:207; Turner 1949). Historically, a few attestations are also known from St Kitts, Barbados and Haiti (Anglade 1998:39; Philip Baker, p c). These naming customs, it seems, can relatively unequivocally be traced to Kwa, where similar naming systems exist in Twi and Fante (Akan), Ewe (Gbe), and Gã (Westermann 1939:34; Christaller 1875; Turner 1949; Bastide 1971:56; Christaller 1875; Redden et al. 1963:103). Meanwhile, Turner (1949:31), who did look for them in several other areas, did not find them elsewhere in Africa. Not only the practice as such, but also the names themselves, can be traced to Kwa, with contributions from both Akan and Gbe.

---

44 Hurbon (1993:75) suggests, however, that the features of the *nago* cult present in Haiti had been incorporated in the *rada* rituals before the practitioners left Africa, and it would thus not be directly indicative of a Yoruba component in Haitian culture. The fourth cult, *petro* consists of seemingly locally developed traditions.

45 The three latter are suggested by Schwegler (p c) to be cognate with *Cassewina*.

Turner (1949:43-190) is particularly valuable in that it contains about 3 500 personal names of African origin used in Gullah-speaking areas. Of these, approximately 1 250 are attested as names in various African languages,[46] summarised as follows:

AFRICAN LANGUAGE FAMILY	SHARE (N≈1 250)	MAJOR INDIVIDUAL CONTRIBUTORS
Mande	30,1%	Mende (11,0%)
Delto-Benuic	26,4%	Yoruba (19,8%),
Bantu	17,4%	Kikongo (11,8%), Kimbundu (3,9%)
Gbe	14,6%	Ewe (9,6%), Fon (5,0%)
Kwa	6,9%	Twi (5,8%)
Atlantic	4,7%	Wolof (2,1%), Fulfulde (1,6%)

As for Africans anthroponyms elsewhere, Emanuel (1972) discusses ten names from the US Virgin Islands.[47] Among these, he suggests that two are derived from Bantu, one from Fon and seven from Twi.

6.7.6 Physical anthropology

Few comparisons in this area seem to have been made between Creole-speaking populations and their putative African ancestors. The ones known to me were all carried out in Portuguese colonies, possibly because of the more favourable political climate offered by a fascistoid régime. None of these studies came to surprising conclusions. Studying the physical anthropology of the Angolares, Paulo (1959) and Almeida (1956) both claimed to find resemblances between these and populations in Angola. Another study from the same era, referred to in Meintel (1984:23) shows blood group correspondences between Cape Verdeans and members of various Senegambian ethnicities, such as Yolof, Bambara, Lebu, Fulfulde and Mandinka.

6.7.7 Dances, games, etc.

Dances are often of Bantu origin in Haiti, according to Bastide 1971:110, 177), but he also mentions one of Ewe origin (p 177).

If the African names of dances are anything to go by, these are about equally divided between Bantu and Kwa both in Haiti FC and in the Lesser Antilles FC varieties. For other Creoles, the number of dance names in *Afrolex* are too limited to allow any conclusions, though there may be an over-representation of Bantu terms in this semantic area.

6.7.8 Other cultural manifestations

Bastide (1971:54-57) enumerates a number of features of Surinamese cultures that bear witness to strong historical ties with Africa:

- Among the maroons, family organisation is matrilinear (Richard Price, p c). Bastide (1971:54-55) mentions only in passing that this is the case of many African cultures, but that Ewe kinship is patrilinear (p 70).[48] However, Saramaccan culture is characterised by 'double descent'; although the child belongs to its mother's clan, it inherits certain taboos and 'magical objects' from its father's clan – just as among the Akans (p 55). For the Boni, just as among the Akan peoples, there is also a restriction on marrying one's brother's widow (p 55).
- Surinam Maroon Burials include an interrogation with the dead (sic!) in order to determine the precise cause of death. Again, this is also the case in Akan cultures (p 58).
- Saramaccan sculpting, finally, has been claimed to be influenced by Akan aesthetic traditions, although there seems to be some evidence to the contrary (p 61).

---

46 The others are used as such in the Gullah-speaking area only, but are suggested by Turner to derive from other nouns in their respective source languages.

47 Actually 11, but he does not claim that /di/, which he suggests derived from the verb 'to eat' in Twi, would function as an anthroponym in Akan.

48 According to Beck (1998), Akan peoples are matrilineal.

As can be seen, the suggested link is usually to Kwa-speaking areas, more specifically to Akan, rather than to Gbe cultures.

As for matrilinearity, Schwegler (1998a:247) points out that this is also true of Kikongo-speaking societies, as well as (until the early 20th century) of the village where Palenquero SC is spoken. As we have just seen, though, other parts of Africa are matrilinear as well, and only with more detailed evidence, as just presented in favour of the Akan-Surinam link above, can Palenquero matriliearity with certainty be ascribed to Kikongo influence.

6.7.9 Summary of non-linguistic features

As opposed to the sections on linguistic features, I have not made an attempt to be exhaustive with regard to the cultural and folkloristic aspects. Part of the reason for including a section on the subject is merely to point at the possibility of backing historical/demographic data with this type of evidence. A comparison with the discussion on demographics earlier in this chapter shows that what little data I have compiled here on the origins of various cultural and other non-linguistic features basically matches the demographic profile of each territory.

FEATURE	LANGUAGE	GROUP	SUGGESTED SUBSTRATE INFLUENCE
Burial traditions	Surinam Maroon ECs	EC	+Akan
Kinship	Surinam Maroon ECs	EC	+Akan, -Gbe
Religion	Haiti FC	FC	+Gbe (+Bantu)
Religion	Ndyuka EC	EC	+Akan/ +Gbe/ +Bantu
Onomastics (day-names)	St Kitts EC	EC	+Kwa
Onomastics (day-names)	Barbados EC	EC	+Kwa
Onomastics (day-names)	Jamaica EC	EC	+Kwa
Onomastics (day-names)	Surinam ECs	EC	+Kwa
Onomastics (day-names)	Gullah EC	EC	+Kwa
Onomastics (in descending order)	Gullah EC	EC	Mande, Yoruba, Kikongo
Onomastics	Virgin Islands EC	EC	+Akan
Physical anthropology	Angolar PC	PC	+Bantu
Physical anthropology	Cape Verde PC	PC	+Atlantic, +Mande
Dances	Haiti FC	FC	+Bantu
Oral literature (Anansi stories)	Gullah EC	EC	+Akan
Oral literature (Anansi stories)	Western Caribbean ECs	EC	+Akan
Oral literature (Anansi stories)	Leeward Islands ECs	EC	+Akan
Oral literature (Anansi stories)	Surinam ECs	EC	+Akan
Oral literature (Anansi stories)	Haiti FC	FC	+Akan
Oral literature (Anansi stories)	Guiana FC	FC	+Akan
Oral literature (Anansi stories)	Lesser Antilles FC	FC	+Akan
Oral literature (Anansi stories)	Negerhollands DC	DC	+Akan
Oral literature (Anansi stories)	Papiamentu SC	SC	+Akan
Oral literature (Anansi stories)	Guyana EC	EC	+Akan
Oral literature (Buki stories)	Louisiana FC	FC	+Wolof
Oral literature (Buki stories)	Haiti FC	FC	+Wolof
Oral literature (Hyena trickster)	Upper Guinea PCs	PC	+Upper Guinea
Oral literature (Elephant trickster)	Lesser Antilles FC	FC	+Bantu
Oral literature (Bizongo the werewolf)	Haiti FC	FC	+Bantu

Table continued overleaf

FEATURE	LANGUAGE	GROUP	SUGGESTED SUBSTRATE INFLUENCE
Cultural similarities	Saramaccan EC	EC	+Slave Coast
Cultural similarities	Surinam EC	EC	+Akan
Cultural similarities	Barbados EC	EC	+Akan
Cultural similarities	Gullah EC	EC	+Akan
Cultural similarities	Jamaica EC	EC	+Akan
Cultural similarities	San Andrés EC	EC	+Akan
Cultural similarities	St Lucia FC	FC	+Akan
Cultural similarities	Haiti FC	FC	+Fon
Cultural similarities	Palenquero SC	SC	+Bantu
Oral tradition	Palenquero SC	SC	+Kikongo
Cryptolectal glossonym	Jamaica EC	EC	+Akan
Cryptolectal glossonym	Surinam ECs	EC	+Akan
Cryptolectal glossonym	Ndyuka EC	EC	+Gbe

Chapter 7

Summary and discussion of the results

The following table summarises the substrate influences suggested this far:

AREA	FEATURE	LANGUAGE	GROUP	SUGGESTED SUBSTRATE INFLUENCE
Core lexicon	1sg	Lower Guinea PC	PC	(+Ewe, +Gã, +Efik, +Igbo, +Tiv, +Yoruba, +Kikongo)
Core lexicon	1sg	Upper Guinea PC	PC	(+Balanta, +Mandinka)
Core lexicon	2pl	Barbados EC	EC	+Igbo
Core lexicon	2pl	Gullah EC	EC	+Igbo
Core lexicon	2pl	Surinamese ECs	EC	+Igbo
Core lexicon	2pl	West Africa EC	EC	+Igbo
Core lexicon	2pl	Western Caribbean ECs	EC	+Igbo
Core lexicon	2pl	Príncipe PC	PC	+Edo
Core lexicon	2pl	São Tomé PC, Príncipe PC	PC	+Umbundu, +Kimbundu
Core lexicon	2pl:IMPERATIVE	Palenquero SC	SC	+Kikongo
Core lexicon	2pl=1pl	Haiti FC (centre)	FC	+Ewe
Core lexicon	2sg	Surinamese ECs	EC	+Igbo
Core lexicon	2sg	Western Caribbean ECs	EC	+Igbo
Core lexicon	3pl	Berbice DC	DC	+Ijo
Core lexicon	3pl	Angolar PC	PC	+Kikongo, +Kimbundu
Core lexicon	3pl	São Tomé PC, Príncipe PC, Annobón PC	PC	+Edo, +Kimbundu
Core lexicon	3pl	Palenquero SC	SC	+Kikongo, +Kimbundu, +Chokwe
Core lexicon	3pl	Papiamentu SC	SC	+Wolof, +Edo
Core lexicon	3sg	Berbice DC	DC	+Ijo
Core lexicon	All bound morphemes	Berbice DC	DC	+Ijo
Core lexicon	Exceptionally high number of basic vocabulary items	Berbice DC	DC	+Ijo
Core lexicon	Exceptionally high number of basic vocabulary items	Angolar PC	PC	+Kimbundu
Core lexicon	Generic/impersonal pronoun	Gulf of Guinea PCs	PC	+Edo, +Wano, +Igbo, +Izi, +Yoruba
Core lexicon	Intensifying morpheme	Saramaccan EC	EC	+Fon
Core lexicon	Interrogatives	Berbice DC	DC	+Ijo
Core lexicon	Interrogatives	Saramaccan EC	EC	+Fon
Core lexicon	Interrogatives	Angolar PC	PC	+Kimbundu
Core lexicon	Most numerals	Angolar PC	PC	+Kimbundu
Core lexicon	Pluraliser	Berbice DC	DC	+Ijo
Core lexicon	Pluraliser	Palenquero SC	SC	+Bantu
Core lexicon	Sentence negation	Upper Guinea PCs	PC	(+Mandinka)
Lexicon	Lexicon (in descending order)	Negerhollands DC	DC	Bantu, Kwa, Delto-Benuic
Lexicon	Lexicon (in descending order)	Barbados EC	EC	Kwa/Delto-Benuic, Bantu
Lexicon	Lexicon (in descending order)	Gullah EC	EC	Mande/Bantu[1], Atlantic
Lexicon	Lexicon (in descending order)	Leewards Islands ECs	EC	Kwa, Delto-Benuic, Bantu
Lexicon	Lexicon (in descending order)	Surinamese ECs	EC	Kwa, Bantu, Delto-Benuic
Lexicon	Lexicon (in descending order)	Western Caribbean ECs	EC	Kwa, Delto-Benuic, Bantu
Lexicon	Lexicon (in descending order)	Guiana FC	FC	Kwa, Delto-Benuic, Bantu/Mande
Lexicon	Lexicon (in descending order)	Haiti FC	FC	Kwa (mostly Gbe), Bantu, Delto-Benuic
Lexicon	Lexicon (in descending order)	Lesser Antilles FCs	FC	Bantu, Kwa, Atlantic
Lexicon	Lexicon (in descending order)	Louisiana FC	FC	Bantu, Mande, Atlantic

1 Depending on whether the words "used only in stories, songs and prayers" (mostly of Mande origin) are included or not.

Area	Feature	Language	Group	Suggested substrate influence
Lexicon	Lexicon (in descending order)	Annobón PC	PC	Delto-Benuic, Bantu
Lexicon	Lexicon (in descending order)	Cape Verde PC	PC	Mande, Atlantic
Lexicon	Lexicon (in descending order)	Guinea-Bissau PC	PC	Atlantic, Mande
Lexicon	Lexicon (in descending order)	Príncipe PC	PC	Delto-Benuic, Bantu
Lexicon	Lexicon (in descending order)	São Tomé PC	PC	Bantu, Delto-Benuic
Lexicon	Lexicon (in descending order)	Palenquero SC	SC	Bantu
Lexicon	Lexicon (in descending order)	Papiamentu SC	SC	Kwa, Bantu
Lexicon	Oldest lexical stratum	ECs	EC	43% Kwa (mostly Akan), 17% Bantu, 21% Delto-Benuic, 10% Atlantic, 8% Mande
Lexicon	Oldest lexical stratum	Gulf of Guinea PC	PC	49% Delto-Benuic, 44% Bantu
Lexicon	Oldest lexical stratum	Upper Guinea PC	PC	54% Mande, 42% Atlantic
Lexicon	Oldest lexical stratum	FCs	FC	15% Atlantic, 7% Mande, 20% Kwa (mostly Gbe), 13% Delto-Benuic, 44% Bantu
Phonetics	Aspiration	Cameroon EC	EC	-Kwa, -Susu, -Isekiri
Phonetics	Aspiration	Gullah EC	EC	-Kwa, -Susu, -Isekiri
Phonetics	Aspiration	Cape Verde PC	PC	+Wolof, +Kisi
Phonology	Coarticulated stops	Gullah EC	EC	+Lower Guinea, -Akan
Phonology	Coarticulated stops	Surinamese ECs	EC	+Lower Guinea, -Akan
Phonology	Coarticulated stops	West African ECs	EC	+Lower Guinea, -Akan
Phonology	Coarticulated stops	Príncipe PC	PC	+Lower Guinea, -Akan
Phonology	Denasalisation	Saramaccan EC	EC	(+Atlantic, +Kikongo, +Kimbundu)
Phonology	Denasalisation	Louisiana FC	FC	(+Atlantic), (+Kikongo), (+Kimbundu)
Phonology	Denasalisation	Angolar PC	PC	(+Atlantic, +Kikongo, +Kimbundu)
Phonology	Denasalisation	Guinea-Bissau PC	PC	(+Atlantic, +Kikongo, +Kimbundu)
Phonology	High nasal vowels	Negerhollands DC	DC	(+Mande, +Kwa, +SW Delto-Benuic)
Phonology	High nasal vowels	Jamaica EC	EC	(+Mande, +Kwa, +SW Delto-Benuic)
Phonology	High nasal vowels	Krio EC	EC	(+Mande, +Kwa, +SW Delto-Benuic)
Phonology	High nasal vowels	Surinamese ECs	EC	(+Mande, +Kwa, +SW Delto-Benuic)
Phonology	High nasal vowels	Haiti FC	FC	(+Mande, +Kwa, +SW Delto-Benuic)
Phonology	High nasal vowels	Lesser Antilles FC	FC	(+Mande, +Kwa, +SW Delto-Benuic)
Phonology	High nasal vowels	Papiamentu SC	SC	(+Mande, +Kwa, +SW Delto-Benuic)
Phonology	Interdental fricatives	Angolar PC	PC	+Ndingi Kikongo
Phonology	Lack of /z/	Berbice DC	DC	+Atlantic, +Akan, -Gbe, , +Ijo
Phonology	Lack of /z/	Negerhollands DC	DC	(+Atlantic, +Akan, -Gbe, , +Ijo)
Phonology	Lack of /z/	Surinamese ECs	EC	+Akan
Phonology	Lack of /z/	West African ECs	EC	+Atlantic, +Akan, -Gbe, +Ijo
Phonology	Lack of /z/	Cape Verde PC	PC	(+Atlantic, +Akan, -Gbe, , +Ijo)
Phonology	Lack of /z/	Guinea-Bissau PC	PC	+Atlantic, +Akan, -Gbe, +Ijo
Phonology	Merger of /p/ and /f/	Cameroon EC	EC	(+Kwa, +Adamawa Fulfulde, +Izi)
Phonology	Merger of /p/ and /f/	Jamaica EC†	EC	(+Kwa, +Adamawa Fulfulde, +Izi)
Phonology	Merger of /p/ and /f/	Saramaccan EC (Líbase dialect)	EC	(+Kwa, +Adamawa Fulfulde, +Izi)
Phonology	Merger of /r/ and /l/	Surinamese ECs	EC	+Bantu, +Gbe, -Akan, -Atlantic, -Delto-Benuic
Phonology	Merger of /r/ and /l/	Gulf of Guinea PCs (except Príncipense)	PC	+Bantu, +Gbe, -Akan, -Atlantic, -Delto-Benuic
Phonology	Merger of /v/ and /b/	Negerhollands DC	DC	(+Akan, -Gbe, +various language from all areas)
Phonology	Merger of /v/ and /b/	ECs	EC	(+Akan, -Gbe, +various language from all areas)
Phonology	Merger of /v/ and /b/	Gullah EC	EC	+Akan, -Gbe, +various language from all areas
Phonology	Merger of /v/ and /b/	Surinamese ECs[2]	EC	+Akan, -Gbe, +various language from all areas

[2] English-derived lexical component only.

AREA	FEATURE	LANGUAGE	GROUP	SUGGESTED SUBSTRATE INFLUENCE
Phonology	Merger of /v/ and /b/	Cape Verde PC	PC	(+Akan, -Gbe, +various language from all areas)
Phonology	Merger of /v/ and /b/	Guinea-Bissau PC	PC	+Akan, -Gbe, +various language from all areas
Phonology	Merger of /v/ and /b/	Gulf of Guinea PCs except Príncipe PC	PC	(+Akan, -Gbe, +various language from all areas)
Phonology	Merger of /v/ and /b/	Papiamentu SC	SC	+Akan, -Gbe, +various language from all areas
Phonology	Palatalisation	Gulf of Guinea PCs except Príncipe PC	PC	+Ewe, +Igbo, +Etsako, +Kikongo
Phonology	Palatalisation	Príncipe PC	PC	+Edo
Phonology	Post-vocalic /r/	Guiana FC	FC	+Atlantic
Phonology	Post-vocalic /r/	Haiti FC (north)	FC	+Atlantic
Phonology	Post-vocalic /r/	Louisiana FC	FC	+Atlantic
Phonology	Prenasalised fricatives	Palenquero SC	SC	+Bantu?
Phonology	Prenasalised stops	Negerhollands DC†	DC	(+Upper Guinea, +Bantu)
Phonology	Prenasalised stops	Gullah EC	EC	+Upper Guinea, +Bantu
Phonology	Prenasalised stops	Jamaican Maroon Spirit EC	EC	+Upper Guinea, +Bantu
Phonology	Prenasalised stops	Surinamese ECs	EC	+Upper Guinea, +Bantu
Phonology	Prenasalised stops	West African EC	EC	+Upper Guinea, +Bantu
Phonology	Prenasalised stops	Gulf of Guinea PC	PC	+Upper Guinea, +Bantu
Phonology	Prenasalised stops	Palenquero SC	SC	+Upper Guinea, +Bantu
Phonology	Prenasalised stops	Papiamentu SC†	SC	(+Upper Guinea, +Bantu)
Phonology	stop+liquid clusters	Jamaica EC	EC	+Gbe (+Dagaari, +Baule)
Phonology	Syllable structure	Negerhollands DC	DC	+Kwa, +Isoko
Phonology	Syllable structure	ECs	EC	-Atlantic
Phonology	Syllable structure	FCs	FC	+Atlantic
Phonology	Vowel aperture	Negerhollands DC	DC	+Bantu, -Kwa, -Delto-Benuic
Phonology	Vowel aperture	Ndyuka EC	EC	+Bantu, -Kwa, -Delto-Benuic
Phonology	Vowel aperture	Sranan EC	EC	+Bantu, -Kwa, -Delto-Benuic
Phonology	Vowel aperture	Louisiana FC (basilect)	FC	+Bantu, -Kwa, -Delto-Benuic
Phonology	Vowel aperture	Annobón PC	PC	+Bantu, -Kwa, -Delto-Benuic
Phonology	Vowel aperture	Guinea-Bissau PC	PC	+ various Atlantic and Mande languages
Syntax	3pl=pl	Negerhollands DC	DC	+Ewe, +Twi, +Igbo, +Fulfulde
Syntax	3pl=pl	Bahamas EC	EC	+Ewe, +Twi, +Igbo, +Fulfulde
Syntax	3pl=pl	Gullah EC	EC	+Ewe, +Twi, +Igbo, +Fulfulde
Syntax	3pl=pl	Guyana EC	EC	+Ewe, +Twi, +Igbo, +Fulfulde
Syntax	3pl=pl	Leeward Islands EC	EC	+Ewe, +Twi, +Igbo, +Fulfulde
Syntax	3pl=pl	West Africa EC	EC	+Ewe, +Twi, +Igbo, +Fulfulde
Syntax	3pl=pl	Western Caribbean EC	EC	+Ewe, +Twi, +Igbo, +Fulfulde
Syntax	3pl=pl	Windward Islands EC	EC	+Ewe, +Twi, +Igbo, +Fulfulde
Syntax	3pl=pl	Guiana FC	FC	+Ewe, +Twi, +Igbo, +Fulfulde
Syntax	3pl=pl	Haiti FC	FC	+Ewe, +Twi, +Igbo, +Fulfulde
Syntax	3pl=pl	Louisiana FC	FC	+Ewe, +Twi, +Igbo, +Fulfulde, +Fante, +Gã, +Aja, +Gẽ, +Yoruba
Syntax	3pl=pl	Gulf of Guinea PC	PC	+Yoruba, +Ewe, +Fante, +Gã, +Aja, +Gẽ (+Edo?)
Syntax	3pl=pl	Papiamentu SC	SC	+Ewe, +Twi, +Igbo, +Fulfulde, +Yoruba
Syntax	Conjunction from 3sg	Saramaccan EC	EC	(+Lower Guinea)
Syntax	Conjunction from 3sg	Príncipe PC	PC	(+Lower Guinea)
Syntax	Internal NP syntax	Annobón PC	PC	+Bantu
Syntax	Negation	Berbice DC	DC	+Ijo
Syntax	Negation	Gulf of Guinea PCs	PC	+Wolof, +Kisi, +Abri, +Ewe, +several Delto-Benuic languages, +almost any Bantu language
Syntax	Negation	Palenquero SC	SC	+Wolof, +Kisi, +Abri, +Ewe, +several Delto-Benuic languages, +almost any Bantu language

AREA	FEATURE	LANGUAGE	GROUP	SUGGESTED SUBSTRATE INFLUENCE
Syntax	Negation	Papiamentu SC	SC	+Wolof, +Kisi, +Abri, +Ewe, +several Delto-Benuic languages, +almost any Bantu language
Syntax	Postpositions	Berbice DC	DC	+Ijo
Syntax	Postpositions	Surinamese ECs	EC	+Mande, +Gur, +Kru, +Kwa
Syntax	PROG as FUT	Belize EC	EC	(+Kisi, +Fante, +Gã, +Igbo)
Syntax	PROG as FUT	Jamaica EC	EC	(+Kisi, +Fante, +Gã, +Igbo)
Syntax	PROG as FUT	Haiti FC	FC	+Kisi, +Fante, +Gã, +Igbo
Syntax	PROG as FUT	Louisiana FC	FC	+Kisi, +Fante, +Gã, +Igbo
Syntax	PROG as FUT	Guinea-Bissau PC	PC	+Kisi, +Fante, +Gã, +Igbo
Syntax	Reduplication	Jamaica EC	EC	+Kwa, +Delto-Benuic
Syntax	Reduplication	Nigeria EC	EC	+Kwa, +Delto-Benuic
Syntax	Reduplication	Surinamese ECs	EC	+Kwa, +Delto-Benuic
Syntax	Reduplication	Guinea-Bissau PC	PC	+Atlantic
Syntax	Reflexivisation	Nigeria EC	EC	+Kwa, +Delto-Benuic, +Atlantic
Syntax	Reflexivisation	Guiana FC	FC	+Kwa, +Delto-Benuic, +Atlantic
Syntax	Reflexivisation	Haiti FC (buttocks)	FC	+Igbo
Syntax	Reflexivisation	Haiti FC (head)	FC	+Atlantic
Syntax	Reflexivisation	Haiti FC (north)	FC	+Kwa, +Delto-Benuic, +Atlantic
Syntax	Reflexivisation	Lesser Antilles FC	FC	+Kwa, +Delto-Benuic, +Atlantic
Syntax	Reflexivisation	Louisiana FC (body)	FC	+Kwa, +Delto-Benuic, +Atlantic
Syntax	Reflexivisation	Louisiana FC (head)	FC	+Atlantic
Syntax	Reflexivisation	Cape Verde PC	PC	+Atlantic
Syntax	Reflexivisation	Guinea-Bissau PC (body)	PC	+Kwa, +Delto-Benuic, +Atlantic
Syntax	Reflexivisation	Guinea-Bissau PC (head)	PC	+Atlantic
Syntax	Reflexivisation	Gulf of Guinea PC	PC	+Kwa, +Delto-Benuic, +Atlantic
Syntax	Reflexivisation	Papiamentu SC	SC	+Kwa, +Delto-Benuic, +Atlantic
Syntax	Verbal serialisation	Berbice DC	DC	+Lower Guinea
Syntax	Verbal serialisation	Negerhollands DC	DC	+Kwa
Syntax	Verbal serialisation	Gullah EC	EC	++Lower Guinea
Syntax	Verbal serialisation	Guyana EC	EC	++Lower Guinea
Syntax	Verbal serialisation	Leeward Islands ECs	EC	++Lower Guinea
Syntax	Verbal serialisation	Surinamese ECs	EC	++Kwa
Syntax	Verbal serialisation	West Africa ECs	EC	++Lower Guinea
Syntax	Verbal serialisation	Western Caribbean ECs	EC	++Lower Guinea
Syntax	Verbal serialisation	Windward Islands ECs	EC	++Lower Guinea
Syntax	Verbal serialisation	Guiana FC	FC	++Lower Guinea
Syntax	Verbal serialisation	Haiti FC	FC	++Lower Guinea
Syntax	Verbal serialisation	Lesser Antilles FCs	FC	++Lower Guinea
Syntax	Verbal serialisation	Louisiana FC	FC	+Lower Guinea
Syntax	Verbal serialisation	Gulf of Guinea PC	PC	++Lower Guinea
Syntax	Verbal serialisation	Upper Guinea PC	PC	-Lower Guinea
Syntax	Verbal serialisation	Palenquero SC	SC	-Lower Guinea
Syntax	Verbal serialisation	Papiamentu SC	SC	+Lower Guinea
Syntax	Verbum dicendi complementation	Berbice DC	DC	+Ijo
Syntax	Verbum dicendi complementation	Negerhollands DC	DC	(+Mande), +Lower Guinea
Syntax	Verbum dicendi complementation	ECs	EC	(+Mande), +Lower Guinea
Syntax	Verbum dicendi complementation	Lesser Antilles FCs	FC	(+Mande), +Lower Guinea
Syntax	Verbum dicendi complementation	Guinea-Bissau PC	PC	(+Mande)
Syntax	Verbum dicendi complementation	Gulf of Guinea PCs	PC	(+Lower Guinea)
Syntax/ Phonology	Agglutination	Surinamese ECs	EC	+Kwa, +Delto-Benuic
Syntax/ Phonology	Agglutination	Gulf of Guinea PCs (especially Príncipe PC)	PC	+Kwa, +Delto-Benuic

7.1 To what extent do demographics and linguistics match?

On the whole, there does seem to be a correlation between the substrate influences identified in the Atlantic Creoles and the demographic reconstruction of the respective creolophone territories. Each case will be discussed separately below, but let us first note that there are three Atlantic Creoles which seem to have an exceptionally homogenous substrate composition.

7.1.1 Three exceptional Creoles

Three Creoles - Berbice DC, Angolar PC, and Palenquero SC - stand out as being exceptionally homogenous with regard to the linguistic features discussed.

Most substrate influences identified for Berbice DC can be traced to Ijo, and none is incompatible with this language. It is striking that there is no proof that Ijo-speakers were ever taken to the Berbice colony but, as Smith (1999) points out, the linguistic evidence is so strong that the conclusion that a contingent of Ijos later lost to history played a crucial role in the formation of the language is inescapable. This is also the generally accepted view - to my knowledge, no writer has ever contested the impact of Ijo on Berbice DC, and indeed, it is often given as an example of a Creole where substrate features are exceptionally easily detected.

The substrate-induced features of Angolar PC, to the extent that these are not shared by the other Gulf of Guinea Creoles, can without exception be attributed to Bantu influence, usually from Kimbundu. Given that Angolar PC is structurally virtually identical to São Tomé PC - at least in Lorenzino's (1998) description - it seems that the impact of Kimbundu has little to do with creolisation, but rather that Angolar is the result of a partial relexification of an already developed Creole, i.e. an early form of São Tomé PC. As mentioned earlier (§6.4.2), Kimbundu-speakers were dominant among slaves imported by the Portuguese from the 1560s, which suggests that Angolar began to form around this time.

Palenquero SC, finally, is also reckoned to be exceptionally influenced by a single language, viz. Kikongo. Again, many of the features discussed here are clearly Kikongo (or at least Bantu) in origin, and none requre recourse to other areas of West Africa. As mentioned above (§6.6.2), Bantu-speakers supplanted Yolofs as the dominant African group in the Cartagena area from the 1580s. The main conclusion to be drawn from that is that the Palenquero maroon group and its language must have crystallised after this date, but before the upheaval created by the numerical dominance of speakers of Bantu languages in the mid-17th century, something that well fits what little documentation there is on the subject (see §6.6.2).

For the other Atlantic Creoles, the picture is considerably more complex.

7.1.2 English Creoles

7.1.2.1 Gullah EC

As mentioned in §6.2.1, Gullah has strong historical links with the anglophone Caribbean, and the overall structure of the language proves that it must have sprung from varieties imported from Barbados, St Kitts and other Antillean islands. Like other New World ECs, it is strongly marked by Lower Guinean languages. The wide range of serialising constructions, the Igbo 2pl pronoun and several other structures establish the Lower Guinean connexion.

Gullah EC is still special among Atlantic ECs in that Upper Guinean languages have left their mark on this Creole. Depending on whether or not one includes Turner's (1949) collection of "words heard only in stories, songs and prayers", Mande or Bantu are the biggest lexical contributors. Also, the lack of aspiration of voiceless plosives is incompatible with most Lower Guinean languages. Nevertheless, the Upper Guinean impact on Gullah EC is quite compatible with the post-formative arrivals of slaves from Senegambia and Sierra Leone (§6.2.1). But again, Gullah EC provides evidence that the essentials of the syntactic structure of proto-Atlantic EC were in place at least before the 1720s, when Upper Guineans (and later Bantus) came to dominate the slave population of the Carolinas, and that the impact of these groups was primarily lexical, and possibly to some extent phonological.

7.1.2.2 Western Caribbean ECs

The Western Caribbean ECs, i.e. Jamaica EC and its close relatives in Belize, the Miskito Coast, and San Andrés and Providence islands and elsewhere, also trace their origins to the Lesser Antilles, and therefore share the same initial substrate composition as the ECs of Barbados and St Kitts. Including this initial period, Lower Guinean languages predominated for most of the time during which we may surmise that proto-Western Caribbean EC formed.

Indeed, every single substrate-induced feature in Western Caribbean ECs discussed is potentially traceable to Lower Guinea and, just like other varieties of New World EC, the Western Caribbean ECs contrast with FCs in having few or no traits that require recourse to other areas of West Africa. There is also a contrast in that ECs generally are more closely aligned with Akan than with Gbe (of the Lower Guinean languages).

Among the putatively Lower Guinean features, several are widespread throughout Lower Guinea. All the others, such as the Igbo pronoun(s), the oldest lexical stratum, and the partial merger of labials, belong to the common core of Atlantic ECs. It is therefore difficult to pinpoint the origin of Western Caribbean ECs beyond the observation that they are more closely connected to Lower Guinean languages than many other New World Creoles.

As with other Atlantic ECs, the relative absence of Bantu influence suggests a crystallisation posterior to the 1640s, when Lower Guineans surpassed Bantus in number (or that the ancestor of Western Caribbean EC was born in Africa; cf §7.2.2).

7.1.2.3 Eastern Caribbean ECs[3]

The Lesser Antillean ECs show indisputable marks of Lower Guinean influence in their lexicon and rich inventory of serial verb constructions. The other features found on the Lesser Antilles are all compatible with a Lower Guinean origin. We encounter once again the Igbo 2pl pronoun on Barbados and islands colonised therefrom (but not on the Leewards, for which St Kitts was the centre of diffusion), but otherwise there is some evidence of Kwa and, more specifically Akan, as having been the major source of substrate features. This goes both for the lexicon in general, and for its presumably oldest layer, as well as for the merger between /b/ and /v/.

All this is compatible with the demographic data insofar as Lower Guineans formed a majority of the imported slaves on both St Kitts and Barbados from the 1640s and onwards. There never were, however, large numbers of Igbos on Barbados who could have introduced the 2pl pronoun. Even more problematic is that Gold Coast imports (responsible for the Akan influence) never exceeded a fifth of the total, nor constituted the largest group on either of these two islands until the last decade of the 17th century. So, while the general character of the Lesser Antilles ECs matches the substratal composition, the presence of an Igbo pronoun and of an early stratum of Akan vocabulary does not (cf §7.2.1).

7.1.2.4 Surinamese ECs

Lower Guineans formed the majority of arrivals in Surinam for most of the 17th and early 18th centuries and, from the 1640s, also in Barbados and St Kitts whose Creoles are ancestral to those of Surinam. Bantus were also well represented throughout most of this period, whereas the Upper Guinean contribution is virtually negligible.

The vast majority of Surinam EC substrate features discussed here can, with reasonable certainty, be traced to Lower Guinea. Only three phonological features are likely to be of Bantu origin (denasalisation, vowel aperture, prenasalised stops), while one other may be so (liquid merger).

Lexically, it is Kwa that has provided the largest number of items, followed by Bantu and Delto-Benuic languages. Inherited lexicon from the ECs of the insular Caribbean includes an important share of Akan lexicon and at least one Igbo personal pronoun (though the Surinam ECs may have one or two more pronouns of Igbo origin). In addition to this, Saramaccan EC has core lexical material (two interrogatives and an intensifying morpheme) from Fon, which are not found elsewhere.

---

3 Though treated as an entity here, the reader will have noticed that the various islands were discussed separately above.

All the syntactic features surveyed occur widely in Lower Guinean languages, although the presence of postpositions and TMA marking of serial verb constructions point more specifically to Kwa.

To the extent that the Kwa influences can be differentiated, it is interesting to note that two features, namely the merger of /b/ and /v/ and the lack of /z/, must be assigned to Akan, while two others, coarticulated stops and the merger of liquids (unless of Bantu origin), suggest the impact of Gbe rather than Akan.

In sum, the presence of Kwa, Delto-Benuic and Bantu traits in the Surinam ECs is expected – all three groups were well represented, and speakers of each formed an absolute majority of the substrate population at various points in time during the 17th or early 18th centuries. The only real surprise is the presence of the Igbo pronoun(s) (§7.2.1) – the proportion of slaves imported from Biafra never exceeded a tenth in Surinam, and dropped to less than 1% in the 1680s.

7.1.2.5 West African ECs

Since the West African ECs are, by and large, Transatlantic imports, a discussion of their linguistic peculiarities and demographic background is of limited relevance here. The most important observations that can be made are (i) that the substrate features that these languages display are also found in the New World, which in itself is an argument for importation from the Americas rather local genesis, and (ii) that the substrate features are reminiscent of Lower Guinean languages rather than of Mande and Atlantic, which are spoken in Sierra Leone. Again, this speaks against Hancock's (e.g. 1986) scenario of Krio EC having originated locally.

7.1.3 French Creoles

7.1.3.1 Louisiana FC

In Louisiana FC, the demographic data would lead us to expect an unusually high proportion of Upper Guinean features and a near complete absence of Bantu influence, and this is indeed largely what we do find.

The high proportion of Bantu lexical items obviously requires a comment, however. First of all, the total number of Louisiana FC Africanisms in *Afrolex* is only 13. Secondly, those of Bantu origin are, without exception, attested also in Haiti FC, from which they may have been introduced to Louisiana by the immigrants fleeing the Haitian revolution at the eve of the 19th century. The Mande items, by contrast, are not used in Haiti, and this further underlines the importance of Upper Guinean languages in Louisiana.

One other feature was tentatively ascribed to Bantu influence, namely the reduction of four degrees of vowel aperture to three. Although a small number of Bantus were indeed present in Louisiana, it must be borne in mind that other languages, including some from Upper Guinea, could have had a similar influence (§3.1.1).

The remaining two phonological features, as well as the five syntactic ones, are all compatible with Upper or Lower Guinean origins.

7.1.3.2 Haiti FC

The oldest lexical layer of Haiti FC, with its strong Bantu component, must have been brought to that country from the Lesser Antilles. To this was apparently added a Gbe component, since Gbe is the dominant overall contributor of lexical Africanisms in Haiti FC.

Most of the structural parallels between Haiti FC and African languages point to Lower Guinea, which is unsurprising, given that Lower Guineans alone dominated the slave population of Haiti for most of the colonial period. Although it might be a pure coincidence, it is interesting to note that no less than three of the features that are not more widely attested match Igbo,[4] with two others being more generally Lower Guinean. So far as I am aware, Igbos were never well represented in the servile work force in Haiti. Four of the structural features are also compatible with one or more Atlantic languages. If these are indeed to be traced to Atlantic, it seems

4 3pl=pl, PROG as FUT and reflexive 'buttocks'.

reasonable to assume that they entered the language in the 1680s, the only period when speakers of Atlantic languages were numerically well represented.

Phonologically, Haiti FC presents the same problem as Lesser Antilles FC, in that the lack of syllable restructuring is unexpected given the strong Lower Guinean and Bantu presence. For Haiti, however, the period when extensive settlement began was characterised by a strong presence of speakers of Atlantic languages and, as we saw in §6.7.2, these arrivals did leave their mark on Haitian culture.

Despite the emphasis on Fon in the works of Lefebvre (e.g. 1993, 1998), no specific structural similarities with that language were observed.

7.1.3.3 Lesser Antilles FCs

The Lesser Antilles FCs display three putatively African-derived syntactic features, all of which are readily attributable to Lower Guinean languages. One phonological trait, the marginal presence of high nasal vowels, is also compatible with Lower Guinean influence. What is striking, once again, is the relative lack of syllable restructuring which would be expected from a predominantly Atlantic substrate, but not from one composed mainly of Lower Guinean languages. Also noteworthy is the strong representation of Bantu vocabulary. A comparison with Haiti FC (§5.1.2.1) suggests that the Bantu lexicon does indeed belong to the oldest stratum. As we have already seen, the dominance of Bantu-speakers predates that of Lower Guineans, which may be taken to suggest that the lexicon of Lesser Antilles FC crystallised earlier than the syntax. I have no explanation to offer for the lack of syllable restructuring or tones (cf §7.2.1).

7.1.3.4 Guiana FC

Given the demographic data presented in §6.3.4, we would expect Guiana FC to be heavily marked by Lower Guinean languages, with little or no influence from Bantu. Indeed, the substrate influences identified are, for the most part, compatible with this expectation. The one exception is syllable structure, including post-vocalic rhotics, tentatively assigned to Atlantic. As we have seen, speakers of Atlantic were in place very early. More surprising is the fact that Bantu lexical items are numerically second only to Lower Guinean items, given that Bantus were virtually unrepresented in French Guiana prior to the 1730s. It should be remembered, however, that *Afrolex* contains only 21 Africanisms from Guiana FC. Also, Mande and Atlantic (i.e. Upper Guinean) lexicon taken together surpass the Bantu component. Furthermore, some of the Bantu words have more or less equally plausible etymologies in languages from other areas.

7.1.4 Portuguese Creoles

7.1.4.1 Upper Guinea PCs

From all that is known about the Upper Guinea PCs, it is clear that substrate influences from Lower Guinea and Buntu are out of the question, which leaves us with Atlantic and Mande languages. The few demographic/historical data that there are, do indicate the presence of both on the Cape Verde islands, but there is nothing to suggest how their proportions varied over time.

It is important to recognise that most of Guinea-Bissau is Atlantic-speaking, so that many Atlantic influences in Guinea-Bissau PC could be considered *ad*stratal rather than *sub*stratal. While the African component of the Guinea-Bissau PC lexicon is predominantly Atlantic, it is of crucial importance to note not only that the proportions are reversed in Cape Verde PC, but also that Mande words predominate in the shared lexicon (and therefore presumably represent the oldest layer). These items are unlikely to have entered Guinea-Bissau PC other than by way of the Cape Verdes and that, in turn, suggests that the proto-Upper Guinea PC arose on the islands, rather than on the mainland. If, as has been suggested (§5.1.1.7), the sentence negation of the two languages is derived from Mandinka, that would strengthen the case.

While the lexicon points to a Mande dominance in Upper Guinea PC formation, all phonological and syntactic features examined – with the possible exception of *verbum dicendi* complementation – are more easily ascribed to Atlantic than to Mande. Again, this could be due to adstrate influence in the case of Guinea-Bissau PC, but not for the insular varieties.

Unfortunately, then, only three such features were found in Cape Verde PC, viz. corporal reflexivisation, aspiration and partial lack of /z/, and for none of these do I have negative evidence which enables me to definitely exclude Mande sources.

7.1.4.2 Gulf of Guinea PCs

The Gulf of Guinea PCs demonstrate a mix of Lower Guinean and Bantu influences, just as might be expected from the geographical location of the islands. It was suggested in Parkvall (1999d) that the Lower Guinean component chronologically preceded the Bantu one. This is reflected in a smaller proportion of Bantu-like features on the varieties spoken on Príncipe and Annobón, which were peopled from São Tomé PC before the massive influx of Bantu-speakers on that island, and also in the reduced proportion of Bantu items in the shared (and thus presumably oldest) vocabulary in comparison to the overall proportion of Bantu words. Most of the African-derived pronoun forms in the Gulf of Guinea PCs are also Delto-Benuic rather than Bantu, although the 2pl of São Tomé and Príncipe PC (§5.1.1.3.11) suggests that Bantu speakers had some involvement even in the original Creole genesis. The palatalisation strategy of Príncipe PC is also more similar to Edo, while that on the other islands is closer to Kikongo. Again, this fits well the suggested scenario in which additional Bantu influence affected São Tomé PC after its daughter varieties had separated from it.

All in all, most of the syntactical features discussed can be traced to Delto-Benuic languages, while Bantu has primarily affected the phonology.

7.1.5 Dutch Creoles

7.1.5.1 Negerhollands DC

Negerhollands DC would, from the demographic reconstruction, seem to be a simple case – the Kwa (and, in particular, Akan) dominance appears to have been rather massive throughout the peopling of St Thomas. The only other expected contributors would be Bantu and Delto-Benuic languages. Indeed, most of the features discussed can be ascribed to Kwa, and two of these – partial merger of /s/ and /z/ and /b/ and /v/ respectively – point to Akan rather than Gbe, something that is very much in line with the demographic data.

Two phonological features, however – namely the three degrees of vowel aperture and the possible existence of prenasalised stops – suggest Bantu rather than Kwa influence. Interestingly, so do the few African lexical items (about two dozen) of which I am currently aware. While slightly more than half of these words have also been attested in neighbouring ECs, from where they might have been borrowed into Negerhollands DC, among the items which have not been recorded in any EC in the area, Bantu words in fact predominate.[5] The only period in the history of Negerhollands in which we would expect Bantu languages to have had a decisive impact are the two decades between 1700 and 1720.

7.1.5.2 Skepi DC

For the now extinct Skepi DC, the only person who has access to any data on it has chosen to make only very small portions of these publicly available and, thus, no conclusions regarding that language can be drawn here.

7.1.6 Spanish Creoles

7.1.6.1 Papiamentu SC

Papiamentu also had a dominant Lower Guinean component in its substrate composition. For most of the 17th and early 18th centuries, Lower Guinea – and in particular the Slave Coast – was the major supplier of slaves to Curaçao, but there was also a sizeable Bantu contingent, with the number of Senegambians being virtually negligible.

---

5 Note, however, that we are dealing with less than ten words here.

The number of attested lexical Africanisms in Papiamentu SC with relatively certain etymologies is remarkably low – only about 15 items. The two major contributors that can be identified are Kwa (usually Gbe rather than Akan) and Bantu. Their relative proportions match the demographic data well. The 3pl pronoun is problematic, since neither speakers of Wolof nor Edo, the potential sources suggested in §5.1.1.3.8 above, seem to have been numerically strong on Curaçao.

The phonological and syntactical features discussed are by and large compatible with the dominance of Slave Coast peoples. The only remarkable features are the circumverbal negation and the possible former existence of prenasalised stops, both of which may more likely be the result of Bantu influence, and the merger of /b/ and /v/. The latter would not be expected from Gbe-speakers, but could be due to speakers of a large number of other languages from all over West Africa as well as, of course, the Spanish-speakers who contributed most of the Papiamentu SC lexicon.[6]

7.2 Concluding discussion

The first thing that I myself learnt from this study is that there are far fewer clearly substrate-induced structures in the Atlantic Creoles than I had expected to find. When I decided on this subject, I did so because I saw Creoles as languages that were somehow exceptionally "mixed" (although even then, I was not prepared to see them as outright combinations of lexifier vocabulary and substrate grammar, as some more radical scholars do). I have since realised, however, that mixedness by no means is what characterises Creoles in comparison to older languages.

Even though I am still vehemently opposed to the view propagated by the superstratist school, according to which substrate influences are virtually non-existent in Creoles (see e.g. McWhorter & Parkvall 1999), the amount of grammar or phonology that can unequivocally be traced to languages other than the one which provided the bulk of the lexicon is clearly fairly limited, at least in the Atlantic area. Yet, in many a radical Creole, the structural features that allow themselves to be unequivocally traced to the lexifier are equally limited in number. Instead, what is characteristic of Creoles, and what sets them apart from other languages, is the reduction associated with pidginisation, followed by the expansion associated with creolisation. The fact that the expansion draws on all resources available in the environment, including both the lexifier and the substrates, often obscures the Pidgin past of contemporary Creoles somewhat but, in most cases, it is accessible for observation and analysis. Although that was not its original purpose, this study has strengthened my conviction that pidginisation (and expansion) – and not mixedness – is what creolistics should focus on.

The main conclusion that can be drawn from this study is one that is far from spectacular – the substrate influences that are found in Atlantic Creoles match quite well the ethnolinguistic composition of their creators during the first couple of decades or so of language contact. This, I believe, is what most people would have expected even before or without having undertaken a study of this kind. Nevertheless, by amassing, setting out and discussing all these features which are potentially or actually attributable to substrate influence in a single volume, I hope to have made a significant advance in the study of the African contribution to Atlantic Creoles.

7.2.1 Some mysteries

The enigmas are relatively few. One is the preponderance of Kwa, and more specifically Akan, in Atlantic ECs in general, and also the widespread 2pl pronoun /unu/ (and variants thereof) from Igbo. Neither is compatible with any known or reconstructed demographical dominance of these two groups in any subsequently EC-speaking area. We might also expect the development of a proto-EC on St Kitts (Baker 1999a) to have led to the same Bantu dominance in the oldest lexical layer as suggested for the FCs.

---

6 But note that the merger also affects the Portuguese lexicon, in which case a lexifier origin, albeit possible, is less likely.

Also problematic are the differences in phonology between FCs on the one hand, and ECs and other Atlantic Creoles on the other. As discussed in Parkvall (1999a), FCs are, in many respects, "less African" than ECs - in their lack of prenasalised and coarticulated stops, in their relatively intact syllables structure (and in particular the absence of paragoge), their absence of tones,[7] and the lack of traces of mergers of liquids or labials. And, yet, they are not necessarily "more European" (see Parkvall 1998). Neither problem is easily explained.

7.2.2 Why the Lower Guinean bias?

Lower Guinea was clearly the major supplier of slaves to the Atlantic plantation colonies, and it is, therefore, hardly surprising that this is reflected in the Creole languages. As we have seen, there are indeed features in some Creoles that derive from Upper Guinean and Bantu languages. And yet, for most Creoles, the small number of such features is hardly proportionate to the number of slaves that were imported from these areas. I have no certain answer as to why this should be so. One possible reason could be that I, just like my predecessors, have proved unable to take off my "Kwa glasses", and that the Lower Guinean bias exists more in the eye of the beholder than in reality - Kwa (usually including Delto-Benuic) has more than once routinely been invoked as the major substrate component in a variety of Creoles without the alternatives having been seriously considered. A second possible reason might be that non-Kwa languages are more compatible with Western European syntax, so that the structures they had to offer are similar to those provided by the lexifier, and we would thus not have a case of substrate influence as defined in chapter 2. Serial verbs, for instance, are, from the European point of view, one of the most conspicuous substrate influences in Atlantic Creoles, and they could not have been provided by Upper Guinean or Bantu languages for the simple reason that these do not have such constructions. A third possible reason is the existence of a Lower Guinean *Sprachbund*, in which many features of Kwa are shared by Delto-Benuic and Kru, and often even the peripheral Bantu languages of Nigeria and Cameroon. Kwa-speakers would thus have been supported, so to speak, in establishing features of their own languages in the emerging Creoles, by slaves from other areas of Lower Guinea. While the Bantu languages are also *relatively* homogeneous, this is in stark contrast to Upper Guinea, where Atlantic and Mande in many respects are typological mirror images of one another. Since most deliveries of slaves from this area would have been mixed, i.e. would have included speakers of both Mande and Atlantic languages, they might be thought of having neutralised each others' potential influences, as it were. Also, it could be suggested that Lower Guinean languages, in being more analytic than at least those of the Atlantic and Bantu groups, would be more suitable candidates for substrate transfer, since it is generally accepted that bound morphemes transfer less easily than free ones in a contact situation. Finally, it should be borne in mind that the better availability and quality of Lower Guinean language materials may have led to the traditional Kwa bias in creolistics - Christaller (1875, 1933) and Westermann (1930, 1939) are among the very best early descriptions of any West African language and, apart from Yoruba and Wolof, good dictionaries and grammars of other relevant West African languages were skeletal, rare or non-existent until comparatively recently.

While the Lower Guinean contribution may have been exaggerated - or at least routinely emphasised - it remains the case that someone familiar with Atlantic Creoles will immediately feel "at home" when browsing though a grammar of Twi, Ewe or Yoruba, whereas grammars of Wolof, Grebo or Umbundu will not provide the Creolist with the same feeling.

On the other hand - but with the exception of the last point - the above would only explain the relative lack of Upper Guinean and Bantu *structures*, not the Lower Guinean bias in phonology and lexicon. Moreover, there certainly are features in Upper Guinea and Buntu which would be prime candidates for transfer even in ECs and FCs. Given that both French and Bantu languages

---

7 The presence of phonemic tones - or at least pitch accents - in many Atlantic Creoles of non-French lexicon is a feature that is without doubt an Africanism. Tones are not investigated in this study, however, because virtually all potential substrates are tone languages, with the exception of a few of the Atlantic family in the extreme north-west Tones would thus be of limited use in determining the precise African connexions of Atlantic Creoles, although the possibility that the tonelessness of FCs and of Upper Guinea PCs is due to influence from this family cannot be excluded.

offered a postverbal negation, that Bantu speakers dominated the French slave labour force in the early days, and that the oldest lexical layer of FCs was suggested above to be Bantu, and furthermore, given the occurrence of circum- or postverbal negations in Gulf of Guinea PCs and New World SCs, it would not be surprising if FCs had circum- or postverbal negations. Yet, they do not. Upper Guinean languages also offered other structures that might have been transferred into Caribbean Creoles, but which remain unattested there.

If one applies the principles set out in chapter 2, substrate influence is not easy to detect in a Creole with an exclusively Upper Guinean substrate such as Cape Verde PC. For instance, Lang (1999) is a paper specifically devoted to the non-Portuguese features of Cape Verdean, and even among those, little, if anything, can with certainty be ascribed to any of the substrates. Not even Quint (*in press*), a book much concerned with African influences in Cape Verdean, has been able to find more traces of Upper Guinean languages than I have presented here.[8]

There exists the possibility that at least some Creoles arose in Africa rather than in the Caribbean. This has been suggested earlier by e.g. Parkvall (1995c) and McWhorter (1997a). For the ECs, McWhorter's scenario would neatly explain both the Akan bias and the presence of Igbo items. There are, however, also arguments against this scenario (Huber 1999). If ECs arose in Africa, while FCs did not, this might also explain the less conspicuous African character of certain aspects of Atlantic FCs, notably their phonology.[9] The FC genesis in Senegal suggested in Parkvall (1995c) would, on the other hand, explain much of the FC phonological facts (including the lack of tones), but this is compatible with neither the Bantu lexicon, nor the Lower Guinean syntactic features such as verb serialisation.

7.2.3 Some speculative reconstructions

If we assume that every single feature discussed in this thesis was incorporated in the Creole concerned in the decade when slaves from the area from which the feature in question is assumed to have been introduced were in a majority, and if we choose year zero as the decade when colonisation began,[10] we can calculate the period of time theoretically elapsed before the various features were introduced. This calculation - which obviously needs to be taken with more than a grain of salt - excludes features which could have been incorporated at any time, i.e. when the substrate composition matches the linguistic structure throughout the period studied. The average interval which results from this calculation is about 25 years.

Out of a total of 75 feature tokens considered for this arithmetical exercise, 44 are postulated to have arisen within 25 years, while 31 are assumed to have been transferred later. The distribution of these within the various linguistic levels is as follows:

LEVEL	LESS THAN 25 YEARS	MORE THAN 25 YEARS	TOTAL
Lexicon	39%	61%	100%
Phonology	50%	50%	100%
Syntax	81%	19%	100%
Total	59%	41%	100%

This suggests that lexicon is the component that is most easily added to the Creole after crystallisation which, of course, conforms to the generally accepted common wisdom that lexicon is the subsystem of any language that is the most flexible and most easily affected by contact. Among the languages considered here, this is especially evident in Gullah EC which, although clearly structurally affiliated with the ECs of the insular Caribbean, has received a considerable lexical component from Upper Guinean languages, and this must represent a post-formative addition. Even more spectacular, of course, is the Kimbundu addition to the lexicon of Angolar

8 With the exception that Quint sees a considerable influence of Mande languages on its TMA system, a conclusion which I do not share.

9 Credit goes to Stéphane Goyette (1999) who - independently of me - arrived at the same tentative conclusion.

10 The starting year here includes the time passed even before the ancestral Creole was implanted in the area where it is now spoken. Thus, the starting point for all ECs and FCs is taken to be the start of colonisation of St Kitts, rather than the first settlement of Jamaica, Haiti or Surinam.

PC.[11] On the other hand, the Bantu lexicon that is shared by FCs of the Lesser Antilles and Haiti must stem from the very earliest period of Afro-French language contact on St Kitts, when Bantus formed the majority of the slave population for a relatively brief period of time, and this would seem to rather suggest that lexical crystallisation occurs before the grammar jells. As we would expect, the core lexicon, including pronouns, is frequently established early, witness the widespread presence of 2pl /unu/ (and varieties thereof) in Atlantic ECs.

If lexicon can be affected by new arrivals for a rather long time while syntax jells relatively early, phonology seems to occupy an intermediate position. The Surinamese ECs provide a good illustration of this. While sharing with other ECs several phonological features of Akan origin that presumably date back to an early period, later Bantu arrivals have also left their mark.

The syntactic traits are interesting in that a vast majority of them best match the substrate composition of the period before the 25-year average. The average syntactical feature, according to this *highly speculative* reconstruction, arose after about 20 years of language contact, with some variation as illustrated in the following table.

FEATURE	SUGGESTED TIME SPAN
Complementation (§4.4)	13 years
Plural marking (§4.12)	18 years
Serial verbs (§4.6)	19 years
Reflexives (§4.1)	25 years
TMA (§4.10.1)	30 years

Very interestingly, as shown in Parkvall (1998), the typical colony established by Europeans in the Caribbean area did not have a majority of non-Europeans in its population until about 33 years, on average, after each colony's foundation. This suggests that *motivation* (cf Baker 1995) was a more important factor in Creole genesis than *demographic imbalance* (cf discussion in Parkvall 1998).

Baker (1995:6-7) examined the first attestations of a variety of features in seven Pidgins and Creoles of English and French lexicon in the Atlantic, Indian and Pacific Oceans.[12] The average feature discussed by Baker surfaces in the textual sources some 58 years after the first textual attestation and 79 years after the start of colonisation. Though I would like to emphasise once again that my arithmetic exercise is utterly speculative, some credibility is lent to it by the fact that the order of attestation in Baker's material for those features that both he and I have considered is essentially the same – i.e. overt complementation appears before overt number marking, and both predate the development of most of the TMA system. Baker does not discuss verb serialisation or reflexive marking, but at least the latter has been argued by Carden & Stewart (1988) and Carden (1989) to appear gradually, after an initial period of use of bare pronouns with a reflexive reading (something that is still reflected in quite a number of Creoles) – i.e. it appears relatively late, just as the speculative reconstruction above would predict.

The likelihood that the basic structure of the Creoles was fixed at a relatively early date is strongly supported by the structural parallels between relatively isolated varieties such as Annobón PC and the Surinamese ECs, and their respective relatives on São Tomé and the Antilles. And yet, the Bantu lexical dominance in the FCs seems to suggest that a core lexicon was established even earlier than many of the structural characteristics.

Some substrate features were no doubt present in the Pidgins that I assume preceded the Atlantic Creoles, just as some substrate-induced traits can be found in any documented Pidgin. As Baker (n d:15ff) points out, however, Pidgins often contain so little structure that there is, so to speak, not much space for substrate features to manifest themselves. Rather, other aspects of substrate influence surface as the Pidgin expands into a Creole, for I would suggest – and this is

---

11 As is the Portuguese lexicon of Saramaccan EC, which most probably postdates the structural crystallisation of the language (Bakker, Smith & Veenstra 1995:168; McWhorter 1997b:13-19; Parkvall 1999c:33; Smith 1987b), but this is somewhat peripheral to the present study, since Portuguese is not a West African language.

12 Viz. Sranan EC, the FCs of the Lesser Antilles and Mauritius, and the Pidgin Englishes of China, Hawaii, Melanesia and Eastern Australia.

something that I intend to develop in future publications - that this expansion draws on all potential sources, including both the lexifier,[13] the substrates and universals. Some of the expansion takes place rather rapidly, whereas developing contact languages can manage without certain other features for quite some time, just as there are older languages that fulfil what is required of them without having e.g. overt number marking. In older languages, grammaticalisation is normally not triggered by communicative needs, but functions in a rather random way. To some extent, this is true of expanding Pidgins as well, or, as Manessy (1995:36) puts it - grammatical features *"ne se développent pas pour que les gens se comprennent mieux, mais parce qu'ils se comprennent mieux"*. It is uncommon, and almost unheard of among non-Pidgins, however, for a language to lack grammaticalised TMA marking or a full set of personal pronouns, and, with regard to features such as these, it could perhaps be said that expansion in Creoles is the only case of communicatively motivated grammaticalisation that there is.

Pronouns are something that even Pidgins normally have, while TMA markers are something that seems to develop later (witness their relative scantiness in most Pidgins, and their comparatively late attestation dates as set out in Baker 1995). While several pronominal forms are directly borrowed from African languages, no TMA marker can convincingly be shown to derive from an African language (§5.1.1). This could be taken to suggest that substrate influence is primarily exerted in the early period of Creole formation.

Apart from reflexivisation, mentioned above, the use of 3pl for nominal plural marking might potentially be a case of late substrate influence. Its absence in many of the world's languages proves it to be a feature that human language, regardless of whether it has gone through pidginisation or not, can manage without. Indeed, overt plural marking has been shown to be a late development in the Indian Ocean FCs (Baker & Corne 1982), and as we have already seen, it was moderately grammaticalised in Negerhollands DC, which could be taken to suggest a relatively late development. Also, one of the African languages that best matches the Atlantic Creole pluralisation strategy is Yoruba, speakers of which did not arrive in large numbers in the Caribbean until the mid-18th century (§6.1.2 and §6.7.4). If the possible aspect-prominence (§4.10.3) is to be seen as modelled on West African languages, that too would be a likely candidate for relatively late manifestation of substrate influence since, in its earliest stages, the Creole-to-be would not have had aspect marking in the first place.[14] Reduplication, conspicuously absent in most Pidgins, would also seem to be a candidate for relatively late transfer.

In sum, then, we obviously can learn something about language restructuring from the study of Atlantic Creoles and their input components. Yet, these languages are far from ideal. The vast majority of them have for most of their history coexisted with their respective lexifiers (or other European languages) in a socially very uneven relationship which has tended to eradicate some of the more un-European traits. Even more crucially, Atlantic Creoles are the outcome of contact between lexifiers which were all Indo-European and substrates which were all Niger-Congo. Moreover, the apparently most important West African languages are more analytical than most, which could make the analytical structures which I attribute to restructuring look like the substrate transfers they are not.

It might be that more far-reaching theoretical conclusions would require a wider range of input languages. But then, again, no single P/C constitutes the perfect test-bed. Hawaiian EC is probably the Creole with the most varied substrate composition, but emerged in a setting where

13 For which reason it is all too tempting - but not necessarily correct - to see any lexifier feature in a Creole as a direct legacy of the lexifier (as has been done in e.g. DeGraff 199a, 2000), while it may in fact be an expansion-related borrowing (see Goyette 2000 for an ingenious demonstration of one such case).

14 There is some reason to believe that aspect (progressive) marking in Creoles postdates the emergence of tense (past) marking. For one thing many Pidgins mark temporal, but not aspectual distinctions overtly. Secondly, in Pidgins and Creoles which have both tense and aspect marking, the latter tends to be inherited from a lexifier aspect marker (as opposed to recreated from other material) less often than the former. Thirdly, if two closely related Creoles have almost, but not quite, the same inventory of TMA markers (e. g. Upper Guinean PCs, Caribbean FCs, Saramaccan EC versus Sranan EC), it is often the A rather than the T marker that differs. Finally, where robust historical documentation exists, a stable and grammaticalised tense marker is usually attested before an aspect marker is.

formal education in the lexifier was provided. Other P/Cs which have arisen in relative isolation from their respective lexifiers usually tend to have relatively homogeneous substrates.

While the firm conclusions which can be drawn from this study are relatively few, my hope is that the wealth of data examined in these pages represents a major advance both towards a reasoned assessment of the nature and extent of African influence in Atlantic Creoles and towards the ultimate goal of creolistics, as I see it, of achieving a full understanding of how these languages originated and evolved.

References

Aboh, Enoch Oladé 1998 Focus constructions and the focus criterion in Gungbe. *Linguistique Africaine* 20 [Pagination refers to MS version].

Abondolo, Daniel 1998 Introduction. Abondolo, Daniel (ed.) *The Uralic languages*, London & New York: Routledge, 2-42.

Adam, Lucien 1883 *Les idiomes négro-aryen et maléo-aryen: essai d'hybridologie linguistique*. Paris: Maisonneuve.

Adams, Emilie 1991 *Understanding Jamaican Patois*. Kingston: Kingston Publishers.

Adamson, Lilian & van Rossem, Cefas 1995 Creole literature. Arends, Muysken & Smith (eds), 75-84.

Adamson, Lilian & Smith, Norval 1995 Sranan. Arends, Muysken & Smith (eds), 219-32.

Adone, Dany & Plag, Ingo (eds) 1994 *Creolization and language change*. Tübingen: Niemeyer.

Agbedor, Paul 1996 The syntax of Ewe personal pronouns. *Linguistique Africaine* 16:19-51.

Agheyisi, Rebecca 1971 *West African Pidgin English: simplification and simplicity*. PhD thesis, Stanford University.

Akhras, Edward 1998 Vowel harmony as an areal feature in Indo-European languages and dialects. MS.

Albuquerque, Luís de 1989 A colonização de São Tomé e Príncipe: os capitães do século XV. Albuquerque, Luís de (ed.) *Portugal no Mundo* 2:171-97. Lisbon: Publicaçoes Alfa.

Albuquerque, Luís de & Santos, Maria Emília Madeira (eds) 1991 *História Géral de Cabo Verde*. Vol. 1. Lisbon & Praia: Centro de Estudos de História e Cartografia Antiga/Instituto de Investigação Científica Tropical/Direcção Géral do Património Cultural de Cabo Verde.

Al-Hassan, Bello 1997 *Reduplication in the Chadic Languages*. Frankfurt: Peter Lang.

Alleyne, Mervyn 1980 *Comparative Afro-American*. Ann Arbor: Karoma.

---- 1993 Continuity versus creativity in Afro-American language varieties. Mufwene (ed.), 167-81.

---- 1996 *Syntaxe historique créole*. Paris & Schœlcher: Éditions Karthala/Presses Universitaires Créoles.

---- 1998 Two opposite processes in the historical construction of creole languages. Paper presented at the conference *Degrees of Restructuring in Creole languages*, Regensburg, June 1998.

Allsopp, Richard 1976 The case for Afrogenesis. Paper presented at the Society for Caribbean Linguistics conference, University of Guyana, August 11-14, 1976.

Allsopp, Richard (ed.) 1996 *Dictionary of Caribbean English usage*. Oxford: Oxford University Press.

Almada, Maria Dulce de Oliveira 1961 *Cabo Verde. Contribução para o estudo do dialecto falado no seu arquipelago*. Lisbon: Junta de Investigação do Ultramar.

Almeida, António de 1956 Contribução para o estudo da antropologica física dos "Angolares" (ilha de São Tomé). In *Conferência Internacional dos Africanistas Ocidentais, 6ª Sessão*, vol. 5, 11-21. Lisbon.

Amastae, Jon 1975 *Dominican Creole phonology*. PhD dissertation, University of Oregon.

---- 1979 Dominican Creole phonology I. *Georgetown University Papers on Language and Linguistics* 15:83-122.

Andrade, Ernesto d' & Kihm, Alain (eds) 1992 *Actas do Colóquio sobre crioulos de base lexical portuguesa*. Lisbon: Edições Colibri.

Anglade, Pierre 1998 *Inventaire étymologique des termes créoles des Caraïbes d'origine africaine*. Paris: L'Harmattan.

Anon. 1961 [1989] *Language Guide (Ga Version)*. Accra: Bureau of Ghana Languages.

Anon. 2000 *Les emprunts linguistiques Européens chez les Myènè du Gabon*. http://mandji.net/mbolo/. Downloaded 2000-06-21.

Ans, André Marcel d' 1968 *Le créole français d'Haïti*. The Hague: Mouton.

Ansre, Gilbert 1971 The Influence of English on West African Languages. Spencer (ed.), 145-64.

Arends, Jacques 1995 Demographic factors in the formation of Sranan. Arends (ed.) 233-85.

---- 1999 The origin of the Portuguese element in the Surinam Creoles. Huber & Parkvall (eds), 195-208.

Arends, Jacques (ed.) 1995 *The early stages of creolization*. Amsterdam: Benjamins.

Arends, J, Muysken, P & Smith, N (eds) 1995 *Pidgins and creoles. An introduction*. Amsterdam: Benjamins.

Arends, J, Kouwenberg, S & Smith, N 1995 Theories focusing on the non-European input. Arends, Muysken & Smith (eds), 99-109.

Arensdorff, L 1913 *Manuel pratique de langue Peulh*. Paris: Librarie Paul Geuthner.

Ariza, Mireille Milfort de 1991 *Le créole haïtien: Variation et prosodie*. Montréal: Centre International de documentation et d'information haïtienne, caraïbéenne et afro-canadienne.

Armstrong, Robert 1984 Idomoid. Bendor-Samuel (ed.) 323-36.

Arnott, D W 1969a Fula. Dunstan (ed.), 55-71.
----. 1969b Tiv. Dunstan (ed.), 143-51.
Atlas 1962 *Atlas lingüístico de la península ibérica 1. Fonética 1.* Madrid: Consejo superior de investigaciones científicas.
Aub-Buscher, Gertrud 1984 Non-Romance elements in the vocabulary of Trinidad French Creole, ms.
Awoyale, Yiwola 1986 Reflexivization in Kwa languages. Dimmendaal, Gerrit (ed.) *Current Approaches to African Linguistics* 3:1-14.
Bailey, Beryl 1966 *Jamaican Creole syntax*. Cambridge: Cambridge University Press.
Baissac, Charles (1880) [1976]: *Étude sur le patois créole mauricien.* Nancy. [Geneva: Slatkine Reprints].
Baker, Philip 1984 Agglutinated French articles in Creole French: their evolutionary significance. *Te Reo* 27:89-129.
---- 1987 Combien y a-t-il eu de genèses créoles à base lexicale française? *Études créoles* 10 (2):60-76.
---- 1993 Assessing the African contribution to French-based Creoles. Mufwene (ed.) 123-55.
---- 1994 Creativity in Creole genesis. Adone & Plag (eds.) 65-84.
---- 1995 Some developmental inferences from historical studies of Pidgins and Creoles. Arends (ed.), 1-24.
---- 1996 On the development of certain prepositional forms in Mauritian and other French creoles. Véronique, Daniel (ed.) *Matériaux pour l'étude des classes grammaticales dans les langues créoles*, Aix-en-Provence: Université de Provence, 41-59.
---- 1999a Investigating the origin and diffusion of shared features among the Atlantic English Creoles. Baker & Bruyn (eds), 315-64.
---- 1999b No creolization without prior pidginization? Paper presented at the *9e Colloque des Études Créoles*, Aix-en-Provence, June 1999.
---- (n d) [c. 1989] *Morphological features of Indian Ocean Creoles and their sources.* Unpublished ms.
---- (ed.) 1995 *From Contact to Creole and beyond.* London: University of Westminster Press.
Baker, Philip & Bruyn, Adrienne (eds) 1999 *St. Kitts and the Atlantic Creoles*. London: Westminster University Press.
Baker, Philip & Corne, Chris 1982 *Isle de France Creoles: affinities and origins.* Ann Arbor: Karoma.
Baker, Philip & Syea, Anand (eds) 1996 *Changing meanings, changing functions.* London: University of Westminster Press.
Bakker, P, Post, M & van der Voort, H 1995 TMA particles and auxiliaries. Arends, Muysken & Smith (eds), 247-58.
Bakker, P, Smith, & Veenstra, T 1995 Saramaccan. Arends, Muysken & Smith (eds), 165-78.
Bal, Willy 1979 *Afro-Romanica Studia.* Albufeira: Edições Poseidon.
Ballong-Wen-Mewuda, J B 1988 Le commerce portugais des esclaves entre la côte de l'actuel Nigéria et celle du Ghana moderne aux XVe et XVIe siècles. Daget, Serge (ed.) *De la traite à l'esclavage. Actes du Colloque International sur la traite des Noirs, Nantes 1985.* Nantes & Paris: Centre des recherches sur l'histoire du monde atlantique/Société française d'histoire d'outre-mer, vol. 1, 121-45.
Bamgboṣe, Ayọ 1966 *A grammar of Yoruba*. Cambridge: Cambridge University Press.
---- 1969 Yoruba. Dunstan (ed.), 163-72.
Banjọ, Ayo 1986 The influence of English on the Yoruba language. Viereck, Wolfgang & Bald, Wolf-Dietrich (eds) *English in contact with other languages*, Budapest: Akadémiai Kiadó, 533-45.
Bannert, Robert 1990 *På väg mot svenskt uttal.* Lund: Studentlitteratur.
Barbot, John 1732 *A description of the coasts of North and South Guinea; and of Ethiopia Inferior; vulgarly Angola [...]*.. London: A & J Churchill.
---- 1746 *A description of the coasts of North and South Guinea; and of Ethiopia Inferior; vulgarly Angola [...].* Churchill, A & J (eds) *A collection of voyages and travels [...].* Vol. 5, 3rd edn, London: Henry Lintot & John Osborn.
Barrena, Natalio 1957 *Gramática Annobonesa*. Madrid: Instituto de Estudios Africanos/Consejo Superior de Investigaciones Científicas.
Barros, Simão [n d] Origens da Colônia de Cabo Verde. *Cadernos Coloniais* 56:3-46.
Bartens, Angela 1995 *Die iberoromanisch-basierten Kreolsprachen.* Frankfurt am Main: Peter Lang.
---- 1996 *Der Kreolische Raum. Geschichte und Gegenwart.* Helsinki: Suomalainen Tiedeakatemia.
---- 1998 Review of Maurer (1995). *Journal of Pidgin and Creole Languages* 13:180-87.
---- 2000 *Ideophones and Sound Symbolism in Atlantic Creoles.* Helsinki: The Finnish Academy of Science and Letters.
Bastide, Roger 1971 *African civilisations in the New World.* London: C Hurst.
Batie, Robert Carlyle 1991 Why sugar? Economic cycles and the changing of staples on the English and French Antilles, 1624-1654. Beckles & Shepherd (eds.), 37-55.

Baudet, Martha 1981 Identifying the African grammatical base of the Caribbean Creoles: a typological approach. Highfield, Arnold & Valdman, Albert (eds) *Historicity and Variation in Creole Studies*, Ann Arbor: Karoma, 104-17.

Baum, Paul 1976 The question of decreolization in Papiamentu phonology. *International Journal of the Sociology of Language* 7:83-93.

Bavin , Edith 1983 Morphological and syntactic devices in Acholi and related Western Nilotic languages. Voßen, R & Bechhaus-Gerst, M (eds) *Nilotic Studies* . Berlin: Dietrich Reimer, vol. 1, 147-68.

Bavoux, Claudine 1993 Francophonie malgache: images et réalités. Robillard & Beniamino (eds), 173-87.

Baxter, Alan 1988 *A grammar of Kristang (Malacca Creole Portuguese)*. Canberra: Australian National University.

Beck, Sanderson 1998 Ethics of Africa and America 30 BC - 1453. <www.san.beck.org/ AB1-AfricaAmerica.html>. Downloaded 2000-06-18.

Beckles, Hilary 1990 *A history of Barbados from Amerindian settlement to nation-state*. Cambridge: Cambridge University Press.

Beckles, Hilary & Shepherd, Verene (eds) 1991 *Caribbean slave society and economy*. New York: New Press.

Belikov, Vladimir (n d) *Fragments of Russenorsk grammar*. Unpublished ms.

Bella, L De Sousa 1946 Apontamentos sôbre a língua dos balantas de Jabadá. *Boletim Cultural da Guiné Portuguesa* 1:729-65.

Bellon, Immanuel 1983 *Twi lessons for beginners*. Accra, Kumasi & London: Presbyterian Book Depot /Longmans, Green.

Bendor-Samuel, John (ed.) 1984 *The Niger-Congo Languages. A classification and description of Africa's largest language family*. Lanham: University Press of America.

Bentley, Holman 1887 *Dictionary and grammar of the Kongo language as spoken at San Salvador, the ancient capital of the old Kongo empire, West Africa*. London: Baptist Missionary Society/Trübner & Co.

Bentolila, Alain (ed.) 1976 *Ti Diksyonnè Kreyòl-Franse. Dictionnaire élémentaire créole haïtien-français*. Port-au-Prince: Éditions Caraïbes.

Bernini, Giuliano & Ramat, Paolo 1998 Markierte Negationsstrukturen in typologischer und arealer Hinsicht. Boeder, W, Schroeder, C, Wagner, K H & Wildgen, W (eds) *Sprache in Raum und Zeit*, Tübingen: Gunter Narr, 3-17.

Berry, Jack 1961 English loanwords and adaptions in Sierra Leone Krio. Le Page (ed.), 1-16.

Bertinetto, Pier Marco 1995 Sum: progressive with future time reference. *Linguist List* 6.221.

---- 2000 The progressive in Romance, as compared with English. Dahl, Östen (ed.) *Tense and aspect in the languages of Europe*. Berlin: Mouton de Gruyter, 559-604.

Bhat, D N S 1974 The phonology of liquid consonants. *Working Papers on Language Universals* 16, 73-104.

----. 1978 A general study of palatalizaion. Greenberg, Joseph (ed.) *Universals of human language*, vol. 2, Stanford: Stanford University Press, 47-92.

Bickerton, Derek 1981 *Roots of Language*. Ann Arbor: Karoma.

---- 1984 The language bioprogram hypothesis. *The Behavioral and Brain Sciences* 7:173-88.

---- 1986 Beyond *Roots*: The five-year test. *Journal of Pidgin and Creole Languages* 1:225-32.

---- 1989 Seselwa serialization and its significance. *Journal of Pidgin and Creole Languages* 4:155-83.

---- 1990 If it quacks like a duck...: a reply to Seuren. *Journal of Pidgin and Creole Languages* 5:293-303.

---- 1993 How new evidence from Hawaii and Suriname supports the Bioprogram. Paper presented at the Conference of the Society for Pidgin and Creole Languages, Amsterdam June 9-12, 1993.

---- 1994 The origins of Saramaccan syntax: A reply to John McWhorter's "Substratal influence in Saramaccan serial verb constructions". *Journal of Pidgin and Creole Languages* 9:65-77.

---- 1998 An old argument revisited. Bruyn, Adrienne & Jacques Arends (eds) *Mengelwerk voor Muysken*, Amsterdam: Institut voor Algemene Taalwetenschap, Universiteit van Amsterdam, 253-56.

Bickerton, Derek & Escalante, Aquilas 1970 Palenquero: A Spanish-based creole of Northern Colombia. *Lingua* 24:254-67.

Bilby, Kenneth 1983 How the "Older Heads" talk. A Jamaican maroon spirit possession language and its relationship to the Creoles of Suriname and Sierra Leone. *Nieuwe West-Indische Gids* 57:37-85.

---- 1992 *Further observations on the Jamaican maroon spirit language*. Paper presented at the 1992 annual meeting of the Society for Pidgin and Creole Linguistics, Philadelphia.

Blench, Roger 1984 Nupoid. Bendor-Samuel (ed.), 305-22.

Blondé, Jacques 1979 La situation du français au Mali. Valdman & Chaudenson (eds.), 377-83.

Bollée, Annegret 1977 *Le créole français des Seychelles*. Tübingen: Max Niemeyer Verlag.

---- 1993 Language policy in the Seychelles and its consequences. *International Journal of the Sociology of Language* 102:85-99.

Boretzky, Norbert 1983 *Kreolsprachen, Substrate und Sprachwandel*. Wiesbaden: Otto Harrassowitz.

---- 1993 The concept of rule, rule borrowing, and substrate influence in Creole languages. Mufwene (ed.), 74-105.

Bouton, Jacques (1640 *Relation de l'établissement des François depuis l'an 1635 en l'isle de Martinique*. Paris: Cramoisy.

Brousseau, Anne-Marie 1994 The phonology of Haitian Creole, French and Fɔngbè. Paper presented at the *Relexification Workshop*, Massachusetts Institute of Technology, Boston 10 January 1994.

Bruyn, Adrienne 1996 On identifying instances of grammaticalization in Creole languages. Baker & Syea (eds), 29-46.

Bruyn, Adrienne & Veenstra, Tonjes 1993 The creolization of Dutch. *Journal of Pidgin and Creole Languages* 8:29-80.

Bull, Benjamin Pinto 1975 *Le créole de la Guinée-Bissau*. Dakar.

Bybee, J, Perkins, R & Pagliuca, W 1994 *The evolution of grammar*. Chicago: University of Chicago Press.

Bynoe-Andriolo, Esla & Yillah, Sorie 1975 Predicate clefting in Afro-European Creoles. *Ohio State Working Papers in Linguistics* 20:234-39.

Byrne, Francis 1987 *Grammatical relations in a radical Creole: verb complementation in Saramaccan*. Amsterdam: Benjamins.

Byrne, Francis & Holm, John (eds) 1993 *Atlantic meets Pacific: a global view of pidginisation and creolisation*. Amsterdam: Benjamins.

Byrne, Francis & Huebner, Thom (eds) 1991 *Development and structures of Creole languages*. Amsterdam: Benjamins.

Cable, George Washington 1886 Creole slave songs. *Century Magazine* 31:807-28.

Calloc'h, J 1911 *Vocabulaire français-ifumu (Batéké) précédé d'éléments de grammaire*. Paris: Paul Geuthner.

Calvet, Louis-Jean & Chaudenson, Robert 1998 *Saint-Barthélemy: une énigme linguistique*. Paris: CIRELFA - Agence de la Francophonie.

Campbell, George 1991 *Compendium of the world's languages*. London & New York: Routledge, 2 vols.

Carden, Guy 1989 Reflexive constructions in *Atipa* and other early Guianese texts. Fauquenoy (ed.), 161-81.

Carden, Guy 1993 The Mauritian 'lekor' reflexive: substrate influence on the target-location parameter. Byrne & Holm (eds), 105-17.

Carden, Guy & Stewart, William 1988 Binding theory, bioprogram and creolization: evidence from Haitian Creole. *Journal of Pidgin and Creole Languages* 3:1-67.

Cardoso, Eduardo Augusto 1989 *O crioulo da ilha de São Nicolau de Cabo Verde*. Praia: Ministério da Educação.

Cardoso, Henrique Lopes 1902 Pequeno vocabulario do dialecto Pepel. *Boletim da Sociedade de Geographia de Lisboa* 20 (10), 121-28.

Carreira, António 1972 *Cabo Verde: formação e extinção de uma sociedade escravocrata, 1463-1878*. Oporto: Imprensa Portuguesa.

Carreira, António & Marques, João Basso 1947 Subsídios para o estudo da língua Manjaca. [n pl]: Centro de Estudos da Guiné Portuguesa.

Carrington, Lawrence 1984 *Saint Lucian Creole: a descriptive analysis of its phonology and morpho-syntax*. Hamburg: Helmut Buske.

Carter, Hazel 1987 Suprasegmentals in Guyanese: some African comparisons. Gilbert (ed.), 213-63.

Carvalho, José Herculano de 1984a *Estudos Linguísticos 1*. Coimbra: Coimbra Editora.

Carvalho, José Herculano de 1984b *Estudos Linguísticos 2*. Coimbra: Coimbra Editora.

Carvalho, José Herculano de 1984c *Estudos Linguísticos 3*. Coimbra: Coimbra Editora.

Cassidy, Frederic 1962 Toward the reconstruction of early English-African Pidgin. *Symposium on Multilingualism (3rd meeting of the Inter-African Committee on Linguistics*. Brazzaville, 267-77.

---- 1964 Toward the recovery of early English-African Pidgin. *Symposium on Multilingualism*. Louvain: Ceuterick, 267-77.

---- 1971 Tracing the Pidgin element in Jamaican Creole (with notes on method and the nature of Pidgin vocabularies). Hymes (ed.), 203-21.

Cassidy, Frederic & Le Page, R B 1967 *Dictionary of Jamaican English*. Cambridge: Cambridge University Press.

Cassidy, Frederic & Le Page, R B 1980 *Dictionary of Jamaican English* (2nd edition). Cambridge: Cambridge University Press.

Castro, Yêda Pessoa de & Castro, Guilherme De Souza 1977 Cultures africaines en Amérique: Une ébauche de recherche conjointe pour localiser les emprunts. Paper presented at the *2nd World Black Festival of Arts and Culture*, Lagos-Kaduna, 15th January-12th February 1977.

Cérol, Marie-Josée 1991 *Une introduction au créole guadeloupéen*. [n pl]: Éditions Jasor.

Chataigner, Abel 1963 Le créole portugais du Sénégal: observations et textes. *Journal of African Languages* 2:44-71.
Chatelain, Héli 1889 *Grammatica elementar do Kimbundu ou lingua de Angola*. Genebra.
Chaudenson, Robert 1974 *Le lexique du parler créole de la Réunion*. Paris: Champion, 2 vols..
---- 1979 *Les créoles français*. Paris: Nathan.
---- 1992 *Des îles, des hommes, des langues*. Paris: L'Harmattan.
---- 1995 *Les créoles*. Paris: Presses Universitaires de France.
Chaudenson, R, Mougeon, R & Béniak, E 1993 *Vers une approche panlectale de la variation du français*. [n pl]: Agence de coopération culturelle et technique.
Chauleau, Liliane 1966 *La société à la Martinique au XVIIe siècle (1635-1713)*. Caen.
Chérubini, Bernard 1985 L'évolution des relations inter-ethniques et la fermentation de la société guyanaise. *Les Dossiers d'Outre-Mer* 81, 95-103.
Childs, Tucker 1995 *A grammar of Kisi*. Berlin & New York: Mouton de Gruyter.
Christaller, J G 1875 *A grammar of the Asante and Fante language called Tshi (Chwee, Twi)*. Basel.
---- 1933 *Dictionary of the Asante and Fante language called Tshi (Twi)*. Basel.
Clements, Clancy 1996 *The genesis of a language*. Amsterdam: Benjamins.
Clements, George 1985 Akan vowel harmony: A non-linear analysis. Goyvaerts, Didier (ed.) *African Linguistics. Essays in memory of M W K Semikenke*, Amsterdam: Benjamins, 55-98.
Colley, Ebrima 1995 *Mandinka grammar manual*. Banjul: Peace Corps.
Collins, Chris 1997 Argument sharing in serial verb constructions. *Linguistic Inquiry* 28:461-97.
Comrie, Bernard (ed.) 1990 *The major languages of South Asia, the Middle East and Africa*. London: Routledge.
Cook, Thomas 1969 Efik. Dunstan (ed.), 35-46.
Cooper, Vincent 1979 *Basilectal Creole, decreolization, and autonomous language change in St. Kitts - Nevis*. Ph.D thesis, Princeton University.
---- 1980 On the notion of decreolization and St. Kitts Creole personal pronouns. Day, Richard (ed.) *Issues in English Creoles*. Heidelberg: Julius Groos Verlag, 39-50.
Corbett, Greville (2000 Are personal pronouns suppletive? Paper presented at *Suppletion 2000*, Stockholm, 26-27 May 2000.
Corcoran, Chris 1998 The place of Guinea Coast Creole English and Sierra Leone Krio in the Afro-genesis debate. Paper presented at the Society for Pidgin and Creole Languages conference, New York, January 9-10, 1998.
Corne, Chris 1999 *From French to Creole*. London: University of Westminster Press.
Corne, C, Coleman, D & Curnow, S 1996 Clause reduction in asyndetic coordination in Isle de France Creole: the "serial verbs" problem. Baker & Syea (eds) , 129-54.
Cornevin, Robert 1982 *Haïti*. Paris: Presses Universitaires de France.
Couto, Hildo Honório do 1999 Reconstructing Kriol syllable structures. <www.unb.br/il/liv/papers/syllab.htm>. Downloaded 1999-06-11.
Cowan, H J K 1965 *A grammar of the Sentani Language*. The Hague: Martinus Nijhoff.
Creissels, Denis 1989 *Aperçu sur les structures phonologiques des langues négro-africaines*. Grenoble: ELLUG.
---- 1991 *Description des langues négro-africaines et théorie syntaxique*. Grenoble: ELLUG.
Crouse, Nellis 1940 *French pioneers in the West Indies 1625-1664*. New York: Columbia University Press.
Cultru, Prosper 1913 Introduction. Jajolet de la Courbe, Michel 1913 *Premier voyage du Sieur de la Courbe fait à la coste d'Afrique en 1685*. Paris: Édouard Champion/Émile Larose, i-lviii.
Cunha, Celso & Cintra, Luís Lindley 1985 *Breve gramática do Português contemporâneo*. Lisbon: Edições João Sá da Costa.
Cunningham, Irma Aloyce Ewing 1992 *A syntactic analysis of Sea Island Creole*. Tuscaloosa & London: University of Alabama Press.
Curtin, Philip 1969 *The Atlantic slave trade: a census*. Madison: University of Wisconsin Press.
Dahl, Östen 1979 A typology of sentence negation. *Linguistics* 17:79-106.
Dalgado, Sebastião Rodolfo 1900 *Dialecto Indo-Português de Ceylão*. Lisbon: Imprensa Nacional.
Dalphinis, Morgan 1985 *Caribbean and African languages. Social history, language and education*. London: Karia Press.
Damoiseau, Robert 1984 *Éléments de grammaire du créole martiniquais*. Fort-de-France: Hatier-Antilles.
Dapper, Olfert 1675 *Africa: being an accurate description of the regions...* Amsterdam: J von Meurs.
David, Bernard & Jardel, Jean-Pierre 1971 *Proverbes créoles de la Martinique*. Fort-de-France: CERAG.
David, Jacques 1975 *French in Africa*. London & Paris: Evans/UNESCO.
Debien, Gabriel 1965 *À la Guyane à la fin du XVIIe siècle: le journal de Goupy des Marets*. Dakar: Université de Dakar.

---- 1974 *L'Esclavage aux Antilles Françaises*. Basse-Terre & Fort-de-France: Société d'histoire de la Guadeloupe/Société d'histoire de la Martinique.

DeBose, C & Faraclas, N 1993 An Africanist approach to the linguistic study of Black English. Getting to the roots of the tense-aspect-modality and copula systems in Afro-American. Mufwene (ed.), 364-87.

DeCamp, David 1960 Four Jamaican creole texts. Le Page & De Camp (eds.), 125-79.

DeCamp, David & Hancock, Ian (eds.) 1974 *Pidgins and Creoles: current trends and prospects*. Washington: Georgetown University Press.

DeGraff, Michel 1999a Morphology in Creole genesis. Paper presented at the *9ème Colloque International des Études Créoles*, Aix-en-Provence, June 1999.

---- 1999b Empirical quicksand. Probing two recent articles on Haitian Creole. *Journal of Pidgin and Creole Languages* 14:359-70.

---- 2000 Creole speakers as a biologically definable class? Morphology in language creation. Paper presented at the Language in Society Workshop, University of Chicago, 10 January 2000. Downloaded 2000-01-21 from http://web.mit.edu/linguistics/www/degraff/uchicago.pdf.

Déjean, Yves 1999 L'archipel nous revient. Créolistes et données. *Études Créoles* 22 (2), 85-114.

Del Castillo Mathieu, Nicolas 1982 *Esclavos negros en Cartagena y sus aportos lexicos*. Bogotá: Instituto Caro y Cuervo.

---- 1984 El lexico negro africano de San Basilio de Palenque. *Thesaurus* 39:80-169.

Delafosse, Maurice 1929 *La langue Mandingue et ses dialectes (Malinké, Bambara, Dioula)*. Vol 1. Paris: Librairie Orientaliste Paul Geuthner.

Demers, Monique 1992 Statut prosodique de la particule discursive *la* en français québécois. *Proceedings of the 1992 annual conference of the Canadian Linguistic Association*, 53-62.

Denis, Béatrice 1998 A comparison of the verb phrase in Jamaican Creole, Sierra Leonean Krio and Nigerian Pidgin. Paper presented at the meeting for the Society for Pidgin and Creole linguistics, New York, January 9-10, 1998.

Derive, Marie-Jo 1990 *Étude dialectologique de l'aire manding de Côte-d'Ivoire, fasicule 1*. Paris: Peeters.

Devonish, Hubert 1989 *Talking in tones: a study of tone in Afro-European Creole languages*. Christ Church & London: Karia Press/Caribbean Academic Publications.

---- 1997 On the Sierra Leone - Caribbean connection: hot on the trail of 'tone shifted' items in Anglo-West African. ms.

Diallo, Alpha Mamadou 1993 Le français en Guinée: une situation de changement. Robillard & Beniamino (eds), 229-42.

---- 1998 Le français et les langues guinéennes: conséquences du contact. Queffélec, Ambroise (ed.) *Le français en Afrique*. Nice: Institut National de la Langue Française, 117-25.

Dialo, Amadou 1990 Le contact wolof/français au Sénégal. Clas, André & Benoît Ouba (ed.) 1990 *Visages du français: Variétés lexicales de l'espace francophone*. Paris: John Libbey, 59-68.

Dillard, Joey 1970 Principles in the history of American English. Paradox, virginity and cafeteria. *Florida Reporter* 8 (1-2), 32-33.

Dixon, R M W 1980 *The languages of Australia*. Cambridge: Cambridge University Press.

Dolbec, Jean & Demers, Monique 1992 Prosodie et fonction discursive: le cas du *la* en français québécois. *Actes du congrès international des linguistes* 15 (2), 39-42. Québec: Presses de l'Universite Laval.

Donicie, Antoon & Voorhoeve, Jan 1963 *De Saramakaanse Woordenschat*. Amsterdam: Bureau voor Taalonderzoek in Suriname van de Universiteit van Amsterdam.

Dookhan, Isaac 1975 *A History of the British Virgin Islands 1672-1970*. Epping: Caribbean University Press/Bowker Publishing Company.

Dorion-Sébeloue, Henriette 1985 La migration guyanaise. *Les Dossiers d'Outre-Mer* 81, 104-111.

Douglass, Frederick (1882 *The life and times of Frederick Douglass 1817-1882*. London: John Lobe.

Drechsel, Emanuel 1996 An integrated vocabulary of Mobilian Jargon, a native American Pidgin of the Mississippi Valley. *Anthropological Linguistics* 38:248-354.

---- 1997 *Mobilian Jargon. Linguistic and sociohistorical aspects of a Native American Pidgin*. New York: Oxford University Press.

Dryer, Matthew 1988 Universals of negative position. Hammond, M, Moravcsik, E & Wirth, J (eds) *Studies in Syntactic Typology*. Amsterdam: Benjamins, 93-124

Dumont, Pierre 1990 *Le français langue africaine*. Paris: L'Harmattan.

Dunn, Richard 1972 *Sugar and slaves. The rise of the planter class in the English West Indies 1624-1713*. London: Jonathan Cape.

Dunstan, Elizabeth 1969 *Twelve Nigerian languages. A handbook on their sound systems for teachers of English*. London & Harlow: Longmans, Green & Co.

Dupont-Gonin, Pierre 1970 *La Guyane française*. Genève: Droz.

Durand, Nathaniel (ed.) 1989 *Twa Kont Donminik*. Roseau: Konmité Pou Etid Kwéyòl.

Duthie, A S 1996 *Introducing Ewe linguistic patterns*. Accra: Ghana University Press.
Dutton, Tom 1983 Birds of a feather: A pair of rare pidgins from the Gulf of Papua. Woolford & Washabaugh (eds.), 77-105.
Dwyer, David 1984 Mande. Bendor-Samuel (ed.), 46-65.
1966 *An introduction to West African Pidgin English*. East Lansing: African Studies Center, Michigan State University/United States Peace Corps.
Dzokange 1979 *Dictionnaire Lingala*. Downloaded 1997-03-27 from: http://bantu.berkeley.edu/CBOLDDocs/DataFiles/Lingala_Dzokange1979.msw.
Ebert, Karen 1991 Vom verbum dicendi zur Konjunktion - Ein kapitel universaler Grammatiken-entwicklung. Bisang, Walter & Rinderknecht, Peter (eds) *Von Europa bis Ozeanien – Von der Autonymie zum Relativsatz: Gedenkschrift für Meinhard Scheller*. Zurich: Seminar für Allgemeine Sprachwissenschaft, 77-95.
Edwards, Jay 1974 African influences on the English of San Andrés island, Colombia. DeCamp & Hancock (eds), 1-26.
Eersel, C H 1984 Stedman's Sranan-notes and queries. Paper presented at the Society for Caribbean Linguistics conference, Jamaica.
Ehrhart, Sabine 1993 *Le créole français de St-Louis (le tayo) en Nouvelle-Calédonie*. Hamburg: Helmut Buske.
Einhorn, E 1974 *Old French: a concise handbook*. Cambridge University Press.
Elia, Silvio 1994 Portugiesisch: Brasilianisch. Holtus, Metzeltin & Schmitt (eds.), 559-75.
Eltis, D, Behrendt, S, Richardson, D & Klein, H 1999 *The Trans-Atlantic slave trade*. CD-ROM. Cambridge: Cambridge University Press.
Elugbe, Ben Ohi 1984 Edoid. Bendor-Samuel (ed.), 291-304.
Emanuel, Lezmore Evan 1972 *Surviving Africanisms in Virgin Islands English Creole*. Cited here from http://angelfire.com/pa/guavaberrybooks/africanisms.html, downloaded 1999-08-04.
Emmer, Peter 1972 De slavenhandel van en naar Nieuw-Nederland. *Economisch- en Sociaal-Historisch Jaarboek* 35:94-147.
Ericsson, Christina & Gustafson-Capková, Sofia 1997 *Stavelsestrukturer i atlantiska kreolspråk*. Stockholm: Institutionen för lingvistik, unpublished MS.
Escure, Geneviève 1991 Verb serialization in Creole oral discourse. Byrne & Huebner (eds.), 179-92.
---- 1986 Belizean Creole. Holm (ed.), 28-70.
Fagerli, Ole 1995 Benefactive constructions. A typological study. *University of Trondheim Working Papers in Linguistics* 25. Dragvoll: Trondheims Universitet.
Faïk, Sully 1979 Le français en Zaïre. Valdman & Chaudenson (eds.), 441-72.
Faine, Jules 1939 *Le créole dans l'Univers. Études comparatives des parlers français-créoles 1: Le mauricien*. Port-au-Prince: Imprimerie de l'État.
Faltz, Leonard 1977 *Reflexivization: a study in universal language*. PhD dissertation, University of California at Berkeley.
Faltz, Leonard 1985 *Reflexivization*. New York: Garland Publications.
Faraclas, Nicholas 1984 Cross River. Bendor-Samuel (ed.), 377-99.
---- 1990 From Old Guinea to Papua New Guinea: A comparative study of Nigerian Pidgin and Tok Pisin. Verhaar, John (ed.) *Melanesian Pidgin and Tok Pisin*. Amsterdam: Benjamins.
Fauquenoy, Marguérite (ed.) 1989 *Atipa revisité ou les itinéraies de Parépou*. Paris: l'Harmattan/Presses Universitaires Créoles.
Fauquenoy-Saint-Jacques, Marguerite 1972 *Analyse structurale du créole guyanais*. Paris: Klincksieck.
---- 1979 Le créole guyanais. Lasserre, Guy (ed.) *Atlas des départements français d'outre-mer 4: La Guyane*, planche 20, 4-5. Bordeaux & Talence: Centre des Études de Géographie Tropicale du Centre National de Recherche Scientifique.
Feldbæk, Ole & Ole Justesen 1980 *Kolonierne i Asien og Afrika*. Copenhagen: Politiken.
Féral, Carole de 1980 *Le pidgin-english camerounais*. Nice: Publication de l'Institut d'Études et de Recherches Interethniques et Interculturelles.
Ferraz, Luís 1974 A linguistic appraisal of Angolar. *Memoriam António Jorge Dias*. Lisbon: Instituto de Alta Cultura, Junta de Investigações Científicas do Ultramar, 177-86.
Ferraz, Luís 1975 African influences on Principense creole. Valkhoff (ed.), 153-64.
---- 1976 The substratum of Annobonese Creole. *International Journal of the Sociology of Language* 7:37-47.
---- 1979 *The Creole of São Tomé*. Johannesburg: Witwatersrand University Press.
---- 1983 The origin and development of four Creoles in the Gulf of Guinea. Woolford & Washabaugh (eds), 120-25.
---- 1987 Portuguese Creoles of West Africa. Gilbert (ed.), 337-360.
Ferraz, Luís & Valkhoff, Marius 1975 A comparative study of São-Toménse and Cabo-Verdiano Creole. Valkhoff (ed.), 15-39.

Ferronha, António Luís (ed.) [n d] *Atlas da Língua Portuguesa na História e no Mundo.* [n pl]: Imprensa Nacional-Casa da Moeda/Comissão Nacional para as Comemorações dos Descobrimentos Portugueses/ União Latina.

Fields, Linda 1995 Early Bajan: Creole or Non-Creole? Arends (ed.), 89-111.

Forget, Danielle 1989 *La*: un marqueur de pértinence discursive. *Revue Québécoise de Linguistique* 18:57-83.

Fouchard, Jean 1979 The slave trade and the peopling of Santo Domingo. *The African slave trade from the fifteenth to the nineteenth century. The general history of Africa. Studies and documents*. Paris. UNESCO, 2:270-88

Fournier, Robert 1996 Des créolismes dans la distribution des déterminants et des complémenteurs en français québécois basilectal. Brasseur, Patrice (ed.) *Français d'Amérique: variation, créolisation, normalisation*. Avignon: Presses de l'Universite d'Avignon, 217-28.

Fox, Barbara 1981 Body part syntax. Towards a universal characterization. *Studies in Language* 5:323-42.

Frajzyngier, Zygmunt 1965 An analysis of intensive forms in Hausa verbs. *Rocznik Orientalistyczny* 29 (2), 31-51.

Frey, Claude 1993 Trois langues et plusieurs normes pour une minorité grandissante des francophones au Burundi. Robillard & Beniamino (eds), 243-59.

Fyle, Clifford & Jones, Eldred 1980 *A Krio-English Dictionary*. New York: Oxford University Press/Sierra Leone University Press.

Gamble, David 1963 Elementary Wolof Grammar. Manessy & Sauvageot (eds.), 131-61.

Garfield, Robert 1992 *A History of São Tomé Island, 1470-1655. The key to Guinea*. San Fransisco: Mellen Research University Press.

Gaston-Martin 1948 *Histoire de l'esclavage dans les colonies françaises*. Paris: Presses Universitaires de France.

Gérmain, Robert 1976) [1988]: *Grammaire créole*. Villejuif: Éditions du Levain [1988: Paris: L'Harmattan].

Gilbert, Glenn (ed.) 1987 *Pidgin and Creole Languages*. Honolulu: University of Hawaii Press.

Gilléron, Jules & Edmont, Edmond 1902-1910 *Atlas linguistique de la France*. 35 vols.+supplement. Paris: Champion.

Gilman, Charles 1993 A Bantu model for the Seychellois 'pour-dire' complementizer. Byrne & Holm (eds.), 49-55.

Givón, Talmy 1975 Serial verbs and syntactic change: Niger-Congo. Li, Charles (ed.) *Word order and word order change*. Austin & London: University of Texas Press, 47-112.

---- 1979 Prolegomena to any sane creology. Hancock, Polomé, Goodman & Heine (eds), Ghent: Story-Scientia, 3-35.

Göbl, László 1934 Ésquisse de la structure grammaticale des patois français créoles. *Zeitschrift für Neufranzösische Sprache und Literatur* 58:257-95.

Gooden, Shelome 1998 Reduplication in Jamaican Creole. Paper presented at the *12th Biennial Conference of the Society for Caribbean Linguistics*, August 1998. Available from the *Creolist Archives* at http://www.ling.su.se/Creole.

Goodman, Morris 1964 *A comparative study of Creole French dialects*. The Hague: Mouton.

---- 1985 Review of Bickerton 1981). *International Journal of American Linguistics* 51:109-37.

---- 1987 The Portuguese Element in American Creoles. Gilbert (ed.), 361-405.

Gorgeon, Catherine 1985 L'Immigration en Guyane. *Les Dossiers d'Outre-Mer 81*, 68-75.

Goslinga, Cornelis 1971 *The Dutch in the Caribbean and on the Wild Coast, 1580-1680*. Assen: Van Gorcum.

---- 1979 *A short history of the Netherlands Antilles and Surinam*. The Hague: Martinus Nijhoff.

Goulden, Rick 1990 *The Melanesian Content in Tok Pisin*. Canberra: Pacific Linguistics, Series B, no. 104.

Goyette, Stéphane 1999 De l'origine des créoles de l'Amérique. Paper presented at the *9e Colloque des Études Créoles*, Aix-en-Provence, June 1999.

---- 2000 Creole Wars: The Prototype Menace. Paper presented at the SPCL meeting, Chicago, January 7-8, 2000.

Granda, Germán de 1974 El repertorio lingüístico de los sefarditas de Curaçao durante los siglos XVII y XVIII y el problema del origen del papiamento. *Romance Philology* 28, 1-16.

---- 1994 *Español de América, español de África y hablas criollas hispanicas. Cambios, contactos y contextos*. Madrid: Editorial Gredos.

Grant, Anthony 1995a *Agglutinated nominals in Creole French. Synchronic and diachronic aspects.* Ph.D thesis, University of Bradford.

---- 1995b Article agglutination in Creole French: a wider perspective. Baker (ed.), 149-76.

---- 1996 The evolution of functional categories in Grand Ronde Chinook Jargon: Ethnolinguistic and grammatical considerations. Baker & Syea (eds), 225-42.

Greeff, Richard 1882 Die Angolares: Neger der Insel São Tomé. *Globus (Illustrierte Zeitschrift für Länder- und Völkerkunde)* 42:362-64, 376-78.
Green, John 1988 Romance Creoles. Harris, Martin & Vincent, Nigel (eds) *The Romance Languages*. London & Sydney: Croom Helm, 420-73.
Green, Katherine 1997 *Non-standard Dominican Spanish: Evidence of partial restructuring*. PhD dissertation, City University of New York. [I only have an electronic copy of this, and since the pagination may be different from the published version, I have used chapter numbering rather than page numbers when referring to this work].
Green, M M & Igwe, G E 1963 *A descriptive grammar of Igbo*. Berlin: Akademienverlag.
Guenier, Nicole 1986 Role of hypercorrection in French Linguistic Change. Fishman, J, Tabouret-Keller, A, Clyne, M, Krishnamurti, B, Abdulaziz, M (eds) *The Fergusonian Impact: In Honor of Charles Ferguson on the Occasion of His 65th Birthday. Vol. 2: Sociolinguistics and the Sociology of Language*. Berlin: Mouton de Gruyter, 121-38.
Guthrie, Malcolm 1953 *The Bantu Languages of Western Equatorial Africa*. Oxford: Oxford University Press.
---- 1967 *Comparative Bantu*. London: Gregg, 4 vols.
Günther, Wilfried 1973 *Das portugiesische Kreolisch der Ihla do Príncipe*. Marburg: Marburger Studien zur Afrika- und Asienkunde
Gyasi, Ibrahim 1991 Aspects of English in Ghana. *English Today* 7 (2), 26-31
Hagemeijer, Tjerk 1999 Serial Verb Constructions and Grammaticalization Paths in São-Tomense. Paper presented at the Society for Pidgin and Creole Languages conference, Los Angeles, 8-9 January 1999.
Hair, P E H 1967 Ethnolinguistic continuity on the Guinea Coast. *Journal of African History* 8:247-68.
Hall, Gwendolyn 1992 *Africans in Colonial Louisiana. The Development of Afro-Creole Culture in the 18th century*. Baton Rouge & London: Louisiana State University Press.
Hall, Robert 1953 Creolized Languages and Genetic Relationships. *Word* 14:367-73.
---- 1966 *Pidgin and Creole Languages*. Ithaca: Cornell University Press.
Hall-Alleyne, Beverly 1990 The social context of African language continuities in Jamaica. *International Journal of the Sociology of Language* 85:31-40.
Hancock, Ian 1969 A Provisional Comparison of the English-based Atlantic Creoles. *African Language Review* 8:7-72.
---- 1975 Some aspects of English in Liberia. Dillard, Joey (ed.) *Perspectives on Black English*, The Hague: Mouton, 248-55.
---- 1980 Malacca Creole Portuguese: African, Asian or European? *Anthropological Linguistics* 17:211-36.
---- 1981 Review article of Fyle & Jones (1981). *English World Wide* 2:245-60.
---- 1986 Domestic hypothesis, diffusion and componentiality. Muysken & Smith (eds), 71-102.
---- 1987 A preliminary classification of the anglophone Atlantic Creoles, with syntactic data from Thirty-three representative dialects. Gilbert (ed.), 264-333.
---- 1996 The special case of Arctic Pidgins. Jahr & Broch (eds.), 15-29.
Hancock, I, Polomé, E, Goodman, M & Heine, B (eds) 1979 *Readings in Creole Studies*. Ghent: Story-Scientia.
Handler, Jerome & Lange, Frederick 1978 *Plantation Slavery in Barbados. An archaeological and historical investigation*. Cambridge & London: Harvard University Press.
Hanotaux, Gabriel & Martineau, Alfred 1929 *Histoire des Colonies françaises et de l'expansion de la France dans le monde*, vol. 1. Paris: Société de l'Histoire/Librairie Plon.
Harries, Helga 1973 Contrastive emphasis and cleft sentences. *Working Papers on Language Universals* 12:85-144.
Hawkins, John 1983 *Word order universals*. New York: Academic Press.
Hazaël-Massieux, Guy 1990 Le guyanais et les langues créoles atlantiques à base française. *Études Créoles* 13 (2), 95-110.
Healy, Maureen 1993 The parallel continuum model for Suriname: a preliminary study. Byrne & Holm (eds), 279-89.
Heine, Bernd 1973 *Pidgin-Sprachen im Bantu-Bereich*. Berlin: Dietrich Riemer.
---- 1976 *A typology of African languages*. Berlin: Reimer.
Heine, B, Güldeman, T, Kilian-Hatz, C, Lessau, D, Roberg, H, Schladt, M & Stolz, T 1993 *Conceptual Shift. A lexicon of grammaticalization processes in African languages*. Cologne: Institut für Afrikanistik, Universität zu Köln.
Heine, Bernd & Reh, Mechthild 1984 *Grammaticalization and reanalysis in African languages*. Hamburg: Helmut Buske Verlag.
Hellinger, Marlis 1979 Across language boundaries. The Creole of Belize (British Honduras). Hancock, Polomé, Goodman, & Heine (eds.), 314-33.
Hemmerson, Michael 1674 *West-Indiansk reese-beskriffning, från åhr 1639 till 1645*. N. pl.

Herskovits, Melville & Frances 1936 *Suriname Folklore*. New York: Columbia University.
Herzfeld, Anita 1986 The creoles of Costa Rica an Panama. Holm (ed.), 131-56.
Highfield, Arnold 1979 *The French dialect of St. Thomas, U.S. Virgin Islands. A descriptive grammar with texts and glossary*. Ann Arbor: Karoma.
Hill, Donald 1974 More on truth, fact and tradition in Carriacou. *Caribbean Quarterly* 20 (1), 45-59.
Hock, Hans Heinrich 1991 *Principles of historical linguistics*. 2nd revised and updated edition. Berlin: Mouton de Gruyter.
Hodges, Tony & Newitt, Malyn 1988 *São Tomé and Príncipe. From plantation colony to microstate*. Boulder & London: Westview Press.
Hoffman, Carl & Schachter, Paul 1969 Hausa. Dunstan (ed.), 73-84.
Holloway, Joseph & Vass, Winifried 1993 *The African Heritage of American English*. Bloomington & Indianapolis: Indiana University Press.
Holm, John 1983 On the relationship of Gullah and Bahamian. *American Speech* 58:303-18.
---- 1986a Central American English: an introduction. Holm (ed.), 6-27.
---- 1986b Nicaragua's Miskito Coast Creole English. Holm (ed.), 95-114, 123-30.
---- 1987 Creole influence on Popular Brazilian Portuguese. Gilbert (ed.), 406-29.
---- 1988 *Pidgins and Creoles*, vol. 1. Cambridge: Cambridge University Press.
---- 1989 *Pidgins and Creoles*, vol. 2. Cambridge: Cambridge University Press.
---- 1992 Popular Brazilian Portuguese: A semi-creole. Andrade & Kihm (eds.), 7-66.
---- 1993 Phonological features common to some West African and Atlantic Creole languages. Mufwene (ed.), 317-27.
---- 1999 Copula patterns in Atlantic and Non-Atlantic Creoles. Rickford & Romaine (eds.), 97-119.
---- (ed.) 1986 *Central American English*. Heidelberg: Julius Groos Verlag.
Holm, John & Shilling, Allison 1982 *Dictionary of Bahamian English*. New York: Lexik House Publishers.
Holm, John et al. 1997 Passive-like constructions in English-based and other creoles. Schneider, Edgar (ed.) *Englishes Around the World* 1, 71-86. Amsterdam: Benjamins.
Holtus, G, Metzeltin, M & Schmitt, C (eds.) 1994 *Lexikon der Romanischen Linguistik*, vol. 6-2. Tübingen: Max Niemeyer Verlag.
Honychurch, Lennox 1975) [1984]: *The Dominica Story. A history of the island*. Roseau: Dominica Institute.
Hornot, A. 1776 *Anecdotes Américaines, ou Histoire abrégée des principaux événements arrivés dans le Nouveau Monde depuis sa découverte jusqu'à l'époque présente*. Paris: Librairie Vincent.
Houdaille, Jacques 1973 Quelques donnés sur la population de St-Domingue au XVIIIe siècle. *Population* 4-5:859-72.
Houis, Maurice 1963 *Étude descriptive de la langue Susu*. Dakar: IFAN.
---- 1980 Langues africaines et créoles. Interférences et économie. *Études Creoles* 3 (2), 9-26.
Huber, Magnus 1996 The grammaticalization of aspect markers in Ghanaian Pidgin English. Baker & Syea (eds.), 53-70.
---- 1998a The origin and development of Krio: new linguistic and sociohistorical evidence. Paper presented at the Society for Pidgin and Creole Linguistics conference, New York, January 9-10, 1998.
---- 1998b Restructuring in vitro: Evidence from early Krio. Paper presented at the conference *Degrees of Restructuring in Creole languages*, Regensburg, June 1998.
---- 1998c *Ghanaian Pidgin English*. PhD thesis, Universität Essen.
---- 1999 Atlantic English Creoles and the Lower Guinea Coast: a case against Afrogenesis. Huber & Parkvall (eds.), 81-110.
Huber, Magnus & Parkvall, Mikael (eds) 1999 *Spreading the Word*. London: Westminster University Press.
Hull, Alexander 1979 On the origin and chronology of the French-based Creoles. Hancock, Polomé, Goodman & Heine (eds.), 201-15.
Hurault, Jean 1983 Eléments de vocabulaire de la langue boni (aluku tongo). *Amsterdam Creole Studies* 6:1-41.
Hurbon, Laënnec 1993) [1995] *Voodoo: truth and fantasy*. London: Thames and Hudson.
Huttar, George 1975 Sources of Creole semantic structures. *Language* 51:684-95.
---- 1981 Some Kwa-Like Features of Djuka Syntax. *Studies in African Linguistics* 12:291-323.
---- 1985 Sources of Ndjuka African vocabulary. *Nieuwe West-Indische Gids* 59:45-71.
---- 1993 Identifying Africanisms in New World languages: how specific can we get? Mufwene (ed.), 47-63.
Huttar, Mary & George 1997 Reduplication in Ndyuka. Spears & Winford (eds), 395-414.
Hymes, Dell (ed.) 1971 *Pidginization and creolization of languages*. Cambridge: Cambridge University Press.
Ingram, David 1989 *First language acquisition. method, description and explanation*. Cambridge: Cambridge University Press.
Innes, Gordon 1966 *An introduction to Grebo*. London: School of African and Oriental Studies.

---- 1967 *A practical introduction to Mende*. London: School of African and Oriental Studies.
Jabłonska, A 1969 The Sino-Russian mixed language in Manchuria. *University of Hawaii Working Papers in Linguistics* 3:135-64.
Jadfard, Roseline 1997 *Kréòl. Guide pratique de conversation en créole guyanais*. Kourou: Ibis Rouge.
Jahr, Ernst Håkon & Broch, Ingvild (eds.) 1996 *Language contact in the Arctic. Northern Pidgins and contact languages*. Berlin & New York: Mouton de Gruyter.
James, C L R 1991 French capitalism and Caribbean slavery. Beckles & Shepherd (eds), 130-35.
Jansen, B, Koopman, H & Muysken, P 1978 Serial verbs in Creole languages. *Amsterdam Creole Studies* 2:125-59.
Jenewari, Charles 1984 Ijoid. Bendor-Samuel (ed.), 105-18.
Jennings, William 1993a The demographics of Creole genesis: implications of socio-historic and population studies from the theories of Creole origin. Paper presented at the Societye for Pidgin and Creole Languages conference, Amsterdam, June 10-12, 1993.
---- 1993b *La genèse du cayennais: Étude de sa démographie et de l'évolution de son système verbal*. MA thesis, University of Auckland.
---- 1995a The first generation of a Creole society: Cayenne 1660-1700. Baker (ed.), 21-40.
---- 1995b Saint-Christophe: site of the first French Creole. Baker (ed.), 63-80.
---- 1997 The use of censuses in the study of creole genesis. Examples from Cayenne and Saint-Christophe. Paper presented at the Society for Pidgin and Creole Languages conference, London, June 26, 1997.
---- 1999 L'eugénique et le multilinguisme: l'analyse approfondie d'une plantation guyanaise en 1690 et ses résultats dans le contexte des études créoles. Paper presented at the *9e Colloque des Études Créoles*, Aix-en-Provence, June 1999.
Jones, Adam 1985 Brandenburg sources for West African History 1680-1700. Wiesbaden: Franz Steiner.
Jones, Eldred 1971 Krio: An English-based language of Sierra Leone. Spencer (ed.), 66-94.
Joseph, Brian & Zwicky, Arnold (eds) 1990 *When verbs collide*. Columbus: Department of Linguistics, Ohio State University.
Josselin de Jong, J P B de 1926 *Het Huidige Negerhollandsch (teksten en woordenlijst)*. Amsterdam: Koninklijke Akademie van Wetenschappen.
Kahrel, Peter & van den Berg, René (eds) 1994 *Typological studies in negation*. Amsterdam: Benjamins.
Karam, Antoine 1986 Les esclaves de la sucrerie Noël. Bruleaux, A-M, Calmont, R & Mam-Lam-Fouck, S (eds) *Deux siècles d'esclavage en Guyane française 1652-1848*,. Cayenne & Paris: CEGER/L'Harmattan, 63-75.
Kelly, John 1969 Urhobo. Dunstan (ed.), 153-61.
Kemmer, Suzanne 1993 *The middle voice*. Amsterdam: Benjamins.
Kephart, Ron 1991 Creole French in Carriacou, Grenada: Texts and Commentary. *Florida Journal of Anthropology* 16, special publication no. 7, 81-89.
Kihm, Alain 1988 Conflation as a directive process in creolization. Boretzky, N, Enninger, W & Stolz, T (eds) *Beiträge zum 4. Essener Kolloquium über Sprachkontakt, Sprachwandel, Sprachwechsel, Sprachtod*. Bochum: Brockmeyer, 11-137.
---- 1994 *Kriyol Syntax. The Portuguese-based creole language of Guinea-Bissau*. Amsterdam: Benjamins.
Kirk-Greene, Anthony 1971 The influence of West African languages on English. Spencer (ed.), 123-44.
Klingler, Tom 1992 A descriptive study of the Creole speech of Pointe Coupee Parish, Louisiana, with focus on the lexicon. PhD thesis, University of Indiana.
---- 1997 Louisiana Creole: The multiple geneses hypothesis reconsidered. Paper presented at the Annual Meeting of the Society for Pidgin and Creole Languages conference, London, June 27, 1997.
---- 2000 Louisiana Creole: The multiple-genesis hypothesis reconsidered. *Journal of Pidgin and Creole Languages* 15:1-35.
Koefoed, Geert 1979 Some remarks on the baby talk theory and the relexification theory. Hancock, Polomé, Goodman & Heine (eds.), 37-54.
Koefoed, Geert & Tarenskeen, Jacqueline 1996 The making of a language from a lexical point of view. Wekker, Herman (ed.) *Creole Languages and Language Acquisition*. Berlin & New York: Mouton de Gruyter, 119-38.
Kós-Dienes, Dora 1984 Sketch of the TMA system of Yoruba. Dahl, Östen (ed.) *Selected Working Papers from the Tense-Mood-Aspect Project*. Stockholm: Institutionen för Lingvistik, 121-26.
Kouwenberg, Silvia 1994a On morphology in creole. Paper presented at the Society for Pidgin and Creole Languages conference, Boston 7-8 January 1994.
---- 1994b Berbice Dutch. Kahrel & van den Berg, 237-66
---- 1994c *A grammar of Berbice Dutch creole*. Berlin & New York: Mouton de Gruyter.
---- 1995 Berbice Dutch. Arends, Muysken & Smith (eds), 233-43.

---- 1996 Berbice Dutch Creole. Mühlhäusler, P, Tryon, D & Wurm, S (eds) *Atlas of Languages of Intercultural Communication in the Pacific, Asia, and the Americas*. Berlin & New York: Mouton de Gruyter, 1347-56.

Kouwenberg, Silvia & LaCharité, Darlene 1998 Iconic inflectional versus non-iconic derivational reduplication in Caribbean Creole languages. http://www.ling.su.se/Creole/archive/kouwenberg_lacharite.html.

Kouwenberg, Silvia & Murray, Eric 1994 *Papiamentu*. Munich & Newcastle: Lincom Europa.

Kouwenberg, Silvia & Muysken, Pieter 1995 Papiamento. Arends, Muysken & Smith (eds.), 205-18.

Kramer, Marvin 1998 Transitivity in Saramaccan adjective, passive and shared object constructions. Paper presented at the Society for Pidgin and Creole Languages conference, New York, January 9-10, 1998.

Kwofie, Emmanuel 1978 *Teaching a foreign language to the West African student*. Champaign & Edmonton: Linguistic Research Incorporated.

Ladefoged, Peter 1968 *A phonetic study of West African languages*. Cambridge: Cambridge University Press.

Ladhams, John 1999a The Pernambuco connection? An examination of the nature and origin of the Portuguese elements in the Surinam Creoles. Huber & Parkvall (eds.), 209-40.

---- 1999b Response to Norval Smith. Huber & Parkvall (eds.), 299-304.

Lafage, Suzanne 1979 Rôle et place du français populaire dans le continuum des langues africaines en Côte d'Ivoire. *Le français moderne* 47 (3), 208-19.

---- 1985 *Français écrit et parlé en pays éwé (Sud-Togo)*. Paris: SÉLAF.

---- 1990 Afrika. Holtus, G, Metzeltin, M & Schmitt, C (eds) *Lexikon der Romanistischen Linguistik*, Tübingen: Max Niemeyer Verlag, vol. 5, 767-87..

Lalla, Barbara 1986 Tracing elusive phonological features of Early Jamaican Creole. Holm, John & Görlach, Manfred (eds) *Focus on the Caribbean*. Amsterdam: Benjamins, 117-32.

Lalla, Barbara & d'Costa, Jean 1990 *Language in Exile. Three Hundred Years of Jamaican Creole*. Tuscaloosa: University of Alabama Press.

Laman, Karl Edvard 1912 *Lärobok i Kongospråket (Kikongo)*. Stockholm: Svernska Missionsförbundets expedition.

---- 1936 *Dictionnaire kikongo-français avec une étude phonétique décivant les dialectes les plus importants de la langue dite kikongo*. Brusells: Institut Royal colonial Belge.

Lang, George 1994 *Ladinização* and Capeverdian Creole genesis. Paper presented at the meeting of the Society for Caribbean Linguistics, Georgetown (Guyana), August 1994.

Lang, Jürgen 1993 Das Verbalsystem des kapverdischen Kreols (Variante von Santiago) . Perl, M, Schönberger, A & Thiele, P (eds) *Portugiesich-basierte Kreolsprachen. Akten des 2. Gemeinsamen Kolloquiums der deutschsprachigen Lusitanistik und Katalanistik (Berlin, 10.-12. September 1992); lusitanischer Teil*, Frankfurt am Main: TFM/Domus Editoria Europaea, 137-66.

---- 1999 O crioulo de Santiago (Cabo Verde exotismo de aparência românica. Paper presented at the *Coloquio sobre Crioulos de Base Lexical Portuguesa*, Lisbon, 29-30 April 1999.

Larsen, Kay 1928 *Dansk Vestindien 1666-1917*. Copenhagen: C A Reitzels Forlag.

Lasserre, Guy (ed.) 1979 *Atlas des départements français d'Outre-Mer 3: La Guyane*. Paris: Centre National de Recherche Scientifique/Institut Géographique National.

Laver, J D M 1969 Etsako. Dunstan (ed.), 47-55.

Lefebvre, Claire 1991 *Take* serial verb constructions in Fon. Lefebvre (ed.), 37-78.

---- 1993 The role of relexification and syntactic reanalysis in Haitian Creole: methodological aspects of a research program. Mufwene (ed.), 254-79.

---- 1998 *Creole genesis and the acquisition of grammar*. Cambridge: Cambridge University Press.

---- (ed.) 1991 *Serial verbs: grammatical, comparative and cognitive approaches*. Amsterdam: Benjamins.

Léger, Catherine 1999 Sum: homophonous markers. *Linguist List* 10 (1176).

Leitch, Miles 1994 Babole. Kahrel & van den Berg, 190-210.

Lenz, Rodolfo 1928 *El papiamento, la lengua criolla de Curazao*. Santiago de Chile: Imprenta Bolcells.

Le Page, Robert 1960 An historical introduction to Jamaican Creole. Le Page & De Camp (eds.), 1-125.

---- (ed.) 1961 *Creole Language Studies* 2. London: Macmillan.

Le Page, Robert & DeCamp, David (eds) 1960 *Jamaican Creole*. London: Macmillan.

Leslau, Wolf 1952 The influence of Sidano on the Ethiopic language of Gurege. *Language* 28, 63-81.

Lewis, Anthony 1997 Negation and speaker proficiency in Palenquero Creole Spanish. Paper presented at the Society for Pidgin and Creole Languages conference, London, June 26, 1997.

Lewis, M B 1947 Teach yourself Malay. London: Hodder & Stoughton.

Lichtveld, Lou 1931 Op zoek naar de spin. *West-Indische Gids* 12:209-30, 305-24.

Liniger-Goumaz, Max 1988 *Brève histoire de la Guinée Équatoriale*. Paris: l'Harmattan.

Lipski, John 1985 *The Spanish of Equatorial Guinea*. Tübingen: Niemeyer.

---- 1989 *The speech of the Negros Congos of Panama*. Amsterdam: Benjamins.
---- 1992 Pidgin English usage in Equatorial Guinea (Fernando Poo). *English World-Wide* 13:33-57.
---- 1994 *Latin American Spanish*. London & New York: Longman.
---- 1999 Chinese-Cuban Pidgin Spanish. Implications for the Afro-Creole debate. Rickford & Romaine (eds.), 215-33.

Loftman, Beryl 1953 *Creole languages of the Caribbean area*. MA thesis, Columbia University.

Long, E 1775 *The history of Jamaica*. London: T Lowndes. 3 vols.

Lord, Carol 1993 *Historical change in serial verb constructions*. Amsterdam: Benjamins.

Lorenzino, Gerardo 1993 African versus Austronesian substrate influence on the Spanish-based creoles. Byrne & Holm (eds), 399-408.
---- 1998 *The Angolar Creole Portuguese of São Tomé: its grammar and sociolinguistic history*. PhD dissertation, City University of New York.

Ludwig, Ralph 1996 *Kreolsprachen zwischen Mündlichkeit und Schriftlichkeit. Zur Syntax und Pragmatik atlantischer Kreolsprachen auf französischer Basis*. Tübingen: Gunter Narr.

Ludwig, R, Montbrand, D, Poullet, H & Telchid, S 1990 *Dictionnaire créole-français, avec un abrégé de grammaire créole et un lexique français-créole*. 2e édition revue et corrigée. Paris & Pointe-à-Pitre: Servédit/Jasor.

Lumsden, John 1994 Semantic representations and relexification. Paper presented at the *Relexification Workshop*, Massachusetts Institute of Technology, Boston 10 January 1994.
---- 1999 The role of relexification in Creole genesis. *Journal of Pidgin and Creole Languages* 14:225-58.

Lumsden, John & Claire Lefebvre 1990 Predicate-cleft constructions and why they aren't what you might think. *Linguistics* 28:761-82.

Ly, Abdoulaye 1955 *L'Évolution du commerce français d'Afrique noire dans le dernier quart du XVIIe siècle. La Compagnie du Sénégal 1673 à 1696*. Bordeaux: Thèse pour le Doctorat ès Lettres, Université de Bordeaux.

Lyovin, Anatole 1997 *An Introduction to the Languages of the World*. New York: Oxford University Press.

Macedo, Donaldo Pereira 1979 *A linguistic approach to the Capeverdean language*. BA thesis, University of Massachusetts/MA thesis, New York University.

Mackenzie, D. N. 1990 Pashto. Comrie (ed.), 132-150.

Maddieson, Ian 1984 *Patterns of Sounds*. Cambridge: Cambridge University Press.

Maduro, Antoine 1953 *Ensayo pa yega na un ortografia uniforme pa nos Papiamentu*. Willemstad: M S L Maduro.

Mafeni, Bernard 1969 Isoko. Dunstan (ed.), 115-24.
---- 1971 Nigerian Pidgin. Spencer (ed.), 95-112.

Maher, Julianne 1993 Antillean Creole on St. Barthélemy. Byrne & Holm (eds.), 409-17.
---- 1994 A French source for Creole *ka*? Paper presented at the Society for Pidgin and Creole Linguistics conference, Boston 7-8 January 1994.
---- 1997 French and Creole on St. Barthélemy and St. Thomas. Valdman (ed.), 237-53.

Maia, António da Silva 1964 *Lições de Gramática de Quimbundo*. 2nd edn Cucujães: The author.

Manessy, Gabriel 1985 Remarques sur la pluralisation du nom en créole et dans les langues africaines. *Études Créoles* 8 (1-2), 129-43.
---- 1989 Dire que ... (de l'origine des creoles atlantiques). *Linguistique* 25 (2), 19-43.
---- 1994 *Le français en Afrique noire. Mythe, stratégies, pratiques*. Paris & St-Denis: L'Harmattan/ Université de la Réunion.
---- 1995 *Créoles, pidgins, variétés véhiculaires. Procès et genèse*. Paris: CNRS.

Manessy, Gabriel & Sauvageot, Serge (eds.) 1963 *Wolof et Sérèr. Étude de phonétique et de grammaire descriptive*. Dakar: Faculté des Lettres et Sciences humaines, Université de Dakar.

Manfredi, Victor 1984 Igboid. Bendor-Samuel (ed.), 337-58.
---- 1993 Verb focus in the typology of Kwa/Kru and Haitian. Byrne & Winford (eds), 3-51.

Manigat, Max 1998 Le Kikongo dans le vocabulaire Créole Haïtien. http://www.ahad-kreyol.org/Newsletter/number14/kikongo.htm. Downloaded 1998-10-19.

Manning, Patrick 1982 *Slavery, colonialism and economic growth in Dahomey, 1640-1960*. Cambridge: Cambridge University Press.
---- 1990 *Slavery and African life: Occidental, Oriental and African slave trades*. Cambridge: Cambridge University Press.

Marchese, Lynell 1984 Kru. Bendor-Samuel (ed.), 119-39.

Markey, T. L. 1979 Editor's note and Notes. Schuchardt, Hugo 1979 *The ethnography of variation. Selected writings on Pidgins and Creoles*. Ann Arbor: Karoma, xix-xxii + 109-33..

Marques, João Basso 1947a Aspectos do problema da semelhança da língua dos papéis, manjacos e brames. *Boletim Cultural da Guiné Portuguesa* 2 (5), 77-109.

Marques, João Basso 1947b Familiaridade idiomática entre Cobianas e cassangas. *Boletim Cultural da Guiné Portuguesa* 2 (8), 875-913.

Marroquim, Mário 1934) [1945]: *A língua do Nordeste (Alagoas e Pernambuco)*. [2nd ed.]. São Paulo: Companhia Editora Nacional.

Marshall, Margaret 1991 The Creole of Mon Louis Island, Alabama, and the Louisiana connection. *Journal of Pidgin and Creole Languages* 6:73-87.

Massignon, Geneviève 1962 *Les parlers français d'Acadie: enquête linguistique*. 2 vols. Paris: Klincksieck.

Mata, Inocência 1988-89 A língua portuguêsa em São Tomé e Príncipe. *A Lusofonia: unificação ortografica e politica linguisticocultural* 4-5, 159-64.

Mathews, Samuel Augustus 1822 *The Willshire squeeze, a ballad founded upon facts, to which are added, specimens of the Negro familiar dialect and proverbial sayings, with songs*. Demerara: Guiana Chronicle Office.

Maurer, Philippe 1985 Le système temporel du papiamento et le système temporel proto-créole de Bickerton. *Amsterdam Creole Studies* 8:41-66.

---- 1987 Der Vergleich der Tempussysteme des Papiamentu und der Palenquero: Argument für die Monogenese? *Linguistische Studien 172, Reihe A, Arbeitsberichte*, 18-36.

---- 1992 L'Apport lexical bantou en angolar. *Afrikanistische Arbeitspapiere* 29:163-74.

---- 1995 *L'Angolar: Un créole afro-portugais parlé à São Tomé*. Hamburg: Buske.

---- 1997 Tense-aspect-mood in Principense. Spears & Winford (eds), 415-35.

---- 1998 El papiamentu de Curazao. Perl & Schwegler (eds), 139-218.

McWhorter, John 1992 Substratal influence in Saramaccan serial verb constructions. *Journal of Pidgin and Creole Languages* 7:1-53.

---- 1995 Sisters under the skin: A case for genetic relationship betwen the Atlantic English-based Creoles. *Journal of Pidgin and Creole Languages* 10:289-333.

---- 1996 The diachrony of predicate negation in Saramaccan Creole: Synchronic and typological implications. *Studies in Language* 20:275-301.

---- 1997a It happened at Cormantin: locating the origin of the Atlantic English-based Creoles. *Journal of Pidgin and Creole Languages* 12:59-102.

---- 1997b *Towards a New Model of Creole Genesis*. New York: Peter Lang.

---- 1998 Identifying the Creole Prototype. Vindicating a typological class. *Language* 74:788-818.

---- 1999a A Creole by any other name: streamlining the terminology. Huber & Parkvall (eds.), 5-28.

---- 1999b The Afrogenesis hypothesis of plantation Creole origin. Huber & Parkvall (eds.), 111-52.

---- [*forthcoming*] Defining Creole as a Synchronic Term. Neumann-Holzschuh & Schneider (eds).

McWhorter, John & Parkvall, Mikael 1999 *Pas tout à fait du français – une étude créole*. Paper presented at the *9e Colloque des Études Créoles*, Aix-en-Provence, June 1999.

McWilliams, Richebourg Gaillard (ed.) 1953) [1988]: *Fleur de Lys and Calumet. Being the Pénicault Narrative of French Adventure in Louisiana*. Tuscaloosa: University of Alabama Press [Original written by André Picault 1698-1721; transation includes comments by McWilliams].

Megenney, William 1982 La influencia del portugués en el palenquero colombiano. *Divulgaciones Etnológicos* 2:25-42.

---- 1984 Africa en Venezuela: Su herenca lingüistica y su cultura literaria. *Montalbán* 15:207-60.

---- 1985 La influencia criollo-portuguesa en el español caribeño. *Anuario de Lingüística Hispánica* 1:157-80.

---- 1989 Black rural speech in Venezuela. *Neophilologus* 73:52-61.

---- 1992 Some lexical linkages between Africa and Venezuela. *Neophilologus* 76:383-91.

---- 1993 Elementos crioll-portugueses en el español dominicano. *Montalban* 25:149-71.

Meier, P, Meier, I, & Bendor-Samuel, J 1975 *A Grammar of Izi*. Norman: Summer Institute of Linguistics.

Meintel, Deirdre 1975 The Creole dialect of the island of Brava. Valkhoff (ed.), 205-56.

---- 1984 *Race, culture, and Portuguese colonization in Cabo Verde*. Syracuse: Maxwell School of Citizenship and Public Affairs.

Mello, Heliana 1996 *The genesis and development of Brazilian Vernacular Portugueuse*. PhD thesis, City University of New York. Also available at http://www.ling.su.se/Creole/Papers_On-Line.html.

Melzian. H. 1937 *A concise dictionary of the Bini language of southern Nigeria*. London: Kegan Paul.

Mendonça, Renato 1933) [1973]: *A Influência Africana no Português do Brasil*. [4th edition: Rio de Janeiro: Civilização Brasileira].

Mettas, Jean 1978 *Répertoire des expéditions négrières françaises au XVIIIe siècle*. Vol. 1. Paris: Société Française d'Histoire d'Outre-Mer.

---- 1984 *Répertoire des expéditions négrières françaises au XVIIIe siècle*. Vol. 2. Paris: Société Française d'Histoire d'Outre-Mer.

Migeod, F W H 1908 *The Mende Language*. London: Kegan Paul, Trench, Trübner & Co.

Morais-Barbosa, Jorge 1975 Cape Verde, Guinea-Bissau and São Tomé and Príncipe: the linguistic situation. Valkhoff (ed.), 133-51.

Morais-Barbosa, Jorge 1992 Towards a functional identification of moneme categories in the Portuguese Creole of São Tomé. Andrade & Kihm (eds.), 177-89.

Morton-Williams, Peter 1964 The Oyo-Yoruba slave trade 1670-1830. *Journal of the Historical Society of Nigeria* 3:25-45.

Moseley, Christopher & Asher, R E (eds) 1994 *Atlas of the world's languages*. London & New York: Routledge.

Mufwene, Salikoko 1987 An issue on predicate-clefting. Evidence from Atlantic Creoles and African languages. Maurer, Philippe & Stolz, Thomas (eds) *Varia Creolica*, 71-89. Bochum: Studienverlag Dr N Rockmeyer.

---- 1990 Serialisation and subordination in Gullah: toward a definition of serialization. Joseph & Zwicky (eds), 91-108.

---- 1991a Is Gullah decreolizing? A comparison of a speech sample of the 1930s with a sample of the 1980s. Bailey, G, Maynor, N & Cukor-Avila, P (eds) *The Emergence of Black English*, Amsterdam: Benjamins, 213-30..

---- 1991b Some reasons why Gullah is not dying yet. *English World-Wide* 12:215-43.

---- 1991c Pidgins, Creoles, typology, and markedness. Byrne & Huebner (eds), 123-43.

---- 1993 Creole genesis: a population genetics perspective. Paper presented at the Society for Pidgin and Creole Languages conference, Amsterdam, June 9-12, 1993.

---- 1996 The founder principle in creole genesis. *Diachronica* 13:83-134.

---- 1997a Kitúba. Thomason (ed.), 173-208.

---- 1997b Jargons, Pidgins, Creoles, and Koines: what are they? Spears & Winford (eds), 35-70.

---- (ed.) 1993 *Africanisms in Afro-American language varieties*. Athens: University of Georgia Press.

Mufwene, Salikoko & Gilman, Charles 1987 How African is Gullah, and why? *American Speech* 62:120-39.

Munro, Pamela 1976 *Mojave syntax*. New York: Garland.

Munteanu, Dan 1996 *El papiamentu, lengua criolla hispánica*. Madrid: Editorial Gredos.

Muysken, Pieter 1988 Are Creoles a special type of language? Newmeyer, F (ed). *Linguistics: The Cambridge Survey 2: Linguistic Theory: Extensions and Implications*. Cambridge: Cambridge University Press, 285-301.

Muysken, Pieter & Meijer, Guus 1979 Introduction. Hesseling, Dirk Christiaan 1979 *On the Origin and Formation of Creoles: A Miscellany of Articles*. Ann Arbor: Karoma, ix-xxi.

Muysken, Pieter & Smith, Norval 1990 Question words in Pidgin and Creoles languages. *Linguistics* 28:883-903.

Muysken, Pieter & Smith, Norval 1994 Reflexives in the Creole languages: an interim report. Adone & Plag (eds), 45-64.

Muysken, P & Smith, N (eds.) 1986 *Substrata versus universals in Creole genesis*. Amsterdam: Benjamins.

Muysken, Pieter & Veenstra, Tonjes 1995 Serial verbs. Arends, Muysken & Smith (eds), 289-301.

Mühlhäusler, Peter 1997 *Pidgin and Creole linguistics. Expanded and revised edition*. London: University of Westminster Press.

Müller, W J 1676 *Die Afrikanische auf der Guineischen Gold-Cust gelegende Landschaft Fetu*. Hamburg.

Naro, Anthony 1978 A study on the origins of pidginization. *Language* 54:314-47.

Navarro Tomás, Tomás 1953 Observaciones sobre el papiamentu. *Nueva Revista de Filología Hispánica* 7.

Ndiaye, Moussa 1996 Quelques faits de contact linguistique franco-wolof. *Revue québécoise de linguistique théorique et appliquée* 13:107-19.

Negreiros, Almada 1895 Os Angolares. Negreiros, Almada: *História ethnographico da Ilha de S. Thomé*. Lisbon: Antica Casa Bertrand-José Bastos.

Netscher, P M 1888 *Geschiedenis van de koloniën Essequebo, Demerary en Berbice*. The Hague: Martinus Nijhoff.

Neumann, Ingrid 1985 *Le créole de Breaux Bridge, Louisiane*. Hamburg: Buske.

Neumann-Holzschuh, Ingrid 1987 *Textes anciens en créole louisianais*. Hamburg: Buske.

Neumann-Holzschuh, Ingrid & Schneider, Edgar (eds) [*forthcoming*] Degrees of restructuring in Creole languages. Amsterdam: Benjamins.

Neves, Carlos Agostinho das 1989 *S. Tomé e Príncipe na segunda metade do séc. XVIII*. Lisbon: Instituto de História de Além-Mar

Niedzielski, Henry 1989 A French based pidgin in Burundi. Pütz, Martin & Dirven, René (eds) *Wheels within wheels*. Frankfurt: Peter Lang, 81-107.

Noll, Volker 1999 *Das brasilianische Portugiesisch: Herausbildung und Kontraste*. Heidelberg: Universitätsverlag C Winter.

Nunes, Mary L 1963 The phonologies of Cape Verdean dialects of Portuguese. *Boletim de Filologia* 21:1-56.

Oldendorp, C G A 1777 *Geschichte der Mission der evangelischen Brüder auf den caraïbischen Inseln S.Thomas, S.Croix und S.Jan*. Barby: Christian Friedrich Laur.
Omoruyi, Thomas 1986 Pluralization strategies in Edo. *Journal of West African Languages* 16 (2), 61-75.
Opubor, Alfred 1969 Itsekiri. Dunstan (ed.), 125-32.
Orjala, Paul Richard 1970 *A dialect survey of Haitian Creole*. PhD thesis, Hartford Seminary.
Owens, Jonathan 1996 Arabic-based Pidgins and Creoles. Thomason (ed.), 125-72.
Papy, Louis 1955 La Guyane Française. *Cahiers d'Outre-Mer* 8 (31), 209-32 + 8 (32), 369-400.
Parkvall, Mikael 1995a Is Afrogenesis possible in the case of French Creoles? Paper presented at the *2nd Westminster Creolistics Workshop*, London, April 1995.
---- 1995b The role of St. Kitts in a new scenario of French Creole genesis. Baker (ed.), 41-62.
---- 1995c *A dual approach to French Creole genesis*. MA thesis, Stockholms Universitet, Institutionen för lingvistik.
---- 1998 Reassessing the role of demographics in language restructuring. Paper presented at the conference *Degrees of Restructuring in Creole languages*, Regensburg, June 1998. Also in Neumann-Holzschuh, Ingrid & Edgar Schneider (eds.) [*forthcoming*]
---- 1999a Feature selection and genetic relationships among Atlantic Creoles. Huber & Parkvall (eds), 29-66.
---- 1999b A note on the peopling of English St. Kitts. Baker & Bruyn (eds), 63-74.
---- 1999c Feature selection and genetic relationships among Atlantic Creoles. Huber & Parkvall (eds), 29-66.
---- 1999d Diakroni och dialektskillnader i guineabuktskreolska. Unpublished ms.
---- 1999e On the alleged creole past of Brazilian Portuguese. *Colóquio sobre crioulos de base lexical portuguesa*, Lisbon, April 1999.
---- 1999f Afrolex 1.15. Lexical africanisms in Atlantic Creoles and related varieties. ms.
---- [*forthcoming*] Reduplication in the Atlantic creoles and other contact languages. Kouwenberg, Silvia (ed.) *Twice as meaningful*. London: Battlebridge.
Parsons, Elsie Clews 1918 *Folk-lore of Andros Islands, Bahamas*. Lancaster & New York: American Folk-lore Society.
---- 1933 *Folklore of the Antilles, French and English*, vol 1. New York: American Folklore Society/G E Stechert & Company.
---- 1936 *Folklore of the Antilles, French and English*, vol 2. New York: American Folklore Society/G E Stechert & Company.
---- 1943 *Folklore of the Antilles, French and English*, vol 3. New York: American Folklore Society.
Patrick, Peter 1995 Recent Jamaican words in sociolinguistic context. *American Speech* 70:227-64.
Patterson, Orlando 1967 *The sociology of slavery*. London : MacGibbon & Kee.
---- 1973 The socialization and personality structure of the slave. Comitas, Lambros & Lowenthal, David (eds) *Slaves, free men, citizens. West Indian perspectives*. Garden City: Anchor Books, 21-43.
Paulo, Leopoldina Ferreira 1959 *Comparação de alguns caracteres antropológicos entre nativos de S. Tomé*. Lisbon: Trabalhos do Centro de Estudos de Etnologia do Ultramar.
Peace Corps 1995a *Wollof-English Dictionary*. Banjul: Peace Corps, The Gambia.
---- 1995b *Mandinka-English Dictionary*. Banjul: Peace Corps, The Gambia.
Pereira, Dulce 1999 Um crioulo de outro planeta. Paper presented at the *Coloquio sobre Crioulos de Base Lexical Portuguesa*, Lisbon, 29-30 April 1999.
Perl, Matthias 1982 Acerca de alguns aspectos históricos do Português crioulo em África. *Biblos* 58:1-12.
---- 1992 Spanisch: Areallinguistik VI. Karibik (Inselwelt). Holtus, G, Metzeltin, M & Schmitt, C (eds) *Lexikon der Romanischen Linguistik vol. 6-1*. Tübingen: Max Niemeyer Verlag, 540-59.
---- 1994 Sprachvariation. Holtus, Metzeltin & Schmitt (eds), 585-91.
---- 1998 Português popular brasileiro (PPB) e *español popular caribeño* (EPC L2, resultado do substrato ou semi-crioulo? Große, Sybille & Zimmerman, Klaus (eds) *"Substandard" e mundança no português do Brasil*. Frankfurt am Main: TFM, 415-30.
Perl, Matthias & Schwegler, Armin (eds.) 1998 *América negra: panorámica actual de los estudios lingüísticos sobre variedades hispanas, portuguesas y criollas*. Frankfurt-am-Main & Madrid: Vervuert/ Iberoamericana.
Petersen, Bernard von 1855 *En historisk beskrivning om de dansk-vestindiske Öer St. Croix, St. Thomas og St Jan*. Copenhagen: C W Stinck.
Petitjean-Roget, Jacques 1980 *La société d'habitation à la Martinique – Un demi-siècle de formation 1635-1685*. Paris: Librairie Honoré Champion.
Peukert, Werner 1978 *Der atlantische Sklavenhandel von Dahomey 1740-1797*. Wiesbaden.
Peytraud, Lucien (1897 *L'esclavage aux Antilles françaises avant 1789*. Paris.

Phillip, Hilary 1988 *Description du créole de la Grenade*. Grenoble: Thèse de doctorat (langues et lettres), Université de Grenoble.
Plag, Ingo 1995 The emergence of *taki* as a complementizer in Sranan. Arends (ed.), 113-48.
Plag, Ingo & Uffman, Christian 1998 Phonological restructuring in creole: The development of paragoge in Sranan. Paper presented at the conference *Degrees of Restructuring in Creole languages*, Regensburg, June 1998.
Plungian, Vladimir 1997 *Tense, aspect and mood in Dogon*. Paper presented at Stockholm University, September 1997.
Pompilus, Pradel 1979 La langue française en Haïti. Valdman & Chaudenson (eds), 119-43.
Poplack, Shana & Tagliamonte, Sali 1996 Nothing in context. Variation, grammaticization and past time marking in Nigerian Pidgin English. Baker & Syea (eds), 71-94.
Porras, Jorge 1992 Relexification in Palenquero. Hirschbühler, Paul & Koerner, Konrad (eds) *Romance Languages and linguistic Theory*, 195-204.
Post, Marike 1992 The serial verb construction in Fa d'Ambu. Andrade & Kihm (eds), 153-69.
---- 1995 Fa d'Ambu. Arends, Muysken & Smith (eds.), 191-204.
Postma, Johannes Menne 1990 *The Dutch in the Atlantic Slave Trade 1600-1815*. Cambridge: University Press.
Poullet, Hector, Telchid, Sylviane & Montbrand, Danièle 1984 *Diksyonnè kréyòl-fwansé*. Fort-de-France: Hatier-Antilles.
Poyen-Bellisle, René de (1894 *Les sons et les formes du créole des Antilles*. Baltimore & Chicago: John Murphy/Chicago University Press.
Price, Richard 1976 *The Guiana Maroons: A historical and bibliographical introduction*. Baltimore: Johns Hopkins University Press.
Prince, Dyneley 1910 Jersey Dutch. *Dialect Notes* 3:459-84.
Prudent, Lambert-Félix 1980 *Des baragouins à la langue antillaise: Analyse historique et Sociolinguistique du Discours sur le Créole*. Paris: Éditions Caraïbiennes.
Pruvost-Beaurain, Jean-Marie (ed.) 1985 *Dictionnaire actuel de la langue française*. Paris: Flammarion.
Pulleybank, Douglas 1990a Niger-Kordofanian languages. Comrie (ed.), 253-64.
---- 1990b Yoruba. Comrie (ed.), 265-84.
Queffelec, Ambroise & Niangouna, Augustin 1990 *Le français au Congo*. Aix-en-Provence: Université de Provence.
Quint, Nicolas [*in press*] *Le cap-verdien: origines et devenir d'une langue métisse*. Paris: L'Harmattan.
Quint-Abrial, Nicolas 1998 *Dicionário Caboverdiano-Português. Variante de Santiago*. CD-ROM edition. Lisbon: Coputação e Linguagem / Priberam Informática.
Quintino, Fernando Rogado 1951 Algumas notas sobre a Gramática Balanta. *Boletim Cultural da Guiné Portuguesa* 6 (21), 1-52.
---- 1961 Conhecimento da língua Balanta através da sua estrutura vocabular. *Boletim Cultural da Guiné Portuguesa* 16 (64), 737-68.
Raimundo, Jacques 1933 *O elemento afro-negro na língua portuguêsa*. Rio: Renascença Editora.
Rambaud, J.-B. 1963 De la détermination en Wolof. Manessy & Sauvageot (eds.), 11-23.
Rask, Rasmus (1828 *Vejledning til Akra-Sproget på Kysten Ginea med et Tillæg om Akvambuisk*. Copenhagen: S. L. Møllers Bogtrykkeri.
Rawley, James 1981 *The Transatlantic slave trade*. New York & London: W W Norton & Co.
Raynal, Guillaume Thomas 1784 *Histoire philosophique et politique des isles françoises dans les Indes occidentales*. Lausanne: Pierre Heubach.
Redden, J E et al. 1963 *Twi basic course*. Washington: Foreign Service Institute, Department of State.
Reinecke, John 1937 *Marginal languages: a sociological survey of the Creole languages and trade jargons*. PhD dissertation, Yale University.
Reinecke, John 1971 Tây Bòi: Notes on the Pidgin French spoken in Vietnam. Hymes (ed.), 47-56.
Rennard, J 1954 *Histoire réligieuse des Antilles françaises des origines à 1914*. Paris: Société de l'histoire des colonies françaises/Librairie Larose.
Rens, Lucian Leo Edward 1953 *The historical and social background of Surinam's Negro English*. Amsterdam: North Holland.
Révah, Israel 1963 La question des substrats et superstrats dans le domaine linguistique brésilien. *Romania* 84:433-50.
Richardson, David 1989 Slave exports from West and West-Central Africa 1700-1810: New Estimates of Volume and Distribution. *Journal of African History* 30:1-22.
Rickford, John 1974 The insights of the mesolect. De Camp & Hancock (eds), 92-117.
---- 1977 The question of prior creolization in Black English. Valdman, Albert (ed.) *Pidgin and Creole Linguistics*, 190-221. Bloomington: Indiana University Press.

---- 1997 Creolization of AAVE? Sociohistorical and textual evidence. Paper presented at the Society for Pidgin and Creole Languages conference, London, June 26, 1997.
Rickford, John & Handler, Jerome 1994 Textual evidence on the nature of early Barbadian speech, 1676-1835. *Journal of Pidgin and Creole Languages* 9:221-55.
Rickford, John & Romaine, Suzanne (eds) 1999 *Creole genesis, attitudes and discourse*. Amsterdam: Benjamins.
Roberts, Julian 1995 A structural sketch of Pidgin Hawaiian. *Amsterdam Creole Studies* 12:97-126.
Roberts, Peter 1988 *West Indians and their languages*. Cambridge: Cambridge University Press.
Robertson, Ian 1983 The Dutch linguistic legacy in Guyana - Berbice and Skepi Dutch. *Carib* 3:11-23.
---- 1989 Berbice and Skepi Dutch. A lexical comparison. *Tijdschrift voor de Nederlandse Taal en Letterkunde* 105:3-21.
---- 1993 The Ijo element in Berbice Dutch and the pidginization/creolization process. Mufwene (ed.), 296-316.
Robertson, Ian 1994 Berbiciaansche woorde. *Amsterdam Creole Studies* 11:67-74.
Robillard, Didier de & Beniamino, Michel 1993 *Le français dans l'espace francophone. Description linguistique et sociolinguistique de la francophonie.* Vol. 1. Paris: Honoré Champion.
Rogozinski, Jan 1992 *A brief history of the Caribbean from the Arawak and the Carib to the present.* New York & Oxford: Facts on File.
Rooij, Vincent de 1997 Shaba Swahili: Partial creolization due to second language learning and substrate pressure. Spears & Winford (eds.), 309-39.
Rosenfelder, Mark [n d] *Numbers from 1 to 10 in Over 3800 Languages.* http://www.zompist.com/numbers.shtml. Downloaded 1999-03-02.
Ross, Alan & Moverley, A W 1964 *The Pitcairnese language.* London: André Deutsch.
Rougé, Jean-Louis 1988 *Petit dictionnaire étymologique du Kriol de Guinée-Bissau et Casamance.* Bissau: Instituto Nacional de Estudos e Pesquisa.
---- 1994 À propos de la formation des créoles du Cap Vert et de Guinée. *Papia* 3 (2), 137-49.
---- 1999 D'où viennent les verbes? Paper presented at the *Coloquio sobre Crioulos de Base Lexical Portuguesa*, Lisbon, 29-30 April 1999.
Rout, Leslie 1976 *The African experience in Spanish America 1502 to the present day.* Cambridge: Cambridge University Press.
Rowlands, E C 1959 *A grammar of Gambian Mandinka*. London: School of Oriental and African Studies.
----. 1969 *Teach yourself Yoruba.* London: English Universities Press.
Ruhlen, Merritt 1973 Nasal Vowels. *Working Papers on Language Universals* 12:1-36.
----- 1975 *A guide to the languages of the world.* Stanford: Stanford University.
---- 1976 The geographical and genetic distribution of linguistic features. Juilland, A, Devine, A M & Stephens, L (eds) *Linguistic studies offered to Joseph Greenberg on the occasion of his sixtieth birthday.* Saratoga: Anma Libri, vol. 1, 137-60.
Russell, Thomas 1868 *The etymology of Jamaican grammar, by a young gentleman.* Kingston: De Cordova, McDougall. Also available at http://www.ling.su.se/Creole/Old_Books.html.
Sabino, Robin 1988 The copula in vernacular Negerhollands. *Journal of Pidgin and Creole Languages* 3:199-212.
---- 1992 A point of detail: serial verbs in Negerhollands. MS.
---- 1994 They just fade away. Language death and loss of phonological variation. *Language in Society* 23:495-526.
Saint-Jacques-Fauquenoy, Marguerite 1974 Guyanese: a French Creole. DeCamp & Hancock (eds), 27-37.
Saint-Quentin, Auguste de 1872 Étude sur la grammaire créole. Saint-Quentin, Alfred de: *Introduction à l'histoire de Cayenne, suivie d'un recueil de contes, fables et chansons en créole avec traduction en regard,* Antibes: J. Marchand Imprimeries, 103-69.
Samarin, William 1990-91 The origins of Kituba and Lingala. *Journal of African Languages and Linguistics* 12:47-77.
Samb, Amar 1983 *Initiation à la grammaire wolof.* Dakar: Institut Fondamental d'Afrique Noire.
Sandoval, A de 1627) [1956]: *De instauranda aethiopum salute*. Bogotá: Emprensa nacional de publicaciones. [Original version published by F. de Lira, Seville].
Santos, Rosine 1979 A origem do crioulo. *Primeiro Colóquio Linguístico sobre o Crioulo de Cabo Verde*. Praia: Ministerio de Educação e Cultura.
Sauvageot, Serge 1965 *Description synchronique d'un dialecte wolof: le parler du Dyolof.* Dakar: Thèse de doctorat, Université de Dakar/IFAN.
Saxena, Anju 1995 Unidirectional grammaticalization: diachronic and cross-linguistic evidence. *Sprachtypologie und Universalienforschung* 48:350-372.

Scantamburlo, Luigi 1981 *Gramática e dicionário da língua criol da Guiné-Bissau (GCr)*. Bologna: Editrice Missionaria Italiana.

Schadeberg, Thilo 1982 Nasalization in Umbundu. *Journal of African Languages and Linguistics* 4:109-32.

Schiller, Eric 1990 On the definition of serial verb constructions. Joseph & Zwicky (eds), 34-64.

Schmied, Josef 1991 *English in Africa. An introduction*. London & New York: Longman.

Schuchardt, Hugo 1888 Kreolische Studien 7: Über das Negroportugiesische von Annobom. *Sitzungsberichte der Wienische Akademie von Wissenschaften* 116 (1), 193-226.

---- 1914 Die Sprache der Saramakkaneger in Surinam. Amsterdam: Koninklijke Akademie van Wetenschappen te Amsterdam.

Schwegler, Armin 1991 Zur Problematik der afroportugiesischen Kontaktsprache in Amerika: Neues aus El Palenque de San Basilio (Kolumbien). *Lusorama* 15:54-79.

---- 1993a Subject pronouns and person/number in Palenquero. Byrne & Holm (eds), 145-61.

---- 1993b Rasgos (afro-) portugueses en el criollo del Palenque de San Basilio (Colombia).. Díaz Alayón, Carmen (ed.) *Homenaje a José Pérez Vidal*. La Laguna: Litografía A Romero, 667-96.

---- 1996a *Chi ma nkongo: lengua y rito ancestrales en El Palenque de San Basilio (Colombia)*. 2 vols. Frankfurt & Madrid: Vervuert.

---- 1996b La doble negación dominicana y la génesis del español caribeño. *Hispanic Linguistics* 8 (2).

---- 1998a El Palenquero. Perl & Schwegler (eds.), 219-91.

---- 1998b El vocabulario africano de Palenque. Segunda parte: compendio alfabético de palabras (con etimologías). Ms.

---- 1999 On the (African) origin of Palenquero subject pronouns. Ms. [*Version of 1999-09-22 quoted here, and numbers refer to sections rather than pages*].

Sebba, Mark 1984a Serial verb or syntactic calque: the great circuit of *say*. Paper presented to the Society for Caribbean Linguistics, Jamaica.

---- 1984b Serial verbs: something new out of Africa. *York Papers in Linguistics* 11.

---- 1987 *The syntax of serial verbs: an investigation into serialisation in Sranan and other languages*. Amsterdam: Benjamins.

---- 1997 *Contact languages: Pidgins and Creoles*. New York: St. Martin's Press.

Sebeok, Thomas (ed.) 1971 *Current trends in linguistics, vol. 7: Linguistics in subsaharan Africa*. The Hague & Paris: Mouton.

Senghor, Léopold Sedar 1963 L'Harmonie vocalique en Sérère. Manessy & Sauvageot (eds), 287-91.

Seuren, Pieter 1990a Serial verb constructions. Joseph & Zwicky (eds), 14-33.

---- 1990b Still no serials in Seselwa: a reply to 'Seselwa serialization and its significance' by Derek Bickerton. *Journal of Pidgin and Creole Languages* 5:271-92.

---- 1993 The question of predicate-clefting in the Indian Ocean Creoles. Byrne & Winford (eds), 53-64.

Sheridan, Richard 1974 *Sugar and slavery. An economic history of the British West Indies, 1623-1775*. Lodge Hill: University of the West Indies.

Shi, Dingxu 1991 Chinese Pidgin English: its origin and linguistic features. *Journal of Chinese Linguistics* 19:1-40.

---- 1993 Learning Pidgin English through Chinese characters. Byrne & Holm (eds), 459-65.

Shillingford, Toni Christine 1970 *French Creole folktales from Dominica. An analysis of their content and form*. Mona: Unpublished MA thesis, University of the West Indies.

Silva, Baltasar Lopes da 1957 *O dialecto crioulo de Cabo Verde*. Lisbon: Imprensa Nacional.

Silva, Izione Santos 1985 *Variation and change in the verbal system of Capeverdean Crioulo*. Washington: PhD, Georgetown University.

Singler, John 1986 Remarks in response to Derek Bickerton's "Creoles and universal grammar: the unmarked case?". *Journal of Pidgin and Creole Languages* 1:141-45.

---- 1993a African influence upon Afro-American language varieties. A consideration of sociohistorical factors. Mufwene (ed.), 235-53.

---- 1993b Primary source evidence as to the character of early plantation life in the Caribbean: Goupy des Marets' manuscript. Paper presented at the Society for Pidgin and Creole Languages conference, Amsterdam, June 10-12, 1993.

---- 1993c The African presence in Caribbean French colonies in the seventeenth century: documentary evidence. Montreal: Département de linguistique, Université du Québec à Montréal.

---- 1994 Creole genesis in the French Caribbean. Paper presented at the *Relexification Workshop*, Massachusetts Institute of Technology, Boston 10 January 1994.

Smith, Michael Garfield 1962 *Kinship and Community in Carriacou*. New Haven & London: Yale University Press.

Smith, N V 1967 *An outline grammar of Nupe*. London: School of African and Oriental Studies.

Smith, N V 1969 Nupe. Dunstan (ed.), 133-41.

Smith, Norval 1987a [A list of Kwa words in Surinamese creoles]. MS.
---- 1987b *The genesis of the Creole languages of Suriname*. Doctoral dissertation, Universiteit van Amsterdam.
---- 1997 Ingredient X: the common core of African words in the Atlantic Creoles. Paper presented at the Society for Pidgin and Creole Languages conference, London, June 27, 1997.
---- 1999 Pernambuco to Surinam 1654-1665? The Jewish slave controversy. Huber & Parkvall (eds), 251-98.
Sousa, Celso Batista de 1990 *S Tomé e Príncipe. Do descobrimento ao medado do século XVI: Desenvolvimento interno e irradiação no Golfo da Guiné*. M A thesis, Universidade de Lisboa.
Spears, Arthur 1990 Haitian Creole Tense, Mood and Aspect. Singler, John (ed.) *Pidgin and Creole Tense-Mood-Aspect systems*. Amsterdam: Benjamins, 119-42.
---- 1993 Where did Haitian Creole come from? Mufwene (ed.), 156-66.
Spears, Arthur & Winford, Donald (eds) 1997 *The structure and status of pidgins and creoles*. Amsterdam: Benjamins.
Spears, Richard 1967 *Basic Course in Mende*. Chicago: Northwestern University.
Speedy, Karin 1994 *Mississippi and Têche Creole. A demographic and Linguistic case for separate genesis in Louisiana*. Auckland: M A thesis, University of Auckland.
Spence, Nicol 1990 'Sporadic' Changes in Jersey French. Green, John & Ayres-Bennett, Wendy (eds) *Variation and change in French*. London & New York: Routledge, 210-25.
Spencer, John (ed.) 1971 *The English language in West Africa*. London: Longman.
Stein, Peter 1984 *Kreolisch und Französisch*. Tübingen: Max Nimeyer.
---- 1995 Early Creole writing and its effects on the discovery of Creole language structure. Arends (ed.), 43-61.
---- 1998 Au milieu du gué: Quelques réflexions à propos de l'origine et de l'avenir des langues créoles. Paper presented at the conference *Degrees of Restructuring in Creole languages*, Regensburg, June 1998.
Stein, Robert Louis 1979 *The French Slave Trade in the Eighteenth Century*. Madison: University of Wisconsin Press.
Stewart, John 1971 Niger-Congo, Kwa. Sebeok (ed.), 179-212.
Stevens, John 1998 Summary of responses to Spanish [v]. *Linguist List* 9.636, 1998-05-01.
Stolz, Thomas 1986 *Gibt es das kreolische Sprachwandelsmodell?* Frankfurt: Peter Lang.
---- 1987a Kriôl und sein Substrat: Evidenz aus dem TMA-system. *Linguistische Studien 172, Reihe A, Arbeitsberichte*, 66-78.
---- 1987b In dubio pro substrato: ein Einblick in die Negation in portugiesisch-basierten Kreols. *LAUD A 177*. Duisburg: Universität Duisburg Gesamthochschule.
---- 1998 UND, MIT und/oder UND/MIT? Koordination, Instrumental und Komitativ - kymrisch, typologisch und universell. *Sprachtypologie und Universalieforschung* 51 (2), 107-130.
Stolz, Thomas & Stein, Peter 1986 Language and history in the former Danish Antilles: non-linguistic evidence for a diachronic description of the Negro-Dutch language. *Amsterdam Creole Studies* 9:103-22.
Storm van s'Gravesande, Laurens 1911 *The rise of British Guiana*. London: The Hakluyt Society. 2 vols.
Sundiata, Ibrahim 1990 *Equatorial Guinea. colonialism, state terror, and the search for stability*. San Fransisco & Oxford: Boulder.
Sunshine, C, Wheaton, P & Kamke, J (eds.) 1982 *Grenada - the peaceful revolution*. Washington: EPICA (=Ecumenical Program for Interamerican Communication and Action) Task Force.
Swartenbroeckx, Pierre 1973 *Dictionnaire kikongo et kituba-français*. Bandundu. Downloaded 1997-03-27 from http://bantu.berkeley.edu/CBOLDDocs/DataFiles/Kongo.Swart1973.prf.
Swift, L B & E W A Zola 1963 *Kituba basic course*. Washington: Foreign Service Institute.
Sylvain, Suzanne 1936 [1979]: *Le créole haïtien: morphologie et syntaxe*. Wetteren & Port-au-Prince: Imprimerie de Meester [Geneva: Slatkine Reprints].
Söderberg, Bertil & Wikman, Ragnar 1966 *Kikongo*. Stockholm: Svenska Bokförlaget.
Tallant, Robert 1946 [1994]: *Voodoo in New Orleans*. New York: Macmillan [Gretna: Pelican Publishing Co].
Taylor, Douglas 1951 Structural outline of Caribbean Creole I: Morphology. *Word* 7:43-59.
---- 1971 Grammatical and lexical affinities of Creoles. Hymes (ed.), 293-96.
---- 1977 *Languages of the West Indies*. Baltimore: Johns Hopkins University Press.
Tchang, Laurent 1990 Un exemple de continuité culturelle: La figure de Tortue dans la littérature orale guyanais. Étude d'un conte. *Études Créoles* 13 (2), 124-53.
Tenreiro, Francisco 1961 *A Ilha de São Tomé*. Memórias da Junta de investigações do Ultramar 24.
Tertre, du (1667-1671) [1973]: *Histoire Générale des Antilles habitées par les Françoys*. 3 vols. Paris: Jully.
Thiele, Petra 1987 Zur Spezifizierung von Substrateinflüssen auf die Entwicklung der Portugiesisch-basierten Kreolsprachen Westafrikas. *Linguistische Studien 172, Reihe A, Arbeitsberichte*, 79-91.

Thomas, Hugh 1997 *The slave trade*. London: Picador.
Thomas, John J 1869 [1969]: *Theory and practice of Creole grammar*. Port of Spain: The Chronicle publishing office [New edition with an introduction by Gertrud Aub-Büscher: London: New Beacon Books].
Thomas, Northcote 1910 *Anthropological report on the Edo-speaking peoples of Nigeria, part II: Linguistics*. London: Harrison & sons.
Thomason, Sarah (ed.) 1996 *Contact languages. A wider perspective*. Amsterdam: Benjamins.
Thomason, Sarah & Kaufman, Terrence 1988 *Language contact, creolization, and genetic linguistics*. Berkeley: University of California Press.
Thompson, Robert Wallace 1961 A note on some possible affinities between the Creole dialects of the old world and those of the new. Le Page (ed.), 107-13.
Tinelli, Henri 1981 *Creole phonology*. The Hague: Mouton.
Tinhorão, José Ramos 1988 *Os Negros em Portugal. Uma presença silenciosa*. Lisbon: Caminho.
Todd, Loreto 1982 *Cameroon*. Heidelberg: Julius Groos Verlag.
Trask, Larry 1993 *A dictionary of grammatical terms in linguistics*. London & New York: Routledge.
Turiault, Jean-Jacques (1875-6 Étude sur la langage créole de la Martinique. *Bulletin de la Société Académique de Brest* 25 (1), 401-516 + 25 (2), 1-111.
Turner, Lorenzo D 1949 *Africanisms in the Gullah dialect*. Chicago: Chicago University Press.
Ultan, Russell 1973 Some reflections on vowel harmony. *Working Papers on Language Universals* 12, 37-67.
United Nations High Commissioner for Human Rights 1999 *Universal declaration of human rights*. http://www.unhchr.ch/udhr/navigate/alpha.htm. Downloaded 1999-02-19.
UPSID = *UCLA Phonological Segment Inventory Database*. [The sample is essentially the same as presented in Maddieson 1984), but I used an expanded version containing 450 languages, which was kindly supplied by Olle Engstrand.]
Valdman, Albert 1970 *Basic course in Haitian creole*. Bloomington & The Hague: Indiana University Publications/Mouton.
---- 1971 The linguistic situation in Haiti. Hymes (ed.), 61-62.
---- 1973 Some aspects of decreolisation in Creole French. Sebeok, Thomas (ed.) *Current trends in linguistics* 11:507-36. The Hague: Mouton.
---- 1978 *Le créole: Structure, statut et origine*. Paris: Klincksieck.
---- 1983 Creolization and second language acquisition. Roger Anderson (ed. *Pidginization and creolization as language acquisition*. Rowley: Newbury House, 212-43.
---- (ed.) 1997 *French and Creole in Louisiana*. New York: Plenum Press.
Valdman, Albert & Chaudenson, Robert (eds.) 1979 *Le français hors de France*. Paris: Champion.
Valdman, Albert & Klingler, Tom 1997 The structure of Louisiana Creole. Valdman (ed.), 109-44.
Valente, José Francisco 1964 *Gramática Umbundu – A língua do centro de Angola*. Lisbon: Junta de Investigações do Ultramar.
Valkhoff, Marius 1966 *Studies in Portuguese and Creoles*. Johannesburg: Witwatersrand University Press.
---- (ed.) 1975 *Miscelânea Luso-Africana*. Lisbon: Junta de Investigações Científicas do Ultramar.
van den Eynde, Karel 1960 *Fonologie en morfologie van het Cokwe*. Louvain: Katolieke Universiteit te Leuven.
van der Voort, Hein 1996 Eskimo Pidgin in West Greenland. Jahr & Broch (eds), 157-258.
---- 1997 New light on Eskimo Pidgins. Spears & Winford (eds), 373-94.van Diggelen, Miep 1978 Negro-Dutch. *Amsterdam Creole Studies* 2:69-100.
van Ginneken, J 1923 *Handboek der Nederlandsche Taal*. Nijmegen.
van Lier, R A J 1971 *Frontier Society. A Social Analysis of the History of Surinam*. The Hague: Martinus Nijhoff.
Van Name, Addison 1869-70 Contributions to Creole Grammar. *Transactions of the American Philological Association* 1:123-67.
van Rossem, Cefas, & van der Voort, Hein (eds) 1996 *Die Creool Taal*. Amsterdam: Amsterdam University Press.
Veenstra, Tonjes 1994 The acquisition of functional categories. Adone & Plag (eds), 99-117.
---- 1996 *Serial verbs in Saramaccan. Predication and Creole genesis*. [n pl] Holland Institute of Generative Linguistics.
Vila Vilar, Enriqueta 1977 *Hispano-America y el comercio de esclavos. Los asientos portugueses*. Seville: Escuela de Estudios Hispano-Americanos de Sevilla.
Vincent, Diane 1994 Les problèmes d'arrimage entre les études discursives et prosodiques: le cas du *la* ponctuant. *Langues et linguistique* 20:201-12.
Vitale, Anthony 1980 Kisetla: linguistic and sociolinguistic aspects of a Pidgin Swahili of Kenya. *Anthropological Linguistics* 22 (2), 47-65.

Voorhoeve, Jan 1971 Varieties of Creole in Suriname. Church Creole and pagan cult languages. Hymes (ed.), 305-15.
---- 1973 Historical and linguistic evidence in favour of the relexification theory in the formation of creoles. *Language in Society* 2:133-45.
Wangkheimayum, Bharati & Sinha, Anjani Kumar 1997 Tense and agreement in Nagamese. Paper presented at the Society for Pidgin and Creole Languages conference, London, June 27, 1997.
Warantz, Elissa 1986 The Bay Islands English of Honduras. Holm (ed.), 71-94.
Ward, Ida 1952 *An Introduction to the Yoruba Language*. Cambridge: Heffer.
---- 1963 A short phonetic study of Wolof (Jolof) as spoken in the Gambia and in Senegal. Manessy & Sauvageot (eds), 57-73.
Wartburg, Walther von 1964 *Französisches etymologisches Wörterbuch: eine Darstellung des galloromanischen Sprachschatzes*, vol 11-2. Basel: Zbinden.
Washabaugh, William 1986 The off-shore island Creoles: Providencia, San Andres and the Caymans. Holm (ed.), 157-79.
Watts, David 1987 *The West Indies: patterns of development, culture and environmental change Ssince 1492*. Cambridge: Cambridge University Press.
Weinreich, Uriel 1953 *Languages in contact: findings and problems*. The Hague: Mouton.
Wells, J C 1982 *Accents of English*. Cambridge: Cambridge University Press. 3 vols.
Welmers, William 1946 *A descriptive grammar of Fanti*. Baltimore: Linguistic Society of America.
---- 1952 Notes on the structure of Bariba. *Language* 28:63-81.
---- 1971 Niger-Congo, Mande. Sebeok (ed.), 113-140.
---- 1973 *African language structures*. Berkeley: Univeristy of California Press.
---- 1976 *A grammar of Vai*. Berkeley: University of California Press.
Westermann, Diedrich 1924 *Die Kpelle-Sprache in Liberia. Grammatische Einführung, Texte und Wörterbuch*. Berlin & Hamburg: Verlag von Dietrich Reimer/C. Boysen.
---- 1930 *A study of the Ewe language*. London: Oxford University Press.
---- 1939 *Die Ewe-Sprache in Togo*. Berlin: Walter de Gruyter.
---- 1947 *Pluralbildung und Nominalklassen in einigen afrikanischen Sprachen*. Berlin: Deutschen Akademie der Wissenschaften zu Berlin.
Westermann, Dietrich & Ward, Ida 1933 *Practical phonetics for students of African languages*. London: Oxford University Press.
Westermann, Dietrich & Bryan, M A 1952 *The languages of West Africa*. London: Oxford University Press.
Whitehead, Henry 1932 Negro dialect of the Virgin Islands. *American Speech* 7:175-79.
Whitehead, J 1899 Grammar and dictionary of the Bobangi language. London: Kegan Paul, Trench, Trübner & Co. for the Baptist Missionary Society. [The version used here is the one found at http://bantu.berkeley.edu/CBOLDDocs/DataFiles/Bobangi.JW1899.msw. Downloaded 1997-03-27.]
Wilkinson, Henry 1933) [1958]: *The adventures of Bermuda. A history of the island from its discovery until the dissolution of the Somers Islands Company in 1684*. London: Oxford University Press.
Williams, Jeffrey 1993 Documenting the Papuan-based Pidgins of insular New Guinea. Byrne & Holm (eds.), 355-67.
Williams, Selase 1993 Substantive Africanisms at the end of the African linguistic diaspora. Mufwene (ed.), 406-22.
Williamson, James 1923 *English colonies in Guiana and the Amazon 1604-1668*. Oxford: Clarendon Press.
Williamson, Kay 1969a Igbo. Dunstan (ed.), 85-96.
---- 1969b Ijo. Dunstan (ed.), 97-114.
---- 1984 Niger-Congo overview. Bendor-Samuel (ed.), 3-45.
Wilson, W A A 1962 *The Crioulo of Guiné*. Johannesburg: Witwatersrand University Press.
Winer, Lise 1993 *Trinidad and Tobago*. Philadelphia & Amsterdam: John Benjamins.
Winford, Donald 1996 Common ground and Creole TMA. *Journal of Pidgin and Creole Languages* 11:71–84.
---- 1999 Tense/aspect and substrate influence in the formation of Sranan. Paper presented at the SPCL meeting, Los Angeles, 8-9 January 1999.
Wittmann, Henri 1996 Les créolismes syntaxiques du français magoua parlé aux Trois-Rivières. MS.
Wittmann, Henri & Fournier, Robert 1983 Le Créole, c'est du français, coudon! *Revue de l'Association Québécoise de Linguistique* 3:187-202.
Woolford, Ellen & Washabaugh, William (eds.) 1983 *The social context of creolization*. Ann Arbor: Karoma.
Wurm, Stephen 1996 The Taimyr Peninsula Russian-based pidgin. Jahr & Broch (eds), 79-90.
Zang Zang, Paul 1998 *Le français en Afrique. Norme, tendances, évalutives, dialectalisation*. Munich: Lincom.
Ziegler, Douglas-Val 1981 Be-Twi-N the lines: some Akan linguistic influences in the New World. *Anthropological Linguistics* 23:203-08.

Index of authors' names
(including correspondents)

D

E

F

G

H

N

O

P

Q

R

S

T

U

V

W

Y

Z